ADVANCED TEXTBOOKS IN ECONOMICS

VOLUME 2

Editors:

C. J. BLISS

M. D. INTRILIGATOR

Advisory Editors:
S. M. GOLDFELD
L. JOHANSEN
D. W. JORGENSON
M. C. KEMP
J.-C. MILLERON

NORTH-HOLLAND PUBLISHING COMPANY
AMSTERDAM · LONDON

AMERICAN ELSEVIER PUBLISHING CO., INC.
NEW YORK

LECTURES ON MICROECONOMIC THEORY

LECTURES ON MICROECONOMIC THEORY

E. MALINVAUD

Institut National de la Statistique et des Études Économiques, Paris

Translation by MRS. A. SILVEY

NORTH-HOLLAND PUBLISHING COMPANY
AMSTERDAM · LONDON

AMERICAN ELSEVIER PUBLISHING CO., INC.
NEW YORK

This book was originally published by Dunod, Paris, 1969, under the title:
Leçons de Théorie Microéconomique.

Library of Congress Catalog Card Number: 79–166312
North-Holland ISBN for this series: 0 7204 3600 1
North-Holland ISBN for this volume: 0 7204 3602 8
American Elsevier ISBN: 0 444 10389 9

1st edition 1972
2nd printing 1973

PUBLISHERS: M N
NORTH-HOLLAND PUBLISHING COMPANY – AMSTERDAM
NORTH-HOLLAND PUBLISHING COMPANY LTD. – LONDON

SOLE DISTRIBUTORS FOR THE U.S.A. AND CANADA:
AMERICAN ELSEVIER PUBLISHING COMPANY, INC.
52 VANDERBILT AVENUE, NEW YORK, N.Y. 10017

PRINTED IN SCOTLAND

Preface

The aim of this book is to help towards the understanding of micro-economic theory, particularly where it concerns general economic equilibrium. I shall deal with the structure of the theory and briefly discuss its motivation. But I shall make only passing remarks about its practical relevance or about the precepts that have been deduced from it for applied economics.

The present edition is a rather extensive revision and adaptation of lectures first prepared as an introduction to the course given by M. Allais at the Ecole Nationale de la Statistique et de l'Administration Economique, Paris. It is addressed to students who dispose of a good background in mathematics and have been introduced to economic phenomena and concepts. But their power of abstraction is not considered as high enough to allow them to take immediate full advantage of the most rigorous and condensed works such as that of Debreu.[†]

The theoretical exposition does not attempt to achieve the greatest generality that is possible today. Most of the results could be strengthened. But a complete catalogue of the known theorems would be tedious and of only secondary interest to the student. Those who wish to specialise in microeconomic theory must refer to the original works for those questions which they want to investigate more deeply.

On the other hand, the various chapters do cover almost completely the different viewpoints that have contributed to our precise understanding of general equilibrium. The choice of topics reflects somewhat my main interest; but this has not apparently resulted in any major omission from what is presently accepted as the content of microeconomic theory. I have moreover refrained from presenting at length my own research. The scope of these lectures is satisfactorily defined by the table of contents, without the need for further discussion here.

It follows from my purpose that the proofs of all the principal results should

---

[†] Debreu, *Theory of Value: an axiomatic analysis of economic equilibrium*, John Wiley and Sons, Inc., New York, 1959.

v

be given or at least outlined, since they are essential for the understanding of the properties involved. It makes it equally desirable that the level of rigour currently achieved by microeconomic theory should be respected. Therefore the assumptions used in each proof have been stated explicitly even when they could have been eliminated by resort to a more powerful argument. In short, the accent is placed on the logical structure of the theory rather than on the statement of its results.

As thus described, the text should be useful to those who are solidly equipped in mathematics, are ready to make the effort required to understand existing microeconomic theory and are not prepared to be content with less rigorous presentations, which are naturally easier but also are responsible for some confusion.

The historical development of microeconomic theory has been only occasionally touched on. To trace and describe the origin of each result would have been to overburden the exposition. The few references given in the various chapters do not pretend to do justice to the authors of the most important contributions, but rather to give the student some indications as to how he may follow up certain questions. If the references are so spotty this may be mainly because I had no time for preparing a complete bibliography. On the other hand I did not think this book was a proper place for flattering my colleagues by extensive display of what each of them has achieved. When the book will be used for a course, the teacher will be well advised to prepare a reading list appropriate to the specific needs of his students.

It is a pleasure to acknowledge that once again Mrs. Anne Silvey was good enough to prepare the English translation of my work and to make it both fluent and accurate.

Contents

Preface   v

Chapter 1. Conceptual framework of microeconomic theory   *1*
  1. Object of the theory   1
  2. Goods, agents, economy   2
  3. Possible interpretations of the concept of a good   5
  4. Descriptive relevance of the accounting economy   9
  5. The demands of rigour and simplicity   10

Chapter 2. The consumer   *12*
  1. Outline of the theory   12
  2. The utility function   14
  3. Utility function and preference relation   16
  4. The feasible set   20
  5. Assumptions about the utility function   24
  6. The existence of equilibrium and demand functions   26
  7. Marginal properties of equilibrium   29
  8. The case where the marginal equalities are sufficient to determine equilibrium   31
  9. The study of demand functions   34
 10. Cardinal utility   39
 11. The axiom of revealed preference   40

Chapter 3. The producer   *43*
  1. Definitions   43
  2. The validity of production functions   48
  3. Assumptions about production sets   51
  4. Equilibrium for the firm in perfect competition   55
  5. The case of additional constraints   59
  6. Supply and demand laws for the firm   61
  7. Cost functions   64
  8. Short and long-run decisions   69
  9. Monopoly   70

Chapter 4. Optimum theory   *76*
  1. Definition of optimal states   76
  2. Prices associated with a distribution optimum   79

 3. A geometric representation   81
 4. The optimality of market equilibria   85
 5. Production optimum   86
 6. Increasing returns and concave isoquants   92
 7. Pareto optimality   93
 8. Optimum and social utility function   96
 9. The relevance of optimum theory   99
10. Separation theorem justifying the existence of prices associated with an optimum   101

Chapter 5. Competitive equilibrium   *105*
 1. Introduction   105
 2. Equilibrium equations for a distribution economy   106
 3. Equilibrium equations for an exchange economy   109
 4. Value, scarcity and utility   113
 5. Value and cost   117
 6. Equilibrium equations in a private ownership economy   123
 7. Prices and income distribution   125
 8. The existence of a general equilibrium   130
 9. The uniqueness of equilibrium   136
10. The realisation and stability of equilibrium   138

Chapter 6. Imperfect competition and game situations   *144*
 1. The general model of the theory of games   145
 2. Bilateral monopoly   147
 3. Duopoly   150
 4. Coalitions   153
 5. Arbitrage and exchange between individuals   155
 6. The core in the exchange economy   157

Chapter 7. Economies with an infinite number of agents   *163*
 1. 'Atomless' economies   163
 2. Convexities   165
 3. The theory of the optimum   168
 4. Perfect competition in atomless economies   170
 5. Domination and free entry   174
 6. Return to the theories of monopoly and duopoly   181

Chapter 8. Determination of an optimum   *184*
 1. The problem   184
 2. General principles   185
 3. Tâtonnement procedure   187
 4. A procedure with quantitative objectives   190
 5. A procedure involving the use of a model by the planning board   193
 6. Correct revelation of preferences   197

Chapter 9. External economies, public goods, fixed costs   *200*
 1. General remarks   200
 2. External effects   203
 3. Collective consumption   211
 4. Public service subject to congestion   218
 5. Public service with fixed cost   219

Chapter 10. Intertemporal economies   *230*

              (A) A date for each commodity   231

1. Market prices and interest rates   231
2. The consumer   234
3. The firm   237
4. A positive theory of interest   239
5. Optimum programmes and the discounting of values   242
6. Optimality in Allais' sense   244

              (B) Production specific to each period   248

1. The analysis of production by periods   248
2. Intertemporal efficiency   250
3. Interest and profit   253
4. Short-sighted decisions and transferability of capital   257
5. Efficient stationary states and proportional growth programmes   260
6. Capitalistic optimum   262
7. The theory of interest once again   265
8. Stationary equilibria   270

Chapter 11. Uncertainty   *273*

1. States and events   273
2. Contingent commodities and plans   275
3. The system of contingent prices   277
4. Individual behaviour in the face of uncertainty   280
5. Linear utility for the choice between random prospects   282
6. The existence of a linear utility function   285
7. Risk premiums and the degree of aversion to risk   290
8. The exchange of risks   292
9. Individual risks and large numbers of agents   294
10. Profit and allocation of risks   296

Conclusion   *298*

Appendix. The extrema of functions of several variables with or without constraint on the variables, by J.-C. Milleron   *299*

1. Useful definitions   299
2. Unconstrained maximum of a function of several variables   302
3. Extremum subject to constraints of the form $g_j(x) = 0; j = 1, 2, \ldots, m$ 304
4. Extremum subject to constrainst of the form $g_j(x) \geqslant 0; j = 1, \ldots, m$ 309

Index   *315*

Conceptual framework of microeconomic theory

1. Object of the theory

L. Robbins put forward the following definition: 'economics is the science which studies human behaviour as a relationship between ends and scarce means which have alternative uses'.† Such a statement does not make it clear that economics is a social science which studies the activity of men living in organised communities. It also risks failure to make sufficient distinction between economics and political science, since the terms 'ends' and 'means' may be interpreted in a very general sense.

In a work which follows marxist thinking, O. Lange writes: 'Political economy, or social economy, is the study of the social laws governing the production and distribution of the material means of satisfying human needs.'‡ There is nothing to say about this very compact definition except that the terms 'social laws' and 'material means' are capable of misinterpretation. The social nature lies in the analysed phenomena, production and distribution, rather than in the permanent relations which we establish between them, and which we call laws. 'Material means', also called 'goods', must be interpreted sufficiently widely to include, for example, the provision of services.

Here we propose the alternative, more explicit definition: *economics is the science which studies how scarce resources are employed for the satisfaction of the needs of men living in society: on the one hand, it is interested in the essential operations of production, distribution and consumption of goods, and on the other hand, in the institutions and activities whose object it is to facilitate these operations.*

The most cursory observation of economic life under the differing regimes which exist today reveals a juxtaposition of large numbers of individuals,

† L. Robbins, *Essay on the Nature and Significance of Economic Science*, MacMillan, London, 1932.

‡ Lange, *Political Economy* (English translation), Pergamon Press, Oxford, 1963.

each acting with some autonomy but within a complex institutional framework which organises their mutual interdependences.

So, in so far as it is a positive, that is, explanatory science, economics must analyse the behaviour of agents who enjoy some freedom but are subject to the constraints imposed on them by nature and institutions. It must investigate the consequences of such individual behaviour for the state of affairs which is realised in the community.

In so far as it is a normative science, economics must also investigate the best way of organising production, distribution and consumption. It must give the conceptual tools which enable us to assess the comparative advantages of different forms of organisation.

In its pursuit of this double activity, positive and normative, our science has come to attribute a central role to the prices which regulate the exchange of goods among agents. For the individual, these prices reflect more or less exactly the social scarcity of the products which he buys and sells. This is why the study of the price system is just as important as the study of production and consumption.

The main object of the theory in which we are interested is the analysis of the simultaneous determination of prices and the quantities produced, exchanged and consumed. It is called microeconomic because, in its abstract formulations, it respects the individuality of each good and each agent. This seems a necessary condition a priori for a logical investigation of the phenomena in question. By contrast, the rest of economic theory is in most cases macroeconomic, reasoning directly on the basis of aggregates of goods and agents.

Microeconomic theory has now attained a fairly high level of rigour, in the sense that its main sections are constructed from a consistent set of abstract concepts, which provide a formal representation of the society under study. So the reasoning in these lectures will be based on a single general model to which more specific assumptions will be introduced as we proceed. The first task is to define the elements of this model.

2. Goods, agents, economy

'Goods' and 'agents' are the first two concepts. Bread, coal, electrical power, buses, etc., are considered as goods, the quantity of each being measured in appropriate units. Services such as transport, hairdressing, medical care, etc., are also goods since they satisfy human needs. Labour is a good of particular importance since it is an essential element in all production. In relation to it, we should, properly speaking, distinguish as many goods as there are types of labour. We shall speak of 'commodities' interchangeably with 'goods'. These two terms will be taken as equivalent, at least up to Chapter 10 where it will be convenient to give them different meanings.

The economic activity of individuals is both professional and private; in most cases, professional activity takes place in the context of firms engaged in production; private activity generally occurs within households and involves the consumption of goods for the satisfaction of widely varying needs. It is convenient for the purposes of theory to distinguish the two types of organised cells in which each activity is carried on. So we shall speak of 'producer agents' and 'consumer agents'.

More generally, 'agents' are the individuals, groups of individuals or organisms which constitute the elementary units of activity. To each agent there corresponds an autonomous centre of decision.

Here we shall assume in most cases that the agents can be divided into two categories: 'producers', who transform certain goods into other goods, and 'consumers' who use certain goods for their own needs. The former are also sometimes called 'enterprises' or 'firms'. The latter may represent either individuals, or cells of united individuals who constitute households, or possibly larger social groups pursuing common aims for the direct satisfaction of their needs.

In the model with which we shall mainly be concerned, there exist l commodities, m consumers and n producers. Certain *resources*, which are available *a priori*, can be used either for production or for consumption. Finally, we shall often add to the model the clause that every good has a *price*. Let us briefly examine these notions in turn.

(a) With each commodity, identified by an appropriate index h ($h = 1$, 2, ..., l), there is associated a definite unit of quantity. The commodity is characterised by the property that two equal quantities of it are completely equivalent for each consumer and each producer. When taking the normative standpoint, we also assume that two equal quantities of the same good are socially equivalent.

We shall often have to consider 'complexes of goods', a complex being defined as a set of quantities of the l commodities, for example, $z_1, z_2, ..., z_l$. It is therefore a vector of R^l, z say.

(b) The social organisation of economic activity generally allows individuals to exchange goods among themselves. One of our main objects in these lectures is to understand how these exchanges are carried out. In most of the following chapters, these exchanges conform to prices given to the different goods.

With each commodity, therefore, we associate a *price* which is a positive or zero number. We say, for example, that the price of the hth good is p_h. For the set of goods, we can define a corresponding vector p, the price vector.

By definition, the *value* of a complex z of goods is

$$\sum_{h=1}^{l} p_h z_h,$$

which can obviously be denoted by pz. Two complexes with the same value are considered to be mutually exchangeable. Thus, z^1 and z^2 are exchangeable if $pz^1 = pz^2$.

Suppose that in particular we have the following two complexes:

$$z^1 = (0, 0, ..., 0, 1, 0, ..., 0), \qquad z^2 = (0, 0, ..., 0, x),$$

where the component 1 has the hth position in z^1. The complexes are exchangeable if

$$p_h = p_l x.$$

So the ratio between p_h and p_l defines the quantity of the good l which must be given in exchange for one unit of h.

In what follows we shall be concerned only with the ratios of the values of different complexes. In fact, in our formulations, the vector p will be defined only up to a multiplicative constant, λp representing the same price vector as p, whatever the positive number λ. We shall verify this in each of the following chapters.

It is sometimes convenient to eliminate this indeterminacy by demanding that p satisfy a conventionally chosen condition. Thus, the price of one commodity is often fixed at 1, and the commodity in question is then called the 'numéraire'. For the purposes of theory, there is no necessity to choose a numéraire; we shall not do this except where explicitly mentioned.

(c) With each *consumer* there is associated an index $i(i = 1, 2, ..., m)$. The activity of the ith consumer is represented by the complex x_i whose components x_{ih} define the quantities consumed of the different goods. The x_{ih} are not necessarily positive; for example, we shall often assume that the ith consumer provides labour of a certain description. This will be represented by negative consumption which appears in x_i as a negative component for the good corresponding to labour of this kind.

(d) With each *producer* there is associated an index $j(j = 1, 2, ..., n)$. The jth producer transforms certain goods, called his 'inputs', into other goods, his 'outputs'. Let a_j and b_j be the vectors which represent respectively the complex of inputs (the a_{jh}) and the complex of outputs (the b_{jh}). The jth producer's *net production* of the good h is, by definition, $y_{jh} = b_{jh} - a_{jh}$. It is positive if h is one of his outputs, negative if it is an input. We shall later consider often the complex of net productions and the vector y_j, without involving inputs and outputs explicitly.

(e) *A priori*, the community has at its disposal certain quantities ω_h of the different goods. These are the *initial resources*, the vector ω of which is one of the data of the situation under study.

Like the notions previously introduced, that of initial resources has some flexibility. Thus, we might conceivably represent the labour provided by the individuals of the community in two ways. As we have just said, this can be considered as negative consumption by consumers. It can also be considered as an initial resource available to the economy. According to the latter point of view, if h represents labour of a certain kind, x_{ih} is zero while ω_h represents the total quantity of that labour provided by the individuals of the community.

We shall have to introduce many variants of the general model. For example, we shall sometimes assume that the initial resources are privately owned and are therefore in the possession of individual consumers. We shall often simplify our theoretical study by considering a model with no producers, where only the distribution or exchange of goods among consumers is analysed.

Having introduced these initial ideas, we can define formally what we mean by the 'economy'. In fact the definition will vary according to the particular model. Obviously we shall come to elaborate our representation of consumers and producers and to add new concepts. But at this very early stage, we can say that an *economy* is defined by a list of goods, a list of consumers, a list of producers, and a vector ω of initial resources. A *state of the economy* is then defined when particular values are given for the m vectors x_i and the n vectors y_j. In positive theory, where the aim is also to explain how prices are determined, we shall have to introduce a vector p (specified up to a multiplicative constant) when we define a state of the economy.

In this general conceptual context, there are two types of objective for microeconomic theory. In the first place, it must *describe* the activity of agents, that is, it must provide models which explain in abstract terms how each consumer i determines x_i and how each producer j determines y_j, and it must also describe how all the x_{ih} and all the y_{jh}, and possibly also prices p_h, are simultaneously determined. (It must therefore place itself at the level of the individual agent in a partial perspective as well as at the level of the whole economy). This is the objective of *equilibrium theory*, first partial, then general equilibrium.

In the second place, it must look for an *optimal organisation* of production, consumption and exchange, and then study the properties of a state of the economy in which this optimal organisation is realised. This is the objective of *optimum theory*, also called welfare theory.

These are the questions which we shall be discussing in the course of these lectures. Our immediate task is to examine the validity of the general conceptual framework on which all later analysis will be based.

3. Possible interpretations of the concept of a good

What kind of picture of economic reality can we derive from these general concepts?

They present us with a community composed of two types of individual, consumers and producers, and of these two types alone. At a given instant, the community finds itself in possession of certain initial resources involving a finite number of goods. It is about to engage in the operations of production, distribution and consumption.

We propose to discover *a priori* how consumers and producers will act when they find themselves in an institutional framework to which we shall later give formal representation. We wish to know what prices will be established for the exchange of goods. We wish to find what might be the best system of production and consumption. In doing this, we appear to assume that the community will act once for all, as if it were taking part in a game with fixed rules.

It is up to each of you to consider, throughout the coming lectures, how far this picture approximates to reality. It is not my purpose to discuss it much further. However, it must be emphasised that these concepts have greater flexibility than may appear at first. In particular, let us examine the definition of goods.

(i) *Quality of goods*

Each commodity must be perfectly homogeneous since two equal quantities of it must be equivalent. In actual fact, many products show a more or less immense range of qualities. Two foodstuffs of the same kind may differ in flavour or nutritive content. Two machines designed for the same tasks may differ in durability, power consumption or ease of operation.

However, the concept of a commodity can be adapted to this diversity among products of the same kind. Two different qualities of the same product or service may in fact be represented by two different commodities. Of course the number of goods then becomes much greater than that of products and services. But there is no reason why l should not be very large.

The model is therefore still appropriate unless the range of qualities of some products appears perfectly continuous, which is never properly speaking true, but may represent the real situation better than a very large number of distinct qualities. For example, if the specification of a crude oil is defined by its composition in terms of certain elements whose number is r, then a distinct quality corresponds to each of the points of a bounded region of r-dimensional space. The qualities are no longer finite in number.

Our model does not cover such cases. However, the theories can be generalised, subject to certain conditions, so that the restriction is not too serious.†

---

† See, for example, G. Debreu, 'Valuation equilibrium and Pareto optimum', *Proceedings of the National Academy of Sciences of the U.S.A.*, vol. 40, pp. 588-592, 1954.

(ii) *Location*

We assume goods to be directly exchangeable, and this is not the case if they are available in different places. Two equal quantities of the same good are not really equivalent if they are not available in the same place. This does not destroy the usefulness of the concept of a good since we may consider the same product available in two different places as two distinct goods. Transport of the product from the first place to the second is then a productive activity with the first good as input and the second as output.

As in the case of qualities, it is restrictive to assume the number of locations finite, but this is not a serious restriction both because, for the most part, economic activity is concentrated in relatively few geographical centres, and because the theories discussed later will be capable of generalisation subject to some fairly natural additional assumptions.

(iii) *Date*

Two equal quantities of the same product which are available at different times are not really equivalent, so that these quantities must be considered to correspond to different commodities.

Obviously the model does not require that we confine our discussion to operations relating to a single period. We can multiply the number of periods at will, provided that we simultaneously multiply the number of commodities. However, to keep within the terms of the model just defined, we must adopt a discrete representation of time and put a limiting terminal date to the future.

We have already said that it is permissible to represent the range of goods by continuous variables. So we can consider time t as a real variable belonging to a certain interval and let the function $z_q(t)$ denote quantities of the product q at each instant t.

Also, we may prefer unlimited future time to choosing a finite number of dates, which implies that the future period to be considered has a definite limiting horizon. Under certain additional assumptions, the theories with which we shall be concerned can be generalised to the case where time is represented by an unlimited sequence of periods

$$t = 1, 2, ..., \text{etc.}$$

However, the generalisation is not straightforward and often leads to weaker results.†

Thus, subject only to the reservation that qualities, locations and periods are finite in number, the conceptual framework introduced above easily takes account of the actual diversity of products and services.

Suppose that the index $q = 1, 2, ..., Q$ characterises both the nature and

---

† See, for example, on optimum theory, E. Malinvaud, 'Capital Accumulation and Allocation of Resources', *Econometrica*, April 1953 and July 1962.

quality of products and services, that there are S locations represented by an index $s = 1, 2, ..., S$ and T periods represented by $t = 1, 2, ..., T$. The index h now represents (q, s, t) and $l = QST$. The quantity x_{ih} denotes the ith consumer's consumption of the product whose nature and quality is q, available at place s in period t.

We shall not go on reminding ourselves that the positive or normative theories we are discussing can be interpreted so as to take account of the diversity of locations and times, since this would become tedious. But there is an accompanying risk of unwittingly disguising difficulties, since some of the assumptions to be adopted may become more restrictive when several places and several dates are distinguished. An example of this will be given shortly. But the student must ask himself throughout the lectures how far the various assumptions adopted are appropriate to a space-time economy. In Chapter 10 we shall have occasion to examine more closely the complications which arise from the progress of time.

To enlarge on the above remarks, we now ignore differences of quality and location. So the index h stands for the double index (q, t). Our theories have an *a priori* standpoint. Their aim is, for example, to explain how production, consumption and price will be determined. In a time perspective, this means (i) that the periods $t = 1, 2, ..., T$ are future periods and (ii) that consumption, production and price are determined simultaneously for all periods.

To choose x_i is to choose all the components x_{iqt} which refer to multiple products and services, but also at multiple future dates. Thus, x_i is a *consumption programme or plan* which relates to all the periods considered. Similarly, to explain the simultaneous determination of the x_i, the y_j and p is to explain how, at the moment considered, the programmes of all agents and prices are determined for all future periods.

To suppose that a price vector p exists at a certain instant is to suppose that, at that instant, there exist well-defined prices for each index (q, t), that is, for each product and each future date. So, corresponding to each product q, there are as many prices as there are dates. The price p_{qt} is that price which must be paid now (at the moment considered) to obtain delivery at time t of a unit of the product q. It is therefore a 'forward price'.

To assume the existence of forward prices for all dates and all products, as we do here for a time economy, is clearly more restrictive and perhaps much less realistic than to assume the existence of actual prices for all products in an economy without time. 'In fact', the sceptic might say, 'in what actual exchanges do forward prices apply? Are they as numerous as the theory would like them to be?' This demonstrates that doubts may be expressed as to the relevance of some possible temporal interpretations of our theories. But such doubts do not destroy its usefulness, though they may sometimes restrict its field of application.

4. Descriptive relevance of the accounting economy

Enough has been said about the concept of a good. Now we must say a little about the most obvious omissions from our representation of the economy.

It is an economy with no public bodies and in particular, with no government agencies. Of course, there is no reason why the institutional rules which govern it should not be decided by some political power with its attendant administration. But our model ignores the fact that certain public bodies also participate directly in the production and consumption of goods. In order to ensure the satisfaction of collective needs, these organisations acquire some of the goods produced and themselves carry out some production operations. As we shall see later, this situation is easily explained: the market economy, which has a certain efficiency in the satisfaction of individual needs, does not as spontaneously ensure the satisfaction of collective needs, which must be taken over by agents representing all interested parties. However, at this stage we ignore the existence of collective needs. We shall return to this simplification later (cf. Chapter 9).

For the moment, we have taken account only of operations on goods and services within the economy. We can introduce income formation in a fairly natural way; the price of the work done by a consumer is the rate of re-muneration for his labour; the value of the net production of a firm constitutes its profit, which is distributed to consumers if they hold the property of the firm.† Indeed, microeconomic theory is much concerned with this aspect of the distribution of incomes. However, its representation of income-formation ignores the many transfers which take place in modern societies: taxes raised to cover the cost of collective services, graduated taxation and subsidies to ensure a more equitable distribution of incomes, etc. Similarly, the model does not represent the multifarious financial operations which actually take place.‡

In our economy, prices are defined only up to a multiplicative constant and can be referred to any numéraire. In real life, prices are expressed as a function of money, which serves as a medium of exchange. Economic science must explain how their absolute level varies, that is, it must explain changes in the purchasing power of money, since such changes affect very many phenomena.

We shall abstract here from this aspect of reality. To visualise the world represented by our model, one might consider that commodities are directly exchanged, as in a 'barter economy'. Better justice is done to the conceptual power of the model if we assume an 'accounting economy', in which the value

---

† Similarly, a representation of 'rent' will be given in Chapter 5.

‡ Taxes and transfers have some part to play in Chapter 9. We shall also see in Chapter 10 that the time version of the model involves borrowing and lending operations: but it does so in a very summary way, without taking account of the liquidity of the various debts.

of each economic operation is properly recorded in accounts that are held for each agent and use the 'numéraire' as unit of value. In such an economy rules are imposed on the accounts of each agent, for instance consumer *i* may be required to balance his budget.

Finally, we are interested in a closed economy with no relationships with other economies. Our community cannot take advantage of the trade possibilities offered by the international market. Its price structure is completely independent of foreign price structures.

These various simplifications can be justified by the requirements of teaching; one cannot introduce everything all at once in a lecture course without running the risk of swamping the audience completely. Monetary theory, public finance and international trade are dealt with elsewhere in economic literature.

However, it must be pointed out that at present there exists no microeconomic theory which has the degree of rigour that we adopt and which recognises explicitly the existence of public bodies, monetary operations and external trade. Just as physics has not yet integrated the theories of electromagnetism and gravitation, so our science has not yet managed fully to integrate the microeconomic theory of the accounting economy with the macroeconomic theories of money, public finance and international trade.

But clearly, this does not destroy the usefulness of microeconomics as it exists today. Its relevance, although somewhat limited by the above simplifications, still persists since the theory as presently constructed does give a correct analysis of the principal phenomena and questions relating to the production and consumption of goods. It gives a conceptual frame of reference which often proves essential, and which no economist can afford to neglect, whatever his speciality.

5. The demands of rigour and simplicity

I have set myself two rules in these lectures. In the first place, I aim at rigour in order clearly to reveal the logical connection between certain formulations and assumptions and the properties deduced from them. In the second place, I aim at simplicity. When dealing with each of the important properties deduced by microeconomic theory, I try to select from all the presently available variants that which seems to be the best compromise between the greatest generality and the greatest simplicity. I therefore avoid those formulations which try to remain closer to reality but can do so only at the price of considerable complexity. I also refrain from listing the different variants, thus embarking on distinctions which are of interest only to specialists.

Such a course has the drawback that it does not lead to the greatest generality which is presently possible. You must see this clearly.

Thus, I shall be led to state precisely and to discuss assumptions that will be useful at one time or another in proofs. In order to reveal the nature of these assumptions more clearly, I shall give counter-examples, that is, situations in which they are not naturally satisfied. However, I must warn against an error of interpretation. These counter-examples will not necessarily reveal cases where the theory breaks down. There are several reasons for this.

In the first place, in most cases I shall use in each proof only some of the assumptions stated. They will be indicated in the statement of the properties.

In the second place, the sole object of some of the assumptions adopted will be to facilitate the proofs. In the choice between generality and simplicity, I shall often tend to favour the latter. Those who wish to go further must consult the books and articles in which the theory has been more fully elaborated.

In the third place, the assumptions in question always take the role of sufficient conditions for the validity of the results. In most cases, it would be wrong to take them as necessary, since, among these assumptions, there are few which could not be replaced by others whose content would be less restrictive from some points of view although often more restrictive from others.

Having completed these lectures, but as yet lacking knowledge of the extensive underlying literature, you may be tempted to say 'microeconomic theory assumes that . . .'. When you feel this temptation, I beg you to say instead 'in his presentation of microeconomic theory Malinvaud assumes that . . .'. If you then think that the restriction is serious, look for generalisations which do not involve it.

2

The consumer

1. Outline of the theory

Our first task is to make a detailed study of a formulation which applies to consumer activity and constitutes the basic element for the development of positive and normative theories concerning the whole economy. We have a double objective.

In the first place, we must represent human needs and take account of the fact that they can be satisfied more or less well, more or less completely. This representation will serve for explanation of the choices made by consuming individuals or households. It will also contribute to normative theories, when we try to classify states of the economy according as they satisfy individual needs more or less well or badly.

In the second place, we must find out how consumers act when placed in the institutional context which we attribute to the economy as a whole when discussing general equilibrium. At this stage, we assume that well defined prices, which for the consumers are given, govern exchanges that are otherwise free.

To achieve the second objective, we must start with the representation of needs. So the study of the laws of consumer behaviour is the natural objective of the present chapter.

In short, the purpose of the model to be discussed here is to explain how the vector x_i of the consumption x_{ih} of a particular individual i is determined. For simplicity, the index i is suppressed in this chapter, and we write x rather than x_i for the consumptions vector.

The main elements of the theory will now be stated briefly before it is discussed in detail, to give an indication of the line of development. The idea of the model is very simple: the consumer chooses the best complex x from a set of complexes that are feasible for him *a priori*. Let us define what is meant by a feasible complex and how the *preferences* of a particular individual are represented.

The consumer is subject to physical constraints and to an economic constraint:

(i) The vector x must belong to a set X which is given *a priori* and may depend on the particular consumer i under consideration. The definition of the set X takes account of the physical limitations on the consumer's activity. For instance, if the particular individual does not contribute to production, then X may simply be the subset of R^l consisting of the vectors with no negative component. But X is often defined more strictly to exclude the vectors x that do not ensure the satisfaction of certain elementary needs. Thus the model may involve the idea of a subsistence standard, which may be either biological or based on social conventions. However, it will often be evident that this idea of a subsistence standard is ignored for the sake of simplicity in these lectures.

(ii) In addition, the consumer has a limited 'income' R and must act within a market where each commodity h has a well-defined price p_h. So the value of x must not exceed R:

$$px = \sum_{h=1}^{l} p_h x_h \leqslant R \tag{1}$$

For the model in this chapter, R and the p_h are exogenous data.

(iii) The consumer's preferences among different vectors x, which satisfy his needs more or less well, are represented by a real function $S(x_1, x_2, ..., x_l)$ called the 'utility function' or 'satisfaction function' and defined in X. The values $S(x^1)$ and $S(x^2)$ of this function corresponding to two different complexes x^1 and x^2 measure as it were to what extent each of these complexes satisfies the consumer.† Therefore when we say that $S(x^1) > S(x^2)$, we are saying that the consumer prefers x^1 to x^2. It follows that, from all the feasible complexes, he chooses that one which maximises $S(x)$.

An *equilibrium* for the consumer is therefore a vector x^0 which maximises S subject to the double constraint expressed by (1) and the fact that x belongs to X.

So the function S, the set X, the vector p and the number R are taken as exogenous in the theory. On the other hand, the x_h are endogenous quantities, that is, quantities whose determination is explained by the theory.

Obviously the vector x chosen by the consumer depends on S, X, p and R. But generally we are content to make clear the dependence on prices p_h and income R, since they are subject to variation with other variables of the general economic environment in which the consumer acts. (In fact, p and R will be treated as endogenous in general equilibrium theory.)

Assuming that the vector x^0 maximising S is unique, we shall discuss the

---

† Here and throughout the lectures, superscripts are used for particular vectors such as x^0, y^1, y^2, ... etc.

vector function $\xi(p, R)$ whose components are the real functions $\xi_h(p_1, p_2, \ldots,$ $p_l, R)$ that determine the x_h° from the p_h and R. The function ξ_h will be called the consumer's *demand function* for commodity h.

In the course of this chapter, we must first make the initial concepts of the model more precise, that is, we must define more clearly and discuss briefly the nature of the two constraints and of the utility function. We must then show that, under certain conditions, the model allows us to determine the equilibrium x^0, and to determine it uniquely. Finally we must find certain general properties of demand functions, properties which remain true independently of the particular specification of the set X and the function S.

In considering the initial concepts we shall have to spend more time on the definition of the function S than on that of the two constraints. So we start by discussing utility.

2. The utility function

A quick survey of the history of economic science will give us a better idea of the sense in which the economist understands the term utility or satisfaction.

The first theories of general equilibrium date from the end of the eighteenth and the beginning of the nineteenth century.† They concentrated almost solely on production; price, value and the distribution of income were explained by costs, and mainly by the amounts of labour involved. Of course, the goods produced had to have utility for the consumer. To their 'exchange value' determined by costs there must correspond a 'use value'. But the appropriate conclusions were not drawn from this observation.

The main contribution of the so-called 'marginalist' school was to show how the conditions under which production responds to consumers' needs could be integrated in an analysis of general equilibrium. The 'theory of marginal utility' was put forward independently and almost simultaneously by three economists: the Englishman Stanley Jevons (1871), the Austrian Carl Menger (1871) and the Frenchman Léon Walras (1874). But there had been a whole current of thought leading up to it.‡

It is fairly natural to say that an individual acquires a good only if its price is less than its use value. Similarly, from the collective point of view, there is no apparent advantage in providing a good for an individual if its cost of production is greater than its utility to him.

But the marginalists emphasised the fact that the utility of a given quantity

---

† The most typical date is certainly 1817, the year of publication of David Ricardo's treatise, *The Principles of Political Economy and Taxation*, New edition, C.U.P., Cambridge, 1951.

‡ See the note on the theory of utility, pp. 1053-73 in Schumpeter, *History of Economic Analysis*, George Allen and Unwin, London, 1954.

of a good to be supplied to a consumer depends on the quantity of the same good already in his possession. The third glass of water or the third overcoat have less utility than the first. If the consumer acquires goods at fixed prices, the exchange value must correspond to the marginal utility, that is, to *the utility of the last quantity bought.*

Jevons, Menger and Walras represented the utility of the commodity h by a function $u_h(x_h)$ of the quantity consumed of the good, this function having a continuous derivative u_h', which must be decreasing in most cases and measures marginal utility, by definition. The utility that the consumer derives from the whole complex x is then

$$S(x) = \sum_{h=1}^{l} u_h(x_h).$$ (2)

Let us consider this formulation. We can imagine small variations with respect to the complex x. Suppose, for example, that there is a positive increase dx_r in the consumption of r and a decrease in the consumption of s (a negative dx_s). The utility of the complex remains unchanged if

$$dS = u_r' \, dx_r + u_s' \, dx_s = 0,$$

that is, if

$$-\frac{dx_r}{dx_s} = \frac{u_s'}{u_r'}.$$ (3)

The derivative u_r' is the marginal utility of the good r. The ratio u_s'/u_r' is called the *marginal rate of substitution of the good s with respect to the good r.* It is the additional quantity of r which will exactly compensate the consumer for a decrease of one unit of s, assuming this unit to be infinitely small. When (3) is satisfied, the consumer attributes the same utility to the complex x and the complex $x + dx$, where the vector dx has all zero components other than dx_r and dx_s. We shall see later on in this chapter that, if x is an equilibrium, the two equivalent complexes x and $x + dx$ must also have the same value, and so

$$p_r \, dx_r + p_s \, dx_s = 0,$$

hence

$$\frac{p_s}{p_r} = \frac{u_s'}{u_r'};$$ (4)

the marginal utilities must be proportional to prices.

According to the definition given by (3), the marginal rate of substitution of s with respect to r depends on the quantities consumed of r and s; it does not depend on the quantities x_h relating to other goods. This soon appears unrealistic. For example, the quantity of water which compensates for a quantity of wine will generally depend on the quantity of beer which the consumer possesses.

In order to present marginal rates of substitution without this particular property. Edgeworth introduced in 1881 a formula which has been adopted ever since. Utility is some function of the l arguments x_h, for example $S(x_1, x_2, ..., x_l)$. If this function is differentiable, the marginal rate of substitution of s with respect to r can be defined as the ratio

$$\frac{S'_s}{S'_r}, \tag{5}$$

where S'_s and S'_r denote the partial derivatives of S with respect to x_s and x_r. Here we have a function of all the x_h.

The theory of utility is essentially logical in nature. It can be applied whatever are the motivations of consumer choices since the economist takes the function S as given and does not attempt to explain how it is arrived at. But this fact, which will become quite clear after the following section, did not appear so initially. The theory has wrongly been associated with utilitarian or hedonist philosophy according to which every human action is motivated by the search for pleasure or the desire to avoid pain. There have also been attempts to see in it a debatable psychological theory.

In fact, the word 'utility' may lend itself to such an error of interpretation. The term 'satisfaction', or Pareto's term 'ophelimity', does not seem much better in this respect. But this is of little importance if the technical meaning of these expressions in economics is clearly understood.

3. Utility function and preference relation

The utility function $S(x)$ represents the consumer's preferences. Its essential characteristic from our point of view is that the consumer chooses x^1 rather than x^2 if $S(x^1) > S(x^2)$. We can therefore use the function S to classify complexes in their order of choice by the consumer.

In particular, we can define an indifference surface corresponding to the complex x^0 as the subset $\mathscr{S}_0$ of R_l consisting of the vectors x such that

$$S(x) = S(x^0).$$

There are therefore as many indifference surfaces as there are values of the function S. Two complexes x^1 and x^2 belong to the same indifference surface if and only if the consumer is indifferent between x^1 and x^2.

Obviously indifference surfaces can easily be represented geometrically if $l = 2$, the two goods being, for example, 'foodstuffs' and 'other goods'. On such a diagram we can, if necessary, indicate the direction of increase of the function S.

Clearly the ordered system of indifference surfaces can be represented by functions S other than the particular function on which it was based. If ϕ is some increasing function

$$S^*(x) = \phi[S(x)] \tag{6}$$

has the same indifference surfaces as $S(x)$, classifies them in the same way, and so provides another analytic representation of the same system of preferences.

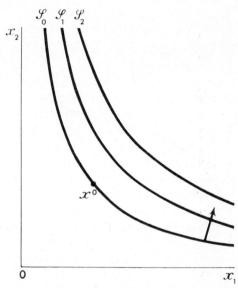

Fig. 1

Conversely, if S^* and S are two utility functions giving the same indifference surfaces, there exists a function ϕ such that (6) is satisfied. (Let I be the interval of the values of $S(x)$; for every s in I, we define $\phi(s)$ as the value of S^* on the indifference surface along which S takes the value s.) If S^* and S classify the indifference surfaces in the same way, then ϕ is increasing.

When we are interested only in the ordered system of indifference surfaces, we say that S is defined up to an increasing function. To recall this indeterminacy, we sometimes describe S as 'relative utility' or 'ordinal utility'. It is then important to verify that the conclusions from our theories do not vary with any change in the definition of utility function.

For the purposes of these lectures, *it will be sufficient that ordinal utility exists*. The student should verify this himself whenever we use the function S. Our theories are based on a given system of preferences rather than on a given function defining use-value in the sense of the nineteenth-century writers.

It might therefore be asked if the introduction of the function S is not superfluous. Since we are interested only in the order of preferences, can we not restrict ourselves to a formal representation of it?

Clearly we can. To see this in detail, let us consider the properties of a system of preferences represented by a utility function. Let $\succsim$ denote the relation defined among the x's of X by

$$x^1 \succsim x^2 \qquad \text{if} \qquad S(x^1) \geqslant S(x^2).$$

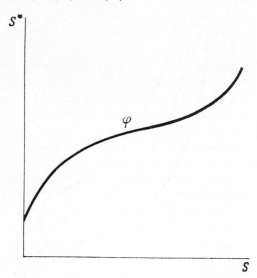

Fig. 2

From this we can derive the following two relations:

$$x^1 \succ x^2 \qquad \text{if} \qquad x^1 \succsim x^2 \qquad \text{but not} \qquad x^2 \succsim x^1,$$

therefore if $\quad S(x^1) > S(x^2)$;

$$x^1 \sim x^2 \qquad \text{if} \qquad x^1 \succsim x^2 \qquad \text{and} \qquad x^2 \succsim x^1$$

therefore if $\quad S(x^1) = S(x^2)$.

We immediately find the following properties of the relation $\succsim$:

A.1 For every pair x^1, x^2 of vectors of X
either $x^1 \succsim x^2$ or $x^2 \succsim x^1$ (the ordering is total)

A.2 For every x of X
$x \succsim x$ (reflexivity)

A.3 If $x^1 \succsim x^2$ and $x^2 \succsim x^3$, then
$x^1 \succsim x^3$ (transitivity).

Instead of starting with the function S, we could have given the relation $\gtrsim$ *a priori*. It would seem reasonable to demand that this relation satisfy the three properties A.1, A.2 and A.3, which would then be taken as axioms, so that $\gtrsim$ would then appear as a relation of the category that mathematicians call 'preorderings'.

This is the approach adopted in the most modern presentations of consumer theory. Only the preordering relation is involved; the notion of utility is not necessarily mentioned.

Why then do we use the utility function as the initial formal concept in the representation of preferences? The reasons are the following.

In the first place, the theory based on the utility function leads to results, well known in economics, which cannot be obtained directly from the preordering relation. These results are not indispensable for the most essential part of microeconomics. However, economists should known them; they are helpful in the consideration of the structure and bearing of our theories.

In the second place, reasoning based on the utility function will seem more familiar to students than the most modern presentations. There should be less trouble with mathematical difficulties, so that the student is free to concentrate on the economic assumptions and the main logical developments.

In the third place, taking a utility function is not much more restrictive than starting with the set of axioms A.1, A.2 and A.3. In fact, when the set X satisfies fairly unrestrictive general conditions, *we can represent by a continuous utility function every preordering which satisfies the following additional axiom*:†

A.4   For any $x^0 \in X$, the set $\{x \in X / x^0 \gtrsim x\}$ of all the x's which are not preferred to x^0 and the set $\{x \in X / x \gtrsim x^0\}$ of all the x's to which x^0 is not preferred are closed in X.

The extent to which the generality of a preference relation must be restricted in order to justify the introduction of a continuous utility function will be made clear in an example of a preordering which does not satisfy A.4. Suppose then that $l = 2$, that X is the set of vectors neither of whose two components is negative, and consider the relation defined as follows: given x^1 and x^2 in X, we say that $x^1 \gtrsim x^2$ if

$$\text{either} \quad \begin{matrix} x_1^1 > x_1^2 \\ x_1^1 = x_1^2 \end{matrix} \quad \text{and} \quad x_2^1 \geqslant x_2^2.$$

This relation, called the 'lexicographic ordering' does not satisfy A.4. Thus on Figure 3, the set

$$\{x \in X / x \gtrsim x^0\}$$

---

†   For the proof, see Debreu, *Theory of Value*, Section 4.6.

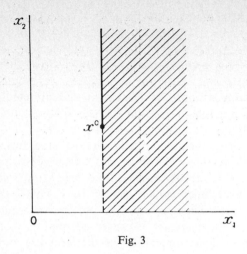

Fig. 3

is shaded; it does not contain that part of its boundary which lies below x^0. In fact, it cannot be represented by a continuous real function S.

Such a preference relation has sometimes been considered; it hardly seems likely to arise in economics, since it assumes that, for the consumer, the good 1 is immeasurably more important than the good 2. We loose little in the way of realism if we eliminate this and similar cases which do not satisfy A.4.

Having reached this point, we have a better understanding of the purely logical nature of the 'theory of utility' on which our reasoning will be based. The consumer's system of preferences is given; we do not have to concern ourselves with the motivation of these preferences and we do not exclude *a priori* any individual ethical system. All that matters is that the axioms A.1 to A.4 should hold. They are philosophically and psychologically neutral, and express a certain internal consistency of choices.†

4. The feasible set

We have said enough about the meaning to be attributed to the representation of preferences in consumer theory. Now we must set certain more precise assumptions about the set X and the function $S(x)$ so that we can

---

† The axioms A.1, A.2 and A.3 have sometimes given rise to discussion. Thus, it has been suggested that the choices of an individual are not always transitive. But the counter-examples given usually depend on an incomplete analysis of the situations among which lack of transitivity is supposed to occur. They seem to have no genuine effect on the force of the axioms, provided that we assume that an individual's system of preferences vary with age, education and other characteristics.

prove certain results about the existence of equilibrium or the properties of demand functions.

In accordance with the principles stated at the end of the first chapter, we shall here present and discuss assumptions which are not all really *necessary* for the validity of the following results, but which will be brought into the proofs as *sufficient* conditions.

To establish the required properties I shall most frequently use the following assumption about the set X of the vectors x representing the feasible consumption complexes.

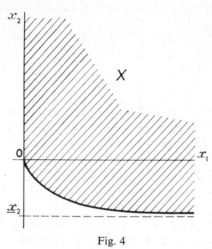

Fig. 4

ASSUMPTION 1. The set X is convex, closed and bounded below. It contains the null vector. If it contains a vector x^1, it also contains every vector x^2 such that

$$x_h^2 \geqslant x_h^1 \quad \text{for} \quad h = 1, 2, ..., l.$$

On Figure 4, which relates to the case of two goods, the shaded part represents a set X which satisfies assumption 1 (obviously the set can be prolonged indefinitely both upwards and to the right). The first commodity can only be consumed, but on the other hand, the consumer may supply certain quantities of the second commodity, which must therefore be considered to represent labour.

Let us examine the clauses of assumption 1 in turn.

You know that a set is said to be *convex* if it contains every vector of the segment (x^1, x^2) whenever it contains x^1 and x^2. This condition, which has often been assumed implicitly in economic theory, does not seem notably to restrict the significance of the results. However, in order that everything should be quite clear, we shall state two cases in which it is not satisfied.

Some goods can be consumed only in integral quantities. If, for example, this is the case for the good 1 when $l = 2$, the set X reduces to a certain number of vertical half-lines; it is not convex (see Figure 5, where the vector x^3 does not belong to X although it lies on the segment joining the two feasible vectors x^1 and x^2). This particular situation is obviously not serious if we have to consider quantities x_1 of the first good which consist of an appreciable number of units; substitution of a convex set for X is then an approximation of the kind permissible in all fields of science. Significant indivisibilities will, however, be ruled out in this chapter and in most parts of our lectures; they are indeed ruled out in most of microeconomic theory.

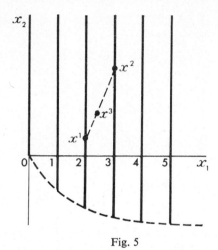

Fig. 5

It was pointed out earlier that goods might be distinguished by their location. Suppose that $l = 2$, and that the goods 1 and 2 represent consumption at Paris and at Lyon respectively. In some applications it will be natural to assume that an individual can consume either at Paris or at Lyon, but not at both simultaneously. The set X then consists of two parts: it is not convex (cf. Figure 6).

To assume that X is closed is to assume that, if each of the vectors x^t of a convergent sequence of vectors ($t = 1, 2, ...$) defines a feasible consumption complex, then the limit vector $\bar{x}$ of x^t also defines a feasible complex. There is no difficulty in accepting this clause.

The fact that X is bounded below means that there exists a vector $\underline{x}$ such that $x_h \geqslant \underline{x}_h$ for $h = 1, 2, ..., l$ and for every x of X. This condition is not restrictive since it is satisfied if the quantities of work supplied by the consumer are bounded above and if the consumption of other commodities cannot be negative.

It seems less satisfying to assume that an individual may have zero consumption of all goods, since this ignores the existence of a biological or sociological subsistence minimum, which the economist should recognise. However, the assumption that the null vector belongs to X simplifies the proofs, and this seems sufficient justification here. Note that, because of this clause, the $\underline{x}_h$ are all negative or zero.

Finally, the last part of assumption 1 means that it is always open to the consumer to accept a supplement of goods even if he does not have to do anything with them. We say that there is *free disposal* of surplus, and shall meet this assumption again in considering the producer. By itself, it eliminates the above two cases of non-convexity, but only postpones the difficulty till later, when assumption 4 on the utility function is formulated.

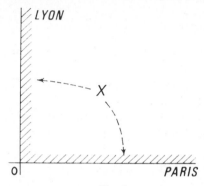

Fig. 6

Apart from the physical constraint expressed by the condition that x belongs to X, the consumer is bound by the economic constraint

$$px \leqslant R \tag{7}$$

where the p_h and R are exogenous data imposed on him.

To assume that price p_h is exogenous is equivalent to assuming that it is not influenced by the more or less large extent of the consumer's demand for the good h or for other goods. This assumption seems admissible in the circumstances. We shall return to it for fuller discussion in relation to the theory of the firm. It is in fact one of the basic elements in the definition of perfect competition.

In accordance with practice, we shall speak of R as the consumer's 'income'. However, when the labour he supplies is considered as negative consumption, R represents resources other than those earned by this labour. Moreover, if the model explicitly involves several periods, R must be interpreted as the total wealth available to the consumer for his consumption during all the periods; the term 'income' is then particularly unsuitable. Throughout the lectures, you must therefore be ready at any time to substitute the term 'wealth' to designate R for that of 'income'.

2

We shall assume that the consumer is subject to a single economic constraint. This assumption may seem unrealistic in certain contexts. For example, if we consider the choice of a consumption programme relating to several periods $t = 1, 2, ..., T$, to restrict ourselves to the constraint (7) means that we suppose that the consumer is free to borrow to cover a temporary deficit and is only required to balance out his operations over all T periods. Substituting the double index (q, t) for h, the restraint (7) becomes

$$\sum_{t=1}^{T} \sum_{q=1}^{Q} p_{qt} x_{qt} \leqslant R.$$

On the other hand, a consumer who can lend, but who can never be a debtor must obey T budget constraints

$$\sum_{\tau=1}^{t} \sum_{q=1}^{Q} (p_{q\tau} x_{q\tau} - R_\tau) \leqslant 0 \qquad t = 1, 2, ..., T$$

where R_τ represents that part of his total resources which is available to him in the τth period.

Let us note moreover that the economic constraint (7) imposes no upper bound on the quantity of commodity h that the consumer can buy on the market, as long as he is ready to pay the price p_h. This excludes any kind of rationing of individual demands.

5. Assumptions about the utility function

We now state three assumptions relating to the function $S(x)$.

ASSUMPTION 2. The function S defined on X is continuous and increasing, in the sense that

$$x_h^1 > x_h^2 \qquad \text{for} \qquad h = 1, 2, ..., l \qquad \text{implies that} \qquad S(x^1) > S(x^2).$$

The continuity of S follows from what was said in Section 4, and in particular from axiom A.4, which we have already discussed. Assumption 2 also supposes that no good is harmful to the consumer. (It must be remembered here that labour is counted negatively so that, for a good h which corresponds to labour, $x_h^1 > x_h^2$ means that the consumer's contribution is smaller in x^1 than in x^2.) The assumption also eliminates the possibility of a state of complete saturation beyond which satisfaction cannot be increased.

ASSUMPTION 3. The function S is twice differentiable. Its first derivatives are never all simultaneously zero.

This assumption is introduced particularly for reasons of mathematical convenience. We use it when we wish to reveal certain marginal equalities and when we employ the analytic calculus in our reasoning. The most modern theoreticians disapprove of it and abstain from its use when proving general results. But research on specific problems or on difficult developments of the theory often makes it.

In the present context, it does not seem very restrictive given that $S(x)$ is assumed to be continuous. However, it is not satisfied in the following example relating to two goods:

$$S(x) = \text{Min} \left\{ \frac{x_1}{a_1}, \frac{x_2}{a_2} \right\},$$

where a_1 and a_2 are two given positive constants. This function, two of whose indifference curves are represented in Figure 7, is not first order differentiable at any point x^0 such that

$$\frac{x_1^0}{a_1} = \frac{x_2^0}{a_2}.$$

In fact, the variation in S around such a point is described by

$$dS = \begin{cases} \dfrac{dx_1}{a_1} & \text{if} & \dfrac{dx_1}{a_1} \leqslant \dfrac{dx_2}{a_1} \\[2ex] \dfrac{dx_2}{a_2} & \text{if} & \dfrac{dx_1}{a_1} \geqslant \dfrac{dx_2}{a_2} \end{cases}$$

Therefore the variation dS is not linear in dx_1 and dx_2, as is required for differentiability.

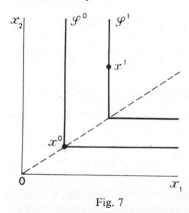

Fig. 7

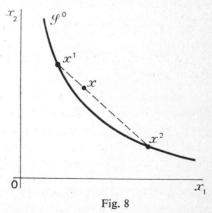

Fig. 8

Such a function may be appropriate to the case of strict complementarity between two goods (for example, oil and vinegar for a consumer who cannot tolerate cooking in oil, but enjoys a vinaigrette dressing of fixed composition). Cases of this kind will be eliminated when we proceed to differential calculus.

The assumption that the derivatives of the differentiable function S are not all simultaneously zero will be useful on occasion later. It does not seem to restrict the nature of the system of preferences. For example, it eliminates a function S^* defined by the transformation $S^* = \phi(S)$ applied to an S satisfying assumption 3, the function ϕ being increasing but having a zero derivative for a particular value of S.

ASSUMPTION 4. The function S is 'strictly quasi-concave'† in the sense that if $S(x^2) \geqslant S(x^1)$ for two different complexes x^1 and x^2, then

$$S(x) > S(x^1)$$

for every complex x of the open interval (x^1, x^2), that is, for every complex x defined by

$$x_h = \alpha x_h^1 + (1 - \alpha)x_h^2 \qquad h = 1, 2, ..., l \tag{9}$$

where α is a positive number less than 1.

Note that $S(x)$ is defined for the vector x with coordinates (9) if X is convex in accordance with assumption 1. A weaker version of assumption 4 is sometimes used. The function S is said to be 'quasi-concave' if $S(x) \geqslant S(x^1)$ with the same conditions for the definition of x^1, x^2 and x. Note also that if S is strictly quasi-concave (or simply quasi-concave) then so also is $S^* = \phi(S)$ whenever ϕ is increasing.

Assumption 4 means that the indifference surfaces are concave upwards (see Figure 8). It is often considered as admissible owing to the fact that a complex x of the segment (x^1, x^2) has a composition which is intermediary to those of x^1 and x^2, and therefore is better balanced than either. It may fall down for example in certain choices relating to the consumer's chosen way of life. An individual may be indifferent as between two complexes, one ensuring a comfortable life dedicated to the arts and the other an adventurous sporting life. But he may prefer one or other of these to an intermediary third complex which does not allow full enjoyment of either way of life. Also, you may verify that the previous examples relating to the non-convexity of X become examples of the non-quasi-concavity of S if there is free disposal of surplus (cf. Figures 5 and 6).

6. The existence of equilibrium and demand functions

We shall now prove that, under certain conditions, an equilibrium exists, so that our theory provides a consistent explanation of consumer behaviour. This will illustrate how to carry out a rigorous proof of a question of economic theory.

PROPOSITION 1. If assumptions 1 and 2 are satisfied, if $p_h > 0$ for $h = 1$, $2, ..., l$ and if $R \geqslant 0$, then there exists a vector x^0 which maximises S in X

---

† The definition of quasi-concave functions introduced here may be compared with the definition of concave functions on p. 300 of the appendix.

subject to the constraint (1). This vector x^0 is such that $px^0 = R$. If, moreover, assumption 4 is satisfied, then x^0 is unique and the demand function $\xi(p, R)$ defining x^0 is continuous for every vector p all of whose components are positive, and for every non-negative number R.

Consider the set P of physically and economically feasible vectors x. This set can be defined as the intersection of X and the set P^* of vectors satisfying

$$\begin{cases} x_h \geqslant \underline{x}_h & \text{for} \quad h = 1, 2, ..., l \\ px \leqslant R \end{cases} \tag{10}$$

(For example, in Figure 9, P is the shaded set, P^* the right-angled triangle containing P and with apex $(0, \underline{x}_2)$.) The set X is closed in view of assumption 1. The set P^* is closed and bounded; for,

$$\underline{x}_h \leqslant x_h \leqslant \frac{R - p\underline{x}}{p_h}. \tag{11}$$

(The second of these inequalities stems from the fact that, in view of (10) and the sign of the p_k,

$$p_h x_h \leqslant R - \sum_{k \neq h} p_k x_k, \qquad - p_k x_k \leqslant - p_k \underline{x}_k \quad \text{and} \quad 0 \leqslant - p_h \underline{x}_h;$$

therefore $p_h x_h \leqslant R - p\underline{x}$.)

Thus P is closed and bounded, that is, it is compact. P is not empty since it contains the null vector, which belongs to X in view of assumption 1 and satisfies the budget constraint (1) whenever R is not negative. S is continuous, in view of assumption 2; now, we know that every continuous function in a non-empty compact set has a maximum.† This is the vector x^0 whose existence we were trying to prove.

We must now show that $px^0 = R$. Suppose $px^0 < R$. There then exists a vector x^1 all of whose components are greater than the components of x^0, and is such that $px^1 \leqslant R$. In view of assumption 1, x^1 is in X and therefore in P; in view of assumption 2, it is preferable to x^0. Therefore x^0 is not the maximum of S in P, which is impossible.

Consider now the case where assumption 4 is satisfied. Suppose that there exists a vector x^1 different from x^0 which also maximises S in P. Obviously $S(x^0) = S(x^1)$, but every vector of the segment (x^0, x^1) then belongs to the convex set P and gives a value of S greater than $S(x^0)$, which is impossible. Therefore the vector x^0 is determined uniquely.

Finally, we must show that $\xi(p, R) = x^0$ depends on p and R continuously.‡ Suppose that this is not the case. Then there exists a sequence of vectors p^t

---

† See, for example, Dieudonné, *Foundations of Modern Analysis*, Academic Press, New York, 1960, theorem (3.17.10).

‡ The proof is rather long and not straightforward and may be omitted on a first reading.

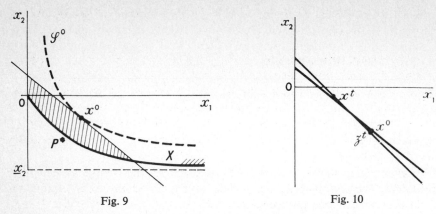

Fig. 9   Fig. 10

and a sequence of numbers R^t tending to p and R respectively (for $t = 1, 2, ...$) but such that

$$x^t = \xi(p^t, R^t)$$

does not tend to x^0. If necessary, after elimination of some of their elements, these sequences can be chosen in such a way that the distance between x^t and x^0 remains greater than a suitably chosen positive number ε.

Consider the vector z^t which is nearest x^0 in Euclidean distance, in the set P^t of vectors z belonging to X and satisfying $p^t z \leqslant R^t$ (see Figure 10). Since P^t is a compact, non-null set and the distance between x^0 and z is a continuous function of z, such a vector z^t does in fact exist. From the definition of x^t,

$$S(x^t) \geqslant S(z^t) \tag{12}$$

and, in view of the above result,

$$p^t x^t = R^t. \tag{13}$$

By similar reasoning to that used to establish the inequalities (11) it can be established that, for all sufficiently large t, the fact that x belongs to P^t implies

$$\underline{x}_h \leqslant x_h \leqslant \frac{R^t - p^t \underline{x}}{p^t_h} \leqslant \frac{R + 1 - 2p\underline{x}}{\frac{1}{2}p_h}.$$

The outside inequalities show that the double sequence consisting of the x^t and the z^t belongs to a compact set (independent of t). It has a limit point which we can denote x^*, z^*.

Because of the choice of the p^t and the R^t, the vector x^* differs from x^0, since the distance between x^* and x^0 is at least ε. The vector x^* belongs to X and satisfies the equality $px^* = R$ because of (13). Therefore

$$S(x^0) > S(x^*) \tag{14}$$

since x^0 is the unique maximum of S in P. The inequality (12) implies

$S(x^*) \geqslant S(z^*)$.

But z^* necessarily coincides with x^0, otherwise there exists a sphere around x^0 which does not intersect $p^t x \leqslant R^t$ for an infinite sequence of values of t. There then exists a vector u, all of whose components are positive, such that $p^t(x^0 - u) > R^t$ for the same sequence of values of t, and therefore also such that $px^0 \geqslant R + pu$. Since this is impossible, z^* must coincide with x^0. Inequalities (14) and (15) are therefore contradictory: this completes the proof of proposition 1.

Proposition 1 shows that, if assumptions 1, 2 and 4 are satisfied, the demand functions $\xi_h(p_1, p_2, ..., p_l : R)$ defining the components of x^0 are themselves continuous and well-defined for all values of the p_h and of R such that

$p_h > 0$ for $h = 1, 2, ..., l$

$R \geqslant 0$.

It would have been preferable to be able to state that the ξ_h are defined and also continuous when some of the p_h are zero. But this requires more complex assumptions. If some of the p_h are zero, the set P^* and therefore also P are not bounded above. In this case, some of the ξ_h may tend to infinity as some of the p_h tend to zero. We shall ignore this case in what follows and shall on occasion discuss situations where some prices are zero, while the demands remain finite.

7. Marginal properties of equilibrium

Assuming now that the utility function is differentiable (assumption 3) we shall establish certain classical relations between prices and marginal rates of substitution relating to a consumer equilibrium x^0. To do this, we shall consider the case where x^0 *lies within* X. We shall then discuss necessary modifications to the relations if the equilibrium point lies on the boundary of the set of feasible consumptions.

If assumptions 1 and 2 are satisfied and if x^0 lies within X, then this vector is a local maximum of $S(x)$ subject to the *'budget constraint'* $px = R$. If, moreover, $S(x)$ is differentiable, the classical maximisation conditions must necessarily be realised (see theorems VI and VII in the appendix, relating to the extrema of functions of several variables).

In view of the first order conditions (theorem VI), there exists a number λ (a Lagrange multiplier) such that the first derivatives of

$$S(x) - \lambda(px - R) \tag{16}$$

with respect to the x_h are all zero at x^0, that is, such that

$$S'_h - \lambda p_h = 0 \qquad \text{for} \qquad h = 1, 2, ..., l. \tag{17}$$

These equalities imply that *the marginal rate of substitution of any good s with respect to any good r is equal to the ratio between the price of r and the price of s*:

$$\frac{S'_s}{S'_r} = \frac{p_s}{p_r} \tag{18}$$

(here S'_r and p_r are assumed to differ from zero).

We note here that the marginal rates of substitution are invariant with respect to any change in the specification of the function S representing a given system of preferences. If $S^* = \phi(S)$ is substituted for S, then $S^{*'}_h = \phi' . S'_h$; ratios such as (18) are unaffected and the Lagrange multiplier λ is multiplied by the value of ϕ' for $S(x^0)$.

We can interpret (17) as implying that, in the space R^l, the vector p, normal to the budget constraint, is collinear with the normal at x^0 of the indifference surface containing this point. It is equivalent to say that this indifference surface is tangential to the plane representing the budget constraint (see Figure 9 where this property is clearly shown for the case of two goods).

The second order conditions (theorem VII) relate to the matrix of the second-order derivatives of the 'Lagrangian' expression (16). The derivatives with respect to the x_h are here equal to those of $S(x)$. Let S''_{hk} be the value at x^0 of the second derivative of S with respect to x_h and x_k. The second order conditions imply that the quadratic form $\sum_{hk} u_h S''_{hk} u_k$ is negative or zero for every vector u such that $\sum_h p_h u_h = 0$, that is, for every vector u normal to p. (Obviously this property expresses the fact that, in the budget plane, the variations of S in the neighbourhood of x^0 which are zero at the first order, are negative or zero at the second order.)

It is clearly restrictive to assume that x^0 lies within X since this requires that the individual chooses to consume positive amounts of all those goods which he cannot himself supply. If x^0 lies on the boundary of X, some of the constraints to which he is subject must be expressed by inequalities rather than by equalities. The necessary conditions for maximisation must then be found in the Kuhn-Tucker theorem (theorem VII in the Appendix) rather than in the classical results used here.

To avoid too much complication, we shall now consider the case where the set X is the positive orthant, that is, it imposes the condition that none of the components of x is negative. Given assumption 1, this case assumes that the individual considered cannot supply any good. It is easy to think of less particular cases which can be treated in the same way as this one.

In this case x^0 is a maximum of $S(x)$ subject to the $l + 1$ constraints expressed by

$$R - px \geqslant 0$$
$$x_h \geqslant 0 \qquad \text{for} \qquad h = 1, 2, ..., l.$$

For the application of theorem XI we then find ourselves in the particular case discussed in p. 312 of the Appendix. There necessarily exists a non-negative Lagrange multiplier λ such that the derivatives with respect to the x_h of

$$S(x) + \lambda(R - px) \tag{19}$$

are all non-positive at x^0, and also are zero for the h's corresponding to positive components x_h^0 of x^0.

We can then divide the l goods into two categories:

(i) the h goods whose consumption is positive in the equilibrium ($x_h^0 > 0$), differentiation of (19) giving (17):

$$S_h' - \lambda p_h = 0, \tag{20}$$

(ii) the k goods for which consumption is zero ($x_k^0 = 0$), the condition then becoming

$$S_k' - \lambda p_k \leqslant 0. \tag{21}$$

Consider first a pair of goods r and s which are both consumed in the equilibrium. Since equalities (17) are satisfied for these two goods, the marginal rate of substitution of s with respect to r is the ratio of p_s and p_r. The relation previously obtained remains unchanged.

Consider now a pair (h, k), where h represents a good consumed and k a good which is not consumed. Relations (20) and (21) imply

$$\frac{S_k'}{S_h'} \leqslant \frac{p_k}{p_h}. \tag{22}$$

The marginal rate of substitution of k with respect to h is less than or at most equal to the relative price of k with respect to h (the price of k is too high for the consumer to wish to consume it). Figure 11 illustrates a case of this type, where the good 2 is not consumed at x^0. The modification to the marginal equality appears very natural.

8. The case where the marginal equalities are sufficient to determine equilibrium

The budget constraint and the marginal equalities (17) define the following system of $l + 1$ equations:

$$\begin{cases} \dfrac{\partial}{\partial x_h} S(x_1, x_2, ..., x_l) - \lambda p_h = 0 & h = 1, 2, ..., l \\[2mm] \displaystyle\sum_h p_h x_h = R \end{cases} \tag{23}$$

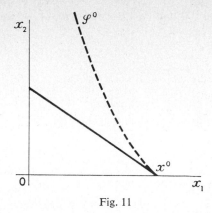

Fig. 11

We can consider this system as allowing us to find the $l + 1$ unknowns which are *a priori* the l quantities x_h and the Lagrange multiplier λ. The system has a solution if the equilibrium x^0 lies within X.

Conversely, is every solution of this system an equilibrium point for the consumer? Is it sufficient that a vector x^0 satisfy the marginal equalities and the budget constraint for it to be an equilibrium point? When discussing the theory of the optimum we shall need to know in which cases the answer to this question is in the affirmative. This motivates the following proposition:

PROPOSITION 2. *If assumptions 1 to 4 are satisfied, and if no price p_h is negative, then a vector x^0 which lies in the interior of X and satisfies system (23) for an appropriate value of λ is an equilibrium point for the consumer.*

To prove this proposition,† we must establish that $px^1 > R$ for every x^1 of X such that

$$S(x^1) > S(x^0). \tag{24}$$

Before considering such an x^1, we shall show that $px \geqslant R$ *for every x such that* $S(x) = S(x^0)$. If dt is a positive infinitesimal, the quasi-concavity of S (assumption 4) implies

$$S[dtx + (1 - dt)x^0] > S(x^0),$$

or

$$\frac{S[x^0 + (x - x^0)\,dt] - S(x^0)}{dt} > 0.$$

In the limit, when dt tends to zero, the following inequality must apply:

$$\sum_{h=1}^{l} S_h'(x^0) \cdot (x_h - x_h^0) \geqslant 0. \tag{25}$$

In system (23) λ *is positive* since the p_h are non-negative, the fact that S is

---

† The proof is rather long. The reader may go straight on to Section 9 if he so wishes.

increasing (assumption 2) implies that none of its first derivatives is negative and assumption 3 excludes the case where all these derivatives are zero. The marginal equalities (23) and inequality (25) then imply $p(x - x^0) \geqslant 0$, and so $px \geqslant px^0 = R$.

Consider now a vector x^1 of X such that $S(x^1) > S(x^0)$. Then the quasi-concavity of S implies that $S(x) > S(x^0)$ for every vector x of the open interval (x^0, x^1). Since x^0 lies within X there exists, centred on x^0, a cube with side 2ε entirely contained in X. Consider then a vector x^* of the interval (x^0, x^1) and such that

$$|x_h^0 - x_h^*| < \frac{\varepsilon}{2} \qquad h = 1, 2, ..., l.$$

Let us also define the vector $\hat{x}$ as

$$\hat{x}_h = \frac{x_h^0 + x_h^*}{2} - \frac{\varepsilon}{2} \qquad h = 1, 2, ..., l.$$

We see immediately that $\hat{x}$ is in the cube and therefore in X, and moreover that $\hat{x}_h < x_h^0$ and $\hat{x}_h < x_h^*$ for all h.

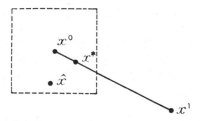

Fig. 12

Let us now prove the inequality $px^* > R$. We know that

$$S(x^*) > S(x^0)$$

and that $S(\hat{x}) < S(x^0)$. So in the interval $(\hat{x}, x^*)$ there exists a vector $\tilde{x}$ such that $S(\tilde{x}) = S(x^0)$. In view of what we established at the beginning of this proof, $p\tilde{x} \geqslant R$, which implies $px^* > R$ since $\tilde{x}_h < x_h^*$ for all h.

Since $px^* > px^0$ and since x^* is contained in the interval (x^0, x^1), it necessarily follows that $px^1 > px^0 = R$, which is the required result.†

---

† It is clear from this proof that, without bringing in the assumption that x^0 lies in the interior of X, we found that x^0 minimises px in the set of x's such that $S(x) \geqslant S(x^0)$. But if we wish to establish that x^0 also maximises $S(x)$ in the set of x's such that $px \leqslant px^0$ we must introduce the condition that x^0 lie in the interior of X, or other less restrictive conditions which need not be mentioned here.

9. The study of demand functions

Up till now we have been concerned with how to characterise and determine consumer equilibrium. But we have spent little time on the demand functions $\xi_h(p, R)$, that is, the functions which define how the equilibrium varies with the exogenous variables p and R. We must now investigate this question.

We start with an initial property which is easily established.

PROPERTY 1. The demand functions are homogeneous of degree zero with respect to prices p_h and income R.

For, suppose that all the p_h and R are simultaneously multiplied by the same positive number α. Neither the function to be maximised nor the domain defined by the constraints will be changed since p and R occur only in the homogeneous linear inequality $px \geqslant R$. The equilibrium is therefore unchanged.

Property 1 shows that the choice of the 'numéraire' does not affect demand functions. If it did not hold, we could not maintain the statement in the first lecture that prices are defined only up to a multiplicative positive constant.

It is sometimes said that property 1 establishes *the absence of money illusion*. In fact, it would not hold if a change in the monetary unit used as numéraire affected consumer behaviour in respect of the demand for goods.

In order to reveal two less immediate properties of demand functions, we shall now carry out a local study of the $\xi_h(p, R)$, assuming that S is increasing and twice differentiable (assumptions 2 and 3). We shall moreover introduce an assumption that will make $\xi_h(p, R)$ not only continuous but also differentiable.

Suppose therefore that the p_h and R vary by infinitely small quantities dp_h and dR; let us find conditions relating to the quantities dx_h by which the components x_h^0 of x^0 then vary. We confine ourselves here to the case where x^0 is a point in the interior of X and so necessarily satisfies (23). In short, we shall investigate how the solution of system (23) varies when p and R vary by dp and dR.

Differentiating (23), we obtain

$$\begin{cases} \sum_k S''_{hk} \, dx_k - d\lambda p_h - \lambda \, dp_h = 0 & h = 1, 2, ..., l \\ \sum_h p_h \, dx_h + \sum_h dp_h x_h = dR, \end{cases}$$

where S''_{hk} denotes the value at x^0 of the second derivative of S with respect to x_h and x_k. We can also use the matrix form

$$\begin{bmatrix} S'' & -p \\ -p' & 0 \end{bmatrix} \begin{bmatrix} dx \\ d\lambda \end{bmatrix} = \begin{bmatrix} \lambda I & 0 \\ x' & -1 \end{bmatrix} \begin{bmatrix} dp \\ dR \end{bmatrix} \tag{26}$$

where p' and x' represent the transposes of the column vectors p and x. This system will determine dx and $d\lambda$ if and only if the matrix on the extreme left is non singular, or, what amounts to the same thing, if the *matrix* $\begin{bmatrix} S'' & - \text{grad } S \\ (- \text{grad } S)' & 0 \end{bmatrix}$ is *non singular*. This is the condition for $\xi(p, R)$ to be differentiable. (The property is maintained if S is replaced by another function S^* deduced from S by a transformation ϕ having a positive derivative.)

Let

$$\begin{bmatrix} U & - v \\ - v' & w \end{bmatrix} \tag{27}$$

denote the inverse of the matrix on the left of (26). We can write

$$\begin{bmatrix} dx \\ d\lambda \end{bmatrix} = \begin{bmatrix} U & - v \\ - v' & w \end{bmatrix} \begin{bmatrix} \lambda I & 0 \\ x' & - 1 \end{bmatrix} \begin{bmatrix} dp \\ dR \end{bmatrix}$$

and consequently

$$dx = \lambda U \, dp + v(dR - x' \, dp). \tag{28}$$

(As an exercise, the reader may verify that λU and v are invariant when S is replaced by another function S^* deduced from S by a transformation having a positive derivative.)

Formula (28) expresses dx as the sum of two terms, the first involving dp, the second $dR - x' \, dp$. The latter quantity is the amount by which the increase in income exceeds the increase in the cost of acquiring x^0. For this reason it is called the *compensated variation in income* (the subtraction of $x' \, dp$ 'compensates' for the variation in the cost of x). We shall denote $dR - x' \, dp$ by $d\rho$ in what follows.

We note that $d\rho = 0$ is equivalent to $\sum_h p_h \, dx_h = 0$ since $R - px = 0$; it therefore follows from (23) that $d\rho = 0$ is equivalent to

$$dS = \sum_h S'_h \, dx_h = 0.$$

The variation in utility is zero at the same time as the compensated income change.

We can write

$$dx = \lambda U \, dp + v \, d\rho. \tag{29}$$

The first term is called the *substitution effect*, the second the *income effect*.

This equation will be more clearly understood if it is interpreted in the simple case where there exist only two goods and where only the price of the first varies

$$(dp_1 < 0, \; dp_2 = 0, \; dR = 0).$$

Consider a graph of (x_1, x_2) with the line AB representing the initial budget equation $px = R$: let N be the point representing the initial equilibrium: let AC be the line representing the new budget equation, and T the new equilibrium. We can draw the line DE parallel to AC but tangent (at P) to the indifference curve passing through the initial equilibrium. The displacement of N to T can be split up as follows:

(i) the displacement of N to P: the 'substitution effect' of good 1 for good 2 following the price variation which makes 2 relatively dearer than 1 (by definition, this effect is measured along the indifference curve passing through N);

(ii) the displacement of P to T: the 'income effect' which follows from the fact that the decrease in p_1 increases the consumer's purchasing power ($d\rho > 0$).

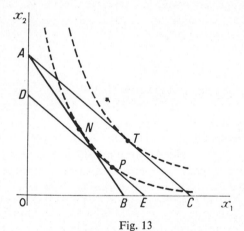

Fig. 13

Since, from (28), $v_1 = \partial x_1 / \partial R$, we can in this case write formula (29) as follows:

$$\frac{\partial x_1}{\partial p_1} = \left(\frac{\partial x_1}{\partial p_1}\right)_{s=Ct} - x_1 \left(\frac{\partial x_1}{\partial R}\right) \tag{30}$$

where $(\partial x_1 / \partial p_1)_{s=Ct}$ conventionally denotes the value of the ratio dx_1/dp_1 when $dp_2 = 0$ and $d\rho = 0$ (and therefore $dR = x_1 \, dp_1$); from (29), this value is equal to λU_{11}.

Since S'' is a symmetric matrix, it follows that U also is symmetric. We can therefore write

$$\lambda U_{hk} = \lambda U_{kh}$$

or, using the conventional notation defined above,

$$\left(\frac{\partial x_h}{\partial p_k}\right)_{s=Ct} = \left(\frac{\partial x_k}{\partial p_h}\right)_{s=Ct}$$

We can state this result as follows:

PROPERTY 2. The demand functions are such that the two 'Slutsky coefficients' characterising the substitution effects respectively of h for k and of k for h are equal.

This property is expressed in terms of the ordinary partial derivatives, which alone are directly observable, as follows:

$$\frac{\partial x_h}{\partial p_k} + x_k \frac{\partial x_h}{\partial R} = \frac{\partial x_k}{\partial p_h} + x_h \frac{\partial x_k}{\partial R}. \tag{31}$$

This is the form in which the *Slutsky equation* is generally written. (E. Slutsky, a Russian economic statistician, published his results in 1915.)

Other interesting properties follow from the way in which equation (28) was derived. First we know that matrix (27) is the inverse of the left hand matrix of system (26). This implies:

$$p'U = 0 \tag{32}$$
$$p'v = 1, \tag{33}$$

equations which may be written as:

$$\sum_{h=1}^{l} p_h \left(\frac{\partial x_h}{\partial p_k} \right)_{S=Ct} = 0 \qquad \text{for } k = 1, 2, \ldots, \tag{34}$$

$$\sum_{h=1}^{l} p_h \frac{\partial x_h}{\partial R} = 1. \tag{35}$$

This last equation expresses a simple fact: when all prices remain unchanged, the value of the change of consumption must be equal to the change of income. A similar, although a bit more complex, interpretation may be given of equation (34).

The second order conditions for an equilibrium also imply that the matrix U, or equivalently the *matrix of the Slutsky substitution coefficients is semi-definite negative*. Indeed, let us write as Z the left hand matrix of (26) and as Z^{-1} the matrix (27). The second order conditions imply that $a'S''a \leq 0$ for any vector a such that $p'a = 0$. We may also write this as:

$$[a' \quad b]Z \begin{bmatrix} a \\ b \end{bmatrix} \leq 0$$

for all vectors $[a' \ b]$ such that $p'a = 0$; or again

$$[\alpha' \quad \beta]Z^{-1} \begin{bmatrix} \alpha \\ \beta \end{bmatrix} \leq 0 \tag{36}$$

for any vector $[\alpha' \ \beta]$ that may be written as $[a' \ b]Z$ with a vector $[a' \ b]$ such that $p'a = 0$. The correspondence between $[\alpha' \ \beta]$ and $[a' \ b]$ implies $a' =$

$\alpha' U - \beta v'$. Hence $p'a = 0$ corresponds to $p'U\alpha - p'v\beta = 0$, which in view of (32) and (33) boils down to $\beta = 0$. Inequality (36) must therefore hold with $\beta = 0$ for any α. It is then simply:

$$\alpha' U \alpha \leqq 0.$$

The matrix U is semi-definite negative, as was to be proved.

In particular its hth diagonal element must be non positive:

$$\left(\frac{\partial x_h}{\partial p_h}\right)_{S=Ct} \leqq 0. \tag{37}$$

We can state equivalently:

PROPERTY 3. The demand for a commodity cannot increase as its price increases when all other prices remain constant and income is raised just enough to compensate for the price increase.

Of course, the expression on the left hand side of (37) is not observable. We shall more commonly be interested in

$$\frac{\partial x_h}{\partial p_h} = \left(\frac{\partial x_h}{\partial p_h}\right)_{S=Ct} - x_h\left(\frac{dx_h}{\partial R}\right).$$

The additional term is negative when $\partial x_h/\partial R > 0$ and $x_h > 0$. The decrease in demand as a function of price is therefore a fairly general law which can fail to hold for a positively consumed good only if a rise in income brings about a lower consumption. However, this latter possibility may arise in the case of so-called *inferior* goods. For the contributions made by the consumer (labour) the substitution and income effects are generally of opposite signs. Demand may therefore increase (and supply decrease) when price (i.e. wage) rises.

Finally, because of property 2, the following definitions are unambiguous:

Two goods h and k are said to be *substitutes* in the neighbourhood of an equilibrium point x^0 if

$$\left(\frac{\partial x_h}{\partial p_k}\right)_{S=Ct} > 0.$$

Two goods are said to be *complements* in the neighbourhood of an equilibrium point x^0 if

$$\left(\frac{\partial x_h}{\partial p_k}\right)_{S=Ct} < 0.$$

The goods h and k are therefore substitutes if a compensated variation in the price of k brings about two variations of opposite signs in the demands for h and k, and therefore some substitution between them. They are complements in the opposite case.

It follows from (34) and (37) that:

$$\sum_{h \neq k} p_h \left(\frac{\partial x_h}{\partial p_k}\right)_{S=Ct} \geqq 0.$$

J. Hicks has interpreted this relation as implying that substitution between different goods is more common than complementarity.

10. Cardinal utility

We have now concluded the programme which we set ourselves for the study of consumption. We have built up the theory by introducing a representation of the market constraints and a system of preferences. The system of preferences can be expressed by a purely ordinal utility function, that is, it can be transformed arbitrarily by an increasing function.

However, on reflection, the reader may hold the opinion that, for each consumer, there exists satisfaction or utility which is not only ordinal, but in a real sense cardinal, or, in the words of M. Allais, that there exists an *absolute satisfaction*. In other words, he may think that, among all the functions S which lead to the same system of preferences, there is one which has deeper significance and which measures better than the others the true utility which the consumer derives from the different consumption complexes. Clearly this point of view does not contradict that adopted in our lectures.

Cardinal utility may possibly give rise to more precise conclusions than simple ordinal utility. In fact, the former allows a type of comparison which is meaningless for the latter, namely the comparison of differences of utility.

More precisely, consider four complexes x^1, x^2, x^3, x^4 and suppose, to fix ideas, that $S(x^2) > S(x^1)$ and $S(x^4) > S(x^3)$. Can we determine if the resulting increase in utility when x^2 is substituted for x^1 is greater than the increase obtained when x^4 is substituted for x^3? Obviously we can, when we believe in a cardinal utility; we need only find out if the following inequality holds:

$$S(x^2) - S(x^1) > S(x^4) - S(x^3). \tag{38}$$

On the other hand, we cannot do so when we know only the preference ordering or an ordinal utility since, for the same complexes x^1, x^2, x^3 and x^4, the direction of an inequality such as (38) varies with the definition of the function S (cf. Figure 14). It depends basically on whether one does or does not accept that comparisons of gains in utility are meaningful, that one should or should not accept the concept of absolute utility.

We note also that inequalities of the type of (38) are unambiguous if S is determined only up to an increasing *linear* function, that is, if $S^*(x) =$

$aS(x) + b$ can be substituted for $S(x)$ in the representation of utilities (a and b are given constants, a being positive). So those who support the concept of absolute utility generally postulate that the corresponding function can be arbitrarily transformed by an increasing linear transformation.

Clearly the distinction between ordinal and cardinal utility recalls the distinction in physics between attributes which are measurable and attributes which are simply referable.

11. The axiom of revealed preference

Before concluding this chapter, we must say something about a proposed approach for the representation of consumer choices. This approach differs from the one we have adopted, but does not contradict it.

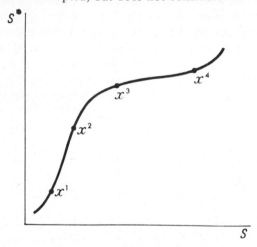

Fig. 14

In the discussion of cardinal utility and ordinal utility, or what amounts practically to the same thing, of cardinal utility and preference relation, an argument often invoked is that ordinal utility only would be 'operational'. It can be determined objectively by the simple observation of behaviour. In order to find a consumer's system of preferences, we need only confront him with a sufficient number of choices among complexes, and observe each time which complex he prefers. On the other hand, we could not learn merely from observation whether his gain in utility when he goes from x^1 to x^2 is greater or less than his gain in utility in going from x^3 to x^4. Cardinal utility would not be operational. The scientist should not introduce to his theories non-operational concepts which do not lend themselves to objective observation.

In 1938, this preoccupation led P. A. Samuelson to question even the notion of a preference relation as defined above. According to Samuelson, we do not really have the possibility of carrying out the experiments necessary for effective observation of consumer preferences. Confrontation of the abstract concept with actual observations is so difficult and so rare that we should avoid using even the notion of a system of preferences.

On the other hand, there is no difficulty in observing a consumer's actual choices when he has a certain income R and is faced with well defined prices p_h. Through his everyday behaviour the consumer 'reveals' his preferences to us without obliging us to think up artificial experiments.

Samuelson recommended therefore that the theory be established directly on the basis of the consumer demand function,† that is, on the vector function $\xi(p, R)$ which defines the complex x chosen by the consumer when the price vector is p and his income is R. (In this theory it is assumed that the vector x chosen by the consumer is determined *uniquely* from p and R.)

Samuelson suggests that x^1 is *revealed to be preferred* to x^2 (which differs from x^1) if there exist p^1 and R^1 such that:

(i) $x^1 = \xi(p^1, R^1)$,

(ii) $p^1 x^2 \leqslant R^1$.

(The consumer, disposing of R^1 and faced with p^1 may acquire either x^2 or x^1; he prefers x^1.)

It may be postulated that these revealed preferences are not mutually contradictory, in other words, that x^2 cannot be revealed to be preferred to x^1 when x^1 is revealed to be preferred to x^2, which is formally expressed by the following condition on the demand function $\xi(p, R)$.

AXIOM P. If, for some vectors p^1 and p^2 and some numbers R^1 and R^2, $p^1 \xi(p^2, R^2) \leqslant R^1$ and $\xi(p^2, R^2) \neq \xi(p^1, R^1)$, then $p^2 \xi(p^1, R^1) > R^2$.

In fact, Samuelson himself did not follow this idea to its conclusion since, in his *Foundations of Economic Analysis*, published in 1948, he presented consumption theory on the basis of ordinal utility.

But it did lead him to investigate more closely the conditions to be satisfied by demand functions if they are to be considered as revealing the existence of a preference relation of the type discussed in Section 3. In other words, he asked under what conditions revealed preferences constitute a complete preordering. H. Houthakker has shown that such a preordering exists whenever the demand functions satisfy an assumption of continuity and the

---

† Previously, G. Cassel put forward a general equilibrium theory based directly on demand functions. But, since he did not require these functions to obey Samuelson's consistency conditions, Cassel could not prove the existence of certain particular properties. For example, he had to postulate the absence of monetary illusion, instead of deducing it as we have done.

following axiom, which, for simplicity, is expressed in terms of complexes and not in terms of the functions themselves†:

AXIOM H. If x^1, x^2, ..., x^r are some r complexes such that x^1 is revealed to be preferred to x^2, x^2 is revealed to be preferred to x^3, ..., x^{r-1} is revealed to be preferred to x^r, then x^r is not revealed to be preferred to x^1.

In short, axiom H implies a kind of transitivity in the relation of revealed preference; it strengthens the axiom proposed by Samuelson.

Houthakker's result shows that, if the demand laws are perfectly known and if they satisfy the very natural conditions mentioned above, then the preference relation also is perfectly known. Contrary to Samuelson's suggestion, therefore, it is possible to determine this relation from direct observation of consumer behaviour without having to confront the consumer with a series of binary choices.

---

† A good survey of the contributions to the theory of revealed preferences is given by Houthakker, 'The Present State of Consumption Theory', *Econometrica*, October 1961.

The producer

1. Definitions

We come now to the activity of producers, also called 'firms'. This will be investigated in two successive stages. First of all we shall study the representation of the technical constraints which limit the range of feasible productive processes. We must then formalise the decisions of the firm which must act within a certain institutional context. Our discussion will be carried on mainly in the context of 'perfect competition', which cannot pretend to be an always valid description of real situations. But it is the ideal model on which the study of the problems of general equilibrium arising in market economies has been based so far.

As in our discussion of consumption theory, we shall omit the index j relating to the particular agent considered. So a_h, b_h and y_h will simply denote input, output and net production of the good h in the firm in question.

For the purposes of economic theory, a detailed description of technical processes is as pointless as knowledge of consumers' motivations. All that matters in this chapter is that we should formalise the constraints which technology imposes on the producer. These can be summarised in a very simple way: certain vectors y correspond to technically possible transformations of inputs into outputs; other vectors correspond to transformations which are not allowed by the technology at the disposal of the firm.

To take account of this, we need only define in R^l the *production set Y* as that set containing the net production vectors which are feasible for the producer. Thus the demands of technology are represented by the simple constraint

$$y \in Y. \tag{1}$$

(We must not forget that Y relates to a particular producer; in general equilibrium theory, each producer j has his own set Y_j.)

Of course, all the technically feasible transformations are not of interest *a priori*; some may require greater inputs and yield smaller outputs than others. The firm's technical experts must eliminate the former in favour of the latter. This is why we can often confine ourselves *a priori* to *technically efficient* net productions. By this we mean any transformation which cannot be altered so as to yield larger net production of one good without this resulting in smaller net production of some other good. Relative to such a transformation, therefore, output of one good cannot be increased without increasing input or reducing output of another good.

Formally, the vector y^1 is said to be technically efficient if it belongs to the set Y of feasible net productions and if there exists no other vector y^2 of Y such that

$$y_h^2 \geqslant y_h^1 \qquad \text{for} \qquad h = 1, 2, ..., l.$$

So the technically efficient vectors y belong to a subset, or possibly to the whole, of the boundary of y in the commodity space.†

In the construction of optimum and equilibrium theories we could impose on ourselves to use the production set Y as the sole representation of technical constraints. This is the method adopted in the most modern approaches to the subject. Following a tradition of almost a century, however, mathematical economists often introduce another more restrictive concept, that of the 'production function', which formalises in particular the idea that marginal substitutions between inputs are feasible.

Actually, in their approach to the problems of general equilibrium economists have alternatively used two types of formalisations, which stress two opposing features of production. One feature is the existence of 'proportionalities' or 'coefficients of production': some inputs must be combined in given proportions, like iron ore and coal in the process of producing pig iron. Another feature is the possibility of substituting an input for another: machines can replace men, one fuel can be substituted for another, more or less fertilizer can be put in a given piece of agricultural land and more or less labour can be spent on it, hence the same crop may be achieved with a little less fertiliser and a little more labour.

Economists such as K. Marx or L. Walras in the first editions of his treatise constructed their systems assuming fixed proportionalities, i.e. complementarity between inputs. Others like V. Pareto have used formalisations implying that substitutabilities are everywhere prevalent. The great advantage of the modern set theoretic approach is to cover both complementarities

† Rigorously, we can confine ourselves to technically efficient vectors only if, corresponding to every y of Y, we can find an efficient y^* such that $y_h^* \geqslant y_h$ for all h. This will be the case if Y is a closed set and if, without leaving Y, we cannot increase one component of y indefinitely without reducing another. It does not restrict the validity of the theory to assume this.

and substitutions. The definition of Y can take into account simultaneously the substitutability of machines for men and the proportionality between iron ore and coal. Hence the theory built directly on Y is fully general in this respect.

When we want to build models that lend themselves to computation for dealing with questions of applied economics, we have the choice today between two types of more specific formalisation: either production functions, usually allowing for large substitutabilities, or fixed coefficient processes combined into 'activity analysis' models.

Lectures such as the present ones should not ignore the production function concept. In fact it will be used extensively with the aim of making exposition easier and to allow the free use of differential calculus. Some essential proofs will be given under the assumption that the sets Y_j can be represented by production functions, even though this assumption is not required for the validity of the result. Production functions must therefore be defined and discussed with some care. Later on we shall point out in passing those places where the use of such functions conceals some difficulty.

A *production function f* for a particular firm is, by definition, a real function defined on R^l such that:

$$f(y_1, y_2, ..., y_l) = 0 \tag{2}$$

if and only if y is an efficient vector, and such that

$$f(y_1, y_2, ..., y_l) \leqslant 0 \tag{3}$$

if and only if y belongs to Y.

For the moment we shall not inquire into the conditions to be satisfied by Y if we are to be able to define such a function. This will be discussed in Section 2.

According to this definition, we can use (1) or (3) equivalently to represent the technical constraints on production† (the function f depends on the particular producer j, as does Y).

Geometric illustrations of the production set and the production function are often fruitful. Suppose, for example, that there are four commodities, the first two of which are outputs of the firm and the last two inputs. Figures 1 and 2 represent two intersections of Y, the first by a hyperplane ($y_3 = y_3^0$; $y_4 = y_4^0$), the second by a hyperplane ($y_1 = y_1^0$; $y_2 = y_2^0$). The first therefore represents the set of the productions that are feasible from the quantities

---

† We may point out that, like the utility function, the production function here is not defined uniquely. For example, if ϕ is a real function with the same sign as its argument, and which is zero when its argument is zero, then $\phi(f)$ corresponds to the same set as f. Since this has already been discussed sufficiently in consumption theory, we shall not lay further stress on it.

$a_3^0 = - y_3^0$ and $a_4^0 = - y_4^0$ of the two inputs; the second represents the set of inputs allowing the quantities $b_1^0 = y_1^0$ and $b_2^0 = y_2^0$ of the two outputs to be obtained. The points satisfying (2) are represented by the North-East boundary on Figure 1 and the South-West boundary on Figure 2. (We note in passing that a set which, like the curve in Figure 2, represents the technically efficient combinations of inputs yielding given quantities of outputs is called an *isoquant*.)

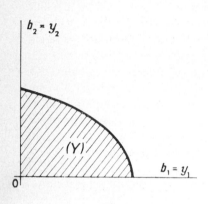

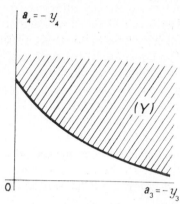

Fig. 1   Fig. 2

The most general form of a production function is that in (2). Slightly more particular expressions are often used. Thus it is often assumed that the firm has only one output, the good 1, to fix ideas; the production function is then given the form:†

$$f(y_1, y_2, ..., y_l) = y_1 - g(y_2, ..., y_l). \tag{4}$$

The technical constraint is

$$y_1 \leqslant g(y_2, ..., y_l) \tag{5}$$

and the expression 'production function' is also used for the function g which defines the output resulting from given quantities of inputs. There should be no real possibility of confusion from this ambiguity.

Note that we could show inputs and outputs explicitly in (5). Thus

$$b_1 \leqslant g(- a_2, - a_3, ..., - a_l) \tag{6}$$

or, after an obvious change in notation,

$$b_1 \leqslant g^*(a_2, a_3, ..., a_l). \tag{7}$$

---

† Obviously this particular form is no longer affected by the indeterminacy already mentioned in relation to the general form (2). Here the function g representing a given set Y is determined uniquely. In fact, even if these are several outputs, in most cases we can solve the equality $f(y) = 0$ for y_1 and so revert to (5).

The function g^* will generally be increasing with the a_h *and the function g will consequently be decreasing with respect to the* y_h, or at least non-increasing.

Later on we shall often assume that the function f is twice differentiable. Let y^0 and $y^0 + dy$ be two neighbouring technically efficient vectors. We can write

$$\sum_{h=1}^{l} f'_h \, dy_h = 0 \tag{8}$$

where f'_h denotes the value at y^0 of the derivative of f with respect to y_h. In particular, if all the dy_h except two, dy_r and dy_s, are zero, then (8) reduces to

$$f'_r \, dy_r + f'_s \, dy_s = 0 \tag{9}$$

or

$$-\frac{dy_r}{dy_s} = \frac{f'_s}{f'_r}. \tag{10}$$

The ratio on the right hand side of (10) can be called the *marginal rate of substitution* between the goods s and r for the producer in question. This expression is similar to that encountered in consumption theory. To avoid confusion, we shall sometimes speak instead of the *marginal rate of transformation*.

In the particular case where f takes the form (4), equalities of the type (10) become

$$-\frac{dy_1}{dy_s} = -g'_s \qquad \text{for} \qquad s \neq 1 \tag{11}$$

and

$$-\frac{dy_r}{dy_s} = \frac{g'_s}{g'_r} \qquad \text{for} \qquad s, r \neq 1. \tag{12}$$

The ratio (11) measures the increase in production resulting from an increase of one unit in the input of s (note that y_s is equal to *minus* the input). It is often called the *marginal productivity* of s. The ratio (12) defines, apart from sign, the additional quantity of input of r which is necessary to compensate in output for a reduction of one unit in the input of s. This is, in fact, a marginal rate of substitution.

We note also that the first derivatives f'_h of the production function f must take non-negative values at every technically efficient point y^0. Consider a small variation dy all of whose components are zero except dy_k, which is assumed positive. Since y^0 is technically efficient, $y^0 + dy$ is not technically possible, that is, $f(y^0 + dy)$ is positive. But, since $f(y^0)$ is zero, $f(y^0 + dy)$ can be positive only if f'_k is not negative.

2. The validity of production functions

We must now investigate the conditions to be satisfied by the production set Y in order that, first of all, there exists a production function f, and in the second place, that this function is differentiable. These conditions are certainly more restrictive than it would appear at first glance.

Differentiability implies that f is continuous and consequently that Y is a closed set in R^l. This property is not restrictive; if the vectors $\{y^1, y^2, ...,\}$ of a convergent sequence each define a feasible production then the limiting vector certainly corresponds in reality to a feasible production.

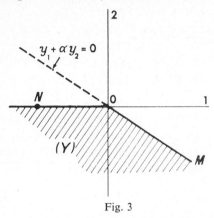

Fig. 3

But the continuity of f implies also that every point y^* on the boundary of y satisfies $f(y^*) = 0$ since it can be approached both by a sequence of vectors y such that $f(y) \leqslant 0$ and by a sequence of vectors such that $f(y) > 0$. So the definition of f implies that every point y^* on the boundary of Y is technically efficient. Moreover, differentiability assumes that, with respect to any technically efficient vector, the marginal rates of substitution are all well-defined. Taken literally, these consequences are difficult to accept.

(i) In the first place, the domains of variation of all, or some, of the y_h may be limited. For example, technology may demand that some good r occurs only as input and some other good s only as output. So the inequalities $y_r \leqslant 0$ and $y_s \geqslant 0$ appear in the definition of Y. (In fact, the second inequality can be eliminated if we assume that the firm can always dispose of its surplus without cost, since this assumption is naturally expressed as: $y^0 \in Y$ and $y_h \leqslant y_h^0$ for all h implies $y \in Y$.) Because of the limits on the domains of variation of some y_h, the set Y has boundaries corresponding to non-technically efficient productions (for example, the half-line ON in Figure 3).

The existence of such boundaries is incompatible with the continuity of f together with the conditions that $f(y) < 0$ is satisfied for every non-technically efficient vector of Y and that $f(y) > 0$ is satisfied for every vector y outside Y. (At a point such as N, $f(y)$ should be equal to a negative number, but should be positive for every point near N whose second coordinate is positive; this is incompatible with the continuity of f at N.)

However, we can take account of these limitations by altering the definition of the production function and explicitly adding inequalities to the formal representations of the set Y and the set of technically efficient vectors. For example, to characterise Y we replace (3) by

$$\begin{cases} f(y_1, y_2, ..., y_l) \leqslant 0, \\ y_h \leqslant 0 \quad \text{for a specified list of goods } h. \end{cases} \tag{13}$$

To characterise the set of technically efficient vectors, (2) is replaced by

$$\begin{cases} f(y_1, y_2, ..., y_l) = 0, \\ y_h \leqslant 0 \quad \text{for the same list of goods } h. \end{cases} \tag{14}$$

Thus, for Figure 3, (13) and (14) become

$$\begin{cases} y_1 + \alpha y_2 \leqslant 0, \\ y_2 \leqslant 0, \end{cases} \tag{15}$$

and

$$\begin{cases} y_1 + \alpha y_2 = 0 \\ y_2 \leqslant 0. \end{cases} \tag{16}$$

This complication will not be taken into account in our discussion of the general theories. That is, we shall proceed as if the limits on the domains of variation of the y_h are never in force. As we saw in consumption theory, certain new particular features are revealed if we take account of constraints expressed by inequalities, but this does not alter basically the nature of the results. We shall presently return to this point.

(ii) In the second place, in some productive operations the different goods which constitute inputs must be combined in fixed proportions. This is particularly the case for most of the raw materials used in many industrial processes.

When such proportionality ratios exist, the isoquants do not have the same form as in Figure 2. If there is free disposal of surplus, they look like the isoquant in Figure 4. Apart from the surplus of one of the two inputs, a_3 and a_4 must take values whose ratio corresponds to that defined by the half-line OA. Except at the point A, the half-lines AN and AM correspond to non-technically efficient productions. At the point A, the first derivatives of f with respect to y_3 and y_4 are not continuous. (The situation is similar to that in Chapter 2, with the utility function (8) illustrated in Figure 7.)

The real situation is sometimes less clear-cut than Figure 4 assumes, since there may be available to the firm two or more production techniques each requiring fixed proportions of inputs, the proportions differing for the different techniques. Figure 5 relates to an example of two techniques, the first represented by the point A, the second by the point B. The firm can employ the two techniques simultaneously to produce the same quantities of outputs. For example, if each technique can be employed on a scale reduced by one half relative to that represented by A or B (the assumption of constant returns to scale, to be defined presently) then the same output can be obtained by simultaneous use of the two techniques on this new scale; the point on Figure 5 corresponding to this method of production is the midpoint of AB.

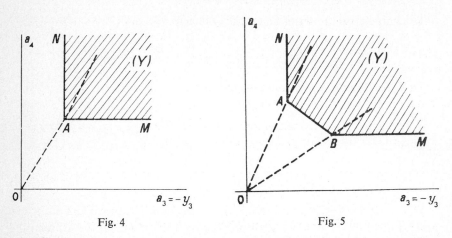

Fig. 4   Fig. 5

Similarly, each point on AB defines a possible combination of the two techniques yielding the same output as A or B. In this case, the first derivatives of f are in fact continuous at each point within AB, but not at A nor at B.

In order formally to represent such situations as those of Figures 4 and 5, we can add other constraints to the equation $f(y) = 0$ to characterise the set of technically efficient vectors. For example, if, as in Figure 4, there must be a fixed proportion between y_3 and y_4, we write:

$$y_4 = \alpha y_3. \tag{17}$$

In the case of two techniques, as in Figure 5, the supplementary constraints may be

$$- \beta y_3 \leqslant - y_4 \leqslant - \alpha y_3. \tag{18}$$

The theory becomes very complicated if such constraints are taken into account. For this reason, they are better ignored in a course of lectures whose aim is to provide the student with a sound grasp of the general logic of the theories to be discussed rather than the difficulties which are encountered in their rigorous exposition. The changes in production theory introduced by their presence will be described briefly.†

Finally, we see that the above-mentioned difficulties can be avoided if we base our reasoning directly on the set Y of feasible productions and on the set of technically efficient productions rather than on the production function. This is the approach adopted in the most modern treatments of the theories with which we are concerned here.

As when a utility function is substituted for a preordering of consumer choices, the substitution of a production function for a production set makes exposition easier since it allows the use of the differential calculus and of fairly standard types of mathematical reasoning. Moreover, this approach alone leads to certain results which every economist must know. Knowledge of these results is essential for the student, even if their application is somewhat restricted by the simplifications required to justify the production function.

3. Assumptions about production sets

We must now discuss certain assumptions which are frequently adopted about production sets or production functions.

ADDITIVITY. If the two vectors y^1 and y^2 define feasible productions ($y^1 \in Y$ and $y^2 \in Y$ or $f(y^1) \leqslant 0$ and $f(y^2) \leqslant 0$), then the vector $y = y^1 + y^2$ defines a feasible production (therefore $y \in Y$ or $f(y) \leqslant 0$).

This appears a natural assumption. For, it seems that we can always realise y by realising independently y^1 and y^2. Additivity fails to hold only if y^1 and y^2 cannot be applied simultaneously. *A priori* there seems no reason for this to be the case.

However, it may happen that the model does not identify all the commodities which in fact occur as inputs in production operations. For example, if the land in the possession of an agricultural undertaking does not appear among the commodities, then additivity does not apply to its production set, since, if the available land is totally used by y^1 on the one hand and by y^2 on the other, realisation of $y^1 + y^2$ requires double the actually available quantity of land. Similarly, if the capacity for work of the head of an industrial firm does not appear among the commodities, and if his capacity limits production, then additivity no longer strictly applies.

---

† It is the aim of a new branch of economic science, 'activity analysis', to integrate into the theory formalisations which describe technical constraints more accurately than do production functions. A very good account of the resulting modifications is given in Dorfman, *Application of Linear Programming to the Theory of the Firm*, University of California Press, Berkeley 1951. See also Dorfman, Samuelson and Solow, *Linear programming and activity analysis*, McGraw-Hill, New York, 1958.

DIVISIBILITY. If the vector y^1 defines a feasible production ($y^1 \in Y$ or $(fy^1) \leq 0$) and if $0 < \alpha < 1$, then the vector αy^1 also defines a feasible production (therefore $\alpha y^1 \in Y$ and $f(\alpha y^1) \leq 0$).

This assumption is much less generally satisfied than the previous one. It assumes that every productive operation can be split up and realised on a reduced scale without changing the proportions of inputs and outputs. Taken literally, it can be said to be rarely satisfied. For every productive operation there is certainly a level below which it cannot be carried out in unaltered conditions. But this indivisibility may vary in its degree of effectiveness and in many industrial operations it appears negligible.

CONSTANT RETURNS TO SCALE.† If the vector y^1 defines a feasible production ($y^1 \in Y$ or $f(y^1) \leq 0$) and if β is a positive number, then the vector βy^1 also defines a feasible production (therefore $\beta y^1 \in Y$ and $f(\beta y^1) \leq 0$).

Obviously the constant returns defined by this assumption imply divisibility. Conversely, additivity and divisibility imply constant returns to scale. For, let k be the integral part of β; we can apply the property of additivity repeatedly, taking the vectors $y^1, 2y^1, ..., (k-1)y^1$ successively for y^2 and thus proving that $2y^1, 3y^1, ..., ky^1$ are feasible; divisibility shows that $(\beta - k)y^1$ is feasible; finally, additivity shows that $\beta y^1 = (\beta - k)y^1 + ky^1$ is feasible.

In practice, we shall consider that returns to scale are constant precisely when additivity and divisibility can be considered to hold, although rigorously, additivity is not necessary.

Consider the particular case where the technical constraints are expressed in the form (5). If the function g is homogeneous of the first degree, then the assumption of constant returns to scale is clearly satisfied.

Conversely, when g is continuous, constant returns to scale imply that

$$g(\beta y_2, ..., \beta y_l) = \beta g(y_2, ..., y_l)$$

for every vector y and every positive number β. In fact the hypothesis implies, by definition,

$$g(\beta y_2, ..., \beta y_l) \geq \beta y_1 = \beta g(y_2, ..., y_l),$$

since βy is feasible whenever y is feasible. Suppose that there exists a vector y^1 and a number $\beta > 0$ such that

$$g(\beta y_2^1, ..., \beta y_l^1) > \beta g(y_2^1, ..., y_l^1) = \beta y_1^1.$$

Then there exists a number $\varepsilon > 0$ such that $\|y - \beta y^1\| < \varepsilon$ implies $g(y_2, ..., y_l) \geq y_1$; it follows then from constant returns to scale that $\|y/\beta - y^1\| < \varepsilon/\beta$

---

† The expression 'constant returns to scale' is explained as follows: if the first good is the sole output, the return with respect to the input l in the productive transformation y^1 is, by definition, the ratio $y_1^1/(-y_l^1)$. This assumption specifies that the volume of output can be changed without changing the return with respect to any of the inputs.

implies $g(y_2/\beta, ..., y_l/\beta) \geqslant y_1/\beta$; hence there exists a vector y^2 near y^1 with all its components greater than the components of y^1 and such that

$$g(y_2^2, ..., y_l^2) \geqslant y_1^2;$$

the vector y^2 is feasible and better than y^1 which is therefore not technically efficient; this contradicts the assumption that $g(y_2^1, ..., y_l^1) = y_1^1$.

To characterise the second of the above assumptions, we often speak of 'non-increasing returns to scale' rather than of divisibility. The relationship with the assumption of constant returns is obvious from the above formulations. However, there must not be any confusion of the assumption of divisibility, or non-increasing returns to scale, with the assumption of 'non-increasing *marginal* returns' with which we shall shortly be concerned.

We also speak of non-decreasing returns to scale when $f(y^1) \leqslant 0$ (or $y^1 \in Y$) and $\alpha > 1$ imply $f(\alpha y^1) \leqslant 0$.

Figure 6 illustrates the three situations for the case of a single input and a single output. The production set bounded by Γ_1 relates to constant returns to scale, that bounded by Γ_2 to decreasing returns and that bounded by Γ_3 to increasing returns (of course, a given production set may come into none of these three categories).

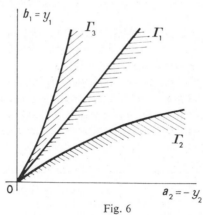

Fig. 6

CONVEXITY. If the vectors y^1 and y^2 define two feasible productions and if $0 < \alpha < 1$, then the vector $\alpha y^1 + (1 - \alpha)y^2$ defines a feasible production.

In short, there is convexity if the set Y contains every segment joining two of its points. Figures 1 and 2 correspond to the intersections of a convex set Y of R^4. Similarly, the sets in Figures 3, 4 and 5 satisfy the assumption of convexity. Finally, in Figure 6, the set bounded by Γ_3 is not convex, and the other two sets are.

Obviously divisibility and additivity imply convexity. Since the null vector naturally belongs to Y, convexity implies divisibility in practice. (To show this, we need only apply the property of convexity, taking the null vector for y^2.)

Convexity has consequences for the second derivatives of the production function. To investigate these consequences, we shall deal with the case of a function of the form

$$y_1 = g(y_2, ..., y_l). \tag{5}$$

Consider two infinitely close vectors y^0 and $y^0 + dy$ which satisfy (5):

$$y_1^0 = g(y_2^0, ..., y_l^0) \tag{19}$$

and

$$y_1^0 + dy_1 = g(y_2^0 + dy_2, ..., y_l^0 + dy_l). \tag{20}$$

If $0 < \alpha < 1$, then $y^0 + \alpha\,dy$ is a possible vector; it therefore satisfies

$$y_1^0 + \alpha\,dy_1 \leqslant g(y_2^0 + \alpha\,dy_2, ..., y_l^0 + \alpha\,dy_l). \tag{21}$$

Let us assume that the second derivatives of g are continuous. Expanding the right hand sides of (20) and (21) up to the second order, and taking account of (19), we obtain

$$dy_1 = \sum_{h=2}^{l} g_h'\,dy_h + \frac{(1 + \varepsilon)}{2} \sum_{h=2}^{l} \sum_{k=2}^{l} g_{hk}''\,dy_h\,dy_k \tag{22}$$

and

$$\alpha\,dy_1 \leqslant \alpha \sum_{h=2}^{l} g_h'\,dy_h + \frac{\alpha^2(1 + \eta)}{2} \sum_{h=2}^{l} \sum_{k=2}^{l} g_{hk}''\,dy_h\,dy_k. \tag{23}$$

Here g_h' is the value at y^0 of the first derivative of g with respect to y_h. Similarly g_{hk}'' is the value at y^0 of the second derivative of g with respect to y_h and y_k. The two numbers ε and η are infinitely small with the dy_h.

Subtracting (22) multiplied by α from (23), and taking account of the fact that $0 < \alpha < 1$, we have

$$\sum_{h=2}^{l} \sum_{k=2}^{l} g_{hk}''\,dy_h\,dy_k \leqslant 0 \tag{24}$$

(the multiplier $\alpha(\alpha - 1 + \alpha\eta - \varepsilon)$ is certainly negative if the dy_h are sufficiently small).

Since *a priori* the dy_h can have any values, *convexity implies that the matrix G'' of the second derivatives g_{hk}'' is negative definite or negative semi-definite.*

Conversely, it can be shown that, if G'' is negative definite for any system of values given to $y_2, y_3, ..., y_l$, then the assumption of convexity holds.

The condition on G'', which we have just established, is a general form of the assumption of *non-increasing marginal returns*. In particular, this condition implies

$$g_{hh}'' \leqslant 0 \qquad h = 2, ..., l,$$

that is,

$$\frac{\partial(-g'_h)}{\partial(-y_h)} \leqslant 0.$$

The marginal return to $h (\partial g/\partial a_h = -g'_h)$, also called the marginal productivity, is therefore a decreasing function of the quantity of input h used $(a_h = -y_h)$.

We should point out that diminishing marginal returns and constant returns to scale are not contradictory, as can be verified from the function $y_1 = \sqrt{y_2 y_3}$. Also, additivity and divisibility imply both constant returns to scale and convexity, therefore non-increasing marginal returns.

To conclude our discussion, we return to the two reasons mentioned earlier for departures from additivity and divisibility.

The fact that certain factors available in limited quantities have not been taken into account explicitly in the formulation of the model obviously does not affect the marginal returns to the other factors. On the other hand, this fact may explain why we choose functions for which returns to scale are diminishing, while additivity implies constant returns.

The presence of considerable indivisibilities may explain the appearance of production functions with increasing returns to scale for which the assumption of non-increasing marginal returns is not satisfied.

M. Allais suggests that we distinguish two situations. In some branches of production, divisibility can be considered to be approximately satisfied to a sufficient extent. In this situation we usually find that production is carried on by a relatively large number of technical units functioning in similar conditions. The technology of this branch satisfies the assumption of constant returns to scale. M. Allais uses the term 'differentiated sector' to cover all productive activity of this kind.

In other fields, considerable indivisibilities exist. The market for each of the goods produced is then served by a very small number of very large technical units. To represent this situation, M. Allais assumes that a single firm exists in each such field, all of which constitute what he calls the 'undifferentiated sector'.

This distinction will be taken again later, notably in Chapter 7 when we shall consider economies involving a large number of agents.

4. Equilibrium for the firm in perfect competition

When dealing with the consumer, we reduced the problem of choosing the best consumption complex to that of maximising a utility function. We shall now assume that the firm tries to maximise the net value of its production:

$$py = \sum_{h=1}^{l} p_h y_h = \sum_{h=1}^{l} p_h b_h - \sum_{h=1}^{l} p_h a_h. \tag{25}$$

This expression, which is the amount by which the value of outputs exceeds the value of inputs also defines the 'profit' that the firm derives from production. In fact, the microeconomic theory with which we are concerned considers the behaviour of the firm to be motivated by its desire to realise the greatest possible profit subject to the constraints imposed by technology and the institutional environment. This assumption, adopted in all theories of general equilibrium, has been subject to criticism. However, no alternative has so far been suggested which stands up to examination and can provide the basis for a general theory. Also, some criticisms arise from misunderstanding of the wide generality of the model under study. In order to avoid the same errors, we shall later discuss the definition of 'profit' when time and uncertainty are taken into account. For our present purposes it is sufficient that the assumption of profit maximisation seems to afford the best way for a simple systematisation of the behaviour of firms.

Again, we consider the firm to be in a situation of *perfect competition* if:

— the price of each good is perfectly defined and exogenous for the firm, and therefore independent of its production decisions;

— and if, at this price, the firm can acquire any quantity it requires of a good, or dispose of any quantity it has produced.

Of course, this is an abstract model of real situations. Basically, it assumes that the firm is small relative to the market, so that its actions have no influence on prices. Moreover, it assumes that the demands and supplies emanating from other agents are completely flexible so that they can react instantly to any supply or any demand emanating from the particular firm. This model is clearly inappropriate to the 'undifferentiated sector'. At the end of this chapter we shall discuss the case of the firm in a monopolistic situation and in Chapter 6 we shall briefly consider the formulations proposed for other situations of imperfect competition.

Adopting the assumptions of profit maximisation and perfect competition, and using a production function representing the technical constraints, we can easily determine equilibrium for the firm. We need only maximise py subject to the constraint

$$f(y_1, y_2, ..., y_l) = 0. \tag{26}$$

(In what follows, we assume that no price p_h is negative, so that the firm loses nothing by limiting itself to technically efficient net productions. Obviously we also assume that the price vector is not identically zero.)

If we follow the same approach as for consumption theory, we should now investigate the existence and uniqueness of equilibrium. We shall not do this, which in any case raises some difficulties of principle (see the footnote at the start of Section 6). So we shall go straight on to consider the marginal equalities satisfied in the equilibrium.

Maximisation of (25) subject to the constraint (26) is a simple case of the classical problem of constrained maximisation. The necessary first order conditions for a vector y^0 to be a solution imply the existence of a Lagrange multiplier λ such that

$$p_h = \lambda f'_h \qquad h = 1, 2, ..., l \tag{27}$$

where f'_h is the value at y^0 of the derivative of f with respect to y_h. For the application of theorem VI of the Appendix, it is assumed here that the f'_h are not all simultaneously zero. It follows from the remark at the end of Section 1 that the f'_k are not negative and consequently that λ is positive.

Conditions (27) imply

$$\frac{f'_s}{f'_r} = \frac{p_s}{p_r}. \tag{28}$$

In the equilibrium, the marginal rate of substitution between the two commodities r and s must equal the ratio of the prices of these commodities.

In particular, if the production function is

$$y_1 = g(y_2, y_3, ..., y_l), \tag{29}$$

conditions (27) become

$$p_1 = \lambda \qquad \text{and} \qquad p_h = - \lambda g'_h \qquad \text{for} \qquad h \neq 1,$$

and so

$$- g'_h = \frac{p_h}{p_1} \qquad h = 2, 3, ..., l. \tag{30}$$

The marginal productivity of commodity h must equal the ratio between its price and that of the output.

As in consumption theory, we can find the necessary second order conditions for a profit maximum. With the general form of the production function, (26) say, these conditions require

$$\sum_{h,k=1}^{l} f''_{hk} \, dy_h \, dy_k \geq 0 \tag{31}$$

for every set of dy_h such that

$$\sum_{h=1}^{l} f'_h \, dy_h = 0, \tag{32}$$

where, of course, f''_{hk} denotes the value at y^0 of the second derivative of f with respect to y_h and y_k (see theorem VIII in the Appendix).

In the particular case of the production function (29), the second order conditions imply more simply that

$$\sum_{h,k=2}^{l} g''_{hk} \, dy_h \, dy_k \leq 0 \tag{33}$$

for every set of dy_h's (where $h = 2, 3, ..., l$). For, we can always associate with these dy_h's a number dy_1 such that (32) is satisfied; (33) then follows from (31). *So we come back to the assumption of non-increasing marginal returns, which is therefore satisfied in the neighbourhood of an equilibrium for the firm.*

These second order conditions reveal an important point: the firm cannot be in competitive equilibrium at a point in the production set where returns to scale are locally increasing. Let us take the case of the production function (29) and assume that from y^0, inputs are increased by the quantities $y_2^0 \, d\alpha$, ..., $y_l^0 \, d\alpha$. Let dy_1 be the corresponding increase in output. We can say that the returns to scale are locally increasing if $dy_1/d\alpha$ is an increasing function of $d\alpha$. If we consider a limited expansion of dy_1 and ignore the case where the second order term is zero, we see that the multiplier of $d\alpha$ in the expression for $dy_1/d\alpha$ is

$$\sum_{h,k=2}^{l} g_{hk}'' y_h^0 y_k^0.$$

It cannot be positive without contradicting the necessary second order condition.

Thus competitive equilibrium is incompatible with such increasing returns to scale, which are often characteristic of the sector in which very large production units predominate. The maintenance of equilibrium for this sector demands forms of institutional organisation other than perfect competition (see, for example, the case of monopoly in Section 9 below, or the management rule for certain public services given in Chapter 6, Section 6).

We can also now consider the inverse problem and prove that the marginal conditions (27) are sufficient for an equilibrium of the firm if the assumption of convexity is satisfied. The following property therefore matches proposition 2 in Chapter 2, relating to the consumer. But its proof is much shorter.

PROPOSITION 1. If the technical constraints are represented by a differentiable production function defining a convex set Y and if the vector y^0 satisfies (26) and (27) with an appropriate positive number λ, then y^0 is an equilibrium for the firm.

Consider a vector y^1 that is technically possible, but apart from that may be any vector:

$$f(y^1) \leqslant 0. \tag{34}$$

Let dt be a small positive number. Because Y is convex, the vector $(1 - dt)y^0 + dt y^1$ is technically possible, and so

$$f[y^0 + (y^1 - y^0) \, dt] \leqslant 0.$$

But $f(y^0) = 0$, hence:

$$\frac{f[y^0 + (y^1 - y^0) \, dt] - f(y^0)}{dt} \leqq 0$$

If dt tends to zero, this inequality holds in the limit, and consequently

$$\sum_{h=1}^{l} (y_h^1 - y_h^0)f_h' \leqslant 0, \tag{35}$$

where f_h' is the value at y^0 of the derivative of f with respect to y_h.

In view of (27), and since λ is positive, (35) implies

$$\sum_{h=1}^{l} p_h(y_h^1 - y_h^0) \leqslant 0.$$

The profit associated with y^1 cannot exceed the profit associated with y^0, which is the required result.

5. The case of additional constraints

We have seen that the production function may be insufficient for complete representation of technical constraints. Without going into details, we shall discuss briefly the treatment of cases where additional constraints must be added.

Suppose first that the constraints are represented by the production function (26) and a second condition:

$$\phi(y_1, y_2 \ldots y_l) = 0 \tag{36}$$

After introduction of a second Lagrange multiplier, the first order conditions become:

$$p_h = \lambda f_h' + \mu \phi_h', \qquad h = 1, 2, \ldots, l, \tag{37}$$

which replaces (27).

Does such a substitution have much effect on our results? Not necessarily. A relatively simple alteration in the properties is sufficient in some cases.

Let us return to the example of four goods and the additional constraint

$$y_4 = \alpha y_3, \tag{38}$$

which expresses strict proportionality between two inputs. System (37) becomes

$$\begin{cases} p_h = \lambda f_h' & \text{for} \quad h = 1, 2. \\ p_3 = \lambda f_3' - \mu \alpha \\ p_4 = \lambda f_4' + \mu \end{cases}$$

Eliminating μ, we obtain

$$\begin{cases} p_h = \lambda f_h' & h = 1, 2. \\ p_3 + \alpha p_4 = \lambda(f_3' + \alpha f_4') \end{cases} \tag{39}$$

This new system has the same form as (27) provided that goods 3 and 4 are replaced by a composite good one unit of which consists of one unit of good

3 and α times one unit of good 4; $f'_3 + \alpha f'_4$ is then the partial derivative of f with respect to the composite good.†

Similarly, no insurmountable problem arises if we take account of constraints expressed by inequalities. Suppose, for example, that there are again four goods and, apart from the production function, the two constraints

$$0 \leqslant -y_4 \leqslant -\alpha y_3. \tag{40}$$

(Goods 3 and 4 are inputs, and the proportion of 4 with respect to 3 is bounded above; see Figure 7.)

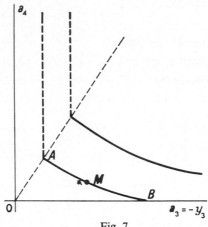

Fig. 7

Here we have a case for application of theorem XI of the Appendix. The function to be maximised is

$$p_1 y_1 + p_2 y_2 + p_3 y_3 + p_4 y_4;$$

the constraints are

$$\begin{cases} -f(y_1, y_2, y_3, y_4) \geqslant 0 \\ -y_4 \geqslant 0 \\ y_4 - \alpha y_3 \geqslant 0. \end{cases}$$

Let λ, μ_1 and μ_2 be the corresponding Kuhn-Tucker multipliers. The necessary conditions for a maximum are

$$\begin{cases} p_h = \lambda f'_h & \text{for} \quad h = 1, 2 \\ p_3 = \lambda f'_3 + \alpha \mu_2 \\ p_4 = \lambda f'_4 + \mu_1 - \mu_2 \end{cases} \tag{41}$$

---

† The introduction of such a composite good raises no difficulty when we are considering the firm in isolation; but it is usually inappropriate for the discussion of general equilibrium, since goods 3 and 4 may be produced by two distinct firms, or consumed by other agents in a proportion other than α.

where each of the multipliers λ, μ_1 and μ_2 must be non-negative, and must be zero when the corresponding constraint is a strict inequality.

If p_1 or p_2 is positive, as we shall assume, the multiplier λ must be positive and the equilibrium y^0 must strictly satisfy $f(y^0) = 0$. We can then distinguish three cases:

(i) If the equilibrium is such that $0 < - y_4^0 < - \alpha y_3^0$ (the point M on Figure 7), the multipliers μ_1 and μ_2 are zero. System (41) reduces to system (27) exactly as if the constraints (40) did not exist.

(ii) If the equilibrium is such that $y_4^0 = 0$ and $y_3^0 < 0$ (point B on Figure 7), $\mu_2 = 0$ and $\mu_1 \geqslant 0$. After elimination of μ_1, system (27) is replaced by

$$\begin{cases} p_h = \lambda f'_h & h = 1, 2, 3. \\ p_4 \geqslant \lambda f'_4 \end{cases} \tag{42}$$

In particular, if the production function takes the form (5), the marginal productivity $- g'_4$ of good 4 is less than or at most equal to the price ratio p_4/p_1.

(iii) If the equilibrium is such that $y_4^0 = \alpha y_3^0 < 0$ (point A in Figure 7), $\mu_1 = 0$ and $\mu_2 \geqslant 0$. System (27) becomes

$$\begin{cases} p_h = \lambda f'_h & h = 1, 2. \\ p_3 + \alpha p_4 = \lambda(f'_3 + \alpha f'_4) \\ p_3 \geqslant \lambda f'_3 \quad \text{and} \quad p_4 \leqslant \lambda f'_4 \end{cases} \tag{43}$$

This brings us back to (39); we can introduce a composite good for the interpretation of the last equality; but we can now identify the individual marginal productivities of inputs 3 and 4 with respect to output 1, namely f'_3/f'_1 and f'_4/f'_1. We see that the marginal productivity of input 3 is at most p_3/p_1, and that of input 4 is at least p_4/p_1. In fact, to increase the input of factor 3 without changing the input of factor 4 is possible but not worth while, whereas to increase the input of factor 4 without changing the input of factor 3 might be worth while but is impossible.

In short, consideration of additional constraints entails some modification in the equilibrium conditions but makes no basic change in their nature.

6. Supply and demand laws for the firm

The theory of the firm must lead to some general properties of supply and demand functions, as happened with the theory of the consumer. In the context of the perfect competition model, the supply function for commodity h defines how the firm's output of this good varies as the prices of all goods vary. Similarly, the demand function for commodity h defines how the firm's input of this commodity varies. We shall deal with these two functions simultaneously by considering net supply, which, by definition, is equal to supply for an output and to demand with a change of sign for an input.

The net supply law for commodity h is therefore that law which defines y_h as a function of the $p_1, p_2, ..., p_l$, the set Y of feasible productions, or the production function f, being fixed. We shall write this law $\eta_h(p_1, p_2, ..., p_l)$, assuming that y^0 exists, and is unique, for every vector p belonging to an l-dimensional domain of R^l.† We can easily establish the following three properties.

(i) *The net supply function is homogeneous of degree zero* with respect to $p_1, p_2, ..., p_l$ and for any multiplication of these prices by the same positive number. This is an obvious property since the constraint, $y \in Y$ or $f(y) = 0$, does not involve p and the function to be maximised is homogeneous in p. If y^0 maximises py subject to the constraint, it also maximises αpy when α is positive.

Just as in consumption theory, this homogeneity of net supply functions shows that the choice of numéraire does not affect equilibrium. Again it can be described as 'the absence of money illusion'.

(ii) *The substitution effect of h for k is equal to the substitution effect of k for h.* Consider the increase in the supply of h when the price of k diminishes. When the net supply functions are differentiable, we can characterise this 'substitution effect' of h for k by the partial derivative of η_h with respect to p_k. Property (ii) then expresses the following equality:

$$\frac{\partial \eta_h}{\partial p_k} = \frac{\partial \eta_k}{\partial p_h} \qquad h, k = 1, 2, ..., l. \tag{44}$$

---

† In fact, this assumption is more restrictive than appears at first sight. For example, if the production function satisfies the assumption of constant returns to scale and is expressed in the form (5) or (29), the derivatives g'_h are homogeneous of degree zero and can therefore be expressed as functions of the $l - 2$ variables $y_2/y_l, ..., , y_{l-1}/y_l$. Now, there are $l - 1$ equations (30), necessary for equilibrium and also sufficient in the case of convexity. If the p_h are chosen freely, these equations will not generally have a solution. In the particular case where the p_h are such that a solution exists, y^0 say, then every proportional vector αy^0 will also be a solution ($\alpha > 0$).

In economic terms these formal difficulties have the following significance. The decision to produce can be split into two stages: (i) the choice of the technical coefficients $y_1/y_l, ..., y_{l-1}/y_l$, (ii) the determination of the volume of production. In the case of constant returns to scale, the two stages are independent of each other and, once the best technical coefficients are chosen, profit is proportional to the volume of production. If it is positive, no equilibrium exists since it is always advantageous to increase production. If it is negative, only zero production gives an equilibrium which does not obey the marginal equalities (30). If profit is zero, then any level of production is optimal.

The most modern versions of microeconomic theory take account of these difficulties: net supply functions can be defined only for a subset of the values that are *a priori* possible for p and can then be multivalued. So the term 'supply correspondences' rather than 'supply functions' is used.

To establish this property, we differentiate the system consisting of (27) and (26) and obtain

$$
\begin{cases}
\lambda \sum_{k=1}^{l} f''_{hk}\,\mathrm{d}y_k + f'_h\,\mathrm{d}\lambda = \mathrm{d}p_h & h = 1, 2, \ldots, l, \\
\sum_{h=1}^{l} f'_h\,\mathrm{d}y_h = 0,
\end{cases}
\tag{45}
$$

which can be written in matrix form:

$$
\begin{bmatrix} \lambda F'' & f' \\ [f']' & 0 \end{bmatrix}
\begin{bmatrix} \mathrm{d}y \\ \mathrm{d}\lambda \end{bmatrix}
=
\begin{bmatrix} \mathrm{d}p \\ 0 \end{bmatrix},
\tag{46}
$$

with the obvious notation. This equality shows that the left hand side of (44) is the element on the hth row and kth column of

$$
\begin{bmatrix} F'' & f' \\ [f']' & 0 \end{bmatrix}^{-1}
\tag{47}
$$

while the right hand side is the element on the kth row and the hth column. Now, the matrix (47), which we assume here to exist, is clearly symmetric, which proves the equality.

This property shows that we can say unambiguously whether two goods are substitutes or complements for the particular firm. We need only look at the sign of the partial derivative $\partial \eta_h / \partial p_k$. More precisely, we say that two outputs or two inputs h and k are complements if this derivative is positive, and are substitutes if it is negative.

(iii) *When the price of a good increases, the net supply of this good cannot diminish.* For the proof of this property we can use the second order condition for an equilibrium and establish that the partial derivative of η_h with respect to p_h is not negative. The reasoning is similar to that used for consumer demand (cf. property 3 in Chapter 2, Section 9). We can also proceed directly on the basis of finite differences, which makes the result clearer and more general.

Consider two price vectors, p^1 and p^2 say, and two corresponding equilibria, y^1 and y^2. Since y^1 maximises $p^1 y$ in the set of the feasible y's and since y^2 is feasible, we can write

$$
p^1 y^2 \leqslant p^1 y^1
\tag{48}
$$

and also

$$
p^2 y^1 \leqslant p^2 y^2
$$

or equivalently,

$$
- p^2 y^2 \leqslant - p^2 y^1.
\tag{49}
$$

Adding (48) and (49), we obtain

$$
(p^1 - p^2) y^2 \leqslant (p^1 - p^2) y^1
$$

or

$$(p^1 - p^2)(y^1 - y^2) \geqslant 0. \tag{50}$$

This is the general form of the relation of *comparative statics*, which must be obeyed in the comparison of two different equilibria for the same firm.

In particular, if p^1 and p^2 are identical except where price p_h is concerned, the inequality becomes:

$$(p_h^1 - p_h^2)(y_h^1 - y_h^2) \geqslant 0.$$

This establishes property (iii).

7. Cost functions

Suppose that the prices p_h of the different commodities are given and that the firm produces only one good, the good 1 to fix ideas. *The cost function relates to the quantity produced y_1, the minimum value of the input mix which yields this production.*

The theory of the firm is often built up on the initial basis of the cost function. This greatly simplifies the analysis, but is subject to criticism on two counts.

In the first place, the relationship between the value of input complex and the quantity produced depends on the prices p_h of the different inputs, so that the cost function changes when these prices change. The production set or production function are more fundamental since they represent the technical constraints independently of the price system.

In the second place, a production theory based on the analysis of costs is out of place in a general equilibrium theory which treats prices as endogenous and not determined *a priori*. Since our aim is to lead up to the study of general equilibrium, we must start with production sets or functions.

However, an examination of cost functions reveals certain useful classical properties which are simple to establish at this point and may be needed later. We assume here that the markets for inputs are competitive so that the p_h are given for the firm ($h = 2, 3, ..., l$).

Since we restrict ourselves to the case of only one output, we can take the production function as

$$y_1 = g(y_2, y_3, ..., y_l). \tag{29}$$

Before defining the cost function, we must first find the combination of inputs which allows production of a given quantity $\bar{y}_1$ of commodity 1 at minimum cost, so we must maximise profit subject to the constraint that $y_1 = \bar{y}_1$. This is a particular case of the problem discussed at the start of

Section 5 where $\phi(y) = y_1 - \bar{y}_1$. Here the system of first order conditions (37) becomes

$$\begin{cases} p_1 = \lambda + \mu \\ p_h = -\lambda g'_h \end{cases} \quad \text{for} \quad h = 2, 3, ..., l.$$

The first equation allows us to find μ and is of no further use. If, as we assume here, the first order conditions are sufficient for cost minimisation, the solution is obtained by determining values of λ and of $y_2, y_3, ..., y_l$ which satisfy

$$\begin{cases} g(y_2, y_3, ..., y_l) = \bar{y}_1 \\ p_h = -\lambda g'_h \quad h = 2, 3, ..., l. \end{cases} \tag{52}$$

When the firm minimises its cost of production, the marginal rates of substitution of inputs are equal to the ratios of their prices; but the marginal productivity of an input, h for example, is not necessarily equal to p_h/p_1. It is equal to p_h/p_1 if $\bar{y}_1$ is the optimal production for the firm selling on a competitive market. But for freely chosen $\bar{y}_1$, in most cases it is not equal to this ratio.

Cost C is defined as

$$C = \sum_{h=2}^{l} p_h a_h = -\sum_{h=2}^{l} p_h y_h. \tag{53}$$

We need only replace the y_h in this expression by their values in the solution of (52) when we want to determine the cost function, which relates the value of the minimum of C with the production level $\bar{y}_1$ (the p_h being considered as given).† This function is often assumed to have the form of the curve C in Figure 8.

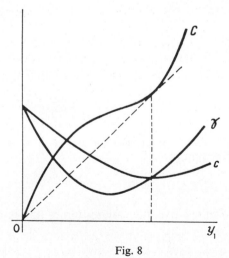

Fig. 8

---

† The term 'cost function' is sometimes also used for the function that relates C to $\bar{y}_1$ and to $p_2, p_3 ... p_l$.

When looking for the equilibrium of the firm, we can work in two stages:

(i) Define the cost function, that is, determine for each value of $\bar{y}_1$ the $y_2, y_3, ..., y_l$ which minimise cost and find the value C corresponding to this minimum cost.

(ii) Choose $\bar{y}_1$ so as to maximise profit $(p_1\bar{y}_1 - C(\bar{y}_1))$.

The solution of stage (ii) is obvious. The first order condition requires

$$p_1 = C'(\bar{y}_1). \tag{54}$$

C' measures the increase in cost resulting from a small increase in production, and is therefore the 'marginal cost'. Equation (54) shows that, *in competitive equilibrium, marginal cost is equal to price of the output*. The second order condition requires that the second derivative of the profit is negative or zero, that is, that marginal cost is increasing or constant.

We shall verify that, in (52), λ equals the marginal cost. When marginal cost is equated to price p_1, the first order conditions for cost minimisation, equations (52), are transformed into first order conditions for profit maximisation, equations (29) and (30).

Let us differentiate (53), the expression for cost, keeping prices p_h constant:

$$dC = - \sum_{h=2}^{l} p_h \, dy_h$$

or, taking account of (52) and, in particular, differentiating the first equation,

$$dC = \lambda \sum_{h=2}^{l} g'_h \, dy_h = \lambda \, d\bar{y}_1. \tag{55}$$

This equation establishes that λ equals marginal cost.

We can also verify that *the assumption of non-increasing marginal returns implies that marginal cost is increasing or constant*. Let us differentiate (52), keeping prices constant:

$$\begin{cases} \sum_{h=2}^{l} g'_h \, dy_h = d\bar{y}_1 \\ d\lambda g'_h + \lambda \sum_{k=2}^{l} g''_{hk} \, dy_k = 0 \qquad h = 2, 3, ..., l. \end{cases} \tag{56}$$

Multiply the hth equation by dy_h; sum for $h = 2, 3, ..., l$; take account of the first equation: we obtain

$$d\lambda \, d\bar{y}_1 + \lambda \sum_{h,k=2}^{l} g''_{hk} \, dy_h \, dy_k = 0. \tag{57}$$

Since marginal cost λ is positive, the assumption of non-increasing marginal returns implies

$$d\lambda \cdot d\bar{y}_1 \geqslant 0 \qquad \text{or} \qquad \frac{d\lambda}{d\bar{y}_1} \geqslant 0, \tag{58}$$

which is the required result.

So a cost curve derived from a production function with non-increasing marginal returns is concave upwards. The classical curve of the cost function, as exhibited in Figure 8, is concave downwards at the start: this corresponds to the range of values of output for which indivisibilities are significant and marginal returns are increasing.

We note also that marginal cost is rigorously constant when the production function satisfies the assumption of constant returns to scale. The function g is then homogeneous of the first degree, and so

$$\sum_{h=2}^{l} g'_h y_h = \bar{y}_1;$$

hence, taking account of the definition of C and the marginal equalities (52),

$$C = \lambda \bar{y}_1.$$

This equation, together with (55) shows that λ, which *a priori* is a function of $\bar{y}_1$, is in fact a constant (always assuming that the p_h are fixed).†

In addition to total cost C and marginal cost C' we often consider *average cost* per unit of output, namely $c = C/\bar{y}_1$. If we differentiate c with respect to $\bar{y}_1$, it is immediately obvious that average cost is increasing or decreasing according as it is greater or less than marginal cost (a typical curve c appears in Figure 8).

It is sometimes convenient to give a diagram representing the last stage in profit maximisation. Let the curves c and γ represent respectively variations in average cost and marginal cost as a function of y_1 for given values of $p_2, p_3, ..., p_l$. The equilibrium point y^0 is determined by the abscissa y_1^0 of the point on the curve γ whose ordinate is p_1. The profit is then y_1^0 times the difference in the ordinates of the points on γ and c with abscissa y_1^0.

Examination of the figure rounds off the preceding analysis, which was limited to finding necessary conditions for a profit maximum at a point y^0 for which constraints other than the production function do not operate. Are these conditions also sufficient, as we assumed earlier when we said that y_1^0 corresponds to the equilibrium?

Ambiguity may exist if several points on γ have p_1 as ordinate. In practice, this is likely to arise only in two ways. In the first place, there may be two such points, one on the decreasing part and the other on the increasing part of the marginal cost curve; the first point cannot correspond to an equilibrium

---

† We saw that the assumption of constant returns to scale would usually not hold if all the factors of production were not accounted for in the model. When defining marginal cost, we assumed that the quantities of all the factors could be freely fixed. This latter assumption is inappropriate to factors such as the work capacity of the managing director. So the case of constant marginal cost is not necessarily frequent in relation to a firm some of whose factors cannot vary. (See below the distinction between long-term and short-term costs.)

since it does not satisfy the second order condition, so that the ambiguity disappears. Also, at the ordinate p_1 the curve γ may be flat (in particular, we saw that marginal cost is constant if the production function satisfies the assumption of constant returns); all the points on this flat section give the same profit; if one of them corresponds to an equilibrium, then the others also correspond to equilibria.

The point or points with ordinate p_1 and lying on the non-decreasing part of γ may not correspond to an equilibrium if it is to the interest of the firm to have zero output y_1. This situation arises if p_1 is less than the minimum average cost c_m and if $y_1 = 0$ implies zero profit, since the points considered then give negative profit.

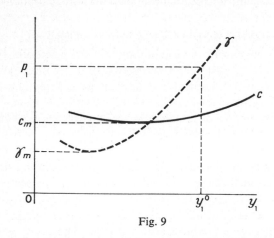

Fig. 9

Finally, if the whole curve γ lies below the ordinate corresponding to p_1, there is no limit on the increase of profit and it is to the interest of the firm to go on increasing production indefinitely. (Of course, in practice it would come up against a limit sooner or later, but the chosen cost function ignores this fact.)

To sum up, for given values of $p_2, p_3, \ldots, p_l$, the value of p_1 may be such that:

(i) the firm should choose $y_1 = 0$ (low price p_1);

(ii) the firm should choose a finite output y_1^0, which may or may not be defined uniquely;

(iii) the firm should increase production indefinitely (high price p_1).

As we said previously, the existence of situations (i) and (iii), together with the multiplicity of equilibria in (ii), are sufficiently real possibilities to make us avoid trying to prove for producer equilibrium a general property of existence and uniqueness corresponding to that stated for consumer equilibrium in proposition I of Chapter 2.

8. Short and long-run decisions

Cost minimisation has just been presented as a stage in profit maximisation. In fact, abandoning the strict model of perfect competition, we sometimes consider that some firms actually behave so as to provide an exogenously determined output and minimise their production cost. System (52) then applies directly to the equilibrium for the firm.

Similarly, in some contexts, the firm does not choose all, but only some of its inputs, the others being predetermined. Thus for the same firm we often distinguish between *long-run decisions* relating to the entire organisation of production (choice of equipment and manufacturing processes) and *short-run decisions* relating to the use of an already existing productive capacity. So for short-run decisions, the inputs relating to capital equipment are fixed.

Such situations can easily be analysed using the principles applied above. Suppose, to fix ideas, that capital equipment is represented by a single good, the lth. Let $\bar{y}_l$ be the predetermined value of y_l. The short-run decision consists of profit maximisation subject to the constraint $y_l = \bar{y}_l$. The *short-run cost function* relates cost C to the value $\bar{y}_1$ of output when $y_l = \bar{y}_l$, the other inputs y_h being fixed so as to minimise cost. Let this function be $C^*(\bar{y}_1, \bar{y}_l)$.

As before, we see that inputs $y_2, y_3, ..., y_{l-1}$, cost C^* and marginal cost λ^* obey the system

$$\begin{cases} g(y_2, ..., y_{l-1}, \bar{y}_l) = \bar{y}_1 \\ p_h = -\lambda^* g'_h \qquad\qquad h = 2, 3, ..., l-1, \\ C^* = -\sum_{h=2}^{l-1} p_h y_h - p_l \bar{y}_l. \end{cases} \qquad (59)$$

Differentiating the first and last equations for given p_h and taking account of the intermediate equalities, we obtain

$$dC^* = \lambda^* \, d\bar{y}_1 - (\lambda^* g'_l + p_l) \, d\bar{y}_l,$$

which replaces (55). The short-run marginal cost is again equal to the equilibrium value of the Lagrange multiplier λ^*. We could also verify that, to determine the value of $\bar{y}_1$ which maximises profit subject to the constraint $y_l = \bar{y}_l$, we must add to (59) the condition that the marginal cost λ^* equals p_1.

Let us illustrate this theory by a diagram in which the different cost functions are represented as a function of y_1. Let cL and γL be the long-run average and marginal cost curves. The long-run equilibrium value of production for price p_1 is determined as the abscissa $\bar{y}_1^L$ of the point on γL whose ordinate is p_1. Also let cC and γC be the short-run average and marginal cost curves. The short-run equilibrium is determined by the abscissa $\bar{y}_1^C$ of the point on γC whose ordinate is p_1.

The long and short-run average cost curves generally have a common point corresponding to the value of $\bar{y}_1$ for which the solution of (52), defining the long-run cost, gives the value $\bar{y}_l$ for y_l. For, the solution of (52) then satisfies (59) with $C^* = C$. Let y_1^0 be this particular value of $\bar{y}_1$. At y_1^0, the equality $p_l = -\lambda^* g'_l$ is satisfied, so that $dC^* = \lambda^* d\bar{y}_1 = dC$. At this point, long and short-run marginal costs are equal, long and short-run average costs are tangential. *A priori*, this may seem an obvious result, since if existing equipment coincides with what the firm would choose in the long run in the same price situation, then short and long-run equilibria must naturally coincide.

Hence, the long-run average cost curve is the envelope of short-run average cost curves (obviously the same property holds for total cost curves). In any case, the short-run cost cannot be lower than the long-run cost since the minimisation which defines the former is subject to one more constraint than that which defines the latter.

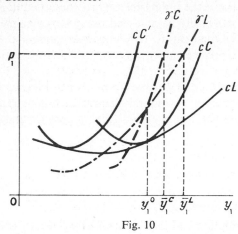

Fig. 10

9. Monopoly

The formal approach developed so far is more or less easily transposed to institutional situations that differ from perfect competition. We may briefly examine here the classical theory of monopoly, leaving for Chapters 6 and 8 the analysis of other situations.

In the applied study of market structures a firm is said to have a monopoly position on the market for commodity h if it supplies alone this commodity and if demand comes from many agents who are individually small and act independently of one another. Classical monopoly theory represents this situation starting from the hypothesis that the same price p_h will apply to the exchange of all units of commodity h but that this price will depend on the quantity y_h that the seller will supply. Thus the monopoly faces a demand whose quantity varies with the price of his product but is otherwise independent of his decision.

The firm facing such a situation necessarily takes account of the fact that the price at which it will dispose of its output depends on the quantity which it puts on the market. We can no longer analyse its behaviour on the assumption that it considers price as exogenous. We have to adopt a formal model other than that of perfect competition.

Suppose, for example, that the firm produces good 1 and sells it on a market where there are many buyers whose demand depends on price p_1 and not on other prices.† We can represent this demand by a relation between p_1 and y_1:

$$p_1 = \pi_1(y_1), \tag{61}$$

where π_1 is the function defining the price at which the monopolist can dispose of the volume of production y_1.

It may also happen that a firm is the only one to use a factor h (for example, when it is the only employer of labour in a town). It is said to be in a situation of 'monopsony'. It knows that price p_h depends on the quantity $a_h = -y_h$ which it uses as input. If it takes no account of the possible interdependence of p_h and the prices of other goods, the firm will fix its decisions as a function of a supply law

$$p_h = \pi_h(y_h) \tag{62}$$

representing the behaviour of the agents supplying the factor h and indicating the price p_h which the firm must pay to acquire a quantity $-y_h$ of h.

We note that the case of perfect competition corresponds to the particular situation where π_1 and π_h are constant functions. Therefore we can deal simultaneously with monopoly and with monopsonies concerning one or more factors by treating the case where the firm tries to maximise its profit and takes account of functions π_h relating the price of each good h to its net production y_h ($h = 1, 2, ..., l$).

As a function of y the profit, or net value of production, is

$$\sum_{h=1}^{l} \pi_h(y_h) \cdot y_h. \tag{63}$$

Maximisation of this expression subject to the constraint expressed by the production function implies the following first order conditions:

$$\pi_h + \pi_h' y_h = \lambda f_h' \qquad h = 1, 2, ..., l,$$

where π_h' is the derivative of π_h and λ is a Lagrange multiplier.

---

† The assumption of independence of demand with respect to prices $p_2, ..., p_l$ is made here for the sake of simplicity. It can obviously be eliminated if prices $p_2, ..., p_l$ are independent of the decisions of the firm, that is, if the markets for all goods except the first are competitive.

For what follows, we shall consider the case where prices are non-zero and shall write the above conditions in the form

$$p_h(1 + \varepsilon_h) = \lambda f'_h \qquad h = 1, 2, ..., l, \tag{64}$$

taking account of the fact that p_h is the value of the function π_h and defining ε_h as the inverse of the elasticity of demand (or supply) which occurs in the market for the good h because of agents other than the particular firm under consideration:

$$\varepsilon_h = y_h \frac{\pi'_h}{\pi_h} = \frac{\mathrm{d} \log \pi_h}{\mathrm{d} \log |y_h|}. \tag{65}$$

In the case of perfect competition, market demand and supply are perfectly elastic from the standpoint of the firm; the ε_h are zero. Conditions (64) reduce to the first order conditions (27) obtained earlier.

In order to investigate (64), we shall consider the case where the production function takes the form

$$y_1 = g(y_2, y_3, ..., y_l), \tag{29}$$

the good 1 being the firm's output. Equations (64) imply

$$\frac{p_h(1 + \varepsilon_h)}{p_1(1 + \varepsilon_1)} = - g'_h \qquad h = 2, ..., l \tag{66}$$

provided that $\varepsilon_1 \neq - 1$ in the equilibrium, which we assume for simplicity. The marginal productivity of the factor h is no longer equal to the ratio of prices but to this ratio multiplied by a term depending on the elasticities relating to the factor h and to output.

Consider first the case of a monopsony for which all the ε_h are zero except that relating to a particular input k. Equations (66) then reduce to the perfect competition equations except for the kth, where $- g'_k$ must equal p_k/p_1 multiplied by the term $(1 + \varepsilon_k)$ which is usually greater than 1. The equilibrium is therefore the same as in a situation of perfect competition involving the same prices for all the goods except k, whose price is greater than that actually asked by suppliers. Since, in the competitive situation, the firm's demand η_k can only decrease, the firm in a position of monopsony usually employs a smaller quantity of the factor k than it would employ in competition. For this reason it may be said to be in the interest of the monopsonist to adopt a 'Malthusian policy'.

We could apply the same reasoning to the case of pure monopoly where all the ε_h except ε_1 are zero. However we shall adopt a rather different approach for an alternative presentation of the analysis, which is thus reinforced.

As in the case of perfect competition, we can maximise profit by means of a two-stage procedure involving first cost minimisation and determination of the cost function. For a pure monopoly, cost minimisation is carried out in exactly the same way as for a perfectly competitive firm and the cost function is exactly the same. So we can confine ourselves to the second stage, and find the value of $\bar{y}_1$ which maximises

$$\pi_1(\bar{y}_1) . \bar{y}_1 - C(\bar{y}_1).$$

We can write this expression in its usual form

$$R(\bar{y}_1) - C(\bar{y}_1), \tag{67}$$

where $R(\bar{y}_1)$ denotes the firm's receipts from output $\bar{y}_1$.

Profit maximisation implies that $\bar{y}_1$ is so chosen that

$$R'(\bar{y}_1) = C'(\bar{y}_1) \tag{68}$$

and

$$R''(\bar{y}_1) \leqslant C''(\bar{y}_1). \tag{69}$$

Equation (68) generalises condition (54) obtained for the case of perfect competition.

We can easily compare monopoly equilibrium with equilibrium for the firm in perfect competition. Figure 11 shows the average cost and marginal cost curves c and γ, as well as the curve d representing the demand function $\pi_1(y_1)$, that is, average revenue, and the curve δ representing marginal revenue, that is, the function $\pi_1 + y_1\pi_1'$. Suppose that π_1' is negative, as will necessarily be the case except perhaps for an inferior good; δ then lies below d. According to (68), monopoly equilibrium is determined by the abscissa y_1^* of the point of intersection of γ and δ. If the firm behaves as in perfect competition, that is, if it takes no account of the reaction of price p_1 to its supply y_1, the equilibrium point is determined by the abscissa y_1^0 of the point of intersection of γ and d.

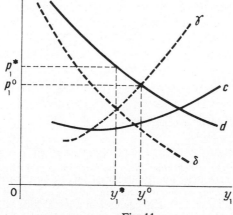

Fig. 11

At the point of intersection of γ and d, the marginal cost must be non-decreasing for y_1^0 to correspond to a true competitive equilibrium. It follows from the fact that d is decreasing and from the respective positions of d and δ that y_1^* is necessarily smaller than y_1^0. *The firm produces less in a position of monopoly than in a situation of perfect competition involving the same prices for it*; this result is similar to that encountered earlier for monopsony.

We can consider R'' as negative in the interpretation of (69) defining the second order condition for a maximum. In particular it will be negative if there is constant elasticity of demand, since then ε_1 is a fixed number, R' is equal to $\pi_1(1 + \varepsilon_1)$ and R'' to $\pi_1'(1 + \varepsilon_1)$. The second order condition is therefore satisfied for any situation where marginal cost is increasing.

But we should point out that this condition may also be satisfied in situations where marginal cost is decreasing. More generally, *monopoly may sometimes allow an equilibrium to be realised which is not possible in perfect competition*. Figure 12 shows an example for a firm with continually decreasing marginal cost, which is possible in the "undifferentiated sector".†

The study of monopoly has taken us outside the field of perfect competition. We could pursue this line in various ways, but the particular aim of this course obliges us to pass on fairly quickly to other more important questions. However, two remarks may usefully be made.

In the first place, it is clear that situations of imperfect competition may involve consumers as well as firms. For example, it is conceivable that a

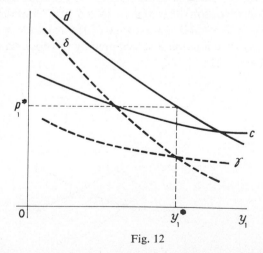

Fig. 12

---

† We should also note that, for the definition of the cost function, second order conditions implying concavity of the isoquants in the neighbourhood of the equilibrium must be satisfied. When this is not so, no equilibrium exists as long as the markets for the factors are competitive: but a monopsony for the firm may allow equilibrium to be realised.

particularly wealthy consumer may have such influence on a market that he has a position of near-monopsony.

In the second place, the theory of imperfect competition cannot depend entirely on the constrained maximum techniques which we have used up till now.

Of course, situations other than those we have considered can be dealt with by constrained maximum techniques, for example, the case of a firm that has a monopoly on each of the two or more independent markets in which its output can be sold. In most cases, profit maximisation leads to price differentiation, the firm releasing to each market a quantity of its product such that marginal revenue from each market equals its marginal cost over all its output.

Generally we can say that constrained maximisation is appropriate to the extent that all agents except at most one adopt a passive attitude, taking the decisions of other agents as given. This is just the situation for a monopoly, since those who demand the product accept as given the price which results from the firm's decision on production. They have no other possible attitude if their number is large and they are all of the same relative importance, and if they are unable to band together in opposition to the monopolist.

But imperfect competition is not limited to such situations. On some markets there are relatively few buyers and sellers; on others, coalitions take place. Other methods of analysis are necessary to deal with such cases.

We shall return to imperfect competition in Chapters 6 and 8 in order to clarify problems of general economic equilibrium. We shall then see how it relates to the theory of games.

4

Optimum theory

Up till now we have been considering the behaviour of a single agent. With the theory of the optimum we approach the study of a whole society. We therefore change our perspective and attack the problems raised by the organisation of the simultaneous actions of all agents.

The classical approach would be first to discuss competitive equilibrium, keeping to the positive standpoint of the previous lectures, and then to go on to the normative standpoint of the search for the optimum. However, we shall reverse the order of these two questions.

Optimum theory involves a rather simpler and more general model than the model on which competitive equilibrium theory is based. It seems plausible that the relationship of the two theories will be more clearly understood if those assumptions which are not involved in optimum theory are introduced in the later discussion of competitive equilibrium.

We are interested, therefore, in the problem of the best possible choice of production and consumption in a given society. Clearly it may appear very ambitious to attempt to deal with this. But it is one of the ultimate objectives of economic science. Preoccupation with the optimum underlies many propositions briefly stated by economists. By providing an initial formalisation and by rigorously establishing conditions for the validity of classical propositions, optimum theory provides the logical foundation for a whole branch of economics.

We must first find out what is meant by the 'best choice' for the society and go on to study the characteristics of situations resulting from this choice.

1. Definition of optimal states

Before fixing a principle of choice, we must again define what are 'feasible' states.

For our present investigation, a 'state of the economy' consists of m consumption vectors x_i and n net production vectors y_j.

We wish to eliminate states which are impossible of realisation whatever the organisation of the society, that is, states which do not obey the physical constraints imposed by nature. So we say that a state is *feasible*:

(i) if it obeys the physical or technological constraints which limit the activity of each agent; in particular,

$$x_i \in X_i \qquad \text{for the consumer } i(i = 1, 2, ..., m) \tag{1}$$
$$y_j \in Y_j \qquad \text{for the firm } j(j = 1, 2, ..., n) \tag{2}$$

(note that we do not introduce the budget constraint for the ith consumer since it is not 'physical', but results from a particular institutional organisation);

(ii) if it also obeys the overall constraints relating to resources and uses for each good, that is, if total consumption is equal to the sum of total net production and of initial resources:

$$\sum_{i=1}^{m} x_{ih} = \sum_{j=1}^{n} y_{jh} + \omega_h \qquad h = 1, 2, ..., l. \tag{3}$$

(We recall that ω_h represents the available initial resources of commodity h. Here it is considered as given.)

How can a choice be made from all the feasible states? The following two principles are generally adopted.

In the first place, the choice between two states may be based only on the consumption they allow to individuals (the x_{ih}) and not directly on the productive operations involved in them (the y_{jh}). According to this widely adopted rule, consumption by individuals is the final aim of production. Production is not an end in itself.

In the second place, the choice between two states may be based on the preferences of the consumers themselves. For, except in particular cases which our present theory does not deal with,† each consumer i is generally considered to be in the best position to know whether or not some vector x_i^1 is better for him than another vector x_i^2.

For a single consumer the choice is simple, depending on his utility function. One state is preferable to another if it gives a greater utility. A multiplicity of consumers obviously complicates things since their preferences between different states may not agree. Within any human society there exist simultaneously a natural solidarity arising from some coinciding interests and a

---

† In fact, some acts of public intervention are inspired by the concern to protect individuals against their own spontaneous choices (the banning of certain drugs, high duties on alcoholic beverages, compulsory retirement, etc.). Such intervention shows that collective choices do not always respect individual preferences. Public authorities are sometimes said to act for a better satisfaction of 'merit wants' than would result from individual decisions.

rivalry arising from conflicting interests. Clearly, where such conflicts exist, individual preferences do not agree.

For the moment, we shall not attempt to solve this basic difficulty, but rather to circumvent it by confining ourselves to a partial ordering of states. For, without having to settle the difficulty, we can declare one state preferable to another if all the consumers actually do prefer it. Thus, following a suggestion first made by the Italian economist Vilfredo Pareto, we can set the following definition:

A state E^0 is called a 'Pareto optimum' if it is feasible, and if there exists no other feasible state E^1 such that

$$S_i(x_i^1) \geqslant S_i(x_i^0) \qquad for \qquad i = 1, 2, ..., m$$

where the inequality holds strictly $(>)$ for at least one consumer. In other words, E^0 is a Pareto optimum if it is feasible and if, given E^0, the utility of one consumer cannot be increased without decreasing the utility of at least one other consumer.

Generally there is a multiplicity of such optimal states. Each feasible state can be represented by a point in m-dimensional space, taking $S_i(x_i)$ as the ith coordinate (see, for example, Figure 1 representing the case of two consumers). The feasible states generally define a closed set (P in Figure 1) in this space. The points representing optimal states belong to a part of, or possibly the whole, boundary of this set (points on the boundary to the right of A).

Optimum theory establishes a correspondence between optimal states and feasible states realised by the behaviour of the different agents confronted with the same price system. These states are called 'market equilibria'. We shall see later that a general equilibrium of perfect competition is a market equilibrium.

More precisely, *we say that a 'market equilibrium' is a state defined by consumption vectors x_i, net production vectors y_j, a price vector p and incomes*

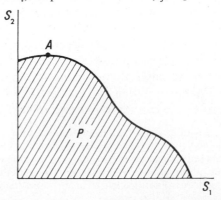

Fig. 1

R_i (*for* $i = 1, 2, ..., m$; $j = 1, 2, ..., n$); *this state satisfies equations* (3) *expressing the equality of supply and demand on the markets for goods; in this state, each consumer maximises his utility subject to his budget constraint and each firm maximises its profit, the price vector p being taken as given by both consumers and producers.*

In this chapter we could work directly on the above model. At the risk of some repetition, it seems preferable to start with two particular cases:

(i) the case of an economy with no production, where the only problem is the distribution of the initial resources among consumers (the term *distribution optimum* will denote a Pareto optimum in such an economy).

(ii) The case of an economy in which we are concerned only with the organisation of production and not with the distribution of the product (the term 'production optimum' for this case will have to be defined precisely).

In fact, to determine an optimal state, we must solve simultaneously the problems raised by the organisation of production and of distribution. But it is important that the student should understand fully the multiple aspects of the theory with which we are presently concerned, and he seems more likely to achieve this if we proceed in stages than if we only deal directly with the general model.

2. Prices associated with a distribution optimum

We now consider the problem of distributing given quantities ω_h among m consumers, the possibilities and preferences of the ith consumer being defined respectively by a set X_i and a utility function S_i. A state of the economy is now represented by the lm numbers x_{ih}.

First of all we shall discuss *necessary conditions* for a state E^0, defined by consumptions x_{ih}^0, to be a distribution optimum. For this we assume first that, in the space R^l, each vector x_i^0 lies in the interior of the corresponding set X_i, and that each function S_i has first and second derivatives, the first derivatives being neither negative nor all simultaneously zero (assumptions 2 and 3 of Chapter 2). We let S_i^0 denote the value $S_i(x_i^0)$.

For E^0 to be an optimum, it must in particular maximise S_1 over the set of feasible states subject to the constraint that the S_i are equal to the corresponding S_i^0, for $i = 2, 3, ..., m$. In particular, it must be a local maximum under the same constraints. Let us examine the consequences of this property.

Since each x_i^0 lies in the interior of its X_i, the constraints on the feasible states reduce, in a neighbourhood of E^0, to the equalities (3) between total demands and resources, i.e. in this case:

$$\sum_{i=1}^{m} x_{ih} = \omega_h \qquad h = 1, 2, ..., l. \tag{4}$$

In order that E^0 should maximise S_1 locally subject to the constraints (4) and

$$S_i(x_i) = S_i^0 \qquad i = 2, 3, ..., m, \tag{5}$$

there must exist Lagrange multipliers $- \sigma_h$ (for $h = 1, 2, ..., l$) and λ_i (for $i = 2, 3, ..., m$) such that the expression

$$\sum_{i=1}^{m} \lambda_i S_i(x_i) - \sum_{h=1}^{l} \sigma_h \sum_{i=1}^{m} x_{ih}, \tag{6}$$

where $\lambda_1 = 1$ by convention, has zero first derivatives with respect to the x_{ih} in E^0.† So there must exist λ_i's and σ_h's such that

$$\lambda_i S'_{ih} = \sigma_h \begin{cases} h = 1, 2, ..., l \\ i = 1, 2, ..., m, \end{cases} \tag{7}$$

where S'_{ih} is the value at x_i^0 of the derivative of S_i with respect to x_{ih}. (Since $\lambda_1 = 1$ and the S'_{1h} are not all simultaneously zero, at least one of the σ_h is not zero, none of the σ_h is negative and consequently all the λ_i are positive.)

The equalities (7) imply

$$\frac{S'_{is}}{S'_{ir}} = \frac{S'_{\alpha s}}{S'_{\alpha r}} \qquad \begin{cases} r, s = 1, 2, ..., l \\ i, \alpha = 1, 2, ..., m \end{cases} \tag{8}$$

(provided that S'_{ir} and $S'_{\alpha r}$ are not zero).

The marginal rate of substitution of s with respect to r must therefore be the same for all consumers, and this must hold for every pair of goods (r, s). This fairly immediate result is easily explained.

Suppose that, for a particular pair of goods (r, s), the marginal rate of substitution of s with respect to r is not the same for two consumers i and α, but is, for example, higher for i. It then becomes possible to alter the distribution of goods so as to increase S_i and S_α simultaneously without affecting the situation of any other consumer. We need only increase x_{is} by the infinitely small positive quantity dv and increase $x_{\alpha r}$ by the infinitely small positive quantity du, at the same time decreasing $x_{\alpha s}$ by dv and x_{ir} by du. Both utilities actually increase if du and dv are chosen so that

$$\frac{S'_{\alpha s}}{S'_{\alpha r}} < \frac{du}{dv} < \frac{S'_{is}}{S'_{ir}}$$

---

† For the application of theorem 6 of the appendix we must check that the matrix G^0 of the derivatives of constraints (4) and (5) has rank $l + m - 1$. Let u be a vector such that $u'G^0 = 0$; let its h-th element be $v_h(h = 1, 2 ... l)$ and its $(l + i - 1)$-th element be $w_i(i = 2, 3 ... m)$. Corresponding to the derivatives with respect to x_{1h}, the vector $u'G^0$ has the component v_h, hence $v_h = 0$. Corresponding to the derivative with respect to x_{ih}(for $i \neq 1$), it has the component $v_h + w_i S'_{ih}$, hence $w_i S'_{ih} = 0$. But, for a given i, the l derivatives S'_{ih} are not simultaneously zero; hence $w_i = 0$. So the matrix G^0 has rank $l + m - 1$.

for then $dS_i = S'_{is}\,dv - S'_{ir}\,du$ and $dS_\alpha = S'_{\alpha r}\,du - S'_{\alpha s}\,dv$ are both positive. By changing the distribution of the commodities r and s between the consumers i and α we achieve a state preferred by each of the two consumers. So contrary to our initial assumption, the state considered would not be an optimum. (It was by this kind of reasoning that the necessary conditions for a distribution optimum were first established in economic science.)

Equations (7) recall those obtained for consumer equilibrium (see equations (17) and (18) in Chapter 2). If we consider σ_h as the price of commodity h, they imply that, for any consumer, the marginal rate of substitution of a commodity s with respect to a commodity r is equal to the ratio between the price of s and the price of r.

This similarity between the necessary conditions for a distribution optimum and the equations established in consumption theory suggests the existence of a useful property. Could we not prove that, given adequate definition of prices p_h and incomes R_i, the distribution optimum E^0 is an equilibrium for each consumer? Let us try to do this.

We set $p_h = \sigma_h$ and $R_i = px_i^0$. (Instead of setting $\lambda_1 = 1$, as before, we could assign some other positive value to it; this would change proportionately the values of all the σ_h. The resulting arbitrariness is unimportant since, in consumption theory, prices and incomes can be defined only up to a multiplicative constant.)

Can we say that x_i^0 maximises $S_i(x_i)$ subject to the constraint that px_i is at most equal to R_i? We can say so, if the equality between the marginal rates of substitution and the corresponding price ratios, together with the budget equation, constitutes a *sufficient* condition for x_i^0 to be the maximum in question. Proposition 2 in Chapter 2 establishes that this is the case *when the function S_i is quasi-concave*. So we can state:

PROPOSITION 1. If E^0 is a distribution optimum such that, for each consumer i, x_i^0 lies in the interior of X_i and if the utility functions S_i and the sets X_i obey assumptions 1 to 4 of Chapter 2, then there exist prices p_h and incomes R_i such that x_i^0 maximises $S_i(x_i)$ subject to the budget constraint $px_i \leqslant R_i$, for all i. The state E^0, prices p_h and incomes R_i then define a market equilibrium.

3. A geometric representation

A geometric representation due to Edgeworth may clarify proposition 1, and in our case will be all the more helpful because the above statement is rather too restrictive. In fact, we could have obtained a more general property by using more powerful methods of reasoning (see Section 10).

Consider the case of two goods and two consumers. Assume that X_i is the set of vectors x_i with no negative component, that is, that the two goods are only consumed. Let x_{11} and x_{12} represent as abscissa and ordinate respectively on a Cartesian graph the quantities consumed by the first consumer. These quantities are bounded above by ω_1 and ω_2, the total available amounts of goods 1 and 2. Overall equilibrium implies

$$\begin{cases} x_{21} = \omega_1 - x_{11}, \\ x_{22} = \omega_2 - x_{12}. \end{cases}$$

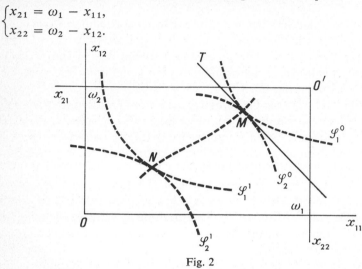

Fig. 2

If M represents the first consumer's consumption complex in a feasible state, we can read the second consumer's consumption complex directly from the graph as the components of the vector MO', or as the coordinates of the point M with respect to a system of rectangular axes centred on O' and directed from right to left for abscissae and downwards for ordinates (system $x_{21}O'x_{22}$ in Figure 2). The first consumer's indifference curves, $\mathscr{S}_1^0$ and $\mathscr{S}_1^1$ say, can be drawn on this graph. The second consumer's indifference curves can be drawn by using the system of axes centred on O'; they are, for example, $\mathscr{S}_2^0$ and $\mathscr{S}_2^1$.

A point M on this graph defines a distribution optimum if it lies within the rectangle bounded by the two systems of axes, if the indifference curves $\mathscr{S}_1$ and $\mathscr{S}_2$ which contain it are tangential and if no point on $\mathscr{S}_2$ lies on the right of $\mathscr{S}_1$. (Here we take account of the fact that the function S_1 increases from left to right and the function S_2 increases from right to left.)

On Figure 2, the two points M and N correspond to distribution optima. The curve passing through these points is such that it contains all the optima. In the case of this figure, we see that there are multiple optima, but also that every feasible state is not an optimum. If the state of the economy is represented by a point P which does not lie on MN, we could improve the distribution of the goods 1 and 2 between the two consumers and arrive at a new state preferred by both consumers.

If S_1 and S_2 are quasi-concave, the curves $\mathscr{S}_1$ are concave towards O' and the curves $\mathscr{S}_2$ are concave towards O. Given a point M, therefore, we need only verify that the two curves $\mathscr{S}_1^0$ and $\mathscr{S}_2^0$, which contain it, are mutually tangential to establish that M represents a distribution optimum.

If MT is the common tangent at M, the marginal utilities of the two goods are proportional to the components of a vector normal to MT. We can then define p_1 and p_2 as the components of any vector p normal to MT. When the two consumers are assigned the incomes $R_1 = px_1^0$ and $R_2 = px_2^0$ respectively, the consumption zones obeying the budget constraints are bounded by the tangent MT, on the right for the first consumer and on the left for the second. If S_1 and S_2 are quasi-concave, M appears as an equilibrium point for each consumer.

We note also that to two different optima such as M and N on our diagram, there generally correspond different prices and incomes. For the first consumer, the optimum furthest to the right is the most favourable; it is often also the optimum for which the distribution of incomes is most favourable to him (the ratio R_1/R_2 is greatest.)†

The above geometric representation allows rapid examination of cases where the various assumptions adopted for the statement of proposition 1 are not satisfied. Let us briefly consider three of these assumptions.

(i) We assumed S_1 and S_2 to be differentiable. Figure 3 illustrates a case where they are not. The indifference curves are not properly speaking tangential at M. Nevertheless, there exists a line MT entirely on the left of $\mathscr{S}_1^0$ and on the right of $\mathscr{S}_2^0$. So the property which interests us still exists, the

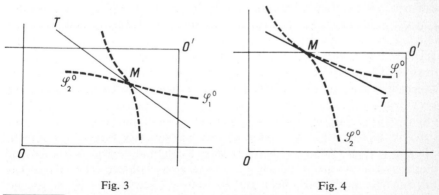

Fig. 3   Fig. 4

---

† We leave it to the reader to construct an example where the point M is more favourable to the first consumer than the point N, while the ratio R_1/R_2 is smaller at M than at N.

point M appearing as an equilibrium for the two consumers whenever prices define the normal to MT and incomes are suitably chosen.

We note also that, in this case, MT may have several positions and consequently that the direction of the price vector is no longer defined uniquely.

(ii) We assumed that, in the optimum E^0, each x_i^0 is contained in the interior of the corresponding set X_i; that is, that the point M of our geometric representation lies within the rectangle with vertices O and O'. Figure 4 represents a case where M lies on the boundary of the rectangle (zero consumption of good 2 by the second consumer). The property established by proposition 1 is still valid, with M constituting an equilibrium point for the first and for the second consumer subject to suitably chosen prices and incomes.

Since S_1 is taken to be differentiable, the direction of the price vector is defined uniquely and, in the equilibrium, we have

$$\frac{S'_{12}}{S'_{11}} = \frac{p_2}{p_1}.$$

But, for the second consumer, the equality is replaced by an inequality

$$\frac{S'_{22}}{S'_{21}} \leqslant \frac{p_2}{p_1}.$$

In this equilibrium, where his consumption of the second good is zero, the second consumer considers the marginal rate of substitution of good 2 relative to good 1 to be less than, or at most equal to, its relative price. We investigated this situation in Chapter 2, Section 7.

(iii) As the above two examples suggest, we could eliminate almost completely from the proof of proposition 1 the assumptions that the S_i are differentiable and that x_i^0 is contained in the interior of X_i. We also assumed that the indifference curves were concave to the right for the first consumer and concave to the left for the second. We can easily construct examples where this condition is not satisfied and the property under discussion still applies. But we could not dispense completely with the assumption in the statement of a general property. This will be demonstrated by the following example.

In Figure 5, the point M is a distribution optimum. At this point, the indifference curve $\mathscr{S}_1^0$ is concave to the left, contrary to our assumption. The two curves $\mathscr{S}_1^0$ and $\mathscr{S}_2^0$ do in fact have a common tangent MT at M. The marginal rate of substitution of the second good with respect to the first is the same for both consumers. But the state E^0 represented by M can no longer be realised as an equilibrium for each consumer. If a price vector p, normal to MT, is chosen and if incomes px_1^0 and px_2^0 are assigned to the two consumers, then the second will choose the point M, but the first will choose on MT the point N, which, for him, belongs to the most favourable indifference curve. The resulting state will not be feasible since it does not satisfy the necessary equalities of demand and supply, consumption of the first good being too low and consumption of the second too high.

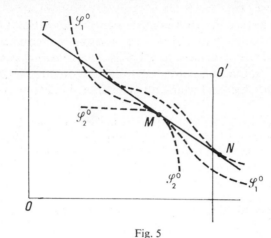

Fig. 5

Of course, this example may be considered to have little relevance if the adopted assumption of concavity is thought to apply to individual indifference curves. We shall return to it in Chapter 7 when discussing the case where there are many consumers.

4. The optimality of market equilibria

We can now establish the converse to proposition 1:

PROPOSITION 2. If E^0 is a feasible state, if there exist prices $p_h \geqslant 0$ ($h = 1$, $2, ..., l$) such that, for all $i = 1, 2, ..., m$, x_i^0 maximises $S_i(x_i)$ in X_i subject to the constraint $px_i \leqslant px_i^0$, and finally, if the S_i and the X_i satisfy assumptions 1 and 2 of Chapter 2, then E^0 is a distribution optimum.

For the proof of proposition 2 we shall assume that, contrary to this proposition, there exists a feasible state E^1 which is better than E^0 in the sense that

$$S_i(x_i^1) \geqslant S_i(x_i^0) \qquad \text{for} \qquad i = 1, 2, ..., m \qquad (9)$$

where the inequality holds strictly for at least one consumer, say the last consumer:

$$S_m(x_m^1) > S_m(x_m^0). \qquad (10)$$

Since x_m^0 maximises S_m subject to the constraint that $px_m \leqslant px_m^0$, the following inequality holds:

$$px_m^1 > px_m^0. \tag{11}$$

We shall show also that

$$px_i^1 \geqslant px_i^0 \qquad \text{for} \qquad i = 1, 2, ..., m. \tag{12}$$

As we have just seen, this inequality certainly holds when $S_i(x_i^1)$ is greater than $S_i(x_i^0)$. Suppose that it does not hold for a consumer i for whom $S_i(x_i^1) = S_i(x_i^0)$. We then have $px_i^1 < px_i^0$. The vector x_i^1 maximises $S_i(x_i)$ subject to the constraint $px_i \leqslant px_i^0$. But this contradicts the result of proposition 1 of Chapter 2 which demands that

$$px_i^1 = px_i^0.$$

(The proposition stipulates that $p_h > 0$ for all h, but $p_h \geqslant 0$ is sufficient for that part of the proof of this proposition with which we are now concerned). This establishes the inequality (12).

The inequalities (11) and (12) imply

$$p\left[\sum_{i=1}^{m} x_i^1 - \sum_{i=1}^{m} x_i^0\right] > 0, \tag{13}$$

which contradicts condition (4) for overall equilibrium:

$$\sum_{i=1}^{m} x_i^1 = \sum_{i=1}^{m} x_i^0 = \omega$$

since, by hypothesis, E^0 and E^1 are two feasible states. This establishes the proof of proposition 2.

We note that the proposition does not involve the assumption that the functions S_i are quasi-concave. Nor does the proof involve some of the properties spelled out in assumptions 1 and 2 of Chapter 2 (the fact that the X_i are convex, closed and bounded below, or that they contain the vector O). So the stated property has wide general validity.

5. Production optimum

We now consider the problem of the organisation of production independently of that of the distribution of goods. We wish to define and characterise situations in which the productive activity of all firms yields the highest possible final productions.

The result of the productive operations is a vector y of total net productions, the sum of the vectors y_j relating to the different firms:

$$y_h = \sum_{j=1}^{m} y_{jh} \qquad h = 1, 2, ..., l.$$

(In most cases, the sum on the right hand side contains both positive terms, for the firms j which have the food h as output, and negative terms for the firms which use the good h as input.)

If, as we have assumed, utilities increase as a function of the x_{ih}, it is always advantageous to replace a vector y^1 of total net productions by another vector y^2 all of whose components are greater. It is therefore natural to make the following definitions.

(a) A state E^0, defined here by the n vectors y_j^0, is *feasible* if $y_j^0 \in Y_j$ (for $j = 1, 2, ..., n$).

(b) A state E^0 is a *production optimum* (or E^0 is said to be *efficient*) if it is feasible, and if there exists no other feasible state E^1 such that

$$y_h^1 \geqslant y_h^0 \qquad \text{for} \qquad h = 1, 2, ..., l$$

where the inequality holds strictly for at least one h.

It is immediately obvious that these definitions are rather simplistic. We often assume that commodities can be grouped into three categories: primary goods, intermediate goods and final goods. Only final goods are considered to be used for consumption while initial resources consist only of primary goods.

If this is so, there are additional conditions for a state E^0 defined by n vectors y_j^0 to be really feasible. Total net production y_q^0 of the primary resource q must be at least $-\omega_q$; total net production y_r^0 of the intermediate good r must be non-negative; finally, net productions of final goods must be such that they can be distributed among consumers so that each consumer is given a consumption vector which is feasible for him.

Moreover, it is not always advantageous to increase the net production of a good h. Suppose, for example, that the feasible state E^1 differs from the feasible state E^0 only in the respect that $y_s^0 = 0$ and $y_s^1 > 0$ for a (non-stockable) intermediate good s. Then E^1 is not really more advantageous than E^0; if E^1 is declared to be optimal, so also should E^0.

This classification of goods into three categories, primary, intermediate and final, has been introduced in detailed theories of the production optimum. It obviously complicates the exposition, but has little effect on the logical structure. So, for simplicity, we shall keep to the definition given above.

As in the case of the distribution optimum, we shall first try to find necessary conditions for a vector y^0 to be a production optimum. For this we shall assume that y_j is restricted only by a differentiable production function

$$f_j(y_j) = 0, \tag{14}$$

4

that is, we ignore the additional constraints that possibly limit production.†
As we have seen, the mathematics becomes very heavy if we take account of
these constraints, and in fact, other methods of reasoning are then required.
We shall return to this point in Section 10, which gives the elements for a
modern proof of the property under discussion.

If E^0 is a production optimum, then it maximises $\sum_j y_{j1}$ subject to the
constraints

$$\sum_{j=1}^{m} y_{jh} = y_h^0 \qquad h = 2, 3, ..., l$$

$$f_j(y_j) = 0 \qquad j = 1, 2, ..., n. \tag{15}$$

Therefore there exist Lagrange multipliers‡

$$\sigma_1 = 1, \qquad \sigma_h \quad \text{and} \quad -\mu_j \ (h = 2, 3, ..., l; j = 1, 2, ..., n)$$

such that the expression

$$\sum_{h=1}^{l} \sigma_h \sum_{j=1}^{n} y_{jh} - \sum_{j=1}^{n} \mu_j f_j(y_j) \tag{16}$$

has zero first derivatives with respect to the y_{jh}; or such that

$$\sigma_h = \mu_j f'_{jh} \qquad \begin{cases} h = 1, 2, ..., l \\ j = 1, 2, ..., n, \end{cases} \tag{17}$$

where f'_{jh} denotes the value at y_j^0 of the derivative of f_j with respect to y_{jh}.
No f'_{jh} is negative, as we saw at the end of the first section of Chapter 3.
Since $\sigma_1 = 1$ and $f'_{j1} \geqslant 0$, then μ_j is necessarily positive.§

For the existence of numbers σ_h and μ_j satisfying (17), it is necessary that

$$\frac{f'_{js}}{f'_{jr}} = \frac{f'_{\beta s}}{f'_{\beta r}} \qquad \begin{cases} r, s = 1, 2, ..., l \\ j, \beta = 1, 2, ..., n. \end{cases} \tag{18}$$

---

† We can write the technical constraint directly in the form of (14) by confining ourselves to 'technically efficient' productions for each firm. In fact, a state E^0 in which $f_j(y_j^0)$
< 0 for a firm j is not a production optimum since y_j^0 can be replaced by a feasible vector
y_j^1 with larger components, without changing the other firms' productions.

‡ For the application of theorem VI of the annex, we require that the f'_{j1} are not all
zero, which is always the case perhaps after a relabelling of the commodity index (the
f'_{jh} are not all zero). Indeed, consider the matrix G^0 of the derivatives of the constraints (15)
and the equation $u'G^0 = 0$ where the vector u has the components $v_h(h = 2 ... l)$ and
$w_j(j = 1, 2 ... n)$. It may be written as:

$$\begin{cases} w_j f'_{j1} = 0 & j = 1, 2 ... n \\ u_h + w_j f'_{jh} = 0 & j = 1, 2 ... n; h = 2 ... l \end{cases}$$

If $f'_{k1} \neq 0$ then $w_k = 0$, hence $u_h = 0$ for all h; hence also $w_j = 0$ for all j (not all derivatives
of f_j are zero). The matrix G^0 has rank $l + n - 1$ as is required.

§ We note that the σ_h and μ_j continue to exist if the arguments of the production functions
are quantities only of those goods which are of interest to the corresponding firms, rather
than quantities of all goods. Equations (17) must be written only for the h's in which the
jth producer is interested; but this does not affect the rest of the proof.

Whenever f'_{jr} and $f'_{\beta r}$ are non-zero, the marginal rate of substitution of the good r with respect to the good s must be the same in all firms, and this must hold for any pair of goods (r, s).

This condition can be obtained directly by showing that, if it is not satisfied for a pair of commodities and a pair of firms, then global net productions can be increased for the two commodities in question by means of infinitely small appropriate variations in the corresponding y_{js}, y_{jr}, $y_{\beta s}$, $y_{\beta r}$. It is sufficient to apply the reasoning used in the discussion of the distribution optimum.

Equations (17) recall those obtained in the investigation of equilibrium for the firm (see equations (27) in Chapter 3). If σ_h is interpreted as the price of commodity h, they imply that, for each firm, the marginal rates of substitution are equal to the corresponding price-ratios.

If we set $p_h = \sigma_h$, equations (17) together with the production functions (14) are equivalent to the first order conditions that y^0 should satisfy in order to be an equilibrium for the firm j in a competitive situation. Now, these first-order conditions are also sufficient for an equilibrium if the production set Y_j satisfies the assumption of convexity (see proposition 1, Chapter 3). We can therefore state the following result which transposes proposition 1 to the theory of the production optimum.

PROPOSITION 3. If E^0 is a production optimum and if, for each firm j, the technical constraints satisfy the assumption of convexity and imply only $f_j(y_j) \leqslant 0$, where f_j is a differentiable function all of whose first derivatives are not simultaneously zero at y_j^0, then there exist prices p_h such that y_j^0 maximises py_j over the set of all technically feasible y_j, and this is true for all j.

In a certain sense, this statement is too restrictive, since it makes assumptions about the technical constraints which could be partly eliminated if a different type of mathematical reasoning were adopted (see Section 10).

The importance of the assumptions for the stated property will be made intuitively obvious if we refer to a convenient geometric representation. Suppose there are only two goods and two firms. To simplify the figure, we shall assume that each firm can produce the two goods simultaneously. (In fact, this can only be advantageous if the firms dispose of inputs which are not represented in the model.)

Consider a Cartesian graph with y_{j1} as abscissa and y_{j2} as ordinate. The vector y_1 with components y_{11} and y_{12} is restricted to belong to a set Y_1 whose boundary $\overline{Y}_1$ only is represented on the diagram (the feasible vectors lie on or below $\overline{Y}_1$). Similarly y_2 is restricted to belong to the set Y_2 whose boundary is $\overline{Y}_2$. The vector y, the sum of y_1 and y_2, is restricted to belong to a set Y which can be constructed, point by point, from Y_1 and Y_2 (this set is said to be the 'sum' of Y_1 and Y_2; it should not be confused with the union of Y_1 and Y_2). The boundary $\overline{Y}$ of Y is clearly the envelope of the curve $\overline{Y}_1 + y_2$ as y_2 varies along $\overline{Y}_2$ (the curve $\overline{Y}_1 + y_2$ is deduced from $\overline{Y}_1$ by a translation of the origin to y_2).

A production optimum is represented by a pair of vectors (y_1^0, y_2^0) whose sum y^0 belongs to the boundary $\overline{Y}$ of Y. For such a state, the tangents to $\overline{Y}_1$ at y_1^0, to $\overline{Y}_2$ at y_2^0 and to $\overline{Y}$ at y^0 are all parallel. (This is a well-known result in geometry which we arrive at easily from our proof of proposition 3.) The marginal rate of substitution of good 2 with respect to good 1 is the same for both firms. The price vector is therefore defined (apart from a multiplicative constant) by the common normal to the three tangents.

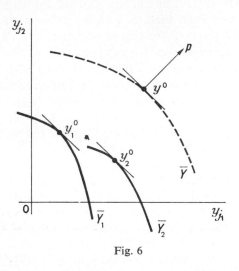

Fig. 6

It is obvious from this type of figure that the assumption of differentiability, necessary for unambiguous definition of the marginal rates of substitution, is not necessary for the existence of prices with respect to which the production optimum corresponds to competitive equilibria for the firms. Figure 7 provides an example of this. For the pair (y_1^0, y_2^0), the direction of the price vector is defined uniquely; for the pair (y_1^0, y_2^*), this direction may vary within a small angle; but in both cases, the property stated in proposition 3 holds. Similarly, it is intuitively obvious that the existence of rigid proportionalities between inputs in certain firms does not affect the property, since its only effect is to give a particular form, illustrated by Figure 4 in Chapter 3, to the corresponding sets Y_j.

Figure 8 refers to the case where a production set (Y_1) is not convex (this set contains the points lying on or below the curve passing through y_1^0). The pair (y_1^0, y_2^0) defines a production optimum. The marginal rates of substitution are the same in both firms. With the corresponding price vector, y_2^0 is an equilibrium point for the second firm; but y_1^0 is not an equilibrium point for the first, since it does not maximise profit py_1 in Y_1 (in fact, it corresponds to a minimum of py_1 along the boundary $\overline{Y}_1$).

This diagram illustrates the difficulty faced by firms in the 'undifferentiated sector' whose production functions do not satisfy the assumption of convexity. A given production optimum may be expressed, for firms in this sector, by vectors y_j^0 which do not maximise their profits. The realisation of such an optimum is incompatible with the purely competitive management of such firms. We shall return to this point in Section 6.

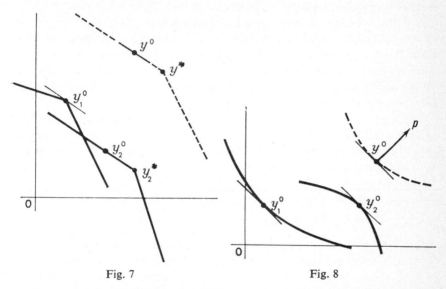

Fig. 7   Fig. 8

Like proposition 1, proposition 3 has a converse which does not involve the assumption of convexity. We shall prove the following result:

PROPOSITION 4. If the y_j^0 are technically feasible, if there exist prices p_h ($h = 1, 2, ..., l$) which are all *positive* and such that each y_j^0 maximises py_j over the set Y_j of technically feasible y_j's, then the state E^0 defined by the y_j^0's constitutes a production optimum.

For, suppose that there exist technically feasible y_j^1's such that

$$\sum_{j=1}^{n} y_{jh}^1 \geqslant \sum_{j=1}^{n} y_{jh}^0 \qquad h = 1, 2, ..., l,$$

where the inequality holds strictly at least once. Since the p_h are all positive, it follows that

$$\sum_{j=1}^{n} py_j^1 > \sum_{j=1}^{n} py_j^0, \tag{19}$$

which obviously contradicts the assumption that each y_j^0 maximises the corresponding quantity py_j over the set of technically feasible y_j.

6. Increasing returns and concave isoquants

Proposition 3 relating to the production optimum excludes indivisibilities or increasing returns, which are in fact important in some branches of industry and some public services. We must clearly investigate the conditions for the efficient participation of such firms in an economy that otherwise uses prices to regulate production decisions.

For this, we shall consider a particular case where a firm (the first) operates in technological conditions which are not compatible with convexity of the set of feasible net productions. The only output of this firm is the good 1; its isoquants are concave upwards, as is required by convexity, but a doubling of all inputs results in more than doubled output. The other firms satisfy the assumptions of the previous section.

This case is clearly particular even for the first firm in that it completely excludes indivisibility of inputs. By examining it, we shall, however, see how the property stated in proposition 3 is affected by 'non-convexities'. We shall also discuss another example of non-convexity in Chapter 9, Section 4.

Let us write the production function of the first firm in the form

$$y_{11} = g_1(y_{12}, y_{13}, ..., y_{1l}), \tag{20}$$

where the function g_1 is assumed to be quasi-concave but not concave (the isoquants are convex upwards but returns to scale are increasing).

If E^0 is a production optimum, there exist σ_h's and μ_j's such that equations (17) are satisfied, since the first part of the proof of proposition 3 does not involve the assumption of convexity. If prices p_h are defined as equal to the σ_h, the marginal productivities of the different inputs in firm 1 are proportional to the prices of these inputs. Since g_1 is quasi-concave, this implies that the vector y_1^0 minimises the cost of production in the set of all feasible vectors y_1 containing the same output y_{11}^0. Moreover, the fact that the $-g'_{1h}$ are equated to the ratios p_h/p_1 ensures that the marginal cost is p_1 (see Chapter 3, Section 7).

Thus, the prices associated with the production optimum E^0 are such that the following two properties hold:

(i) The vector y_1^0 is an equilibrium if the firm acquires its inputs at the price in question and if it is restricted to produce the quantity y_{11}^0 contained in the optimum considered.

(ii) The price of the output is equal to the marginal cost when the quantity produced is y_{11}^0 and the prices of the inputs are the p_h.

So the realisation of the optimum E^0 is compatible with the following management rule for the firm: it should (i) produce an output y^0_{11}, which is fixed for it, (ii) minimise its cost calculated from the prices p_h associated with E^0 (for $h = 2, ..., l$), (iii) sell its product at marginal cost. This management rule is in fact often suggested for public undertakings.

Clearly, this case can be generalised and appropriate management rules found for more complex situations. If, for example, the last input, the good l, is subject to indivisibilities, but if convexity holds for the set of possible vectors y_1 such that $y_{11} = y^0_{11}$ and $y_{1l} = y^0_{1l}$, the rule must specify not only the quantity of output, but also the quantity of the last input. Thus cost minimisation must often be restricted to short-run decisions when longer-run decisions involve indivisibilities.

Also, for any firm with a single output, marginal cost must equal the price of this output, the cost being computed from the vector of the $p_h = \sigma_h$ associated with the production optimum, and this must be so independently of any assumption relating to convexities. The only condition is that marginal cost must be well defined, that is, that the function $C_1(y_{11})$ expressing variations in cost at given prices should be differentiable.

Here we shall conclude our rapid investigation of a case where convexity is lacking. The management rules we have established are less simple than those for market equilibrium. They would certainly be less spontaneously adopted by the firm. They assume previous determination not only of prices, but also of certain quantitative data (the production target y^0_{11}, for example). After the following chapters, the reader will be in a better position to judge how far the presence of indivisibilities prejudices the efficient, decentralised organisation of production.

7. Pareto optimality

We have considered in some detail the theories of the distribution optimum and the production optimum. We can now deal rapidly with the theory of Pareto optimality, which supersedes the previous two analyses.

Suppose then that a state E^0 is a Pareto optimum and that the x^0_i contained in it lie in the interior of the corresponding X_i. The function S_1 must be locally maximised over the set of feasible states subject to the constraint that the S_i are equal to the $S_i(x^0_i)$ for $i = 2, 3, ..., m$. For maximisation, the following constraints apply:

$$S_i(x_i) = S_i(x^0_i) \qquad i = 2, 3, ..., m \qquad (21)$$

$$f_j(y_j) = 0 \qquad j = 1, 2, ..., n \qquad (22)$$

$$\sum_{i=1}^{m} x_{ih} = \sum_{j=1}^{n} y_{jh} + \omega_h \qquad h = 1, 2, ..., l \qquad (23)$$

There necessarily exist Lagrange multipliers† $\lambda_1 = 1$, λ_i (for $i = 2, 3, ...,$ m), $-\mu_j$ (for $j = 1, 2, ..., n$), $-\sigma_h$ (for $h = 1, 2, ..., l$) such that

$$\sum_{i=1}^{m} \lambda_i S_i(x_i) - \sum_{j=1}^{n} \mu_j f_j(y_j) - \sum_{h=1}^{l} \sigma_h \left[\sum_{i=1}^{m} x_{ih} - \sum_{j=1}^{n} y_{jh} \right] \tag{24}$$

has zero derivatives with respect to the x_{ih} and y_{jh} in E^0. In other words, there necessarily exist λ_i's, μ_j's and σ_h's such that E^0 satisfies the system

$$\begin{cases} \lambda_i S'_{ih} = \sigma_h & \text{for} \quad h = 1, 2, ..., l \\ & \qquad\quad i = 1, 2, ..., m \\ \mu_j f'_{jh} = \sigma_h & \qquad\quad j = 1, 2, ..., n. \end{cases} \tag{25}$$

These equalities correspond to (7) and (17) above. They imply

$$\frac{S'_{is}}{S'_{ir}} = \frac{S'_{\alpha s}}{S'_{\alpha r}} = \frac{f'_{js}}{f'_{jr}} = \frac{f'_{\beta s}}{f'_{\beta r}} \qquad \begin{matrix} r, s = 1, 2, ..., l \\ i, \alpha = 1, 2, ..., m \\ j, \beta = 1, 2, ..., n. \end{matrix} \tag{26}$$

The marginal rate of substitution of s with respect to r must be the same for all consumers; it must equal the marginal rate of transformation of s with respect to r, which must be the same for all firms.

This necessary equality of substitution rates and transformation rates can be proved directly by showing that, if the ratio S'_{is}/S'_{ir} exceeds the ratio f'_{js}/f'_{jr}, then S_i can be increased, without changing the utilities of the other consumers, by increasing x_{is} and y_{js} by $f'_{jr} \, du$ and by simultaneously decreasing x_{ir} and y_{jr} by $f'_{js} \, du$, where du is a small enough positive quantity.

If we consider σ_h as the price of commodity h, we can interpret equations (25) as necessary first-order conditions for equilibria for the different consumers and the different firms. So the state E^0 appears as a market equilibrium with prices $p_h = \sigma_h$ if these first-order conditions are sufficient as well as necessary.

We can now state the following result, which synthesizes propositions 1 and 3:

PROPOSITION 5. If E^0 is a Pareto optimum, such that, for each consumer i, the vector x_i^0 is contained in the interior of X_i, if the utility functions S_i and the X_i obey assumptions 1 to 4 of Chapter 2, and if, for each firm j, the technical constraints obey the assumption of convexity and imply only $f_j(y_j) \leqslant 0$, where f_j is a differentiable function all of whose first derivatives are not simultaneously zero at y_j^0, then there exist prices p_h for all goods and incomes R_i for all consumers such that

---

† ⁎ Following the same line of argument as for the distribution optimum, one can prove that the matrix G^0 giving the derivatives of the constraints has rank $l + m + n - 1$, so that theorem VI of the appendix applies.

(i) x_i^0 maximises $S_i(x_i)$ subject to the constraint $px_i \leqslant R_i$, for $i = 1, 2, ..., m$.
(ii) y_j^0 maximises py_j subject to the constraint $f_j(y_j) \leqslant 0$, for all $j = 1, 2, ..., n$.

A geometric representation of the case of a single consumer and a single firm will round off Figures 1 and 5 and may clarify proposition 5.

Let the quantities consumed by the consumer, x_1 and x_2 say, be represented on a graph as abscissa and ordinate respectively. Let $\overline{Y} + \omega$ be the boundary of the set of vectors of realisable consumption, that is, the vectors which can be written $y + \omega$ where y is a vector belonging to Y.

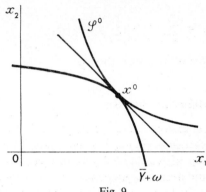

Fig. 9

Let the point x^0 represent the consumption vector of an optimal state. An indifference curve $\mathscr{S}^0$, which must contain no point on the left of $\overline{Y} + \omega$, passes through x^0. If, as is assumed by proposition 5, $\mathscr{S}^0$ is concave upwards and $\overline{Y} + \omega$ is concave downwards, these two curves have a common tangent at x^0 and lie on either side of this tangent. The vector x^0 appears as an equilibrium point for the firm and for the consumer; the price vector is the normal to the tangent and the consumer's income is px^0.

Obviously proposition 5 has a converse.

PROPOSITION 6. If E^0 is a feasible state, if there exist prices $p_h \geqslant 0$ ($h = 1, 2, ..., l$) such that, for all $i = 1, 2, ..., m$, the vector x_i^0 maximises $S_i(x_i)$ over X_i subject to the constraint $px_i \leqslant px_i^0$ and also that, for all $j = 1, 2, ..., n$, the vector y_j^0 maximises py_j over Y_j, if finally, the S_i and the X_i satisfy assumptions 1 and 2 of Chapter 2, then E^0 is a Pareto optimum.

For, suppose that there exists a possible state E^1 such that

$$S_i(x_i^1) \geqslant S_i(x_i^0) \qquad \text{for} \qquad i = 1, 2, ..., m,$$

where the inequality holds strictly for at least one consumer. In the proof of proposition 2 we saw that this implies

$$p\left[\sum_{i=1}^{m} x_i^1 - \sum_{i=1}^{m} x_i^0\right] > 0. \tag{27}$$

Also, since y_j^0 maximises py_j in Y_j and y_j^1 belongs to Y_j, we can state

$$py_j^1 \leqslant py_j^0 \qquad j = 1, 2, ..., n$$

and so

$$p\left[\sum_{j=1}^n y_j^1 - \sum_{j=1}^n y_j^0\right] \leqslant 0. \tag{28}$$

Now, it is clear that (27) and (28) are incompatible with the equilibrium condition

$$\sum_{i=1}^m x_i^1 - \sum_{j=1}^n y_j^1 = \sum_{i=1}^m x_i^0 - \sum_{j=1}^n y_j^0 = \omega. \tag{29}$$

This completes the proof of proposition 6.

8. Optimum and social utility function

Except in the trivial case of a single consumer, there are generally multiple optimal states, as is shown in Figure 2. This results from the fact that we have only a partial ordering of the set of feasible states.

To eliminate this indeterminacy, we must introduce a complete ordering of states. It is desirable in logic that this new ordering should be compatible with the ordering so far used, in the sense that a state E^1 preferred to another state E^2 after the partial ordering should still be preferred to it after the complete ordering.

Starting from this principle, it has sometimes been suggested that states be classified according to the values they give for a *social utility function*, that is, a real function whose arguments are the m values of the individual utilities of the m consumers:

$$U(S_1, S_2, ..., S_m). \tag{30}$$

Then, by definition, the social utility which the community in question attributes to a state E is

$$U[S_1(x_1), S_2(x_2), ..., S_m(x_m)]. \tag{31}$$

The function is usually considered to be differentiable. Let U_i' denote its derivative with respect to S_i. Compatibility of the complete ordering with the partial ordering requires that the U_i' should all be positive, for all possible values of the S_i.

It is obviously a bold step to assume the existence of a social utility function. To define such a function, we must first assign a completely specified utility function to each consumer. We must therefore choose a particular form for S_i, we can no longer be content with 'ordinal utility', but must refer to

'cardinal utility', without which the definition of U becomes ambiguous.†
(Note also that a simple increasing linear transformation applied to one of
the S_i changes the ordering of states which is implied by U. So the term
'cardinal utility' has a narrower meaning here than in Chapter 2.)

In the second place, a social utility function establishes some judgment
between different consumers' gains in utility. Thus, let us consider two
states E^1 and E^2 such that

$$S_i^1 = S_i(x_i^1) = S_i(x_i^2) = S_i^2$$

for all consumers except the first two, and such that $S_1^1 = S_1^2 + dS_1$,
$S_2^1 = S_2^2 + dS_2$, where dS_1 and dS_2 are infinitely small. The function U
will declare these two states equivalent if

$$U_1' \, dS_1 + U_2' \, dS_2 = 0. \tag{32}$$

So a social utility function assumes that, in some sense, a marginal rate of
substitution between the individual utilities of different consumers exists at
the collective level. The choices represented by such a function are not based
solely on consideration of the efficiency of production and distribution;
they also express a value judgment on the just distribution of welfare among
individuals. In other words we may say that a social utility function represents
the accepted ethical principles about equity.

Most theoretical economists balk at the idea of such an *intercomparison of
individual utilities*, asserting that the utilities of two distinct individuals
cannot be compared, and there is no way of going from the one to the other.
This is the 'no bridge' principle. On the other hand, the partisans of the social
utility function claim that, in fact, it is necessary to choose one particular
state from all Pareto optimal states. Such a choice implies, explicitly or implicitly, that there are marginal rates of substitution between the utilities of
different consumers; explicit introduction of the function U makes for a
clearer choice.

We shall now examine the particular condition to be satisfied by a state
which is optimum according to some social utility function. Here we shall
confine ourselves to the first-order conditions for a local maximum of U,
and shall assume that the x_i are contained in the interiors of the respective X_i.

We must find the conditions for a maximum of (31) subject to the constraints (22) and (23) already considered in the section on the Pareto
optimum. If $- \mu_j$ (for $j = 1, 2, ..., n$) and $- \sigma_h$ (for $h = 1, 2, ..., l$) represent

---

† We could dispense both with individual utility functions and with the social utility
function by defining directly a preordering relation in the ml-dimensional space of the x_{ih}
(for $i = 1, 2, ..., m$; $h = 1, 2, ..., l$). This collective preordering ought to be compatible
with the preorderings of individual preferences. However, such an approach does not
eliminate the necessity to arbitrate between consumers.

the corresponding Lagrange multipliers, equation to zero of the appropriate derivatives gives†

$$\begin{cases} U_i' S_{ih}' = \sigma_h & \text{for} \quad h = 1, 2, ..., l \\ & \quad\quad\quad i = 1, 2, ..., m \\ \mu_j' f_{jh}' = \sigma_h & \quad\quad\quad j = 1, 2, ..., n. \end{cases} \quad (33)$$

The second system of equations is identical with that in the conditions (25) for a Pareto optimum. In the first system, the Lagrange multipliers λ_i which, except for λ_1, were indeterminate *a priori*, have been replaced by the known functions U_i'.

For a state to be an optimum according to the function U, not only must the conditions (26) relating to the marginal rates of substitution be satisfied, but also, for each good, the product $U_i' S_{ih}'$ must take the same value for all consumers. (It is sufficient that this condition be satisfied for one good, the numéraire l for example; in view of (25), it is then satisfied for all goods.) We say that the marginal utilities of the different individuals‡ must be inversely proportional to the U_i', that is, to the weight with which the dS_i relating to these individuals occur in the calculation of dU.

The product $U_i' S_{ih}'$ can then be interpreted as the price p_h of commodity h (clearly we could also take for p_h a multiple, independent of h, of $U_i' S_{ih}'$). Under these conditions,

$$dU = \sum_{ih} U_i' S_{ih}' \, dx_{ih} = \sum_{ih} p_h \, dx_{ih}. \quad (33)$$

Therefore the variation in social utility for any infinitely small deviation from the optimum is equal to the variation in the value of global consumption, this value being calculated with the prices associated with the optimum. Conversely we can easily show that, if the social utility function is a quasi-concave function of the x_{ih}, if the X_i are convex, if a feasible state E^0 is a market equilibrium such that §:

$$U_i' S_{il}' = U_\alpha' S_{\alpha l}' \qquad i, \alpha = 1, 2, ..., m, \quad (35)$$

then this is an optimal state according to the social utility function U.

In works of applied economics, different variants of a project are frequently compared on the basis of the increase which each brings about in the value

---

† It is again easy to check that the matrix G^0 of the derivatives of the constraints has rank $l + n$, so that theorem VI of the appendix applies here.

‡ When the good l is the numéraire, S_{il}' is sometimes called the 'marginal utility of money'. We then say that the marginal utilities of money must be inversely proportional to the U_i'.

§ It is sometimes said that, for a market equilibrium satisfying (35), 'the distribution of incomes is optimal'. It is important to avoid confusion about the meaning of this expression and to understand clearly that the criterion of optimality does not relate directly to incomes, but to individual utilities.

of final consumption, or in the value of national income, one or other of these aggregates being calculated at constant prices. The foregoing analysis justifies such a procedure only where the reference state, with respect to which variations are defined, is approximately optimal, particularly in respect of the equity of distribution among consumers.†

For, if two variants of the same project cannot be classified by the Pareto criterion, then one must benefit some consumers while the other benefits other consumers. To refer to the value of global consumption is to assume implicitly that a decrease of 1 in the value of one individual's consumption must be accepted whenever this leads to an increase of more than 1 in the value of any other individual's consumption. This point of view is rejected whenever a variant is chosen on the grounds that it leads to more equitable distribution among individuals.

9. The relevance of optimum theory

Let us now discuss the contribution of optimum theory to the understanding of the problems raised by the production and distribution of goods in society. We are no longer particularly concerned with the assumptions adopted for the proof of the results, but only with the significance of the results themselves.

Proposition 6, preceded by propositions 2 and 4, establishes, under what are in fact very general conditions, that a market equilibrium is a Pareto optimum. So in a certain sense, such an equilibrium is an efficient solution to the problem of organisation of the production and distribution of goods.

However, a market equilibrium E^0 may conceivably be rejected in favour of another state E^1 or E^2. This may happen if the distribution of goods among consumers in E^1 or in E^2 is held to be preferable on grounds of social justice to that in E^0. Of course, for some individuals these new states entail less satisfactory consumption than does E^0. But on the other hand, they afford more satisfactory consumption to other individuals and appear on the whole better according to the social ethic of the particular community (see Figure 10, where the shaded set P corresponds to the feasible states).

Thus, if this ethic is represented by a social utility function, there is no reason *a priori* for the market equilibrium E^0 to coincide with the state E^1 which maximises social utility. The state E^1 will naturally be preferred to E^0 provided that the community's institutions do not prevent its realisation. If it turns out that E^1 is institutionally incapable of realisation, then it is still

† It should also be mentioned that the justification applies only for comparisons between feasible variants. If the labour resources are fully employed, the two variants should use the same labour inputs. Changes in the labour costs, properly valued, have often to be taken into account.

conceivable that another state E^2 may be preferred to E^0, although E^2 is not a Pareto optimum.

But welfare theory also states that, under certain conditions, any Pareto optimum is a particular market equilibrium (see proposition 5, preceded by propositions 1 and 3). This is particularly the case with the socially best optimum, E^1 in our example. Of course, in most cases this market equilibrium need not coincide with the perfect competition equilibrium realised where there is private ownership of primary resources and firms. But can one not conceive of institutions which allow the preferred state E^1 to be realised as a market equilibrium? We shall now discuss briefly how this question may be tackled.

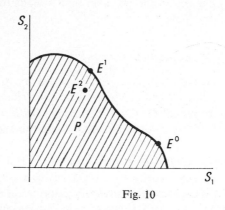

Fig. 10

Proposition 5 establishes that with E^1, the state of maximum welfare, we can associate a price vector p such that, if prices p_h are chosen, if consumers receive incomes $R_i = px_i^1$ and *if E^1 is realised*, then it is to the advantage of no agent to change the consumption vector or the net production vector which the state assigns to him. T. Koopmans suggests that the *price vector be said to 'sustain' the state in question*.

Strictly speaking we have no guarantee that, if prices are fixed at the appropriate p_h and incomes at the R_i, the behaviour of consumers and firms will lead to the automatic realisation of E^1. This would be so only if, for these prices and incomes, the equilibria pertaining to each consumer and to each firm were all determined uniquely. As we have seen, this property of uniqueness may fail to hold, especially for firms. If we wish to realise E^1, and if some of the corresponding individual equilibria are multiple, we must devise some procedure which ensures that each agent chooses the particular vector x_i or y_j which not only constitutes an equilibrium for him but also allows the overall equilibrium E^1 to be realised. (Figure 11 illustrates the difficulty; like Figure 2, it represents a distribution equilibrium M. The particular feature here is that the indifference curve $\mathscr{S}_2^0$ passing through M coincides with the common tangent MT along AB. All the points on AB are therefore equilibria for the second consumer; but only M is compatible with overall equilibrium.)

More generally, it is important to establish a procedure for determining prices, or a procedure for finding simultaneously the preferred state E^1 and its associated prices. This question, which is discussed by the 'economic theory of socialism' will be more conveniently dealt with after the investigation of competitive equilibrium. Chapter 8 will be devoted to it.

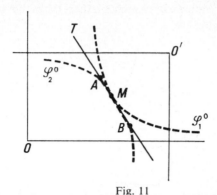

Fig. 11

10. Separation theorem justifying the existence of prices associated with an optimum

In the preceding pages, various figures illustrate the fact that an optimum may appear as a market equilibrium. There is great similarity between these figures, and this suggests that the property results from a single mathematical theorem capable of simple geometric representation. This is in fact true.

So to end this chapter, we shall give another proof of the central property of proposition 5. For this we use the modern formulation which does not involve the use of the differential calculus and which makes the theory more obvious† because of its conceptual simplicity. The crux of the proof is a theorem which will not be proved, but for which some preliminary definitions must be introduced.

A *hyperplane* in R^l is the set P of vectors z such that $pz = a$ where a is a fixed number and p a non-null fixed vector said to be normal to the hyperplane. *The hyperplane P is said to be bounding for the set U if either $pu \leqslant a$ for all the vectors u of U, or $pu \geqslant a$ for all the u of U. The hyperplane P is*

---

† The proof follows almost exactly the argument in Chapter 6 (Section 4) of Debreu, *Theory of Value*, John Wiley and Sons, Inc., New York, 1959.

said to separate the two sets U and V if pu $\geqslant$ a for all the u of U and pv $\leqslant$ a
for all the *v* of *V*, or if *pu* $\leqslant$ *a* for all the *u* of *U* and *pv* $\geqslant$ *a* for all the *v* of *V*
(cf. **Figure 12**).

Given *q* sets U_r (where *r* = 1, 2, ..., *q*) the *sum* of these sets, $\sum_{r=1}^{q} U_r$, is the
set *U* whose elements are all the vectors *u* which can be written $u = \sum_{r=1}^{q} u_r$
where the u_r are vectors belonging respectively to the sets U_r. Similarly, $-U$
is the set of vectors which can be written $-u$, the vector *u* then belonging to
U (note that $U - U$ contains elements other than the null-vector except
when *U* has a single element).

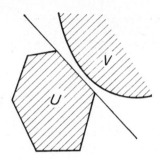

Fig. 12

We can immediately establish

PROPOSITION 7. If *p* is normal to a hyperplane *pz* = *a* which is bounding
for the set $U = \sum_{r=1}^{q} U_r$, then it is also normal to hyperplanes *pz* = a_r bounding
for the U_r (*r* = 1, 2, ..., *q*). If, moreover, *pw* = *a* where *w* is a vector of *U*
corresponding to the vectors w_r of the U_r, then we can take $a_r = pw_r$.

For, consider a particular set U_r and an element u_s^0 in each of the other
U_s (*s* $\neq$ *r*). Suppose, to fix ideas, that *pu* $\leqslant$ *a* for every *u* of *U*. We know
that

$$pu_r \leqslant - \sum_{s \neq r} pu_s^0 + a; \qquad (36)$$

pu_r is therefore bounded above in U_r; let a_r be the smallest of its upper
bounds. The hyperplane *pz* = a_r is bounding for U_r. In the case where *w* is
known to be such that *pw* = *a*, the number a_r is equal to pw_r, since if it is
greater than pw_r there exists in U_r a vector u_r^* such that $pu_r^* > pw_r$; therefore

$$pu_r^* + \sum_{s \neq r} pw_s$$

is greater than pw and therefore than a. But, by hypothesis, this is impossible, since $u_r^* + \sum_{s \neq r} w_s$ belongs to U. If a vector w with the above property is not known, we can still conclude $\sum_r a_r \leqslant a$.

PROPOSITION 8. The sum U of q convex sets U_r is a convex set. If V is convex, so also is $- V$.

To prove that U is convex, we must establish that the vector

$$u = \alpha v + (1 - \alpha)w$$

belongs to U whenever v and w belong to U and that $0 < \alpha < 1$. Let v_r and w_r be the vectors of U_r $(r = 1, 2, ..., q)$ which occur in the sums $v = \sum_r v_r$ and $w = \sum_r w_r$. Convexity of U_r implies that $u_r = \alpha v_r + (1 - \alpha)w_r$ belongs to U_r. In addition, the respective expressions for u and the u_r imply $u = \sum_r u_r$. Therefore the vector u belongs to U.

Similarly we can immediately establish the convexity of $- V$ from the convexity of V.

MINKOWSKI'S THEOREM. Let U be a convex set and z^* a vector which is not contained in U. There exists a hyperplane bounding for U and passing through z^* (that is, such that $pz^* = a$).

This theorem, which we shall not prove,† belongs to a group of mathematical results some of which are known as 'separation theorems'. Let us consider two disjoint convex sets U_1 and U_2. In view of proposition 8, the set $U_1 - U_2$ is convex; it does not contain the null-vector since U_1 and U_2 are disjoint. Therefore, by Minkowski's theorem, there exists a hyperplane $pz = 0$ containing the null vector and bounding for $U_1 - U_2$. According to proposition 7 and the remark at the end of the corresponding proof, there exist two numbers a_1 and $- a_2$ such that $a_1 - a_2 \leqslant 0$, $pv_1 \leqslant a_1$ for every u_1 of U_1 and $p(- u_2) \leqslant - a_2$ for every u_2 of U_2. A fortiori, $pu_2 \geqslant a_1$ for every u_2 of U_2, so that $pz = a_1$ separates U_1 and U_2 (Figure 12 illustrates this property). This reveals the relationship between Minkowski's theorem and separation theorems of convex sets.

We are now in a position to use Minkowski's theorem to prove proposition 5 without using differential calculus.

Let E^0 be the optimum state. Let X_i^0 be the set of vectors x_i which the ith consumer considers as at least equivalent to x_i^0, that is, the subset of X_i

---

† For the proof, see, for example, appendix B to Karlin, *Mathematical Methods in Theory of Games, Programming and Economics*, vol. I, Addison-Wesley Publ. Co., Reading, Mass., 1959.

composed of the x_i's such that $S_i(x_i) \geqslant S_i(x_i^0)$. The convexity of X_i and the quasi-concavity of S_i imply that X_i^0 is convex.

Then let

$$Z^0 = \sum_{i=1}^{m} X_i^0 - \sum_{j=1}^{n} Y_j - \{\omega\}, \tag{37}$$

where $\{\omega\}$ is the set consisting of the single vector ω. The set Z^0 is convex when the convexity of the Y_j is added to the convexity of the X_i and the quasi-concavity of the S_i (cf. proposition 8). Since E^0 is feasible, the null-vector belongs to Z^0 (cf. (23) and the fact that x_i^0 is in X_i^0); but it is not contained in the interior of Z^0; otherwise Z^0 would contain a vector u all of whose components would be negative and there would exist a state E^1 such that $x_i^1 \in X_i^0$; $y_j^1 \in Y_j$ and $\sum_j y_{jh}^1 + \omega_h = \sum_i x_{ih}^1 - u_h$ for all h. The state E^2, defined by $x_1^2 = x_1^1 - u$, $x_i^2 = x_i^1$ $(i = 2, ..., m)$, $y_j^2 = y_j^1$ $(j = 1, 2, ..., n)$ would be feasible and preferred to E^0, which contradicts the optimality of E^0.

Minkowski's theorem therefore establishes the existence of a vector p such that $pz \geqslant 0$ for all z of Z^0. Proposition 7, together with the fact that the x_i^0 and y_j^0 correspond to the null vector in (37), implies

(i') $px_i \geqslant px_i^0$ for all x_i of X_i such that $S_i(x_i) \geqslant S_i(x_i^0)$.

(ii) $py_j \leqslant py_j^0$ for all y_j of Y_j.

To complete the proof of proposition 5 we need only show that it follows from (i') that

(i) $S_i(x_i) \leqslant S_i(x_i^0)$ for all x_i of X_i such that $px_i \leqslant px_i^0$.

In fact an additional condition is required for (i') to imply (i). If we adopt the condition that x_i^0 is contained in the interior of X_i, we can repeat exactly the reasoning in the second part of the proof of proposition 2 of Chapter 2 (after 'consider now a vector x^1 ...'), and the reader may refer back to this.

We can therefore state

PROPOSITION 9. If E^0 is an optimal state such that, for each consumer i, x_i^0 is contained in the interior of X_i, if the S_i and the X_i satisfy assumptions 1, 2 and 4 of Chapter 2, and if the sets Y_j are convex, then there exist prices p_h for all goods and incomes R_i for all consumers such that E^0 appears as a market equilibrium with these prices and incomes.

Comparison with the statement of proposition 5 shows that this is a much more general property, which no longer involves certain rather awkward assumptions which were introduced in order that the usual techniques for dealing with problems of constrained maximisation could be applied.

Competitive equilibrium

1. Introduction

We are now about to make an investigation of the conditions under which the independent decisions of the different agents are finally made compatible and lead to overall equilibrium, called *general equilibrium*. Our context here is that of a competitive economy and we shall have to discuss some more specific assumptions that are necessary for the validity of the proofs to be given or outlined.

The theory that we shall discuss attempts to describe this major phenomenon, which has occupied economists since their science began: in complex societies like ours, how are the division of labour, production, exchange and consumption arrived at without some directing agency to ensure that all the individual actions are consistent? What is the 'invisible hand' ensuring this consistency?

It is also the aim of general equilibrium theory to explain the determination of the prices that are established in the markets and apply in exchanges. These prices are taken as data when consumers' and producers' decisions are being formalised. On the other hand, they are endogenous in any investigation of general equilibrium, which must therefore lead to a theory of price, or a 'theory of value'. So in this chapter we must also answer the question, 'What are the main factors determining price?'

Obviously competitive equilibrium theory does not give exhaustive answers to these two types of question. It is based on a particular representation of social organisation and individual behaviour, and this representation is limited in more than one respect. It ignores situations of imperfect competition; it relates to an economy without money and without under-employment. It therefore gives an imperfect explanation of the consistency of individual decisions, and also as may be of their inconsistency (the case of under-employment). It provides an imperfect picture of price determination. However, it has the great advantage of providing a system and a frame of reference by means of which we can understand the essential articulation, in economies with no central direction, of production, distribution and consumption on the one hand, and of price-formation on the other.

In the study of general equilibrium, as in that of the consumer or the firm, there is said to be *perfect competition* if the price of each good is the same for all agents and all transactions, if each agent considers this price as independent of his own decisions, and if he feels able to acquire or dispose of any quantity of the good at this price. The assumptions defined previously for consumers' and producers' behaviour will again be adopted.†

To simplify the presentation and discussion of the theory, our approach will be similar to that adopted in the chapter on optimum theory. We shall first discuss an economy with no production, and go on to discuss a situation where the productive sphere can be dealt with in isolation. Finally, we shall consider a complex economy with the greatest degree of generality possible in this course of lectures.

There are two advantages in this approach. In the first place, it must reduce the complexity of the mathematics, and lead to better understanding of the problems and the results. In the second place, it leads to the successive discussion of two price theories which were formerly held to conflict, and so allows us a clearer grasp of the synthesis which has now been achieved.

A complete study of general equilibrium theory demands the discussion in turn of questions of economics and questions of logic. We shall try to distinguish them as clearly as possible. For this reason in particular, mathematically difficult problems concerning the existence and stability of equilibrium will be dealt with at the end of the chapter.

2. Equilibrium equations for a distribution economy

We first consider an economy of m consumers, the consumption of the ith consumer being x_{ih}. Overall consistency of the individual decisions is ensured if

$$\sum_{i=1}^{m} x_{ih} = \omega_h \qquad h = 1, 2, ..., l, \tag{1}$$

where ω_h represents the resources of the good h which *a priori* are available in this economy.

There will be market equilibrium if there exist prices p_h and quantities x_{ih} satisfying (1) and if, in addition, each consumer i, considering the p_h as given,

---

† This definition of perfect competition is sufficient for the theoretical model to be discussed, but not for a typology of real situations, since it does not define the required conditions for a competitive equilibrium to tend naturally to be realised. We shall return to this question later (cf. Chapter 7).

maximises his utility $S_i(x_i)$ subject to his budget constraint. So the unknowns of the equilibrium are the $(m + 1)l$ variables p_h and x_{ih}. We must show how the values of these variables are determined.

To do this, we need only return to the theory of consumer equilibrium. Each vector x_i must be an equilibrium for the consumer i with the prices p_h in question; moreover, conditions (1) must be satisfied. We saw how x_i is determined, given the price vector p. Let us assume for the moment that it is determined uniquely. To each price vector there correspond well defined values for the left hand sides of (1). The l conditions (1) can therefore be considered as l equations on the l components of p.

To make this more precise, we must indicate more clearly which variables are exogenous in the equilibrium. We shall do this in two different ways, dealing successively with two non-equivalent systems called the 'distribution economy' and the 'exchange economy' respectively.

In the distribution economy, each consumer i disposes of an 'income' R_i, which is given exogenously. (It is permissible to speak of 'wealth' or 'assets' instead of income.) The consumer i then maximises $S_i(x_i)$ subject to the constraints

$$x_i \in X_i \tag{2}·$$

$$px_i \leqslant R_i. \tag{3}$$

In order to visualise such an economy, we can assume that, besides the m consumers, and independent of them, there are one or more agents in possession of the initial resources ω_h who release these resources at prices such that the consumers demand exactly the quantities ω_h. We can call these new agents 'distributors' and assume, for simplicity, that there is one distributor for each good. Thus the distribution economy is an idealised picture of commercial operations in a society where production and the distribution of incomes are taken out of the market, while prices are fixed so as to ensure that consumers' demands, competitively manifested, absorb exactly the total quantity of goods available after production.

The theory of the consumer is directly applicable in the study of equilibrium for a distribution economy. We can let

$$\xi_{ih}(p; R_i)$$

denote the demand function of the ith consumer for commodity h, this function being assumed to be determined uniquely. The aggregate demand function of all m consumers for commodity h is the sum of the ξ_{ih}. We can write it $\xi_h(p)$, leaving out from the arguments the R_i, which are exogenous data;

$$\xi_h(p) = \sum_{i=1}^{m} \xi_{ih}(p; R_i). \tag{4}$$

The equilibrium conditions (1) are then expressed by a system of l equations on the l prices p_h:

$$\xi_h(p) = \omega_h \qquad h = 1, 2, ..., l. \tag{5}$$

Solution of this system gives the equilibrium prices p_h, the corresponding values of the x_{ih} being given by the functions ξ_{ih}.

Each equation (5) implies that global demand $\xi_h(p)$ equals global supply ω_h in the market for commodity h. The system therefore expresses the requirement that the l prices be determined so as to ensure simultaneous equilibria in the l markets. Let us assume for the moment that this condition defines the vector p uniquely. Let p^0 and x_i^0 denote the equilibrium values of p and x_i.

Like consumer theory, the theory of a distribution economy can provide some general indications of the characteristics of equilibrium and of the changes that occur in it when some of the exogenous data vary.

Suppose, for example, that all the incomes R_i are multiplied by the same number λ. The vectors λp^0 and x_i^0 (for $i = 1, 2, ..., m$) define a new equilibrium. Indeed, the functions ξ_{ih} are homogeneous of degree zero with respect to p and R_i (see property 1 in Chapter 2). The number x_{ih}^0, which is equal to $\xi_{ih}(p^0; R_i)$, is therefore also equal to $\xi_{ih}(\lambda; \lambda p^0 R_i)$. Moreover, by hypothesis, the x_{ih}^0 satisfy conditions (1). Again we find that a change in the unit of account in which the R_i and the p_h are measured does not affect the equilibrium (no money illusion).

Unfortunately it is impossible to obtain more specific results at this level of generality. When discussing the consumer we saw that there are very few general results relating to individual demand functions. The effect of aggregation is to eliminate the general validity of the Slutsky equations (cf. property 2 in Chapter 2).

However, we shall now suggest the probable existence of a particular property of individual demand, a property which may allow aggregation and which will be assumed in Section 10 for the proof of an important result.

By considering infinitely small variations dp and dR_i in p and in R_i, we established that the corresponding variation dx_i in the equilibrium consumption vector x_i satisfies:

$$dx_i = \lambda_i U_i \, dp + v_i(dR_i - x_i' \, dp), \tag{6}$$

where λ_i is a positive number, U_i is a negative semi-definite matrix and v_i is a vector; in addition, λ_i, U_i and v_i depend on the equilibrium under consideration (see equation (27) in Chapter 2).

Suppose now that $dR_i = 0$, and consider the scalar product

$$dp' \, dx_i = \lambda_i \, dp' \, U_i \, dp - dp' \, v_i \cdot x_i \, dp.$$

The first term on the right hand side represents the substitution effect; it is negative or zero, since U_i is negative semi-definite. Actually this term is zero either when dp is proportional to p, or under rather special specifications of the utility function S_i (specifications implying that $a'S_i''a = 0$ for some non zero vector a such that $p'a = 0$). The second term is the income effect. It is certainly negative when dp is proportional to p since $p'v_i = 1$ and $x_i'p = R_i$. It would always be negative if the marginal propensities v_{ih} were proportional to the consumptions x_{ih} (that is, if the income elasticities were all equal, and therefore all equal to 1). To the extent that these elasticities do not vary much from 1, it may appear probable that the scalar product dp' dx_i is negative for any dp. Now, if this is so for each dp' dx_i, it also holds for their sum over all consumers. This is why we sometimes find it admissible to set the following assumption, which recalls the relation of comparative statics established in the theory of the producer (cf. Chapter 3, Section 6).

ASSUMPTION 1. The collective demand functions $\xi_h(p)$ are such that, for any given values of the p_h and the R_i,

$$\sum_{h=1}^{l} d\xi_h(p) \, dp_h < 0 \tag{7}$$

for any infinitely small variations dp_h, not all zero, which are applied to prices p_h in the neighbourhood of the equilibrium.

This assumption allows us to establish an immediate result concerning changes of equilibrium in the distribution economy. If, when the R_i remain fixed, the initial resources are subject to small variations dω_h, then the corresponding variations in equilibrium prices must satisfy the following inequality:

$$d\omega \cdot dp < 0.$$

In particular, if only the quantity ω_k relating to a particular good k increases while the other ω_h remain constant, the equilibrium price p_k^0 must decrease.

3. Equilibrium equations for an exchange economy

The model of equilibrium in a distribution economy has the advantage of simplicity. The proofs of its properties are relatively straightforward.

However, the descriptive value of this model is debatable. The assumption that the 'distributors' are independent of the consumers may be sufficient to describe collectivist societies where there is central direction of production and the markets for consumer goods. On the other hand, it does not appear satisfactory for the representation of societies where the institution of private ownership is predominant. In such societies, incomes depend on prices, while the consumers are also in possession of the primary resources ω_h.

In order to construct a more realistic model in this respect, we shall assume that the ith consumer possesses certain quantities, given *a priori*, of the goods h, ω_{ih} say, and that the consumers own all the initial resources:

$$\sum_{i=1}^{m} \omega_{ih} = \omega_h \qquad h = 1, 2, ..., l. \tag{8}$$

To determine the consumptions x_{ih} is therefore equivalent to determining the quantities of the different goods acquired or disposed of by each individual consumer and owner. The ith consumer acquires $x_{ih} - \omega_{ih}$ if this difference is positive; in the opposite case, he disposes of $\omega_{ih} - x_{ih}$. Here we are dealing with an 'exchange economy'.

For formal purposes, there is only a minor difference between the distribution economy and the exchange economy. While the R_i are exogenous in the former, in the latter they are defined by

$$R_i = \sum_{h=1}^{l} p_h \omega_h \qquad i = 1, 2, ..., m \tag{9}$$

where the ω_{ih} are themselves exogenous.

It follows, however, that the ith consumer's demand is a different function of the price vector p:

$$\xi_{ih}(p; p\omega_i) \tag{10}$$

ω_i being the exogenous vector of the ω_{ih}. So this demand has properties other than those appropriate to the distribution economy. In particular, the ξ_{ih} are now homogeneous functions of degree zero of the p_h for fixed ω_{ih}, where they were not homogeneous functions of the p_h for fixed R_i. Assumption 1 no longer applies, since, in the first place, it was introduced on the assumption that $dR_i = 0$, and no longer holds when $dR_i = \omega_i\, dp$; in the second place, homogeneity of the ξ_{ih} implies that dx_i is zero when dp is a vector collinear with p. Therefore there exist non-null vectors dp such that the scalar product $dp\, dx_i$ is zero, which is contrary to assumption 1.

We again let $\xi_h(p)$ denote the global demand for the good h, that is, the function of p which is the sum of the m functions (10) for i varying from 1 to m, the ω_{ih} being fixed. This will not be the same function of p as in the previous section, but this should not cause any confusion.

The equilibrium equations are then similar to those for the distribution economy:

$$\begin{cases} x_{ih} = \xi_{ih}(p; p\omega_i) & \begin{cases} i = 1, 2, ..., m \\ h = 1, 2, ..., l \end{cases} \\ \xi_h(p) = \sum_{i=1}^{m} \xi_{ih}(p; p\omega_i) = \omega_h & h = 1, 2, ..., l \end{cases} \tag{11}$$

or $(m + 1)l$ equations for the determination of the same number of quantities, the x_{ih} and the p_h.

However, the system of the last l equations determining the p_h does not have the same properties as the corresponding system (5) in the previous section. The $\xi_h(p)$, homogeneous functions of degree zero, actually depend only on the $l - 1$ relative prices p_h/p_l for $h = 1, 2, ..., l - 1$. So system (11) can only determine relative prices, one of the p_h being arbitrary.

Are not these l equations involving $l - 1$ variables incompatible? No, since realisation of $l - 1$ of them entails realisation of the last one. Since each consumer necessarily obeys his budget constraint, the demand functions satisfy

$$\sum_{h=1}^{l} p_h[\xi_{ih}(p; p\omega_i) - \omega_{ih}] \equiv 0$$

identically with respect to the p_h; therefore

$$\sum_{h=1}^{l} p_h[\xi_h(p) - \omega_h] \equiv 0 \tag{12}$$

identically also with respect to the p_h. (This identity is often called *Walras' Law*). In short, the count of the equations and the unknowns together with the homogeneity of the demand functions suggest that the equilibrium equations (11) determine relative prices and consumptions.

Note also that the distribution economy equilibrium and the exchange economy equilibrium are two examples of what we called market equilibria in Chapter 4. There are great similarities between the two models, but they are not identical. This bears out the remark made at the beginning of our investigation of the optimum. Models relating to competitive equilibrium are more strictly specified than those relating to the optimum.

Certain characteristics of equilibrium in an exchange economy will be more clearly understood if we consider more directly the case of two commodities and two consumers whose behaviour accords with the rules of perfect competition. When there are only two consumers, we are confronted *a priori* with a game situation of the type to be discussed later (Chapter 6); perfect competition does not appear likely. So the case of two consumers will be discussed solely as a simple illustration of a theory applying to situations where there are many consumers.

Starting from the first consumer's indifference curves, we can easily determine the equilibrium (x_{11}, x_{12}) corresponding to given prices (p_1, p_2) and given initial resources $(\omega_{11}, \omega_{12})$ (see Figure 1, where the quantities of the two goods are given as abscissa and ordinate respectively). We need only draw the budget line PT normal to the price vector and passing through P, which represents initial resources. The equilibrium point M is the point of

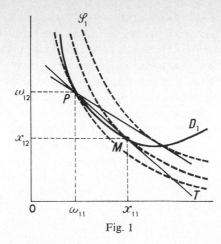

Fig. 1

PT which lies on the highest indifference curve. When prices vary and P remains fixed, the point M moves along a curve D_1 which can be called the 'demand curve' of the first consumer.

On the same coordinate axes we can construct an Edgeworth box diagram similar to that in Figure 2 of Chapter 4 (see Figure 2). The curve D_1 represents the first consumer's demand; a curve D_2 constructed from the second consumer's indifference curves represents the latter's demand in the system of axes centred on O' (with coordinates ω_1, ω_2). The curves D_1 and D_2 both pass through P; any other point of intersection M of these curves represents an equilibrium since it corresponds to the same price vector for both consumers, the vector normal to PM. At such a point M the indifference curves $\mathscr{S}_1$ and $\mathscr{S}_2$ are tangential, so that M does in fact lie on the locus MN of distribution optima.

The same type of 'Edgeworth diagram' can be applied to the distribution

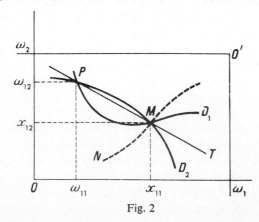

Fig. 2

economy, since we see that the price vector of an exchange economy can be normalised by the rule $p\omega = R$ where R is a given number (the case where the p_h are zero for all non-zero ω_h is of little practical interest). We shall not use this normalisation rule in our investigation of the process by which equilibrium is realized; but there is nothing to prevent its introduction when equilibrium equations only are being considered. Now, every distribution economy is identical with an exchange economy in which prices are normalised in this way; the vector ω_i of resources possessed by the ith consumer is then taken as proportional to the vector ω of total resources, the proportionality coefficient being the ratio between this consumer's income R_i and total income R, the sum of individual incomes. (To attribute the income R_i to the ith consumer is equivalent to giving him a property right over the part $R_i\omega_h/R$ of each primary resource ω_h.) In the case of a distribution economy with only two consumers, we can construct a figure similar to Figure 2. The point P representing resources is then on the diagonal OO' and divides this diagonal in the proportions R_1/R and R_2/R.

To conclude this definition of the exchange economy, we also note the following assumption, which is sometimes adopted and which will be used repeatedly in the following sections:

ASSUMPTION 2 (Gross substitutability). The global demand functions $\xi_h(p)$ are differentiable and such that

$$\frac{\partial \xi_h(p)}{\partial p_k} > 0 \tag{13}$$

for every p with no negative component, for all h and for all $k \neq h$. (Homogeneity of $\xi_h(p)$ then implies that its derivative with respect to p_h is negative.)

Although it is satisfied with certain utility functions, this is a fairly restrictive assumption. For example, it is not satisfied by the demand function represented in Figure 1 since, for small values of p_1/p_2, the ordinate x_2 decreases as p_1 increases. This happens although, when the model contains no other goods, the two goods are necessarily substitutes, in the sense of the definition given in Chapter 2.

4. Value, scarcity and utility

Let us pause to consider the 'theory of value' that follows from the preceding formalisation of an economy with no production. The prices which realise general equilibrium are held to depend on the exogenous elements contained in the model, namely the available resources ω_h, the demand functions $\xi_{ih}(p)$, incomes R_i or the initial possessions ω_{ih} of individuals. In short, prices depend on three factors:

— the degree of *scarcity* of the different goods, as expressed by the quantities ω_h of resources;

— the varying *utility* of these goods, which determines the demand functions ξ_{ih};

— the *distribution* among consumers of claims on collective resources, either direct distribution through the ω_{ih} or indirect distribution through the R_i.

It is the simultaneous interplay of these three factors which conditions the determination of prices.

Can we go further than this general statement and find out how each factor influences the value system? The most natural approach is to see how price reacts to small variations in the exogenous elements of the model. We must first consider the effects of an increase in scarcity of a particular good r, that is, a small negative variation $\partial \omega_r$ in the available quantity of this good, all the other exogenous elements remaining unchanged. We must then consider an autonomous variation $\partial \xi_r$ in the demand function for the good r. Finally we must find the implications of a small change in the distribution of claims.

We shall start by examining conditions under which the following proposition is valid.

PROPOSITION 1. As a good r becomes scarcer, its price increases.

We have already answered this question at the end of Section 2 when we showed that assumption 1 implies this proposition in a 'distribution economy'. For an exchange economy the proposition is ambiguous for two reasons: in the first place, equilibrium prices are determined only up to a positive multiplicative constant; in the second place, a variation $\partial \omega_r$ in the resources of the good r must necessarily be accompanied by a variation in the claims of the different consumers (the ω_{ir}). However, we can still give a valid interpretation of the property if we adopt the gross substitutability of assumption 2.

The problem will be tackled with sufficient generality to lead up to the investigation of the other two properties to be discussed later. Suppose therefore that there are variations $\partial \omega_{ir}$ in the quantities ω_{ir} of a particular good r, and that a change in consumers' needs causes variations $\partial \xi_h$ in the values $\xi_h(p^0)$ taken by the global demand functions at the previous equilibrium prices p_h^0, which are all assumed positive.

These variations will bring about variations dp_h in the equilibrium prices, which will themselves react on global demands. The maintenance of equilibrium requires that the final variation $d\xi_h$ in ξ_h is equal to the variation $\partial \omega_h$ in available resources (the latter is zero for all goods other than r). Consequently we can write

$$d\xi_h = \partial \xi_h + \sum_{k=1}^{l} \frac{\partial \xi_h}{\partial p_k} \, dp_k + \sum_{i=1}^{m} \frac{\partial \xi_{ih}}{\partial \omega_{ir}} \, \partial \omega_{ir} = \partial \omega_h, \tag{14}$$

which can also be written as:

$$\sum_{k=1}^{l} \frac{\partial \xi_h}{\partial p_k}\, dp_k = \partial u_h \qquad h = 1, 2, ..., l \tag{15}$$

with:

$$\partial u_h = \partial \omega_h - \partial \xi_h - \sum_{i=1}^{m} \frac{\partial \xi_{ih}}{\partial \omega_{ir}}\, \partial \omega_{ir}. \tag{16}$$

The coefficients of the dp_k in system (15) must constitute a singular matrix since the p_k are determined only up to a multiplicative constant. In fact, the identity

$$\sum_{k=1}^{l} p_k \frac{\partial \xi_h}{\partial p_k} = 0 \tag{17}$$

follows from the homogeneity of ξ_h (to see this we need only differentiate with respect to λ, in the neighbourhood of $\lambda = 1$, the equality $\xi_h(\lambda p) = \xi_h(p)$, which follows from the theory of the consumer).

Although system (15) is not sufficient for the determination of the dp_h, it must enable the variations $d\pi_h/\pi_h = dp_h/p_h - dp_r/p_r$ in relative prices $\pi_{\theta} = p_h/p_r$ to be determined. Indeed, let us replace in (15) the term

$$\frac{\partial \xi_h}{\partial p_r}\, dp_r \qquad \text{by} \qquad -\sum_{k \neq r} p_k \frac{\partial \xi_h}{\partial p_k} \cdot \frac{dp_r}{p_r},$$

which is equal to it in view of (17). We obtain the system

$$\sum_{k \neq r} p_k \frac{\partial \xi_h}{\partial p_k} \cdot \frac{d\pi_k}{\pi_k} = \partial u_h \qquad h \neq r \tag{18}$$

written for all values of h other than r.

If we adopt assumption 2 of gross substitutability, the matrix of order $l - 1$ whose elements are the coefficients of the $d\pi_k/\pi_k$ has special properties. Its non-diagonal terms are positive. In view of (17), each diagonal term $p_h(\partial \xi_h/\partial p_h)$ is negative and smaller in absolute value than the sum of the non-diagonal terms in the same row. Such a matrix has an inverse whose elements are all negative.† We can therefore write:

larger ?

$$\frac{d\pi_h}{\pi_h} = \sum_{k \neq r} \alpha_{hk} \partial u_k \qquad \text{for} \qquad h \neq r, \tag{19}$$

where the α_{hk} are negative numbers.

Let us now return to the case where the good r becomes scarcer ($\partial \omega_r < 0$ and $\partial \omega_h = 0$ for $h \neq r$), the demand functions remaining unchanged ($\partial_h = 0$ for all h). Equation (16) becomes

$$\partial u_h = -\sum_{i=1}^{m} \frac{\partial \xi_{ih}}{\partial \omega_{ir}}\, \partial \omega_{ir} \qquad \text{for} \qquad h \neq r. \tag{20}$$

---

† See, for example, McKenzie, 'Matrices with dominant diagonals' in Arrow, Karlin and Suppes, *Mathematical Methods in the Social Sciences*, Stanford University Press, 1959.

Now, we can assume that the $\partial \omega_{ir}$ are all negative since their sum is negative, and an obvious change in the distribution of claims would be introduced by the assumption that one of them is non-negative.

Ignoring the possible existence of inferior goods, we can say that the $\partial \xi_{ih}/\partial \omega_{ir}$ are positive and therefore also that the ∂u_h are positive for all h's other than r. In view of (19), the $\mathrm{d}\pi_h/\pi_h$ are all negative, and so

$$\frac{\mathrm{d}p_r}{p_r} > \frac{\mathrm{d}p_h}{p_h} \qquad \text{for} \qquad h \neq r. \tag{21}$$

All relative prices with respect to the good r decrease. *Price p_r increases relatively more than all other prices.*

Consider now the case of an increase in the utility of the good r, all the other exogenous elements of the model remaining unchanged. This is naturally expressed by an increase $\partial \xi_r > 0$ in the demand for r. Walras' law requires that other demands decrease correspondingly. It is therefore appropriate to consider the case where $\partial \xi_h < 0$ for all h's other than r.

In the context of the exchange economy† with, in this case, $\partial \omega_{ir} = 0$, equation (16) shows that ∂u_h is then positive for all $h \neq r$. If there is gross substitutability, the $\mathrm{d}\pi_h/\pi_h$ are all negative, the equality (21) is again satisfied, which justifies

PROPOSITION 2. If the utility of a good r increases, its price increases.

How are prices liable to be affected by a change in the distribution of claims? If one consumer α gains at the expense of another consumer β, global demand will move towards the goods for which α's individual demand is less inelastic than β's. The prices of these goods will then increase.

PROPOSITION 3. If the individuals benefiting from a change in distribution have a particularly high propensity to spend an increment in their resources on the good r, then its price increases.

Let us consider this statement still in the context of an exchange economy. Suppose $\partial \xi_h = 0$ and $\mathrm{d}\omega_h = 0$ for all h, $\partial \omega_{\alpha s} > 0$, $\partial \omega_{\beta s} = -\partial \omega_{\alpha s} < 0$ and $\partial \omega_{ih} = 0$ for all other pairs (i, h). We assume that

$$\frac{\partial \xi_{\alpha r}}{\partial \omega_{\alpha s}} > \frac{\partial \xi_{\beta r}}{\partial \omega_{\beta s}} \tag{22}$$

---

† If we adopt assumption 1 in the context of the distribution economy and assume the demands for only two goods, r and s, vary ($\partial \xi_r > 0$ and $\partial \xi_s < 0$), it is easy to prove that $\mathrm{d}p_r > 0$ and $\mathrm{d}p_s < 0$.

and correspondingly

$$\frac{\partial \xi_{\alpha h}}{\partial \omega_{\alpha s}} < \frac{\partial \xi_{\beta h}}{\partial \omega_{\beta s}} \qquad \text{for} \qquad h \neq r \tag{23}$$

An equation like (16), with the ω_{ir} replaced by the ω_{is}, shows that then the ∂u_h are positive for all h's other than r. If there is gross substitutability, the equality (21) is again satisfied.

This concludes for the moment our discussion of price determination in economies with no production. We have investigated three propositions which are often considered to summarise the 'laws of the market'. However, they have been established on the basis of a certain number of restrictive assumptions, which suggests that they cannot have complete generality. In fact, it is possible to construct examples where they do not hold. Their validity is further limited when possibilities of production exist. However, they apply to the most common situations in practice.

5. Value and cost

Whenever production is taken into account, price must satisfy other properties, which did not come into the above discussion. When dealing with the firm, we saw that, in perfect competition equilibrium, the price-ratios must equal the technical marginal rates of substitution (the f'_{js}/f'_{jr}) and that the price of each good must equal its marginal cost. This shows that the value system also depends on the technical conditions of production. Also, it is to be expected that the price of a good will decrease when discovery of a new process facilitates its manufacture.

In order to understand this other aspect of price formation we shall first consider a case where values depend *only* on technical conditions. Where it applies, this case justifies the 'labour theory of value'.

We make the following assumptions:

(i) Each firm j specialises in the production of a single good r_j (and therefore $y_{jh} \leqslant 0$ for all $h \neq r_j$). We let q_j denote j's production of the good r_j.

(ii) Production is carried on under constant returns to scale. We can then characterise the technical conditions of production by referring to the quantities of inputs yielding an output $q_j = 1$, these quantities being

$$\frac{-y_{jh}}{q_j} = a_{jh} \qquad \text{for} \qquad h \neq r_j \tag{24}$$

(It is customary to let a_{jh} denote the *unit* input of h here. I have sometimes used this notation to denote the total input of h, and the reader should guard against confusion.)

Let a_j be the vector of the a_{jh}, the component r_j being taken as zero, by convention. The production set can be defined by the condition that $y_j \in Y_j$ if and only if the vector a defined by (24) satisfies

$$a_j \in A_j. \tag{25}$$

The new set A_j is therefore the set of input combinations yielding a unit output of r_j.

(iii) All the goods are produced with the exception of one (labour), which we can assume to be the lth good. All production requires this good ($a_{jl} > 0$ for every vector of A_j).

These three assumptions, and especially the last, are obviously restrictive. The last assumption ignores the existence of natural raw materials and the fact that there are many types of labour (in a time analysis, it would be necessary in particular to take account of the fact that two equal quantities of labour provided at two different dates are not substitutable for one another). However, the model based on these assumptions is often very useful as a first approximation. It is in fact a generalisation of the classical model of Leontief.†

Without specifying either the volume and distribution of resources, or consumers' preferences, let us consider a general competitive equilibrium E^0 in an economy whose productive activity satisfies the above conditions. We assume that $p_h^0 \geqslant 0$ for all h and $p_l^0 > 0$ (this is not very restrictive). We also assume that every commodity other than labour is actually produced: for all $h \neq l$ there exists a firm j such that $r_j = h$ and $q_j^0 > 0$. To simplify notation, we take the last commodity as numéraire ($p_l = 1$) and also let p_j denote the price of r_j and f_j the unit input of labour ($f_j = a_{jl}$).

Since E^0 is an equilibrium, we can write

$$\sum_{h=1}^{l-1} p_h^0 a_{jh}^0 + f_j^0 = p_j^0 \quad \text{if} \quad q_j^0 > 0 \tag{26}$$

$$\sum_{h=1}^{l-1} p_h^0 a_{jh} + f_j \geqslant p_j^0 \quad \text{if} \quad a_j \in A_j. \tag{27}$$

The left hand sides represent the unit costs of production. Equation (27) excludes the case where a possible vector a_j allows production of r_j at a cost less than its price, which conflicts with equilibrium since to go on increasing output of r_j using this input combination is technically feasible for j (constant returns to scale) and is associated with infinitely increasing profit. Equation (26) expresses the fact that the price of r_j must cover its cost if the good is produced by j, otherwise it is to the advantage of the firm not to produce at all.

---

† See Leontief, *The Structure of the American Economy, 1919-09*, O.U.P., 1951 and Dorfman, Samuelson and Solow, *Linear Programming and Activity Analysis*, McGraw-Hill, New York, 1958.

Equation (26) implies that $p_h^0 > 0$ for all h, since, for the firm producing this good, $a_{jh}^0 \geqslant 0$ and $f_j^0 > 0$ and therefore $p_j^0 > 0$.

Since every good other than the last is produced by at least one firm, we can write a system of $l - 1$ equations similar to (26), the hth equation corresponding to a j for which $r_j = h$. We can then write this system in matrix form:

$$A^0 p^0 + f^0 = p^0 \tag{28}$$

where A^0 is the square matrix of order $l - 1$ of the a_{jh}^0 chosen in this way, while f^0 and p^0 are the column vectors with $l - 1$ components defined by the f_j^0 and the p_h^0. Equation (28) can also be expressed by

$$(I - A^0) p^0 = f^0. \tag{29}$$

Now, the matrix $I - A^0$ has special properties. Its diagonal elements are positive (we set $a_{jh} = 0$ for $h = r_j$); its other elements are either negative or zero. Moreover, when the elements in the same row are multiplied by the respective positive numbers p_h^0, then the absolute value of the diagonal term is greater than the sum of the others (according to (26), the difference is the positive number f_j^0). It follows that $I - A^0$ has an inverse all of whose elements α_{hj} are non-negative† and which we can write

$$p_h^0 = \sum_j \alpha_{hj} f_j^0. \tag{30}$$

The right hand side of this equality involves only quantities relating to the technical conditions of production. It can be interpreted as expressing the labour theory of value: price p_h^0 is equal to the quantity of labour (the last good) which is used in the production of the good h, either directly in the firm j which manufactures it ($r_j = h$) or indirectly in the firms manufacturing the inputs used by j. This interpretation is clearly revealed in (26) considered as defining price p_j^0; f_j^0 corresponds to the amount of labour used per unit of output in j, while $p_h^0 a_{jh}^0$ corresponds to the amount of labour which has been used, directly or indirectly, to produce the quantity a_{jh}^0 of unit input of the good h in the production of r_j.

This interpretation may be more fully justified as follows. Let q be a $(l - 1)$-component output vector having components q_j for those j occurring in the construction of A^0. Let P be the program defined by these q_j, the respective technical coefficients of A^0 and a zero output for all other producers. Let us moreover choose q in such a way that the final net output x_h is precisely zero for all h (from 1 to $l - 1$) except for $h = r$ for which it is equal to one.

---

† See, for example, the article by McKenzie referred to on p. 115.

5

In order to find this vector q, we can first compute x_h as follows:

$$x_h = q_h - \sum_{j=1}^{l-1} q_j a_{jh}^0$$

or, denoting by x' and q' the row vectors having x_h and q_h as components:

$$x' = q'(I - A^0)$$

hence

$$q' = x'(I - A^0)^{-1}$$

or, equivalently:

$$q_j = \sum_{h=1}^{l-1} x_h \alpha_{hj}.$$

The particular specification chosen for x implies

$$q_j = \alpha_{rj}.$$

The total labour input in program P is then equal to:

$$\sum_{j=1}^{l-1} f_j^0 q_j = \sum_{j=1}^{l-1} \alpha_{rj} f_j^0.$$

which is precisely p_r^0 according to equation (30). The price p_r^0 is the total labour input necessary for a final net output consisting of just one unit of commodity r.

Is this genuinely a case where prices depend *solely* on the technical conditions of production, that is, on the sets A_j? Yes, for we shall see that two competitive equilibria E^0 and E^1 necessarily have the same prices, labour being taken as numéraire, if they involve the same technical sets, and this is so even if they have different vectors ω of resources or different demand functions $\xi_h(p)$. We need only assume that, in E^1 as in E^0, the first $l - 1$ goods are all produced and have non-negative prices.

We first write a system similar to (29) for E^1:

$$(I - A^1)p^1 = f^1. \tag{31}$$

We note also that (27) applied to the a_j involved in the construction of A^1 implies

$$(I - A^1)p^0 \leqslant f^1 \tag{32}$$

Similarly, inverting the roles of E^0 and E^1,

$$(I - A^0)p^1 \leqslant f^0. \tag{33}$$

(29) and (33) on the one hand, and (31) and (32) on the other imply

$$(I - A^0)(p^1 - p^0) \leqslant 0, \tag{34}$$

$$(I - A^1)(p^0 - p^1) \leqslant 0. \tag{35}$$

Since $I - A^0$ and $I - A^1$ have inverses with no negative component, (34) implies $p^1 \leqslant p^0$ and (35) implies $p^0 \leqslant p^1$. These two inequalities are compatible only if $p^1 = p^0$.

We can now consider the following property:

PROPOSITION 4. If technical improvement occurs in the production of the good r, its price decreases relative to the price of labour. Prices of the other products also decrease, or at least do not increase.

A technical improvement is the discovery of a better method of production of the good r. Let k be the firm in which this improvement occurs ($r_k = r$) and a_k^* the new input vector to which it gives rise.

Let E^0 and E^1 denote the equilibria before and after the introduction of this improvement. We can write

$$\sum_{h=1}^{l-1} p_h^0 a_{kh}^* + f_k^* < p_r^0 \tag{36}$$

since the new method allows production of r at lower cost than the previous cost p_r^0. We define the matrix A^* and the vector f^* as identical to A^0 and f^0 except where the production of r is concerned, where we take the a_{kh}^* and f_k^*. As before, the relations (26) apply to the production of the other goods. Taking account of (36), we can write

$$(I - A^*)p^0 \geqslant f^*. \tag{37}$$

By the same reasoning as for (33), we have

$$(I - A^*)p^1 \leqslant f^*. \tag{38}$$

Therefore

$$(I - A^*)(p^1 - p^0) \leqslant 0. \tag{39}$$

Since $I - A^*$ has an inverse with no negative element, $p^1 - p^0$ has no positive component:

$$p_h^1 \leqslant p_h^0 \qquad \text{for all } h. \tag{40}$$

Taking the rth row of (38) and adding it to (36), we have

$$p_r^1 - p_r^0 < \sum_{h=1}^{l-1} a_{kh}^*(p_h^1 - p_h^0).$$

Now, in view of (40), the right hand side cannot be positive. Therefore price p_r^1 is strictly less than p_r^0. This completes the proof of proposition 4.

The model on which our discussion has been based is fairly specialised. It has enabled us to find out how prices are determined without involving the system of quantities produced or consumed in the equilibrium; only unit inputs have been involved.

Obviously things are not so simple if we relax one or other of the three assumptions at the beginning of this section. For example, if there is diversity of non-producible primary factors, their respective prices must be included in relations similar to (26) and (27). Consideration of these relations would no longer alone be sufficient for the determination of prices. The relative scarcity of the different factors would be involved as would the respective utilities of the different products since they require different proportions of the factors; so also would the distribution of claims, since this influences collective demands.

Of course, under different restrictions, properties replacing proposition 4 can be established. But the question clearly becomes more complex. So we shall not attempt to generalise the model step by step by finding out simultaneously how the properties of the price-system are affected.

Instead, we shall proceed directly to general formulation of the equilibrium

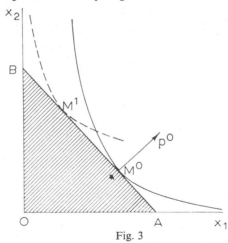

Fig. 3

equations. Then it will be possible for prices to depend simultaneously on the scarcity of resources, the technical conditions of production, the distribution of claims among individuals, and finally, on individual preferences. But they will depend more or less on these various factors, and not always according to simple schemas.

Considering a graphical representation of a very simple case may, however, be a useful complement to the preceding developments. Let us suppose there are just two produced commodities and one consumer. The shaded area of Figure 3 represents the set of feasible consumption vectors when assumptions (i), (ii) and (iii) of pages 117–8 hold. A competitive equilibrium E^0 is a production optimum. Its image M^0 on Figure 3 must therefore be on the boundary AB of this area. The boundary must be a straight line since the price vector does not depend on the input-output combination. The budget line of the consumer must coincide with AB (a line distinct from AB but parallel to it would lead the consumer to demand more or less than is supplied). Hence at M^0 the indifference curve is tangent to AB (see the unbroken line). The price vector p^0 is collinear with the common normal at M^0 to the indifference curve and the production boundary *AB*. If commodity 2 becomes more useful, the indifference map is transformed and a new equilibrium point M^1 is found where more of commodity 2 is produced (see the broken indifference curve). The price vector does not change.

Let us now consider a distribution economy of the type studied in Section 2, an economy with again only two commodities and one consumer. The equilibrium point is imposed by the resources ω_1 and ω_2. For a competitive

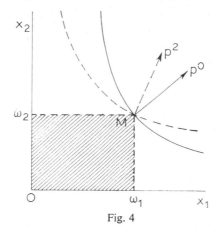

Fig. 4

equilibrium the price vector must be normal at *M* to the indifference curve containing *M*. If commodity 2 becomes more useful, this curve shifts and the price vector rotates so as to increase the relative price of commodity 2 (see Figure 4).

The two preceding cases are extreme polar cases. In the first one quantities change but not prices; in the second one prices change but not quantities. Many models involve an economy where production exists but does not satisfy the assumptions of pages 117–8. If there are just two commodities and one consumer a figure similar to 3 or 4 may again be drawn. The production boundary will then not be a straight line but a convex curve or convex polygonal line. An increase in the usefulness of commodity 2 will usually induce both an increase of its production and an increase of its relative price (see Figure 5).

6. Equilibrium equations in a private ownership economy

When discussing equilibrium for the firm, we let $\eta_{jh}(p)$ represent the net supply function of the firm *j* for the good *h*. We must now include the net supply functions of the individual firms ($j = 1, 2, ..., n$) in the equilibrium equation relating to the good *h*. So we write:

$$\sum_{i=1}^{m} \xi_{ih}(p; R_i) = \omega_h + \sum_{j=1}^{n} \eta_{jh}(p) \qquad h = 1, 2, ..., . \qquad (41)$$

These equations replace equations (5) for equilibrium in an economy with no production.

As before, we must show how consumers' incomes R_i are determined. We shall do this by finding a representation of a private ownership economy where primary resources and firms are owned only by individual consumers. Thus we shall generalise our previous exchange economy.

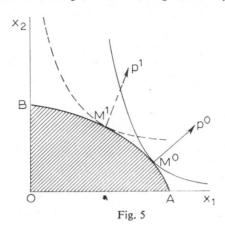

Fig. 5

Suppose that the ith consumer owns the quantity ω_{ih} of the resources of the good h, and a share θ_{ij} of the firm j (for the goods $h = 1, 2, ..., l$ and the firms $j = 1, 2, ..., n$). Since the consumers own all the resources and all the firms, we must have

$$\sum_{i=1}^{m} \omega_{ih} = \omega_h \qquad h = 1, 2, ..., l; \tag{42}$$

$$\sum_{i=1}^{m} \theta_{ij} = 1 \qquad j = 1, 2, ..., n. \tag{43}$$

Under these conditions, the ith consumer's income R_i will be the sum of the values $p_h \omega_{ih}$ of resources and the shares θ_{ij} of the profits of firms. If π_j denotes the profit of the firm j, income R_i is†

$$R_i = \sum_{h=1}^{l} p_h \omega_{ih} + \sum_{j=1}^{n} \theta_{ij} \pi_j \qquad i = 1, 2, ..., m. \tag{44}$$

---

† The last term in (44) represents the 'return to enterprise' received by consumers. It is usual to distinguish the return to labour in the first term. Remaining income corresponds to other natural resources and is called 'rent'. It is useful to recall here that the term 'income' can be replaced by the term 'wealth' in this model that does not involve time explicitly. This explains the absence of the 'return to capital' which will be introduced in Chapter 10, Section B.3.

Finally, profit π_j is equal to the total value of the firm j's net supplies:

$$\pi_j = \sum_{k=1}^{l} p_h \eta_{jh}(p) \qquad j = 1, 2, ..., n. \tag{45}$$

In this private ownership economy, the exogenous data are the ω_{ih} and θ_{ij}, the unknowns are the prices p_h, incomes R_i and profits π_j, that is, there are $l + m + n$ variables. We can consider (41), (44) and (45) as 'the equations of equilibrium'. The system thus defined contains as many equations as there are unknowns.

To find its properties, we must take account of the fact that the functions ξ_{ih} and η_{jh} derive from the behaviour of the consumers and firms. A complete theory must be based on assumptions about the sets X_i and Y_j and the functions S_i. Here we shall confine ourselves to one general remark.

When investigating the behaviour of the consumer and the firm, we found that the demand functions ξ_{ih} are homogeneous of degree zero with respect to p and R_i, and the supply functions η_{jh} are homogeneous of degree zero with respect to p. Under these conditions, the system (41), (44), (45) is homogeneous of degree zero with respect to the unknowns, the p_h, the R_i and the π_j. It determines them only up to a multiplicative constant. Once again we find that the unit of account can be chosen arbitrarily.

But is not this system of $l + m + n$ equations then overdetermined? No, because one of the equations can be deduced from the others. This is 'Walras' law'. In fact, the functions ξ_{ih} satisfy

$$\sum_{h=1}^{l} p_h \xi_{ih}(p; R_i) = R_i \qquad i = 1, 2, ..., m$$

identically. Let us replace R_i by its value as a function of the p_h, this value being obtained from (44) and (45); let us, for simplicity, omit the arguments of the functions. We can write the above equation in the form

$$\sum_{h=1}^{l} p_h \left[\xi_{ih} - \omega_{ih} - \sum_{j=1}^{n} \theta_{ij} \eta_{jh} \right] = 0 \qquad i = 1, 2, ..., m.$$

Summing over i and taking account of (42) and (43), we have

$$\sum_{h=1}^{l} p_h \left[\sum_{i=1}^{m} \xi_{ih} - \omega_h - \sum_{j=1}^{n} \eta_{jh} \right] = 0,$$

which is satisfied identically with respect to p and which implies that realisation of $l - 1$ of the equations (41) entails realisation of the last equation.

7. Prices and income distribution

Every theory of general equilibrium implies a theory of distribution. This will become clear if we examine a particular case of the general model just discussed.

Leaving aside transfer incomes about which they have little to say, theoretical economists have long looked on income as the return for some kind of participation in production. The individuals who own the factors of production—labour of various kinds, land, natural resources, etc.—place quantities of these factors at the disposal of producers and receive their value in return—wages, rent, etc. Since a general equilibrium theory explains how the prices of the factors are determined as well as the prices of the products, it has implications for the distribution of incomes. It shows how the different levels of wages, rents, etc. are fixed relative to each other and allows relative changes in them to be investigated.

In particular, the theory of competitive equilibrium contains a distribution theory. To see this more clearly, let us consider a model involving two factors of production, for example, 'skilled labour' and 'unskilled labour'. We might equally well consider 'labour' and 'land'. Often 'labour' and 'capital' are chosen in such cases. But, in so far as a considerable part of capital is itself produced, time should properly be introduced for a satisfactory theory of the return to capital, and we shall not do this before Chapter 10.

We assume that each individual i ($i = 1, 2, ..., m$) possesses quantities ω_{i1} and ω_{i2} of the two factors; $\omega_{i1} > 0$ and $\omega_{i2} = 0$ for skilled workers, $\omega_{i1} = 0$ and $\omega_{i2} > 0$ for unskilled workers. In addition, n consumable goods are produced ($h = 1, 2, ..., n$). Production is carried on under constant returns to scale and each firm manufactures one and only one product ($j = 1, 2, ..., n$). We also assume that the products are obtained directly from the factors; as we shall see, this is not really restrictive.

Then let q_h be the quantity of h produced, and f_{h1} and f_{h2} the two technical coefficients which represent the quantity of each of the two factors used in producing one unit of h. These coefficients are not fixed *a priori*; but they must satisfy a condition which follows directly from the production function $q_h = g_h(q_h f_{h1}, q_h f_{h2})$, namely

$$g_h(f_{h1}, f_{h2}) = 1 \qquad h = 1, 2, ..., n, \tag{46}$$

g_h being a homogeneous function of degree 1. We also assume that g_h is concave, twice differentiable and even more precisely, that the second derivatives g''_{h11} and g''_{h22} are strictly negative (decreasing marginal returns).

Let us take the second factor as numéraire; let p_h denote the price of h and let s be the price of the first factor. In competitive equilibrium, the price of each product must be equal to its cost, since returns to scale are constant:

$$p_h = f_{h1}s + f_{h2} \qquad h = 1, 2, ..., n. \tag{47}$$

The marginal productivity of each factor must equal its price:

$$p_h g'_{h1} = s \qquad p_h g'_{h2} = 1 \qquad h = 1, 2, ..., n \tag{48}$$

where g'_{h1} and g'_{h2} denote the derivatives of g_h with respect to each of its arguments. We can also write

$$sg'_{h2} = g'_{h1} \qquad h = 1, 2, ..., n. \tag{49}$$

The system of $3n$ equations, (47) and (48), is equivalent to the system (46), (47), (49), since the homogeneity of g_h implies $f_{h1}g'_{h1} + f_{h2}g'_{h2} = 1$. Either of these systems defines the $3n$ variables f_{h1}, f_{h2} and p_h as a function of s.

If we had used a more general model in which the production of each good requires inputs not only of factors but also of products, we should have reached exactly the same result by a reasoning process similar to those in Section 5. For this case, the symbols f_{h1} and f_{h2} in the following equations should be interpreted as the quantities of the factors used directly or indirectly to obtain one unit of final net output of h, where q_h denotes this final output.

In any case, the equalities between resources and uses are

$$\sum_{i=1}^{m} \xi_{ih}(p; R_i) = q_h \qquad h = 1, 2, ..., n \tag{50}$$

$$\sum_{h=1}^{n} q_h f_{h1} = \omega_1 \tag{51}$$

$$\sum_{h=1}^{n} q_h f_{h2} = \omega_2 \tag{52}$$

where ω_1 and ω_2 denote the total resources of the factors 1 and 2, the ξ_{ih} are individual demands, and the R_i are the incomes:

$$R_i = \omega_{1i}s + \omega_{2i} \qquad i = 1, 2, ..., m \tag{53}$$

(since returns to scale are constant, returns to enterprise are zero). The $m + n + 2$ equations (50) to (53) are not independent of the previous equations since the ξ_{ih} satisfy the budget identity

$$\sum_{h=1}^{n} p_h \xi_{ih}(p; R_i) = R_i,$$

and therefore Walras' law

$$\sum_{h=1}^{n} \sum_{i=1}^{m} p_h \xi_{ih}(p; R_i) = \sum_{i=1}^{m} R_i = \omega_1 s + \omega_2,$$

as can be verified by taking account of (47), (50), (51) and (52). So the situation is as if the equalities (50) to (53) constitute $m + n + 1$ additional equations for the determination of the R_i, the q_h and s.

Let us now see how the level of skilled wages, s, varies relative to the level of unskilled wages. We can imagine changes of various kinds in the exogenous elements of the equilibrium. Here we need only consider two types of change, one affecting the scarcity of the factors and the other the needs or tastes of consumers. We shall adopt the same method as in Sections 4 and 5 and trace the effects of variations $\partial \omega_{i1}$, $\partial \omega_{i2}$ or $\partial \xi_{ih}$.

Since the technical conditions, the functions g_h, are now fixed, we can use the system of equations (46), (47) and (49) to express the variations dp_h, df_{h1} and df_{h2} as a function of ds. We obtain immediately

$$dp_h = f_{h1}\, ds, \tag{54}$$

since, when (47) is differentiated, the term $s\, df_{h1} + df_{h2}$ becomes zero: the marginal equations (48), which determine the choice of technical coefficients, imply $s\, df_{h1} + df_{h2} = p_h[g'_{h1}\, df_{h1} + g'_{h2}\, df_{h2}]$; the term in square brackets is zero in view of the production function (46).

Differentiating (46) and the second of equations (48), we have

$$\begin{cases} g'_{h1}\, df_{h1} + g'_{h2}\, df_{h2} = 0 \\ g''_{h12}\, df_{h1} + g''_{h22}\, df_{h2} = -\, g'_{h2}\dfrac{dp_h}{p_h}. \end{cases}$$

Now, g_{h2} is homogeneous of degree zero, which implies

$$g''_{h12}f_{h1} + g''_{h22}f_{h2} = 0.$$

Taking account of (54), the above system becomes

$$\begin{cases} g'_{h1}\, df_{h1} + g'_{h2}\, df_{h2} = 0 \\ f_{h2}\, df_{h1} - f_{h1}\, df_{h2} = \dfrac{g'_{h2}(f_{h1})^2}{g''_{h22}} \cdot \dfrac{ds}{p_h} \end{cases}$$

which gives

$$\begin{cases} df_{h1} = \dfrac{(g'_{h2})^2(f_{h1})^2\, ds}{g''_{h22}p_h} \\ df_{h2} = \dfrac{-\, g'_{h2}g'_{h1}(f_{h1})^2\, ds}{g''_{h22}p_h} \end{cases} \tag{55}$$

(the homogeneity of g_h implies $f_{h1}g'_{h1} + f_{h2}g'_{h2} = 1$). The second derivative g''_{h22} is negative since g_h is concave. Thus df_{h1} has the opposite sign to ds and df_{h2} has the same sign as ds. An increase in the price of the first factor relative to the price of the second brings about substitution of the second factor for the first.

We now turn our attention to the equations defining quantities, and more precisely, to (50), (51) and (53). Using the notation of equation (27) in Chapter 2, and letting ξ_i and f_1 denote the vectors of the ξ_{ih} and the f_{1h}, we can write

$$d\xi_i = \partial \xi_i + \lambda_i U_i f_1\, ds + v_i(dR_i - x'_i f_1\, ds).$$

By differentiating (51) we obtain

$$q'\,df_1 + f_1'\,dq = \partial\omega_1$$

where f_1' is obviously the row vector, the transpose of f_1. If we let u_h denote the (negative) multiplier of ds in the expression for df_{h1}, take account of $dq = \sum_i d\xi_i$ and differentiate (53), we obtain

$$\left[q'u + \sum_{i=1}^{m} \lambda_i f_1' U_i f_1 + \sum_{i=1}^{m} f_1' v_i (\omega_{i1} - x_i' f_1) \right] ds$$
$$= \partial\omega_1 - f_1' \sum_{i=1}^{m} \partial\xi_i - \sum_{i=1}^{m} f_1' v_i (s\partial\omega_{i1} + \partial\omega_{i2}). \tag{56}$$

This expresses ds as a function of the exogenous variations $\partial\omega_{i1}$, $\partial\omega_{i2}$ and $\partial\xi_i$. It is the required equation. Consider first the expression in square brackets which multiplies ds. Its first term is negative, according to our earlier discussion. Its second term cannot be positive since the theory of consumer equilibrium shows that U is negative semi-definite. We can neglect the third term, since it is zero when the v_i are the same for all consumers (equation (51) shows that the sum of the $\omega_{i1} - x_i' f_1$ is zero); for it to be positive, the income-effect for goods which largely use the first factor must be systematically greater among individuals owning this factor than among the rest. Except in very exceptional cases, the expression which multiplies ds must be negative.

We are now in a position to state the effects of exogenous changes on the distribution of incomes.

(i) *If the second factor becomes scarcer*, $(\partial\omega_{i2} < 0$ for all i, where $\partial\omega_{i1} = 0$ and $\partial\xi_i = 0)$, then the right hand side of (56) is positive and ds is negative; *the relative return to the first factor decreases.*

(ii) *If the first factor becomes scarcer* $(\partial\omega_1 < 0$ and $\partial\omega_{i1} < 0$ for all i, where $\partial\omega_{i2} = 0$ and $\partial\xi_i = 0)$, then the right hand side of (56) is negative (in practice, $p'v_i = 1$ implies here $sf_1'v_i = 1 - f_2'v_i < 1$); ds is negative; *positive* *the return to the first factor increases.*

(iii) *If consumers' demands transfer to goods using more of the first factor, then the return to this factor increases.* The budget equation implies $p'\,d\xi_i = 0$, that is, $sf_1'\partial\xi_i + f_2'\partial\xi_i = 0$. The assumption adopted here reduces to $f_1'\partial\xi_i > 0$ and $f_2'\partial\xi_i < 0$; since the $\partial\omega_{ih}$ are all zero, it follows that $ds > 0$. For example, if only one consumer's demands for r and s vary, with $\partial\xi_r > 0$ and $\partial\xi_s = -(p_r/p_s)\partial\xi_r < 0$, then

$$f_1'\,d\xi = \left[\frac{sf_{r1}}{p_r} - \frac{sf_{s1}}{p_s} \right] \frac{p_r\partial\xi_r}{s}$$

will be positive precisely when the first factor represents a greater part of the value of r than it does of the value of s.

The conclusions we have just reached recall those obtained for an economy with no production. Apart from their interest for distribution theory, they contribute to the understanding of the way in which general models synthesize the two price theories discussed in Sections 4 and 5 respectively.

8. The existence of a general equilibrium

In the preceding sections we have discussed the equations of equilibrium, but have not rigorously examined the question whether this system of equations has a solution. We were content to verify that there were as many equations as there were unknowns: $(m + 1)l$ in the distribution economy, $(m + 1)l - 1$ in the exchange economy, after elimination of one equation deducible from the others, $l + m + n - 1$ in the private ownership economy with production. (In the particular case of Section 5 we did not even set out all the equilibrium equations.)

Until recently, microeconomic theory found this sufficient. However, it was known that equality of the number of equations with the number of unknowns was neither necessary nor sufficient for the existence of a solution. But it seemed impossible to establish the existence of a solution for general models in which the relevant functions were not specified exactly.

Mathematical economists have been aware of this gap for about twenty years; they have given rigorous proofs of the existence of equilibrium in a number of general models. Given the mathematical level of these lectures, we cannot ignore such proofs, and shall illustrate their nature by means of a very simple case.

But first, we must demonstrate the importance of existence properties for the microeconomic theory which is our main concern. Suppose we have established that a system of equations representing equilibrium has a solution, however the exogenous elements of the model may be specified. Then we can be certain that our model *always* provides a representation of equilibrium, a representation which may be true or false but exists in any case. On the other hand, if equilibrium does not exist for certain specifications of the exogenous elements, then the model is not valid in these cases; in a certain sense, it is inconsistent. We see why theoreticians, preoccupied with logic, ensure the existence of solutions to the systems of equations by which they represent competitive equilibrium.

The proofs with which we shall be concerned are not trivial. They all depend on the application of 'fixed point theorems' to the models considered. We must say something about these theorems.

Consider, in l-dimensional Euclidean space, the 'parallelepiped' Z of all the points in this space which satisfy the inequalities

$$u_h \leqslant z_h \leqslant v_h,$$

where the u_h and v_h are fixed numbers (obviously $u_h \leqslant v_h$). A simple fixed point theorem can be stated as follows:

BROUWER'S THEOREM.† Given a *continuous* mapping $\phi(z)$ of a parallelepiped Z into itself, there exists a vector z^0 of Z such that $\phi(z^0) = z^0$. The vector z^0 is said to be the *fixed point* of the function ϕ.

The simplest case is that of a real function ϕ defined on the set of real numbers, where Z is an interval, for example [0, 1]. The theorem then states that the graph of this function contains at least one point lying on the first bisector.

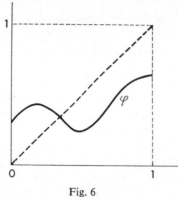

Fig. 6

There have been many extensions of Brouwer's theorem in mathematics. In particular, Kakutani's theorem has often been used in equilibrium theory; but for our present purposes, we do not need to go into such extensions of the theorem.

In fact, we can now prove the existence of equilibrium for a distribution economy.

THEOREM 1. Given non-negative incomes R_i and initial resources ω_h that are all positive, assume that, for every price-vector p with no negative component and for all i, a (partial) equilibrium exists for the ith consumer and is defined uniquely by non-negative functions $\xi_{ih}(p; R_i)$, which are continuous with respect to p. Then there exists a vector p^0 with no negative component and such that

$$\sum_{i=1}^{m} \xi_{ih}(p^0; R_i) \leqslant \omega_h \qquad \text{for} \qquad h = 1, 2, ..., l, \qquad (57)$$

the inequality being replaced by an equality for all h such that $p_h^0 > 0$.

---

† This is an intentionally restrictive statement of the theorem. For an introduction to fixed point theorems, see C. Berge, *Espaces topologiques, Fonctions multivoques*, Dunod Paris, 1959, Chapter VIII, Section 2.

For the proof, we can use directly the global demand functions $\xi_h(p)$ defined by (4) and clearly continuous when the ξ_{ih} are continuous. In l-dimensional space, we shall consider the parallelepiped P defined by

$$0 \leqslant p_h \leqslant \frac{R}{\omega_h}, \tag{58}$$

where R denotes the sum of the m incomes R_i.

Given some vector p of P, consider the functions†

$$\Psi_h(p) = p_h + \xi_h(p) - \omega_h, \tag{59}$$

and

$$\phi_h(p) = \begin{cases} 0 & \text{if} & \Psi_h(p) \leqslant 0, \\ \Psi_h(p) & \text{if} & 0 \leqslant \Psi_h(p) \leqslant \frac{R}{\omega_h}, \\ \dfrac{R}{\omega_h} & \text{if} & \Psi_h(p) \geqslant \dfrac{R}{\omega_h}. \end{cases} \tag{60}$$

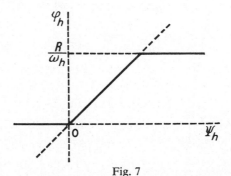

Fig. 7

Consider the vector mapping $\phi(p)$ whose l components are the $\phi_h(p)$ defined above. In going from p to $\phi(p)$, the components that increase correspond to goods for which demand exceeds supply, while the components that decrease correspond to goods for which supply exceeds demand. The mapping ϕ can therefore be considered to describe a fairly natural process of realisation of equilibrium (compare equation (64) given below in Section 10).

This mapping is obviously continuous since Ψ_h is a continuous function of p and ϕ_h is a continuous function of Ψ_h. It transforms every vector of P

---

† The function $\Psi_h(p)$ may seem peculiar because the quantities added in the right hand side of (59) are heterogeneous. It can easily be verified that the following proof applies equally when $\Psi_h(p)$ is defined by

$$\Psi_h(p) = p_h + \lambda_h[\xi_h(p) - \omega_h]$$

where λ_h is some fixed positive number.

into a vector of P. Brouwer's theorem states that it has a fixed point p^0, that is, that there exists a vector p^0 such that

$$\phi_h(p^0) = p_h^0 \qquad h = 1, 2, \ldots, l.$$

Let us examine each of the three possibilities (60) and the corresponding three possibilities for p_h^0 (see Figure 7).

(i) If $p_h^0 = 0$, then $\Psi_h(p^0) \leqslant 0$, and so $\xi_h(p^0) \leqslant \omega_h$; (57) is satisfied.

(ii) If $0 < p_h^0 < R/\omega_h$, then $p_h^0 = \psi_h(p^0)$, and so $\xi_h(p^0) = \omega_h$, as is required by theorem 1 in this case.

(iii) If $p_h^0 = R/\omega_h$, then we must have $\psi_h(p^0) \geqslant R/\omega_h = p_h^0$, and therefore $\xi_h(p^0) \geqslant \omega_h$ and $p_h^0\xi_h(p^0) \geqslant p_h^0\omega_h = R$; therefore

$$\sum_i [p_h^0\xi_{ih}(p^0; R_i) - R_i] \geqslant 0.$$

But, since the l demands ξ_{ih} of the ith consumer are non-negative, the value $p_h^0\xi_{ih}$ of each of them must be at most equal to R_i. Therefore the expression in square brackets in the last inequality is negative or zero, which means that the inequality becomes an equality, and therefore that $\xi_h(p^0) = \omega_h$ (since $p_h^0 > 0$).

This completes the proof of theorem 1.

The property stated in this theorem differs slightly from the definition of equilibrium given in Section 2. However, the difference is only minor since (57) must always take the form of (5), except perhaps when the price of h is zero. But then the good has zero marginal utility for all consumers. If we assume that there is free disposal of surplus, we can still speak of an equilibrium since no-one is interested in the surplus of h, which can be destroyed without cost. In fact, we could take the property stated in theorem 1 as the definition of equilibrium; this has often been done in mathematical economics.

Theorem 1 is weak not in its conclusion, but in its assumptions, which are formulated directly on the demand functions. Their validity could be better assessed if they related to the utility functions S_i and the consumption sets X_i.

We note in passing that, since the ξ_{ih} are non-negative, the theorem ignores services provided by consumers, which are not the object of the distribution operations under consideration.

The most serious assumption relates to the existence and uniqueness of consumer equilibrium, which must be satisfied for any price vector p provided that the latter has no negative component. We proved the existence and uniqueness of an equilibrium for the consumer, subject to certain assumptions (proposition 1 of Chapter 2). Thus we have ourselves determined sufficient conditions for the existence of the ξ_{ih}. However, these conditions assumed that the p_h were all positive while, for theorem 1, we require only that the p_h are not negative. Thus we can deduce the existence of an equilibrium directly from the properties assumed for the X_i and the S_i only if we strengthen the assumptions made in Chapter 2 and carry out slightly heavier proofs.

We note also that, to establish the continuity of the ξ_{ih}, we assumed the X_i to be convex and the S_i to be quasi-concave. Without some such condition, the proof could not be established, as will be shown later in a counter-example.

An assumption used in consumer theory for the proof of the existence of the ξ_{ih} is important for correct appreciation of the relevance of general equilibrium theory. The time has come to say a few words about this.

In Chapter 2 we assumed that the set X_i of possible consumptions for the ith individual contains the null-vector. This ignored the existence of a subsistence standard. It is granted in every society that each individual must be assured of some minimum consumption that depends on the society's stage of development. The set X_i must contain only vectors obeying this subsistence standard; it no longer contains the null-vector.

Under these conditions, equilibrium for the consumer exists only if prices p_h and income R_i are such that X_i has at least one common point with the set of the x_i satisfying $px_i \leqslant R_i$. A new condition, called the *survival condition* must be satisfied for the existence of general equilibrium.

In the distribution economy, a survival condition can be defined as follows. Let λ_i be the smallest number such that the vector $\lambda_i \omega$ belongs to X_i (we assume the existence of such a number, which is certainly not restrictive in practice). A survival condition is:

$$R_i \geqslant \lambda_i R \qquad i = 1, 2, ..., m \tag{61}$$

where, as previously, R denotes the sum of the R_i. Incomes must be so distributed that the part of global income due to each individual gives him the right to a part of the resources which is at least equal to his subsistence standard. In the equilibrium, we necessarily have

$$\sum_{i=1}^{m} p^0 x_i = p^0 \omega,$$

and therefore $R = p^0 \omega$; the survival condition implies $R_i \geqslant p^0 \lambda_i \omega$; the consumer can acquire at least the vector $\lambda_i \omega$ of X_i.

If we wish to take account of this survival condition in the proof of the existence of demand functions (cf. Chapter 2), we must obviously introduce new assumptions which complicate the proof of theorem 1.

Let us now consider a case where no equilibrium exists, namely the case of two identical consumers and two goods ($m = 2$; $l = 2$). The consumption sets X_i contain all the vectors with no negative component.

The indifference curves are the quarter-circles centred on the origin:

$$S_i(x_{i1}, x_{i2}) = x_{i1}^2 + x_{i2}^2,$$

so that the utility functions do not satisfy the assumption of quasi-concavity. The initial resources are $\omega_1 = 4$ and $\omega_2 = 2$. Incomes are such that $R_1 = R_2 = 3$.

We can easily determine the two consumers' demands for each possible price-vector.

(i) If $p_1 < p_2$, then each consumer demands only the good 1, or more precisely,

$$x_{11} = x_{21} = 3/p_1$$
$$x_{12} = x_{22} = 0.$$

This combination maximises S_i over the set of the x_i in the first quadrant which satisfy the budget constraint

$$p_1 x_{i1} + p_2 x_{i2} = 3.$$

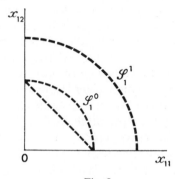

Fig. 8

There is no equilibrium corresponding to such prices since the global demand for 1 is $6/p_1$; the limitation on resources $\omega_1 = 4$ implies that p_1 is positive; therefore p_2 is also positive, which is incompatible with an excess supply of 2 for the second good.

(ii) If $p_2 < p_1$, the consumers demand only the good 2:

$$x_{11} = x_{21} = 0,$$
$$x_{12} = x_{22} = 3/p_2.$$

No equilibrium exists for such a combination of prices.

(iii) If $p_1 = p_2$, then each consumer chooses one or other of the following demands:

$$\text{either} \begin{cases} x_{i1} = 3/p \\ x_{i2} = 0 \end{cases}; \quad \text{or} \begin{cases} x_{i1} = 0 \\ x_{i2} = 3/p \end{cases}.$$

We then have three possibilities for global demand:

$$\begin{cases} x_1 = 6/p \\ x_2 = 0 \end{cases}, \quad \begin{cases} x_1 = 3/p \\ x_2 = 3/p \end{cases}, \quad \begin{cases} x_1 = 0 \\ x_2 = 6/p \end{cases}.$$

No equilibrium is possible with any of them since global available resources are $\omega_1 = 4$, $\omega_2 = 2$.

In this case there is no competitive equilibrium possible for the distribution economy.

We have spent some considerable time in proving the existence of equilibrium in a distribution economy since this proof is a simple prototype of others which are often much heavier and which have been established for other formulations of equilibrium. Such proofs had to be established, once and for all, in economic science, but we cannot devote more time to them than they deserve in a general course.

Indeed, we encounter fairly severe difficulties if we try to apply the approach used so far in these lectures to a closer look at the existence problem for a private ownership economy with production.

One of the difficulties arises when we become aware of the restrictive nature of the assumption that a (partial) equilibrium exists for the firm and is unique for any price vector p. We then want to treat the functions $\eta_{jh}(p)$ as defined only for vectors p that belong to subsets of R^l, and then as being multivalued. This obviously complicates the theory.

However, our conclusions from the investigation of the distribution economy remain basically valid for this more general model. Subject to conditions which, in particular, imply convexity but apart from that are fairly unrestrictive, we can establish the existence of a competitive equilibrium.

As we have already observed when studying the firm, the presence of considerable indivisibilities or increasing returns to scale may prevent the realisation of a competitive equilibrium. This is the major limitation on the theories examined here in so far as they aim to provide a positive analysis of observed reality in decentralised economies. We have already seen that imperfections in competition may facilitate the realisation of an equilibrium. We shall return on several later occasions to the difficulty raised by non-convexities.

9. The uniqueness of equilibrium

By establishing that an equilibrium exists, we fulfil the need to check up on the logical consistency of the theory. But if there exist *several* equilibria that satisfy the model, the theory provides only a partial explanation; it does not indicate which of the equilibria will be realised. A relevant question is therefore to find conditions under which the uniqueness of equilibrium can be proved.

Here we shall confine ourselves to a brief discussion in the context of the distribution and of the exchange economy. Note, however, that in the course of Section 5, when discussing a particular model related to production, we established the uniqueness of the equilibrium price-vector.

That the question is not meaningless is revealed by Figure 9, which reproduces an Edgeworth diagram ($m = 2$; $l = 2$). The two points M and M' both correspond to competitive equilibria since PM and PM' are tangents, at M and M' respectively, to the indifference curves of the two consumers. If prices corresponding to the budget line PT are established, then both consumers accept the point M. If prices corresponding to PT' are established, then the point M' is realised. It has already been pointed out that perfect competition, assumed here, does not hold when there are only two exchanging agents. But obviously the case $m = 2$ is not special for the uniqueness property.

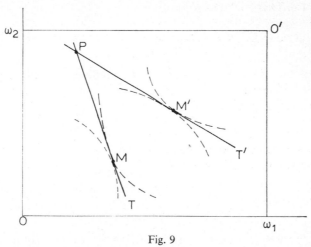

Fig. 9

Such situations do not arise in the exchange economy if the demand functions are defined uniquely and if they satisfy assumption 2 of gross substitutability. Clearly the equilibrium price-vector is fixed only up to a multiplicative constant. So we shall say that uniqueness exists if, given two equilibria E^0 and E^1, then $x_i^1 = x_i^0$ for all i and there exists $\lambda \neq 0$ such that $p^1 = \lambda p^0$.

Suppose then that uniqueness as thus described is not realised. Let p^1 and p^0 be two non-collinear equilibrium vectors. Let r be the good for which the ratio p_h^0/p_h^1 is minimised:

$$p_h^0 \geqslant \frac{p_r^0}{p_r^1} p_h^1 \qquad \text{for all } h, \tag{62}$$

where the inequality holds strictly for at least one h, since p^0 and p^1 are not collinear. Consider now the vector p^*, collinear with p^1, and whose components are the numbers on the right hand side of (62). Gross substitutability implies that the demand for r is higher with prices p_h^* than with prices p_h^0, which contradicts the fact that it equals ω_r in both equilibria E^1 and E^0. In order to show that gross substitutability does in fact have this effect, we need only consider a continuous transformation of the prices of p^0 up to p^*, along which transformation no price increases, and therefore the price of r remains constant. So the demand for r will never decrease; at certain times it must increase, since the price of at least one other good must decrease.

Similarly, we see immediately that equilibrium is unique in the distribution economy if the demand functions are defined uniquely and if a rather more specific assumption than assumption 1 is satisfied:

ASSUMPTION 1'. The collective demand functions $\xi_h(p)$ are such that, for every pair of different vectors p^0 and p^1,

$$\sum_{h=1}^{l} [\xi_h(p^0) - \xi_h(p^1)][p_h^0 - p_h^1] < 0. \tag{63}$$

For, if p^0 and p^1 are the price-vectors of two different equilibria E^0 and E^1, they must be different and must imply the same demands ω_h for each of the goods h. This is contrary to (63).

10. The realisation and stability of equilibrium

Having established the equilibrium equations, Walras, to whom the present theory is essentially due, explains how equilibrium tends naturally to be realised. The following quotation illustrates the importance which he attributes to this explanation. Having just defined a system representing equilibrium in an economy with a productive sector, he writes: 'It remains only to show, for production equilibrium as for exchange equilibrium, that this problem to which we have given a theoretical solution is just that problem which in practice is solved in the market-place by the mechanism of free competition.'[†]

In fact, the theory as presented up to this point shows how the consistency of individual decisions can be ensured if markets are competitive and if equilibrium prices are realised in these markets. But nothing in our previous discussions guarantees that competition tends to establish equilibrium prices. This is the question which now concerns us.

According to Walras, price-adjustments can be formally represented by a 'tâtonnement' process. He suggests that the way prices are determined on Commodity Exchanges or Stock Exchanges is typical of the competitive mechanism. So, systematic analysis of the way an Exchange functions in his view provides systematic analysis of any market.

---

† See L. Walras, *Elements of Pure Economics* (W. Jaffé tr.), George Allen & Unwin, London, 1954.

In an Exchange, all buyers and sellers are present or are at least represented. They come with the intention to buy or to sell, and it depends on the price proposed whether their intentions are realised or not. An initial price is 'called'. Offers to buy and sell are made at this price. If total supply does not equal total demand, a second price is called which may be less than or greater than the first according as supply exceeds or falls short of demand; and so on, until all the buyers and sellers have been able to deal at a price which suits them.

To round off general equilibrium theory from our present standpoint, we must therefore first give a formal definition of the process of tâtonnement, and then find the conditions under which it does in fact lead to equilibrium, that is, we must investigate the 'stability' of equilibrium.

For simplicity, we again confine ourselves to an economy which involves only consumers. If prices are defined by the vector p, the amount by which total demand exceeds total supply is $\xi_h(p) - \omega_h$ for the good h. For a formal representation of the tâtonnement process, it is often assumed to be continuous over time and the rate of revision of p_h is assumed proportional to excess demand $\xi_h - \omega_h$†:

$$\frac{dp_h}{dt} = a_h[\xi_h(p) - \omega_h] \qquad h = 1, 2, ..., l, \tag{64}$$

where a is a positive constant and t denotes time for the realisation of the tâtonnement process.‡

A particular feature of this formulation is that it assumes that the manifested demands depend on the prices called at each moment of time, and not on the way prices move throughout the various adjustments, which is equivalent to assuming that in fact no exchange takes place before equilibrium price is determined. This is not the case in Commodity and Stock Exchanges, since, without exception, contracts are made at each of the prices called. So the demands which are satisfied at the beginning do not appear later, and this modifies equilibrium prices.

To make this last point clear, we need only consider the example of the distribution economy. Suppose that the initial prices p_h^1 are lower than the equilibrium prices p_h^0. Suppose also that only the first consumer's demand is satisfied at the prices p_h^1. He receives quantities ω_h^1 of resources, such that

---

† Of course, (64) applies only so long as p_h is positive, or as the right hand side is positive when p_h is zero. When, at $p_h = 0$, supply is still excessive, there is generally assumed to be no further variation in p_h.

‡ When the theory of the stability, or realisation, of market equilibrium is applied to an economy involving several periods of time, it is assumed that the duration of the tâtonnement process is an infinitesimal fraction of the basic period. This is clearly restrictive because of the lags involved in revisions of supplies by firms. Walras emphasised this point (see Walras, op. cit.).

$p^1 \omega^1 = R_1$. By hypothesis, $p^1 \omega^1 < p^0 \omega^1$ and $p^0 \omega = R$, where R denotes the total income of all consumers. Thus

$$p^0(\omega - \omega^1) < R - R_1.$$

The initial equilibrium prices p_h^0 are therefore too small to ensure equality of demand and supply for the remaining $m - 1$ consumers. New equilibrium prices, differing from the p_h^0 because of the deal concluded by the first consumer, must be defined.

Thus this formulation of the tâtonnement process suggested by Walras and repeated since by most writers in this field,† is a fairly extreme idealisation of the mechanism by which prices are determined. However, it is based on the essential idea that the price of a product must increase or decrease according as the demand for it is greater than or less than the supply.

Some economists have criticised this process on the grounds that the agents responsible for effecting price-revisions are not generally specified in its statement. The criticism obviously does not apply to Commodity Exchanges, but may carry more weight in other cases. In the distribution economy, it is natural to assume that the 'distributors', owners of or agents for the goods to be distributed, themselves alter prices upwards or downwards in the light of the difference they observe between demand and available supply. In the exchange economy, it is necessary to assume the existence of intermediaries between the exchanging parties. This assumption sometimes appears artificial.

Equations (64) representing the tâtonnement process constitute a system of l differential equations in the l unknowns p_h. A value p^0 of p which satisfies equations (5) expressing the equality of global supply and global demand, is an equilibrium value for this system of differential equations. Generally the solution of (64) is a set of l functions $p_h(t)$ which are defined given their initial values $p_h(0)$.

DEFINITIONS. An equilibrium price vector p^0 is said to be *stable* or 'globally stable', if, for any initial prices $p_h(0)$, each price $p_h(t)$ tends to p_h^0 as t tends to infinity, for $h = 1, 2, ..., l$. An equilibrium p^0 is said to be *locally stable* if the $p_h(t)$ tend to the corresponding p_h^0 when the initial values $p_h(0)$ are sufficiently near the p_h^0.

If (64) relates to a single good, the decrease in demand as a function of price is sufficient to ensure local stability of the equilibrium. The question becomes complicated when there are several goods. An adjustment to p_h which seems a correction in the market for h may increase disequilibrium in the markets for other goods. Therefore it is conceivable *a priori* that the adjust-

---

† For other formulations, and a general review of stability theory, see T. Negishi, 'The Stability of a Competitive Economy: A Survey Article', *Econometrica*, October 1962.

ments described by (64) may not ensure stability of competitive equilibrium. However, a certain number of results relating to stability have been established. We shall prove one of them for the distribution economy and then state one for the exchange economy.

THEOREM 2. If the collective demand functions are differentiable and satisfy assumption 1, every equilibrium for the distribution economy comprising prices p_h^0 which are all positive, is locally stable when the price-adjustments satisfy (64). If the demand functions satisfy assumption 1', there is also global stability.

Consider such an equilibrium p^0. In view of assumption 1, there exists a number $\varepsilon > 0$ such that $|p_h - p_h^0| < \varepsilon$ (for all h) implies

$$\sum_{h=1}^{l} [\xi_h(p) - \xi_h(p^0)][p_h - p_h^0] < 0 \tag{65}$$

except when $p = p^0$. (The inequality holds for all $p \neq p^0$ if assumption 1' is satisfied.)

Moreover, since the p_h^0 are positive, ε can be chosen so that

$$|p_h - p_h^0| < \varepsilon \quad \text{implies} \quad p_h > 0.$$

Let us consider the $p_h(0)$ such that

$$|p_h(0) - p_h^0| < \eta \quad h = 1, 2, ..., l, \tag{66}$$

where η is a positive number to be defined later. Let us assume that $p(0)$ differs from the equilibrium vector p^0, otherwise the stability condition is obviously satisfied, with the $p_h(t)$ being continually equal to the p_h^0.

Let $D(t)$ be the positive quantity defined by:

$$D(t)^2 = \sum_{h=1}^{l} \frac{1}{a_h}[p_h(t) - p_h^0]^2. \tag{67}$$

We can immediately find

$$\frac{\mathrm{d}}{\mathrm{d}t}[D(t)^2] = 2 \sum_{h=1}^{l} \frac{1}{a_h}[p_h(t) - p_h^0]\frac{\mathrm{d}p_h}{\mathrm{d}t}$$

or, in view of (64),

$$\frac{\mathrm{d}}{\mathrm{d}t}[D(t)^2] = 2 \sum_{h=1}^{l} [p_h(t) - p_h^0][\xi_h(p) - \xi_h(p^0)]. \tag{68}$$

This equality, together with (65), shows that, outside the equilibrium, the distance $D(t)$ is decreasing. However, to establish this point we must take account of the fact that the inequality (65) in question is only locally applicable.

Suppose now that η is chosen so that

$$a_k\eta^2 \sum_{h=1}^{l} \frac{1}{a_h} < \varepsilon^2 \quad \text{for } k = 1, 2, ..., l \quad \text{and } \eta < \varepsilon.$$

Under these conditions, $|p_h(0) - p_h^0| < \varepsilon$ for all h; (65) applies for $p = p(0)$ and (68) shows that $D(t)$ is decreasing for $t = 0$.

We can also show that $D^2(t)$ is continually decreasing so long as $p(t) \neq p^0$. For, suppose that $D^2(t)$ is no longer decreasing for the first time after the value t_0 of t. The relations (67), (66) and the condition on η show that $D^2(0)$, and consequently also $D^2(t_0)$, are smaller than all the ε^2/a_k (for $k = 1, 2, \ldots,$ l). But it follows from the definition of $D^2(t)$ that $|p_h(t) - p_h^0|^2$ is at most equal to $a_h D^2(t)$; thus $|p_h(t_0) - p_h^0| < \varepsilon$ for all h. It follows therefore from (65) and (68) that $D^2(t_0)$ is decreasing except when $p(t_0) = p^0$, in which case equilibrium is reached.

Thus the non-negative and never increasing quantity $D^2(t)$ tends to a limit. If the limit is zero, $p_h(t)$ tends to p_h^0 for all h, which is what we have to prove. Let us assume that the limit is $\underline{D}^2 \neq 0$. Then there exists a sequence of values t_s (where $s = 1, 2, \ldots$), such that $p(t_s)$ tends to a vector p^1 which differs from p^0. (Here we apply the property that every function defined on the set of positive real numbers and taking values in a compact set of Euclidean space has a point of accumulation; the function is $p(t)$, the compact set is the set of vectors p such that $\underline{D}^2 \leqslant D^2 \leqslant D^2(0)$). If we consider the sequence of values t_s in (68), then by continuity, we can write

$$0 = 2 \sum_{h=1}^{l} [p_h^1 - p_h^0][\xi_h(p^1) - \xi_h(p^0)].$$

In view of the reasons discussed in the previous paragraph, $|p_h^1 - p_h^0| < \varepsilon$ for all h. The above equality is therefore incompatible with (65); this completes the proof of theorem 2.

For the exchange economy, the tâtonnement process described by (64) differs *a priori* from that just discussed since price-revisions entail changes in the value of the resources at the disposal of each consumer. If the good 1 becomes dearer relative to the other goods, there is a resulting change in the distribution of incomes in favour of those consumers for whom the ratio $\omega_{i1}/p\omega_i$ is particularly high. Also, we have already seen that assumption 1, used in the proof of theorem 2, does not hold for the exchange economy.

However, we can immediately deduce a useful result from Walras' law, as expressed by (12). If we take account of (12) in the differential system (64), it implies

$$\sum_{h=1}^{l} \frac{1}{a_h} p_h \frac{dp_h}{dt} = 0, \tag{69}$$

or

$$\sum_{h=1}^{l} \frac{1}{a_h} [p_h(t)]^2 = C, \tag{70}$$

where C is a fixed number. Given the $p_h(0)$, the evolution of the $p_h(t)$ is restricted to (70), which can be considered as fixing a natural normalisation rule for the vector $p(t)$.

We saw that, in the exchange economy, the equilibrium price-vector is defined only up to a multiplicative constant. No equilibrium price-vector p^0 appears stable, or even locally stable, if we keep strictly to the definition of stability given before the statement of theorem 2. But this would be a mistake. When discussing stability in the context of the exchange economy we shall replace the phrase 'for any initial prices $p_h(0)$' by the following: 'for any initial prices $p_h(0)$ satisfying

$$\sum_{h=1}^{l} \frac{1}{a_h}\{[p_h(0)]^2 - (p_h^0)^2\} = 0'. \tag{71}$$

We can then state the following result†:

THEOREM 3. If the global demand functions are differentiable and satisfy assumption 2 of gross substitutability, every equilibrium in the exchange economy is locally stable when the price-adjustments obey (64).

This concludes our investigation of adjustments towards equilibrium. Obviously there must be many possible variants of the theory, but we would gain relatively little in understanding of the real phenomena by digressing for too long in this course on such variants.

---

† For the proof, see, for example, T. Negishi, op. cit.

6

Imperfect competition and game situations

We have just made a study of general economic equilibrium on the assumption that perfect competition regulated the relations between agents. We must now continue with this investigation in the context of different institutional assumptions which represent other aspects of economic organisation as it actually exists. The latter is obviously very complex; not only does it involve the rules and customs governing contracts, but also certain objective situations which allow to individuals or to firms the possibility of contracting on particularly favourable terms.

Unfortunately, economic science has not yet established other general theories whose explanatory power is comparable to that which can be claimed for competitive equilibrium theory. Recent research seems likely to produce useful results, but its exposition here would be premature.

In these lectures, whose aim is the theoretical study of general equilibrium rather than of the multiple possible situations on the individual level, we therefore deal almost exclusively with perfect competition. However, the theory of monopoly has been discussed briefly (see Chapter 3, Section 9). Similarly, we shall now devote some time to some other models of imperfect competition. We shall not attempt a thorough investigation, but only to say enough to clarify the bearing of the theory of competitive equilibrium, and to prepare the student who wants to follow the coming progress in the study of other institutional frameworks.

The common feature of the different situations now to be discussed is that, *when deciding on his own actions, each agent must form some precise idea of the decisions of each of the other agents taken individually.* In perfect competition a consumer or a producer has to know only the prices of the different commodities, as these prices summarise for him the results of the decisions of all the other agents. Similarly, it is enough for a non-discriminating monopolist to know the aggregate demand function for his product without his having to understand the motivations behind the decisions of the various consumers. This is no longer the case in the situations with which we are now concerned.

The theoretical study of these situations was initiated by A. Cournot and J. Bertrand in the mid-nineteenth century. It has been greatly advanced by the recent appearance of the *theory of games*, which offers a general conceptual framework that can accommodate the most widely varying cases. Before embarking on the study of particular situations, we shall introduce some notions borrowed from games theory. Just as we shall not attempt to give a systematic treatment of imperfect competition, so we shall not try to put forward the main body of this theory, but only what is strictly useful for a sound understanding of general economic equilibrium.†

1. The general model of the theory of games

Suppose that a certain number of players take part in a game where they act according to certain rules. The gains that each player will make from the game depend on his own actions and also on those of the other players. If we consider the logical characteristics of the game and ignore the particular social context in which it is usually placed, we find an obvious analogy with the situations we have been discussing. Our agents correspond to the players, our physical or institutional constraints to the rules of the game, and our utilities or profits to the gains from the game. Hence the general concepts of the theory of games apply closely to the study of the economic world.

Let each player or agent be represented by an index r or s ($r, s = 1, 2, ..., n$). The action of r can be represented by a suitable mathematical entity a_r, which is generally a vector in a certain space. The rules or constraints imply that a_r belongs to a set A_r which is given *a priori*:

$$a_r \in A_r \qquad r = 1, 2, ..., n. \tag{1}$$

Finally, the pay-off W_r that the agent r makes from the game is a real function of the actions of all the agents:‡

$$W_r(a_1, a_2, ..., a_n). \tag{2}$$

This is a very summary representation of a game. But, contrary to appearances perhaps, it does not assume that the game consists of a single move in which all the players act simultaneously. In fact, a_r must be interpreted as a

---

† On the theory of games, see, for example, Vajda, *An Introduction to Linear Programming and the Theory of Games*, Methuen, 1960.

‡ Here we ignore chance drawing, or the other random processes of which most games are composed, since they are not involved in the imperfect competition situations in which we are interested. Subject to an assumption about the nature of pay-off functions, the theory of games shows that the logical structure defined above applies to games of chance as well as to purely deterministic games.

'strategy' defining what the player r will do on each turn, in each of the situations in which he may find himself because of the actions of the other players. Suppose, for example, that the game consists of three moves and there are two players A and B, the former coming in on the first and third moves and the latter on the second move; suppose that B must choose between only two actions 1 and 2, and his choice is known to A on the third move. There are then three components in an action a_1 by A: what A does on the first move, what he does on the third when B has chosen 1, what he does on the third when B has chosen 2. In fairly complex games, a_r obviously has a very large number of components; the representation by the A_r and W_r may be very complicated. But this in no way hinders an abstract, general study.

Given this logical structure, *the theory of games proposes to determine which actions the n players adopt, or should adopt, when each of them knows the sets A_s and the pay-off functions W_s of the others together with his own set and his own function.*

Note that the assumption that all the agents know the A_s and the W_s may appear restrictive when applied to the study of economic phenomena. It is a natural assumption to adopt for situations where there are few agents and each can without too much difficulty find out the conditions under which each of the others acts. But clearly this assumption makes the theory of games inadequate for the treatment of the problems raised by the organisation of exchanges of information within large communities (cf. Chapter 8).

If it had been able to provide a general solution to the problem which it set for itself, the theory of games would have become the basis for a large part of microeconomic theory. Unfortunately, it has not fully succeeded in doing so. Its special contribution has been a very considerable clarification of concepts in the questions that it has tackled and in the exhaustive treatment of some simple cases. In particular, the theory of the zero sum two person game,[†] has great elegance. But it scarcely applies to economic situations, and will therefore be ignored here.

Among those concepts capable of general application, that of *non-cooperative equilibrium* deserves particular mention here. Such an equilibrium E^0 is, by definition, a feasible state, that is, a particular specification $a_1^0, a_2^0, ..., a_n^0$ of the $a_1, a_2, ..., a_n$ belonging to their respective A_r's, such that

$$W_r(a_1^0, ..., a_{r-1}^0, a_r, a_{r+1}^0, ..., a_n^0) \leqslant W_r(a_1^0, ..., a_{r-1}^0, a_r^0, a_{r+1}^0, ..., a_n^0) \qquad (3)$$

for all $a_r \in A_r$, and this for all r. In other words, E^0 is a non-cooperative equilibrium if each agent has no interest in changing his action when he considers the actions of the other agents as given.

---

† We have a zero sum two person game if $n = 2$ and if $W_1(a_1^1, a_2^1) \geqslant W_1(a_1^2, a_2^2)$ when and only when $W_2(a_1^1, a_2^1) \leqslant W_2(a_1^2, a_2^2)$.

As we shall see from two examples, non-cooperative equilibrium is not very likely to be realised in many situations where there are few agents, since each agent is then aware that his decision reacts on the decisions of the others.

Let us examine first the cases of bilateral monopoly and of duopoly. We shall later come to the concept of coalition, which is naturally introduced when a non-cooperative equilibrium does not adequately represent the outcome of the game.

2. Bilateral monopoly

Bilateral monopoly exists in the market for a commodity when there is just one buyer and one seller.

In this brief theoretical study we shall assume that the commodity in question is the first ($h = 1$), while all the other markets are competitive. We also assume that both the buyer and the seller are firms, the commodity 1 being an intermediary product, input for the first firm and output for the second. For the buyer ($j = 2$) and the seller ($j = 1$), the prices of goods other than the first are given. These two participants must decide the price p_1 and the quantity exchanged y_1.

Let $C_1(y_1)$ be the cost of production of y_1 for the seller, let $R_2(y_1) - p_1y_1$ be the buyer's profit from his own activity when he uses the quantity y_1. The pay-offs for the two participants are respectively

$$W_1 = p_1y_1 - C_1(y_1), \tag{4}$$
$$W_2 = R_2(y_1) - p_1y_1. \tag{5}$$

We shall assume that C_1 and R_2 are twice differentiable and that $C_1 > 0$ and $R_2'' < 0$.

In order to specify a model of the type introduced in the theory of games, we must also specify the actions a_1 and a_2 of the two firms and the corresponding domains A_1 and A_2. We can conceive of various models representing as many variants of bilateral monopoly, each containing a particular determination of the pair (p_1, y_1) as a function of the actions (a_1, a_2) adopted. We shall keep to a simple case, which is certainly relevant to some actual cases. We shall assume that the first firm, A, determines the price p_1, and the second firm, B, determines the quantity that it acquires, the domains A_1 and A_2 being then defined by $p_1 \geqslant 0$ and $y_1 \geqslant 0$.

Let us first examine the possibility of a non-cooperative equilibrium. If it takes price p_1, fixed by A, as given, the firm B behaves as in perfect competition; it chooses y_1 so that

$$R_2'(y_1) = p_1, \tag{6}$$

or chooses $y_1 = 0$ if $R_2'(0) < p_1$.

If the firm A takes y_1 as given, it is to its advantage to choose the highest possible value of p_1 (this value is infinitely large if A_1 is not bounded) except when $y_1 = 0$, when p_1 can have any value. Strictly speaking, the only possible non-cooperative equilibria correspond therefore to $y_1 = 0$ and $p_1 \geqslant R_2'(0)$, that is, to zero production of the good in question.

This shows that, when the firm A is choosing p_1, it cannot ignore the possible repercussion of its choice on B's demand. Too high a price eliminates the demand altogether.

It could try to maximise profit on the basis that B fixes y_1 according to (6); it would then behave like a monopolist whose demand is defined by this equation. One can easily show that firm A would then produce the quantity y_1^*, the solution of

$$C_1'(y_1) - y_1 R_2''(y_1) = R_2'(y_1)$$

and sell it at the price $p_1^* = R_2'(y_1^*)$.

But B has basically no reason to behave according to (6) since it knows that it has only A to deal with. For instance, it may refuse to buy the total output y_1^* at price p_1^*, having every reason to believe that this attitude will induce A to lower the price.

Before deciding on its behaviour, it is obviously to the advantage of each firm to discover the other's rule of action. It can do this by putting itself in the other's situation and determining its most profitable course of action.

Thus the two firms must realise, either immediately or after some probing, that it is to their mutual advantage to reach some explicit or implicit agreement acceptable to both. It is then of little importance that in principle the first firm fixes p_1 and the second y_1, since they do this jointly with a view to establishing a satisfactory combination (p_1^0, y_1^0).

What will such a combination be? It appears that it must satisfy the following conditions:

(i) it must lead to a value of W_1 at least equal to $- C_1(0)$, since otherwise A has no interest in any exchange with B;

(ii) it must give a value of W_2 at least equal to $R_2(0)$;

(iii) it must maximise W_1 subject to the constraint that W_2 retains the value W_2^0, since otherwise A could suggest to B a combination more satisfactory to itself, and equally satisfactory to B;

(iv) it must maximise W_2 subject to the constraint that W_1 retains the value W_1^0. To make this more precise, let us first consider (iii).

If $y_1^0 \neq 0$, as we shall assume in order to avoid bringing in the Kuhn-Tucker conditions, then (iii) is expressed by the existence of a number λ such that the derivatives of

$$[p_1 y_1 - C_1(y_1)] + \lambda [R_2(y_1) - p_1 y_1]$$

with respect to p_1 and y_1 are simultaneously zero.

The derivative with respect to p_1 is zero exactly when $\lambda = 1$. Equating to zero the derivative with respect to y_1 then implies

$$C_1'(y_1^0) = R_2'(y_1^0),\tag{7}$$

which determines y_1^0 uniquely since C_1' is increasing and R_2' is decreasing.

We obviously arrive at the same result by considering (iv). Finally it appears that (i) and (ii) fix an interval to which p_1^0 must belong, namely

$$\frac{C_1(y_1^0) - C_1(0)}{y_1^0} \leqslant p_1^0 \leqslant \frac{R_2(y_1^0) - R_2(0)}{y_1^0}.\tag{8}$$

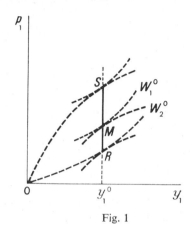

Fig. 1

In short, the combinations (p_1^0, y_1^0) that allow the parties to be in agreement all entail the same production, but price is restricted only to belong to (8). There are usually many such combinations. Their set is said to constitute the *core* of bilateral monopoly.

This set can be represented on a graph with y_1 as abscissa and p_1 as ordinate (cf. Figure 1). Each dotted curve groups the combinations for which W_1, or W_2, has the same given value. The curves $W_1 = $ const. are tangential to the curves $W_2 = $ const. along the vertical with abscissa y_1^0. The core is represented by the interval RS on this vertical, contained between the two curves passing through the origin.

How can p_1 be determined within the interval (8)? Firm A wants the highest price, firm B the lowest price. Within the core, their interests are strictly opposed, and therefore the combination finally established is often said to depend on the respective powers of the two contracting parties.

Each may threaten to disregard the agreement in order to induce the other to accept his demands. But neither has a threat that guarantees him greater gain than he would realise if no exchange took place. So threats are only effective if an agreement is finally obtained.

We conclude this discussion by stating the following conclusions:

(i) non-cooperative equilibrium does not appear to be a useful solution to bilateral monopoly;

(ii) it is to the interest of the parties involved to come to an understanding, so that one of the combinations belonging to the core may be established;

(iii) the use of threats as a means of obtaining a particularly favourable combination involves the risk of disagreement, which may finally result in a combination outside the core.

3. Duopoly

Let us now consider the theory of duopoly, that is, of a market served by two producers, where demand originates from many individually small agents. Economic theory represents this situation under the assumption that the same price will apply to the exchange of all units of the commodity concerned and that demand is competitive in the following sense: the total quantity sold depends on the price of the commodity but on nothing else (buyers' strategy is therefore not involved here).

Let us assume, for convenience, that the market is for the good 1, and that the demand law is decreasing and can be written.

$$p_1 = \pi_1(y_1) \tag{9}$$

as for monopoly. Total production y_1 is realised by the firms 1 and 2 whose outputs are y_{11} and y_{21} respectively.

For this investigation of duopoly, we assume that the prices $p_2, p_3, ..., p_l$ of the other goods are fixed, for example on competitive markets, and that they are independent of p_1 and y_1. Strictly speaking, this can only happen if the good 1 is relatively unimportant so that, in particular, the demands of firms 1 and 2 on the markets for other goods are a negligible part of the market. The function π_1 is obviously defined with reference to the particular values of $p_2, p_3, ..., p_l$.

Let $C_1(y_{11})$ and $C_2(y_{21})$ denote the cost functions of firms 1 and 2. Their respective profits are therefore

$$\begin{cases} W_1(y_{11}, y_{21}) = y_{11}\pi_1(y_{11} + y_{21}) - C_1(y_{11}) \\ W_2(y_{11}, y_{21}) = y_{21}\pi_1(y_{11} + y_{21}) - C_2(y_{21}) \end{cases} \tag{10}$$

The outputs y_{11} and y_{21} appear as the action variables of the two firms, W_1 and W_2 as their respective pay-off functions.

A. Cournot, who first investigated the theory of duopoly, suggested the solution of non-cooperative equilibrium defined in general terms in Section 1 above and which, when applied to duopoly, is known as the *Cournot equilibrium*. This solution assumes that each firm passively observes the other and takes its decision as given, then makes its own decision so as to maximise its gain. The equilibrium is then a pair (y_{11}^0, y_{21}^0) such that y_{11}^0 maximises $W_1(y_{11}, y_{21}^0)$ considered as a function of y_{11}, and y_{21}^0 maximises $W_2(y_{11}^0, y_{21})$ considered as a function of y_{21}.

But it is not at all obvious that, any more than in bilateral monopoly, the firms in this situation will adopt passive attitudes. Figure 2 will make this clear.

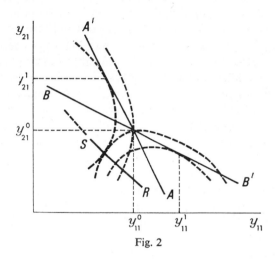

Fig. 2

The curves which are concave downwards represent the contours $W_1 =$ const., the curves which are concave to the left the contours $W_2 =$ const. The curve AA' is the locus of the highest points on the contours $W_1 =$ const. It defines, for each value of y_{21}, the decision of firm 1 if it adopts a passive attitude. Profit W_1 is obviously increasing downwards along a vertical, so that, on a horizontal (y_{21} given), it is to the advantage of firm 1 to choose the point which is tangent to one of the contours $W_1 =$ const. Similarly, the curve BB' joining the points furthest to the right on the contours $W_2 =$ const. defines the decision of firm 2 when it adopts a passive attitude. The Cournot equilibrium is then defined by the point of intersection (y_{11}^0, y_{21}^0) of AA' and BB'.

But firm 1 is usually assumed to know not only its own function W_1 but also its competitor's function W_2. It can then determine BB', which describes the behaviour of firm 2 when the latter is passive. In this situation, it is to the advantage of firm 1 to choose on BB' the point at which it is tangential to a curve $W_1 =$ const., that is, the output y_{11}^1 which in the case of our figure is clearly greater than y_{11}^0.

The firm 1 will probably be aware that it can realise a higher profit than its profit in the Cournot equilibrium. It may therefore decide on the output

6

y_{11}^1, for example. But the same reasoning applies to firm 2, which gains by choosing output y_{21}^1 when it sees that its competitor has a passive attitude. Now, for each producer, the pair (y_{11}^1, y_{21}^1) entails profits that are much lower than those in the Cournot equilibrium.

As in bilateral monopoly, when each participant is aware of the other's situation they must sooner or later reach an explicit or implicit agreement with each other, since only through such an agreement can a struggle damaging to both be avoided, provided that one of them does not think he can eliminate the other from the market. The latter case is excluded here.

What pairs (y_{11}, y_{21}) allow such an agreement to be reached? Those which, in the first place, assign to each firm a profit at least equal to what it would obtain if it withdrew from the market, and which, in the second place, maximise each firm's profit for a given value of the other's profit. These pairs are represented in Figure 2 by the points on the curvilinear segment RS belonging to the curve joining the points of contact of the curves $W_1 = $ const. and the curves $W_2 = $ const., the point R lying on $W_1 = -C_1(0)$ and S on $W_2 = -C_2(0)$. As in bilateral monopoly, the set of pairs represented by the points on RS can be called the *core*.

Within the core, it seems *a priori* that the position of (y_{11}, y_{21}) is indeterminate. Each firm may try to obtain a particularly advantageous combination by threatening not to observe the agreement. But this pays only if the threat does not have to be carried out.

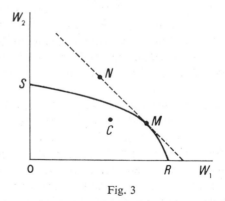

Fig. 3

The realisation of a combination belonging to the core objectifies the agreement between the two firms who do not generally behave, however, as a monopolist would. The latter would try to maximise the total gain $W_1 + W_2$, which in most cases determines a unique pair (y_{11}^*, y_{21}^*) within the core.

This distinction is made clear in Figure 3, where W_1 and W_2 are abscissa and ordinate respectively. The core is represented by RS, which is the right upper boundary of the set of combinations (W_1, W_2) resulting from all the possible choices of y_{11} and y_{21}. (The Cournot equilibrium C is represented by a point which lies inside RS.) The sum $W_1 + W_2$ is maximised for a particular combination M where the tangent to RS is parallel to the second bisector. Now, M is not necessarily equally favourable to both firms; it may very well be rejected by one firm hoping to obtain a more advantageous point on RS.

However, it must be understood that if there is complete collusion between the two firms, they may realise any point on the tangent at M to RS, for example N. They need only agree that one firm should make a direct payment to the other. In the case of our figure, the first pays the second a sum defined by the length of the projection of NM on one or other of the coordinate axes.

Where there is complete collusion, the two firms behave like a single monopolist. The only issue between them is in the division of the total profit, that is, in the discussion of the collateral payment to be made by one to the other. Obviously each can use threats in the course of this discussion, at the risk of breaking the agreement.

4. Coalitions

This examination of the two particular cases of bilateral monopoly and of duopoly has led to conclusions that appear generally valid in any situation where there is a small number of participants. First of all, it is doubtful that a non-cooperative equilibrium will be realised. In the second place, whenever tacit or explicit agreements are made, we can base our reasoning on them, ignoring the action variables proper to each participant; all we are concerned with are the possible combinations of gains at the outcome of the game, which may vary according as collateral payments do or do not enter into consideration.

On the other hand, a common feature of these two cases is that they involve only two players, and therefore every agreement necessarily involves all participants. In a situation where there are three or more agents, coalitions may be formed which group together only some of the agents. *A priori*, the study of such coalitions seems relevant to the clear analysis of the interdependences between the actions of multiple individuals.

Let us first consider the question in general terms before going on to discuss it in the context of the exchange economy.

By definition, a coalition is a subset C of the set I of n players: $I = \{1, 2, ..., n\}$. From the theoretical standpoint it is convenient to keep the term coalition to apply to the whole of I, and also to the set $\{r\}$ consisting of a single player r.

The possibility of coalitions affects the outcome of the game either because only a coalition can achieve a certain result, or because a particular coalition may prevent some other result from being realised. For the discussion of this question, we introduce a simple formulation of the results of the game.

An *imputation* is a set of n real values $(w_1, w_2, ..., w_r, ..., w_s)$ that represents the players' gains at the end of the game. An imputation is 'feasible' if there exists a set of feasible actions of the n players, and, when they are allowed, collateral payments among them, which allow the gains of this imputation to be realised.

Similarly, an imputation $(w_1, w_2, ..., w_n)$ is *feasible for the coalition C* if C can ensure for its members the gains w_r (for $r \in C$), however the players who are not in C may act. We note that an imputation is obviously 'feasible' if it is feasible for a coalition C and is also feasible for the complementary coalition of C.

A coalition may prevent the realisation of a particular imputation if it can procure for its members higher gains than those attributed to them by this imputation. This explains the following formal definition:

The coalition C *blocks the imputation* $(w_1^0, w_2^0, ..., w_n^0)$ if there exists an imputation $(w_1^1, w_2^1, ..., w_n^1)$ that is feasible for C and such that $w_r^1 \geqslant w_r^0$ for every player r of C and $w_r^1 > w_r^0$ for at least one player of C.

Consider, for example, the case of bilateral monopoly, the firm A being player 1 and the firm B player 2. The coalition $\{1\}$ consisting only of player 1 blocks every imputation that assigns to 1 a gain less than $- C_1(0)$; the coalition $\{2\}$ blocks every imputation that assigns to 2 a gain less than $R_2(0)$; the coalition $\{1, 2\}$ formed by the two firms blocks every imputation that does not maximise W_1 for a given value of W_2, or that does not maximise W_2 for a given value of W_1. We see that the core then consists of all the combinations (p_1, y_1) corresponding to imputations that are not blocked by any coalition. We can establish the same for duopoly; hence the following general definition:

The core consists of the set of feasible imputations which are not blocked by any coalition.

The value of this definition derives from the idea that the game should naturally lead to an imputation belonging to the core.

However, there are three situations where this is not the case.

(i) As we saw earlier, the use of threats by some players may destroy the agreements reached and lead to unfavourable results for all the participants.

(ii) When there are more than a few players, the information which each possesses about the situation of the others often becomes very incomplete, and the conclusion of agreements which are fruitful a priori may demand long and costly negotiations. Hence we talk of 'information costs' and 'communication costs', which may sometimes cause the agents to remain with an imputation that does not belong to the core.

(iii) Finally, it may be the case that the core is empty. For every possible imputation there may be a coalition capable of blocking it. We shall not encounter such situations in our discussion of economic theory. However, the fact that they may arise should be borne in mind.†

5. Arbitrage and exchange between individuals

We again turn our attention to general economic models. The introduction of production raises particular problems, which will be referred to at the end of this chapter. So we shall now confine ourselves to the exchange economy defined in Chapter 5. Consumers ($i = 1, 2, ..., m$) are in possession *a priori* of quantities ω_{ih} of the different commodities ($h = 1, 2, ..., l$). Following exchanges, they consume quantities x_{ih} such that each vector x_i belongs to the corresponding set X_i. The vector x_i is the more advantageous the higher the value it gives for the utility function $S_i(x_i)$, which is assumed to be continuous.

We have studied competitive equilibrium in an exchange economy. We can now find the states that are liable to be realised when perfect competition does not necessarily regulate exchanges. Every kind of imperfect competition being permitted *a priori*, we wish to try to discover which states are capable of being established.

We approach this question with no preconceived ideas, as Edgeworth did at the end of the 19th century, and shall follow his line of reasoning.‡ This discussion will help towards a clearer understanding of some aspects of the formation of equilibrium. We shall use part of the terminology adopted by M. Allais for this topic.§

Let there be two individual consumers i and α who own respectively the quantities x_{ih} and $x_{\alpha h}$ of the various goods ($h = 1, 2, ..., l$). These are either the quantities ω_{ih} and $\omega_{\alpha h}$ they owned originally or quantities they have acquired after some exchanges. We assume that they would both benefit from a transaction between them; let z_h denote the quantity of h that i would give to α in this transaction, or $- z_h$ the quantity of the same good given by α to i. Since the operation would be mutually advantageous, $S_i(x_i - z) > S_i(x_i)$ and $S_\alpha(x_\alpha + z) > S_\alpha(z_\alpha)$.

The individuals i and α may be unaware of this possibility of exchange. In this case, any third party who intervenes to enable them to carry out the

---

† For an example of a game with an empty core see Shapley and Shubik, 'Quasi-cores in a Monetary Economy with Nonconvex Preferences', *Econometrica*, October 1966.

‡ Edgeworth, *Mathematical Psychics*, Kegan Paul, London, 1881.

§ Allais, 'Les conditions de l'efficacité dans l'economie'; a paper read to the Rapallo Seminar (Centro Studi e Richerche su Problemi Economico-Sociali) September 1967, parts IV-VI.

operation has the possibility of profiting from it. Since S_i is continuous, there exists a non-zero vector w with no negative component and such that $S_i(x_i - z - w) > S_i(x_i)$. So the three individuals will benefit from a transaction where the quantities of h in their possession will vary by $- (z_h + w_h)$ for i, by z_h for α and by w_h for the middle-man. Such a transaction is called an *arbitrage*.

In the above example, two consumers are involved in the possibility of exchange; this is bilateral arbitrage. In the same way, we can conceive of multilateral arbitrage where the possible exchange involves several consumers. The middleman in the arbitrage is able to profit by it. In what follows, we shall assume either that he is himself one of the agents or that his deducted proceeds w_h are sufficiently small to be ignored.

Here we shall use the term '*stable allocation*' for a state in which no further arbitrage, bilateral or multilateral, is possible; all market dealings are concluded and there is no further possibility of exchange. Obviously there is no reason for such a state to coincide with a competitive equilibrium.

A stable allocation E^0 as thus defined is clearly a distribution optimum. Otherwise there exists another feasible state E^1 preferred by one consumer and judged at least equally good by all the others. To say that E^1 is feasible is equivalent to saying that passage from E^0 to E^1 constitutes an exchange. The possibility of arbitrage (perhaps involving all the consumers) therefore exists. This is contrary to the fact that E^0 is a stable allocation.†

The notion of arbitrage can also be used to describe the process of exchange. If the initial situation, with each consumer owning quantities ω_{ih} is not a stable allocation, certain exchanges and arbitrages take place. The quantities owned by the different individuals are therefore changed as often as necessary for the realisation of a stable allocation. The utility functions S_i cannot decrease during these exchanges. If we also assume that no advantageous possibility remains ignored indefinitely‡ then the process in question is convergent.§

---

† In the definition of arbitrage, strict inequalities have been set for the comparisons of utility levels. If the exchange consisting of going from E^0 to E^1 implies some equalities, small modifications can be made in E^1 and thus a state E^2 can be defined such that all utilities increase in the passage from E^0 to E^2. This possibility is guaranteed by the fact that the functions S_i are continuous and that they can increase in the neighbourhood of E^0 (needs are not completely satiated).

‡ As in the discussion of the core, we assume here that, in the first place, information is sufficiently well transmitted that an informed middleman always exists to undertake an arbitrage, and, in the second place, that no agent absolutely rejects a transaction that is to his advantage, as he might do after having put forward demands unacceptable to the others.

§ It is left to the reader to formulate and prove this property. For a very similar approach to that used here, see Hahn and Negishi, 'A Theorem on Non-Tâtonnement Stability', *Econometrica*, July 1962.

However, the theory as thus constructed is not very specific; it is compatible with multiple paths to a stable allocation. This is illustrated for example by Figure 4, applying to the case of two goods and two agents and assumed to have been constructed within an Edgeworth diagram. *PR* and *PS* are the indifference curves passing through *P*, the point of initial resources. *RS* is the locus of Pareto optima. A path implying three exchanges has been shown (P to E^1, E^1 to E^2, E^2 to E^0). Each exchange improves the utilities of the two consumers. But there are many other possible paths and the final state can be represented by any point within *RS*.

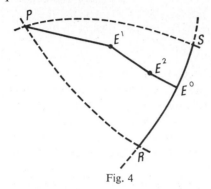

Fig. 4

6. The core in the exchange economy

The segment *RS* in Figure 4 recalls similar segments in Figures 1 and 2. So we may ask if the set of stable allocations does not define a 'core', similar in conception to that introduced by the theory of games.

This is not a purely formal question, since the exchange economy has the same basic nature as a game: in the context of certain constraints, the agents choose actions or strategies which, when taken together, result finally in utility levels S_i, which are completely analogous to the pay-offs W_r in the theory of games.

Of course, we should find it hard to give a formal description of the initial actions of the parties to an exchange—approaches, propositions, counter-propositions, etc. The concept of a 'transaction', which implies an agreement between two parties, is likely to be more fruitful. But this is relatively unimportant. By far the largest part of the theory of games can be built up without reference to the initial actions of the players. It is sufficient to determine the sets of feasible imputations for each of the coalitions.

In the exchange economy, the imputations are the utility levels which result from the consumption vectors. We can therefore reason directly on the basis of the concepts of 'state' or 'allocation': the set of m vectors x_i. The general definitions given previously can easily be transposed.

A coalition is a subset C of the set of m consumers. The state E^0 is feasible for the coalition C if:

$$x_i^0 \in X_i \qquad \text{for} \qquad i \in C \tag{11}$$

$$\sum_{i \in C} (x_{ih}^0 - \omega_{ih}) = 0 \qquad \text{for} \qquad h = 1, 2, ..., l. \tag{12}$$

Conditions (11) and (12) guarantee that it is possible for the members of C acting in common, independently of those who do not belong to C, to obtain the x_i^0.

A state E^0 is 'feasible' if it is feasible for the coalition comprising all the consumers. The feasible state E^0 is 'blocked by the coalition C' if there exists a state E^1 that is feasible for C and is such that:

$$S_i(x_i^1) \geqslant S_i(x_i^0) \qquad \text{for} \qquad i \in C, \tag{13}$$

where the inequality holds strictly for at least one consumer in C. Condition (13) guarantees that the x_i^1 are preferable to the x_i^0 for the members of C.

The 'core' of the exchange economy is naturally the set of feasible states E which are not blocked by any coalition. We can immediately establish for it the following two properties:

PROPOSITION 1. Every state E belonging to the core is a distribution optimum.

If, in fact, a feasible state E is not an optimum, then it is blocked by the coalition of all consumers.

PROPOSITION 2. If the X_i and the S_i satisfy assumptions 1 and 2 of Chapter 2, then every competitive equilibrium E^0 belongs to the core.

For, let p be the price vector corresponding to E^0. Suppose that there exists a coalition blocking E^0. The inequalities (13), of which at least one holds strictly, and the consumers' rule of behaviour then imply:

$$\sum_{i \in C} (px_i^1 - p\omega_i) > 0$$

(the detail of the proof is exactly the same as for proposition 2 of Chapter 4, relating to the optimality of market equilibria). The above inequality contradicts (12), which must be satisfied by E^1 for the existence of C.

Thus propositions 1 and 2 establish that the core is contained in the set of all the distribution optima, but it contains the unique or multiple competitive equilibria.

We can again consider the graphical representation of the core in the case of only two goods and two consumers (see Figure 5, constructed like an Edgeworth graph).

We know that the core is represented by a part of MN, on which lie the distribution optima, that is, the points where the two consumers' indifference curves are mutually tangential. The states represented by points outside MN are just those blocked by the coalition $\{1, 2\}$. The states blocked by the coalition $\{1\}$ are represented by the points on the left of the indifference curve $\mathcal{S}_1^*$ passing through the point P representing the initial distribution of resources between the consumers. Similarly, the states blocked by the coalition $\{2\}$ are represented by the points on the right of the indifference curve $\mathcal{S}_2^*$ passing through P. So finally, the core is the part RS of MN, from the point R of intersection with $\mathcal{S}_1^*$ to the point S of intersection with $\mathcal{S}_2^*$. We see that the competitive equilibrium point M, where the common tangent to two indifference curves passes through P, belongs to the core.

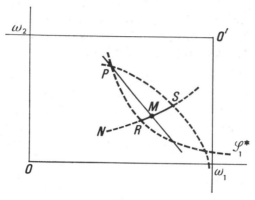

Fig. 5

The similarity between Figure 5 and Figures 1 or 2 shows that we could go on to discuss the exchange of two infinitely divisible commodities between two consumers along the same lines as we discussed bilateral monopoly and duopoly. But enough has already been said about this kind of question.

In the diagram, the set of stable allocations coincides with the core except for the bounding points R and S (but this difference results from a different treatment of the inequalities). We can easily understand the reason for this. Every allocation that does not belong to the core defines a state in which, by hypothesis, there is a possibility of arbitrage. Conversely, every state E^0 of the core (with the exception of R and S) is a stable allocation for the economy in question since to go from the initial state P to E^0 is an advantageous arbitrage, and, once E^0 is reached, no possibility of arbitrage exists.

Is this coincidence general? We shall see that it does not apply to cases of more than two agents because of a difference in point of view for the process through which equilibrium is realised. Let us start by considering a particular case.

Suppose that there are two goods and three agents who initially possess the resources defined by the following vectors:

$$\omega_1 = \begin{bmatrix} 0 \\ 2 \end{bmatrix}, \qquad \omega_2 = \begin{bmatrix} 1 \\ 1 \end{bmatrix}, \qquad \omega_3 = \begin{bmatrix} 1 \\ 1 \end{bmatrix}. \tag{14}$$

We assume that the three agents have identical preferences represented by the utility function

$$S_i(x_i) = x_{i1}x_{i2} \qquad (x_{ih} \geqslant 0). \tag{15}$$

The following two exchanges define a possible path to a stable allocation:

(i) Agents 1 and 2 conclude a transaction in terms of which the second gives 1/4 of good 1 while the first gives 3/2 of good 2. The utility of the first goes from 0 to 1/8, while the second's goes from 1 to 15/8. The quantities in their possession after the exchange are

$$x_1 = \begin{bmatrix} 1/4 \\ 1/2 \end{bmatrix}, \qquad x_2 = \begin{bmatrix} 3/4 \\ 5/2 \end{bmatrix}, \qquad x_3 = \begin{bmatrix} 1 \\ 1 \end{bmatrix}. \tag{16}$$

(ii) Agents 2 and 3 then conclude a transaction in terms of which 3 gives 1/4 of the first good while 2 gives 1/2 of the second good. The utility of 2 goes from 15/8 to 2, and that of 3 from 1 to 9/8. The quantities finally in the possession of the agents are:

$$x_1^0 = \begin{bmatrix} 1/4 \\ 1/2 \end{bmatrix}, \qquad x_2^0 = \begin{bmatrix} 1 \\ 2 \end{bmatrix}, \qquad x_3^0 = \begin{bmatrix} 3/4 \\ 3/2 \end{bmatrix}. \tag{17}$$

We could check that this resulting state E^0 is a stable allocation; it is also a distribution optimum with which we can associate the prices $p_1 = 2, p_2 = 1$. Under our definitions, the state E^0 does not belong to the core since it is blocked by the coalition $\{1, 3\}$. If they combine their initial resources defined by (14), these two agents can realise the allocation

$$x_1^* = \begin{bmatrix} 1/4 \\ 1 \end{bmatrix}, \qquad x_3^* = \begin{bmatrix} 3/4 \\ 2 \end{bmatrix} \tag{18}$$

which is clearly better for them than that defined by (17).

As this example shows, the difference between a core and a set of stable allocations does not lie in the distinction between two methods of approach using the central notions of 'arbitrage' and 'coalition' respectively. Arbitrage can be defined as the operation by which a coalition goes from one allocation to another which is better for its members. The difference lies in the description of the process by which exchanges are carried out.

The idea that the chosen allocation must belong to the core makes the implicit assumption that no operation is concluded which leads to a state outside the core, or that any operation of this type which is concluded can be rescinded in favour of others. Edgeworth introduced the assumption that agents are free to *recontract*, that is, that the contracts agreed at the start of the exchanging process can always be annulled later if more advantageous contracts appear. In our example, agent 1, who initially agreed to the exchange leading to (16) would be free to reverse this decision when agent 3 suggests the more advantageous exchange leading to (18).

A priori, the assumption that contracts are not binding until a state belonging to the core is reached does not appear at all realistic. But it must not be taken too literally. Its meaning is rather that the agents do not commit themselves definitely before they have explored the various contracts that may be offered to them. In fact, looking at the data in our example, we cannot but feel that it is equally unrealistic to assume that agent 1 commits himself definitely to the exchange (i) with agent 2 on such relatively unfavourable terms.

The possibility of recontracting assumed by Edgeworth and by the theory of games is basically similar to Walras' assumption of tâtonnement where contracts are not concluded until equilibrium prices are reached. It assumes that there is a high degree of concerted action among agents, and therefore the theory to which it leads is relatively specific.†

If this possibility is rejected, the stable allocations that can be realised from a given initial situation appear very indeterminate, particularly in economies with a large number of agents. Of course, we know that such an allocation is an optimum and is preferred to the initial situation by each agent for whom it differs from the initial situation. But nothing more precise can be said on the basis of general logical analysis. So, as always, we must choose between the unrestrictive but unspecific theory of stable allocations and the more specific but more restrictive theory of the core.

However, we must again take note here that, if there is a large number of agents, information costs and communication costs may make it ·difficult to discover an allocation belonging to the core. To assume that the state finally chosen is an element of the core is to assume solution of the problem of optimality with which a large part of microeconomic theory is concerned.‡

---

† It may be mentioned here that Walras' assumption has been rejected by some researchers into dynamic processes for an economy where there exist prices known by all the agents, and where definite contracts are concluded between some buyers and sellers before equilibrium prices are determined. These have been called 'non-tâtonnement' processes. See Negishi, 'The Stability of a Competitive Economy; a Survey Article', *Econometrica*, October 1962.

‡ Another useful concept has been introduced in this kind of theory by L. S. Shapley and later developed by Shapley and Shubik (see for instance, *International Economic Review*, October 1969). Let us consider the contribution $g_r(C)$ that individual r will make to the gain of any coalition C into which he would be entering. For any C not containing r, the contribution is equal to the gain achieved by $C \cup \{r\}$ minus that achieved by C alone. (The definition of this contribution is easy when gains are transferable from one individual to another so that the aggregate gain of a coalition makes sense; it may also be made precise when gains are not transferable.) The *value* of what r will eventually get is taken by Shapley as being equal to a properly defined average $\bar{g}_r$ of $g_r(C)$ over the set of all coalitions not containing him. In the game or exchange situation under consideration this average would correspond to a natural measure of the power of the individual r, a measure that would be accepted by him and by others as well, so that a general consensus could be achieved to the effect that he should get precisely $\bar{g}_r$.

In the last two sections we confined ourselves for simplicity to exchange economies. The concepts introduced and discussed can be generalised in various ways to an economy containing producers. The difficulty stems from the fact that profit maximisation is no longer suitable as a criterion of choice for producers since they no longer consider prices as given. The theory must therefore specify how decisions are taken in firms. It is certainly natural to assume that consumers control the firms. But *a priori*, there are various conceivable ways in which this control and its implications may be specified. The simplest is to assume that each firm is the property of a single consumer who is in full control of it and may use its net output either for his consumption or for the exchanges in which he becomes engaged.

Given this personalisation of firms, the theories of the last two sections can be generalised in a very natural way.

Economies with an infinite number of agents

1. 'Atomless' economies

We have so far been arguing on the basis of a general model which can have any number of agents. In particular, the theories of the optimum and of competitive equilibrium have been established without restriction on the integers m and n representing the number of consumers and the number of producers respectively. For simplicity, some of the examples chosen for discussion involved only two agents.

In fact, modern societies are made up of a very large number of individuals, and it is this multiplicity that explains the complexity of the problems raised by the organisation of production and distribution. Economic science must pay great attention to this complexity, which enforces the search for original solutions that are very different from those in technological sciences. In order to appreciate the relevance of the results given in previous chapters, the student must therefore consider them in relation to concrete situations where there are very many consumers and producers.

In addition, we must see whether the multiplicity of agents leads to new results which do not hold for more restricted communities. When m and n are very large, the model has a particular nature, not so far allowed for, which may prove interesting.

In fact we shall see that, under certain conditions, the assumptions of convexity adopted in the previous chapters lose their usefulness, and this obviously increases the validity of optimum theory. Similarly, we shall be able to give precise content to the classical idea that perfect competition tends naturally to be achieved when there is a large number of agents each of whom individually represents only a small part of the market. Finally we shall consider again from a new viewpoint some questions concerning imperfect competition.

For our present purposes we shall give the elements of theories whose complete proofs are too heavy to be included in this course of lectures. However, it is hoped that the origin and the nature of the results will become clear enough.

The name *atomistic economies* has been given to those containing many consumers and producers, none of whom is of sufficient weight for his decisions to have a perceptible effect on general equilibrium. Modern technical literature speaks of *atomless economies*. In spite of appearances, these two expressions mean the same, since the first refers to the fact that there is a very large number of units which individually are small, and the second to the fact that no unit is an undissociable entity of appreciable size relative to the whole. If actual economies do not satisfy these abstract conditions, then this is essentially because of the presence of large firms which are naturally in a situation of imperfect competition. The discussion that follows will then apply fairly well to consumers and to branches of industry where the number of firms is large (M. Allais' differentiated sector); on the other hand, it may have little relevance to sectors where there is a very large degree of concentration. This should be borne in mind.

Let us now examine a mathematical formulation of the atomless economy. Suppose that consumers and producers are grouped into categories so that all individuals in the same category are identical.

Changing our previous notation slightly, we let i denote a particular category of consumers and assume that there are m such categories ($i = 1, 2, ..., m$). A particular consumer in the ith category is now denoted by the double index (i, q) (where $q = 1, 2, ..., r_i$). Similarly j denotes a category of producers ($j = 1, 2, ..., n$) while (j, t) refers to a producer in this category (where $t = 1, 2, ..., s_j$).

The economy can then be defined as follows:

(i) The (i, q)th consumer has a consumption set X_i and a utility function $S_i(x_{iq})$ which, by hypothesis, depend only on the category to which he belongs. Similarly, if consumers have incomes that are fixed exogenously or if they own certain primary resources, then the corresponding numbers R_i or vectors ω_i are identical for all individuals in the same category.

(ii) The (j, t)th producer has a production set Y_j or a production function $f_j(y_{jt})$ which, by hypothesis, depend only on the category j to which he belongs.

The numbers r_i and s_j of individuals composing the different categories are large, since we are dealing with an atomistic economy. In fact, *the results which we shall discuss are valid only in the limit when the number of agents tends to infinity*. Therefore r_i and s_j will tend to infinity. For simplicity, we shall also assume that this tendency is uniform in all categories, for example that the r_i and s_j are all equal to the same number r, which tends to infinity.†

---

† Obviously there are other possible mathematical formulations of atomless economies. For example, recent researches assume that the agents form a continuum on which a measure is defined. The assumption that the agents are identical within certain categories is then replaced by another which can roughly be described as follows: 'We can find as many agents as we want who differ as little as we want from any given agent α, except perhaps for a negligible proportion of agents α'.

2. Convexities

In economies as thus defined, the assumptions of convexity become pointless for welfare theory as well as for competitive equilibrium theory. This becomes clear if we consider groups of identical agents and substitute for individual sets or individual preferences, which may be non-convex,† group sets or preferences which are necessarily convex. The group activity is then represented by a vector that is the arithmetic mean of the vectors representing the activities of the agents who make up the group.

The meaning of this substitution will become clear if we consider in succession the three mathematical entities on which convexity assumptions have been introduced for the proof of certain properties: the consumption sets X_i, production sets Y_j and utility functions S_i.

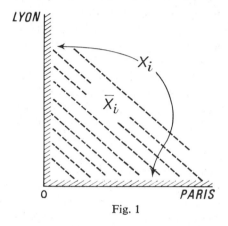

Fig. 1

Suppose first that the set X_i, to which the consumption vector x_{iq} of the agents (i, q) must belong, is not convex. *A priori*, this may be any set; in particular, *it may consist of a discrete collection of points* if the quantities x_{iqh} must be given as integral numbers of units. In fact, the absence of convexity may signify the absence of divisibility. (Figure 1 reproduces Figure 6 of Chapter 2 and applies to the case of two locations, where the consumer is free to choose his domicile but must carry out all his consumption in the same place.)

Then let the mean consumption vector x_i for consumers in the ith category be given by,

$$x_{ih} = \frac{1}{r_i} \sum_{q=1}^{r_i} x_{iqh} \qquad h = 1, 2, ..., l. \tag{1}$$

---

† Here we mean that preferences are convex if the corresponding utility functions are quasi-concave.

The fact that the x_{iq} belong to X_i imposes on x_i only one condition, namely that x_i must belong to the set $\overline{X}_i$, the *convex hull*† of X_i .Formula (1) shows that x_i belongs to $\overline{X}_i$. Conversely, every vector of $\overline{X}_i$ corresponds to feasible average consumptions for the consumers in the ith category, provided that the latter is infinitely large.

For, consider any vector x_i of $\overline{X}_i$. By hypothesis, there exist non-negative numbers λ^s whose sum is 1 and vectors x_i^s belonging to X_i such that

$$x_i = \sum_{s=1}^{\sigma} \lambda^s x_i^s. \tag{2}$$

The vector x_i can therefore be realised in the ith category if the activity of a proportion λ^s of the consumers in this category is defined by the vector x_i^s, for $s = 1, 2, ..., \sigma$.

The proportion λ^s is realisable, at least in the limit as r_i tends to infinity. To verify this, let us write r instead of r_i. For every value of r we define σ integers m_r^s such that $|m_r^s - r\lambda^s| < 1$ and the sum of the m_r^s is equal to r. (To define the m_r^s we need only consider the integral parts n_r^s of the $r\lambda^s$. The difference between r and their sum n_r is integral and less than the number of indices for which $r\lambda^s$ is not integral. We can then take $m_r^s = n_r^s + 1$ for $r - n_r$ of these indices and $m_r^s = n_r^s$ for all the other s.) Consider the mean vector $x_i^{(r)}$ obtained for the category when x_i^s is attributed to m_r^s consumers ($s = 1, 2, ..., \sigma$). We can find directly:

$$|x_{ih}^{(r)} - x_{ih}| = \left| \sum_{s=1}^{\sigma} \left(\frac{1}{r} m_r^s - \lambda^s \right) x_{ih}^s \right| \leqslant \sum_{s=1}^{\sigma} \left| \frac{1}{r} m_r^s - \lambda^s \right| \cdot |x_{ih}^s|.$$

As r tends to infinity, $|(1/r)m_r^s - \lambda^s|$, which is less than $1/r$, tends to zero. Consequently $|x_{ih}^{(r)} - x_{ih}|$ also tends to zero. The vector x_i of $\overline{X}_i$ can therefore always be considered as the limit of a sequence $\{x_i^{(r)}\}$ of feasible mean vectors for the ith category (as r tends to infinity).

Now, the set $\overline{X}_i$, the convex hull of X_i, is necessarily convex.‡ To the extent that we can reason directly on the basis of the mean consumption vectors for the various categories, it becomes pointless to assume convexity of the X_i.

---

† By definition, the convex hull $\overline{A}$ of a set A of R^l is the set of all the elements a of R^l which can be written in the form:

$$a = \sum_{s=1}^{\sigma} \lambda^s a^s,$$

where the λ^s are positive numbers whose sum is 1 and the a^s are elements of A.

‡ In general, let a and b be two vectors:

$$a = \sum_{s=1}^{\sigma} \lambda^s a^s, \qquad b = \sum_{t=1}^{\tau} \mu^t b^t,$$

of the convex hull $\overline{A}$ of a set A to which the a^s and the b^t belong, the λ^s and the μ^t being

The same reasoning can be applied to the production set Y_j of a branch where there is an infinitely large number of firms. If this set is not convex, it can be replaced by its convex hull $\overline{Y}_j$ which is necessarily convex. (Figure 2 represents an example of two goods. The set $\overline{Y}_j$ comprises the dotted area beyond Y_j. The vector y_j^0, which belongs to $\overline{Y}_j$ but is outside Y_j, may be realised, with two thirds of the firms having zero activity and the activity of the remaining third being represented by the vector y_j^1 of Y_j.

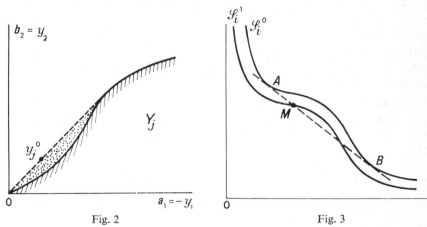

Fig. 2   Fig. 3

Consider now the case of a non-quasi-concave utility function S_i (cf. Figure 3). Can we associate with it another function $\overline{S}_i$ which is quasi-concave and represents the preferences of the ith category among the various *mean* consumption vectors which can be attributed to this category? In fact, it is possible to do so if we make the following two fairly natural assumptions:

(i) In the ith category, goods are so distributed that the utility function $S_i(x_{iq})$ has the same value for all the consumers q. (To make this assumption tenable, we may have to break up the category i into smaller sub-categories.)

(ii) Within the ith category goods are efficiently distributed in the sense that a redistribution cannot be favourable to one consumer without being unfavourable to at least one other consumer; a distribution optimum is realised in the category.

We now ask the question: what is the set of mean consumption vectors x_i in R^l which ensure to the individual consumers a utility level at least equal

positive numbers whose sums are respectively 1. Also let α and β be any two positive numbers whose sum is 1. The vector $\alpha a + \beta b$ necessarily belongs to $\overline{A}$ since we can write it

$$\sum_{s=1}^{\sigma} \alpha\lambda^s a^s + \sum_{t=1}^{\tau} \beta\mu^t b^t,$$

with the $\sigma + \tau$ vectors a^s and b^t of A and the numbers $\alpha\lambda^s$ and $\beta\mu^t$, all positive, whose general sum is 1.

to a given value S_i^0? These are the vectors x_i to which correspond some x_{iq} satisfying (1) and such that

$$S_i(x_{iq}) \geqslant S_i^0. \tag{3}$$

Let U_i^0 be the set of the x_{iq} satisfying (3). We come back to a similar problem to that encountered for X_i. The only difference is that X_i is replaced by U_i^0. So we can conclude that the required set of x_i's is the convex hull $\overline{U}_i^0$ of U_i^0, provided that there is an infinitely large number of consumers in the ith category. (In Figure 3, U_i^0 is the set of vectors on or above the indifference curve $\mathscr{S}_i^0$. The point M belonging to the convex hull of U_i^0 although below $\mathscr{S}_i^0$ ensures the utility level S_i^0 to the consumers if the mean consumptions to which it corresponds are distributed between two subgroups of consumers so that the activity vectors of these subgroups are represented by A and B.)

In short, to the function S_i we can find a corresponding family of sets such as U_i^0. The family of convex hulls $\overline{U}_i^0$ of the U_i^0 defines a system of preferences, which we can represent by a new utility function $\overline{S}_i$ that is necessarily quasi-concave.[†] This function can be chosen so as to coincide with S_i for every vector x_i which, uniformly attributed to the consumers of i, realises a distribution optimum in the ith category; $\overline{S}_i$ is then greater than S_i for those vectors x_i that do not satisfy the latter condition.

3. The theory of the optimum

We shall now briefly discuss welfare theory, in order to see how the above concepts apply. The assumption of convexity was necessary for the proof that every optimum is a market equilibrium, but not, as we recall, for the converse property. In an atomistic economy we can dispense with the assumption completely.

Consider a Pareto optimum E^0 in which all agents in the same category act identically; the vector x_{iq}^0 does not depend on q and can be written x_i^0, while the vector y_{jt}^0 does not depend on t and can be written y_j^0. This assumption may require the subdivision of some of the initial categories, but this is obviously no inconvenience. For simplicity, we also assume that there is the same number of agents in each category ($r_i = s_j = r$). *Without adopting the assumption of convexity for the sets X_i and Y_j or for the functions S_i, we can show that the optimum E_0 is a market equilibrium, at least when r can be considered as infinitely large.*

[†] Assumption 4 of Chapter 2 stipulates that S_i is *strictly* quasi-concave. Given two vectors x^0 and x^1 such that $S_i(x^0) \leqslant S_i(x^1)$, it implies that $S_i(x) > S_i(x^0)$ for every vector x within the segment $[x^0, x^1]$. Ordinary quasi-concavity however implies only that $S_i(x) \geqslant S_i(x^0)$. Only this weaker property holds for $\overline{S}_i$. However, it is sufficient for a certain number of properties, in particular for those relating to the optimum.

In fact, we can associate with the economy under study an imaginary economy comprising m consumers and n producers each representing a particular category. By hypothesis, the ith consumer of the imaginary economy has an activity vector x_i corresponding to a feasible mean consumption vector for the ith category; therefore x_i must belong to the convex hull $\overline{X}_i$ of X_i. Similarly the jth producer has a vector y_j corresponding to feasible average net output vectors for the jth category, and therefore belonging to the convex hull $\overline{Y}_j$ of Y_j. In addition, the ith consumer has a utility function $\overline{S}_i$, necessarily quasi-concave, constructed as was shown earlier. Finally, the primary resources vector of the imaginary economy is ω/r. (It is permissible for us to assume that ω increases with r so that the ratio ω/r remains constant as r tends to infinity.)

To the state E^0 of the initial economy there obviously corresponds a state $\overline{E}^0$ of the imaginary economy; the latter is defined by the vectors x_i^0 and y_j^0. We can establish that this is a Pareto optimum for the imaginary economy.

In fact it is a feasible state since x_i^0 belongs to X_i, which is contained in $\overline{X}_i$. Similarly y_j^0 belongs to Y_j contained in $\overline{Y}_j$. Finally, the equilibrium between resources and uses in the initial economy can be written

$$\omega + r \sum_j y_j^0 = \omega + \sum_j \sum_t y_{jt}^0 = \sum_i \sum_q x_{iq}^0 = r \sum_i x_i^0, \tag{4}$$

or

$$\frac{\omega}{r} + \sum_j y_j^0 = \sum_i x_i^0, \tag{5}$$

which expresses equilibrium between resources and uses in the imaginary economy.

Moreover, no feasible state $\overline{E}^1$ preferable to $\overline{E}^0$ exists for this economy, since this would imply a feasible state E^1, preferable to E^0, for the initial economy, contrary to our original assumption. For, let x_i^1 and y_j^1 be the activity vectors defined by $\overline{E}^1$; since they belong to their respective sets $\overline{X}_i$ and $\overline{Y}_j$, there are corresponding vectors x_{iq}^1 and y_{jt}^1 belonging to the X_i and Y_j, such that, in the limit for infinitely large r,

$$\frac{1}{r} \sum_q x_{iq}^1 = x_i^1, \qquad \frac{1}{r} \sum_t y_{jt}^1 = y_j^1. \tag{6}$$

The x_{qt}^1 can be chosen so that

$$S_i(x_{iq}^1) \geqslant S_i^0 = S_i(x_i^0), \tag{7}$$

since this is just what the assumption that

$$\overline{S}_i(x_i^1) \geqslant \overline{S}_i(x_i^0) = S_i^0 \tag{8}$$

implies. (Since E^0 is a Pareto optimum, the $x_{iq}^0 = x_i^0$ define a distribution optimum in the ith category, so that $\overline{S}_i(x_i^0) = S_i(x_i^0)$). Since at least one of the inequalities (8) holds strictly, we can deduce that at least one of the inequalities (7) also holds strictly. (For brevity, we omit the proof of this.) To verify that E^1, preferred to E^0, is also feasible, we now need only to examine the equilibrium of resources and uses. We see immediately that E^1 is feasible, since an equation similar to (5) holds for $\bar{E}^1$ and, in view of (6), an equation similar to (4) then holds for E^1.

Since $\bar{E}^0$ is optimal in the imaginary economy where the required convexity assumptions are satisfied by $\bar{X}_i$, $\bar{Y}_j$ and S_i, there corresponds to $\bar{E}^0$ a price-vector p such that:

(i) the vector x_i^0 maximises $\bar{S}_i(x_i)$ in $\bar{X}_i$ subject to the constraint $px_i \leqslant px_i^0$ (for $i = 1, 2, ..., m$);

(ii) the vector y_j^0 maximises py_j in $\bar{Y}_j$ (for $j = 1, 2, ..., n$).

We can deduce that E^0 and p also define a market equilibrium in the initial economy; that is,

(i′) the vector x_i^0 maximises $S_i(x_{iq})$ in X_i subject to the constraint $px_{iq} \leqslant px_i^0$ (for all i and all q);

(ii′) the vector y_j^0 maximises py_{jt} in Y_j (for all j and all t).

Let us verify by *reductio ad absurdum* that, for example, (i) implies (i′). If there exists a vector x_{iq}^2 of X_i such that $S_i(x_{iq}^2) > S_i(x_i^0)$ and $px_{iq}^2 \leqslant px_i^0$, we can set $x_i^2 = x_{iq}^2$ and note that x_i^2 belongs to $\bar{X}_i$, and that it satisfies

$$px_i^2 \leqslant px_i^0$$

and

$$\bar{S}_i(x_i^2) \geqslant S_i(x_i^2) > S_i(x_i^0) = \bar{S}_i(x_i^0),$$

which is contrary to (i).

4. Perfect competition in atomless economies

It has long been thought that competitive imperfections tend naturally to disappear in atomistic economies. When they are numerous and individually small, agents could not achieve a better situation than their situation in competitive equilibrium; competitive behaviour would become completely rational for consumers and producers, and no other measures would be necessary except those intended to facilitate the exchange of information and communication between agents. This idea has recently been given a rigorous formulation, which we shall discuss in relation to the *exchange economy*.†
In the following section we shall consider the notions of 'collusion' and 'free entry', which have also some bearing on the present problem.

---

† We shall essentially follow the presentation of this problem by Debreu and Scarf in 'A Limit Theorem on the Core of an Economy', *International Economic Review*, September 1963.

For this discussion, we must obviously investigate competitive equilibria in a model that does not assume *a priori* that perfect competition has been realised. The general concepts of games theory will be our frame of reference.

As we saw in the previous chapter, the 'core', the set of feasible states not blocked by any coalition, must contain the state that will be realised provided that the agents can exchange information and negotiate without cost, assuming also they do not carry out the threats that can be made during the bargaining process. We shall now show that the core tends to be identified with the set of competitive equilibria when the number of agents tends to infinity.

To the previous assumptions relating to the similarity of consumers within categories, we now add the assumption that the vector of the initial resources owned by the agent (i, q) depends only on the category to which he belongs, and is therefore denoted simply by ω_i. For simplicity, we also assume that the *utility functions S_i are strictly quasi-concave and increasing* (quasi-concavity, but not strict quasi-concavity, can be deduced from the fact that there is an infinite number of consumers).

Under these conditions, *every state belonging to the core contains exactly the same consumption vector x_i^0 for all the consumers in the same category i.* To establish this property, we shall consider some feasible state E and let $\underline{x}_i$ denote that vector among the x_{iq} of E ($q = 1, 2, ..., r$) which gives the smallest value of S_i, or any vector of the x_{iq} which minimises S_i, if there are several. It follows that

$$S_i(\underline{x}_i) \leqslant S_i(x_{iq}) \qquad q = 1, 2, ..., r$$

and, in view of the properties assumed for S_i,

$$S_i(\underline{x}_i) \leqslant S_i\left[\frac{1}{r}\sum_{q=1}^{r} x_{iq}\right] \tag{9}$$

where the inequality holds strictly if at least two of the x_{iq} are distinct. Moreover, since E is feasible,

$$\sum_{i=1}^{m}\left[\frac{1}{r}\sum_{q=1}^{r} x_{iq} - \omega_i\right] = 0. \tag{10}$$

Consider the coalition C consisting of m consumers, one from each category, the consumer from the ith category being the one, or one of those, that receive $\underline{x}_i$ in E. If there are two distinct x_{iq}'s in the same category, then C blocks E since, in view of (10), C can attribute the consumption $1/r \sum_q x_{iq}$ to its ith member and in view of (9), this consumption is never less, and sometimes more advantageous than $\underline{x}_i$. Therefore the state E can belong to the core only if all the x_{iq} in the same category are equal.

In short, to represent a state in the core, we need only, for any r, specify m vectors x_i each corresponding to the consumption vectors attributed to all the individuals in the same category. Since this is a feasible state, we must have

$$\sum_{i=1}^{m} (x_i - \omega_i) = 0. \tag{11}$$

In this representation we no longer have to involve the consumers individually.

It is now almost obvious that if, when $r = r^0$, m vectors x_i^0 define a state in the core, then when $r = r^0 - 1$, these vectors also define a state belonging to the core (which we again denote by E^0). Otherwise, for $r = r^0 - 1$, there exists a coalition C blocking E^0; then for $r = r^0$, the same coalition exists and blocks E^0. We can therefore say that *the core for r^0 is contained in the core for $r^0 - 1$*.

The property we are aiming at can now be stated as follows: if assumptions 2 and 4 of Chapter 2 are satisfied, *a state which belongs to the core for all r is a competitive equilibrium*.

This property will first be illustrated by the particular case of two goods and two categories of consumers.†

We can return to Figure 4 in Chapter 6 where the elements relating to the first category of consumers are given with reference to the system of axes centred on O, and those related to the second are given with reference to the system centred on O'. Assuming that M is the only competitive equilibrium point, we must show that, for every other point E^1 there exists a value r^1 of r and a coalition C blocking E^1 in the economy where $r = r^1$. We can obviously confine ourselves to a point on the arc RS representing the core when $r = 1$. Every point outside RS is already blocked when $r = 1$.

Then let E^1 be a point on RS, let $\mathscr{S}_1^1$ and $\mathscr{S}_2^1$ be indifference curves passing through E^1 and let the point P represent the distribution of initial resources. The line PE^1 contains points on the right of $\mathscr{S}_1^1$ and on the left of $\mathscr{S}_2^1$, otherwise E^1 becomes a competitive equilibrium. Suppose, for example, that PE^1 cuts $\mathscr{S}_1^1$ at a point Q lying between P and E^1.

Consider now a coalition C comprising m_1 consumers from category 1 and m_2 consumers from category 2. Suppose that such a coalition attributes the consumption vector x_1 to its category 1 members and x_2 to its category 2 members. It can do this only if these vectors satisfy the equality between global resources and uses within the coalition:

$$m_1 x_{1h} + m_2 x_{2h} = m_1 \omega_{1h} + m_2 \omega_{2h} \qquad h = 1, 2. \tag{12}$$

† Edgeworth put forward the following analysis in 1881 in *Mathematical Psychics*, Kegan Paul, London.

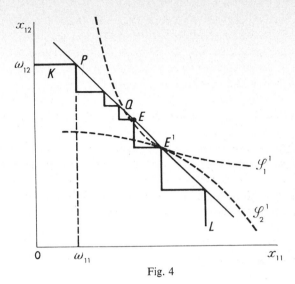

Fig. 4

But also, in the state E^1 which by hypothesis belongs to the core and so attributes the same consumption vectors to all the individuals in the same category:

$$x_{1h}^1 + x_{2h}^1 = \omega_{1h} + \omega_{2h}.$$

Eliminating ω_{2h}, we can write (12) in the form:

$$m_1 x_{1h} = (m_1 - m_2)\omega_{1h} + m_2 x_{1h}^1 + m_2(x_{2h}^1 - x_{2h})$$

$$\text{for} \quad h = 1, 2. \quad (13)$$

Suppose also that, in order to block E^1, the coalition C makes category 2 consumers impartial by attributing to them quantities x_{2h} equal to the x_{2h}^1. Equations (13) then become

$$x_{1h} = (1 - \alpha)\omega_{1h} + \alpha x_{1h}^1 \quad h = 1, 2 \quad (14)$$

where

$$\alpha = \frac{m_1}{m_2}. \quad (15)$$

The equalities (14) determine the quantities which remain available for the other agents once category 2 agents become impartial.

In Figure 4 it is assumed that $r = 3$, and points representing the consumption vectors attributed by different coalitions of this type to category 1 consumers (for $0 \leqslant m_1, m_2 \leqslant 3$) are shown. These points are the N.E. vertices of the stepped line KL. (The points corresponding to $m_1 = 1$ and $m_2 = 2$ or 3 lie outside the figure.)

The coalition C will effectively block E^1 if the point E, whose coordinates are defined by (14), lies on the right of $\mathscr{S}^1_1$. Now, E is a point on the line PE^1. To construct the coalition blocking E^1, we need only find a point on the segment E^1Q which is the weighted mean of P and E^1, weighted respectively by the masses $1 - \alpha$ and α, where α is a rational number. Since Q does not coincide with E^1, there always exists a point on E^1Q which satisfies this condition. The blocking coalition C is a coalition of the previous type for which m_1 and m_2 are the integral numerator and denominator respectively of α. Since $m_1 > m_2$, we need only take $r^1 = m_1$ to have an economy with a number of agents that is sufficient for the blocking coalition to exist.

Figure 4 shows the point E corresponding to $\alpha = 1/3$. In this figure, the state E^1 lies outside the core for $r \geqslant 3$, since it is blocked by the coalition comprising three category 1 and two category 2 consumers. Thus, in this case only the competitive equilibrium E_0 belongs to the core for every possible value of r, which is what we had to prove.

The generalisation to any numbers of goods and consumers is made easy by the following remark.[†] Consider a state E^1 belonging to the core. We know that it gives the same consumption vector x^1_i to all consumers of category i and that it is a Pareto optimum. Hence it is sustained by a price vector p. If E^1 is not a competitive equilibrium, $p(x^1_i - \omega_i)$ differs from zero for some categories; more precisely it must be negative for at least one category, k say, because E^1 fulfils (11). Using this remark and differentiability of S_k one easily finds that E^1 is blocked by a coalition containing $r_0 + 1$ consumers of category k and r_0 consumers of each of the other categories, r_0 being a sufficiently large number. (The proof follows the same approach as for the case of two goods and two consumers; it is left to the reader).

5. Domination and free entry

(i) *General remarks*

We have just seen that, in certain contexts, perfect competition naturally has a special rôle. The same positive approach can be used to investigate this problem more deeply as well as to consider differing contexts.

What happens when 'atoms' are present, that is, when there are agents who each plays an important part in certain markets? Are not these agents in a position to *dominate* the markets in question so long as the other participants are numerous and individually small? Here we interpret this question as follows: in this situation, is the core not systematically favourable to these agents?

[†] This remark is due to P. Champsaur and G. Laroque, who have been able to generalise the same proof to the case of non differentiable preference relations.

In addition, domination does not necessarily result from natural situations; it may arise because of collusion among agents who, taken individually, are small but unite to act as a single agent. They are said to form a 'syndicate'.

In the context of our methodology, the members of a syndicate agree that they will under no circumstance enter a coalition that does not contain them all. So the effect of the formation of a syndicate is to restrict the set of realisable coalitions and probably also the set of coalitions capable of blocking a given imputation. So it may possibly lead to enlargement of the core. This is in fact the reason for forming a syndicate: some of the imputations thus introduced to the core may be favourable to the members of the syndicate, which tries to obtain one of them by means of actions that, however, are not revealed by investigation of the core.

The possibility of collusion is the source of a certain institutional instability in perfect competition. Even when there is a large number of individually small agents, there is the risk of their grouping together so that situations of monopoly, bilateral monopoly, oligopoly, etc., appear.

In order to combat natural monopolies and to avoid what are considered to be the injurious effects of collusion, the advocates of competition have emphasised the importance of 'free entry'; there must be the legal guarantee that each individual wishing to engage in productive or exchange operations has freedom to do so; in a market where a monopolist is operating, the appearance of some independent individuals should be sufficient to prevent the monopolist from exploiting the favourable situation in which he is placed. The concept of free entry is justified theoretically if, even when atoms are present, the core reduces to the competitive equilibrium (or to the set of competitive equilibria) whenever there exists a proportion, however small, of independent agents in competition with the atoms.

It is impossible as yet to give complete circumstantial answers to the many questions raised by the above remarks. Such answers would require examination of the differing situations that can arise in the productive sphere where the main situations of monopoly and oligopoly occur. They demand investigation of indivisibilities and increasing returns, which are the most frequent causes of such situations. For these reasons, the theory is not straightforward.

However, if we adopt the context of the exchange economy, we can carry out two simple analyses whose results provide the basis for reflection and illustrate two ideas which certainly are much more widely valid.†

(ii) *A simple model*

Consider an exchange economy with only two goods and two categories of consumers ($m = 2$). Category 2 is composed, as before, of a number r of

---

† The theoretical research on which this discussion is based obviously relates to more general models than our present one.

identical consumers ($\omega_{2q} = \omega_2$ and $S_{2q} = S_2$, where $q = 1, 2, ..., r$), and r can be an arbitrarily large number. But category 1 has a structure that may tend to favour the effects of domination: it contains an atom controlling a large part k of the resources at the disposal of this category.

More precisely, the atom owns the resources defined by the vector $kr\omega_1$ and has a utility function S_1 while each of the other $(1 - k)r$ individuals has the same utility function S_1 and owns the vector $\omega_{1h} = \omega_1$ (the number k is assumed to be such that kr is integral, and the indices q of the other individuals in question are $q = kr + 1, ..., r$). Two cases will be examined: that in which the atom is the only agent in category 1 (the case of 'monopoly', $k = 1$), and that in which $k < 1$ and each of the other $r(1 - k)$ agents is individually small (the case of free entry).

As before, an Edgeworth box diagram provides a useful picture of these two cases. However, it does not apply directly to our initial formulation of the model.

In the first place, the Edgeworth diagram in the previous section was conceived in terms of a situation where there is the same number r of agents in each of the two categories. It was possible to confine the diagram to the indifference curves of a representative individual of each category, given that the number r was arbitrarily large. We shall continue to represent the second category in this way, but for the first category we must adopt the convention that the same graph may apply for varying values of r.

Now, the limiting process in which r tends to infinity is meaningful only if the respective importance of the two categories remains the same. The first category's resources must increase as quickly as the resources $r\omega_{2h}$ of the second. Thus, in the case of a single type 1 individual, his initial resources and his consumption of the good h will be written $r\omega_{1h}$ and rx_{1h} and no longer ω_{1h} and x_{1h}.

To the extent that r is arbitrary, the figure can be established only if the same indifference curves of agent 1 apply to the vectors x_1 for all values of the number r by which they are multiplied. Therefore *the indifference curves must be homothetic with respect to the origin*. This is obviously a restrictive assumption (in the context of the consumption theory in Chapter 2, it implies that the income-elasticities of demand are all equal to 1). However, it is essential for the simple graphical method adopted here.†

In the second place, in order to reason directly from the Edgeworth diagram, we first established that every imputation belonging to the core attributed precisely the same consumptions to the different individuals in the same category. So two vectors x_1 and x_2, respectively for the consumptions of the

---

† If this analysis for the exchange economy is transposed to a model of production, the assumption that the indifference curves are homothetic is replaced by the assumption of constant returns to scale, which appears less restrictive.

individuals in the two categories, were sufficient to represent an imputation of the core. It is now a more delicate operation to reduce the model in this way. So we shall first confine ourselves to imputations of the core that attribute the same vector x_2 to all agents in category 2, a vector rkx_1 to the atom and the vector x_1 to the other agents in category 1. We shall later consider the question of finding out if the core contains imputations that do not have this property.

(iii) *Preliminary study of the core*

Consider a state E^1 that is assumed to be contained in the core and has the particular property defined above. This state is represented by a point on the Edgeworth diagram. It is blocked neither by the coalition composed of all the individuals nor by coalitions consisting of a single individual. It therefore belongs to the curvilinear segment RS representing the core when $r = 1$. We wish to find out if it is restricted to belong to only a part of RS.

Characterisation of this part of RS will be simplified if we introduce the additional assumption that, when $r = 1$, the competitive equilibrium M is unique and that at a point E on RS the common tangent to the two indifference curves lies on the left of P if E is on the left of M, and on the right of P if E is on the right of M (the diagrams introduced up till now have this property except Figure 10 of Chapter 5).

The quasi-concavity of S_1 and S_2 implies that, if a coalition C blocks E^1, it can do so by attributing the same vector x_2^* to all the individuals in category 2 and the same vector x_1^* to those in category 1, the atom then receiving krx_1^*. The reasoning can be based on either category, but the notation is simpler for the second, whose first m_2 individuals can always be assumed to belong to C. Since C blocks E^1, there exist vectors x_{2q} such that

$$S_2(x_{2q}) \geqslant S_2(x_2^1) \qquad q = 1, 2, ..., m_2. \tag{16}$$

Let

$$x_2^* = \frac{1}{m_2} \sum_{q=1}^{m_2} x_{2q}. \tag{17}$$

The quasi-concavity of S implies

$$S_2(x_2^*) \geqslant S_2(x_2^1) \tag{18}$$

where the inequality holds strictly if at least one of the inequalities (16) holds strictly. In view of (17), it is possible for C to replace the x_{2q} by the same vector x_2^* attributed to all members of category 2, and this does not affect the fact that C blocks E^1.

Thus, by confining ourselves to imputations defined by two vectors x_1^* and x_2^* we can make a complete study of the additional conditions that E^1 must satisfy in order to belong to the core. In particular, this shows that E^1 cannot be blocked by a coalition whose members all belong to the same category i, which requires $x_i^* = \omega_i$ and therefore is contrary to $S_i(x_i^*) > S_i(x_i^1) \geqslant S_i(\omega_i)$.

Consider a coalition C composed of m_2 members of category 2 ($m_2 \leqslant r$) and either m_1 members of category 1 if the atom is excluded ($0 < m_1 \leqslant (1 - k)r$), or $m_1 + 1 - kr$ if the atom is included ($kr \leqslant m_1 \leqslant r$). In both cases, C's resources are then $m_1\omega_1 + m_2\omega_2$; they impose the constraints

$$m_1 x_{1h}^* + m_2 x_{2h}^* = m_1\omega_{1h} + m_2\omega_{2h} \qquad h = 1, 2 \tag{19}$$

similar to (12). Proceeding as at the end of section 4 and assuming in particular that the type 2 consumers have been made impartial by $x_2^* = x_2^1$, which is not restrictive, we obtain equations similar to (14) and (15) defining the consumptions which C can attribute to its type 1 members:

$$x_{1h}^* = x_{1h}^1 + (1 - \alpha)(\omega_{1h} - x_{1h}^1) \qquad h = 1, 2 \tag{20}$$

$$\alpha = \frac{m_2}{m_1}. \tag{21}$$

(iv) *Monopoly and competition*

When category 1 contains only the atom (when $k = 1$), then m_1 necessarily equals r so that α is at most 1. On the other hand, for sufficiently large r, the proportion α can be as near as we please to any number between 0 and 1. In order that E^1 should belong to the core, it is necessary and sufficient that the segment PE^1 contain no point lying above $\mathscr{S}_1^1$, the indifference curve through E^1. Under our adopted assumption this implies that the core does not contain points lying on RS on the left of M, but contains all the points of RS on the right of M (see Figure 5).

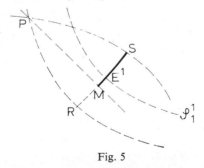

Fig. 5

Here again we find the idea of domination: the atom can obtain more than in the state of competitive equilibrium while the type 2 agents cannot, at least so long as they do not come to an agreement to set up an opposing syndicate.

In the latter case, we revert to an exchange economy with two contracting parties and the core RS already represented in Figure 4 of Chapter 6.

The situation is different if the atom is not the only member of its category ($k < 1$). Here m_1 can not only equal r but can take positive integral values at most equal to $r - kr$. If r is arbitrarily large, α can have any positive value. For example, $\alpha^0 \leqslant 1$ when $m_1 = r$ and $m_2 = \alpha^0 r$, and $\alpha^0 > 1$ when $m_1 = (1 - k)r/\alpha^0$ and $m_2 = (1 - k)r$. This brings us back exactly to the case at the end of Section 4. The core contains only the competitive equilibrium M.

To obtain this result we need only be able to realise the values of α^0 contained in an open interval containing 1. We can therefore confine ourselves without restriction to $\alpha^0 \leqslant 1/(1 - k)$ and realise a number $\alpha^0 > 1$ through $m_1 = (1 - k)r$ and $m_2 = \alpha^0(1 - k)r \leqslant r$. The coalition which blocks the states represented by points on RS to the right of M then contains the set of type 1 individuals other than the atom and an adequate number of type 2 individuals. The set of these other type 1 individuals can therefore constitute another atom without this causing any change in the core.

The idea of free entry is therefore confirmed also. When the resources of category 1 are not wholly owned by a single agent, and the category 2 individuals are numerous and individually small, the only state that is not blocked by any coalition is the competitive equilibrium.

(v) *Further study of the core*

To obtain the above results we assumed the states of the core to be defined simply by two vectors x_1^1 and x_2^1, each type 2 individual receiving x_2^1, the atom krx_1^1 and the other type 1 individuals x_1^1. Are there not other states in the core? We shall eliminate this possibility by considering the situation $k < 1$ (the case of monopoly would require a limiting argument which will not be given here).

Let us therefore consider a possible state E. Let krx_1^1 denote the consumption of the atom, whereas x_{1q} and x_{2q} are the consumptions of the other agents of both types, respectively for $q = kr + 1 = t, \ldots, r$ and $q = 1, \ldots, r$. Since E is feasible, we can write

$$kx_1^1 + \frac{1}{r} \sum_{q=t}^{r} x_{1q} + \frac{1}{r} \sum_{q=1}^{r} x_{2q} = \omega_1 + \omega_2. \tag{22}$$

Let us define the two possibilities:

$$S_1(x_1^1) < S_1(x_{1q}) \quad \text{for all} \quad q = t, \ldots, r, \tag{23}$$

$$S_1(x_1^1) > S_1(x_{1q}) \quad \text{for all} \quad q = t, \ldots, r. \tag{24}$$

If (23) does not hold, let $\underline{x}_1$ and $\underline{x}_2$ be vectors chosen respectively from the x_{1q} and the x_{2q}, and satisfying:

$$S_1(\underline{x}_1) \leqslant S_1(x_{1q}) \quad \text{for} \quad q = t, \ldots, r, \tag{25}$$

$$S_2(\underline{x}_2) \leqslant S_2(x_{2q}) \quad \text{for} \quad q = 1, \ldots, r. \tag{26}$$

Consider the coalition C^1 formed of the (or a) type 1 consumer who receives $\underline{x}_1$ in E and the type 2 consumer who receives $\underline{x}_2$ in E. Equation (22) shows that this coalition can realise

$$x_1^0 = kx_1^1 + \frac{1}{r} \sum_{q=t}^{r} x_{1q} \tag{27}$$

for its first member and

$$x_2^0 = \frac{1}{r} \sum_{q=1}^{r} x_{2q} \tag{28}$$

for its second member. The quasiconcavity of S_1 and S_2 shows that, since (23) does not hold,

$$S_1(x_1^0) \geqslant S_1(\underline{x}_1) \qquad and \qquad S_2(x_2^0) \geqslant S_2(\underline{x}_2)$$

(x_1^0 is a convex combination of x_1^1 and the x_{1q} since there are $r - t + 1 = (1 - k)r$ type 1 individuals apart from the atom). The *strict quasiconcavity* of S_1 and S_2 implies that C^1 blocks E except when the x_{1q} are all equal to x_1^1 and the x_{2q} are all equal to each other, which we can write

$$\begin{cases} x_{1q} = x_1^1 & \text{for} \quad q = t, ..., r \\ x_{2q} = x_2^1 & \text{for} \quad q = 1, ..., r. \end{cases} \tag{29}$$

If E is in the core, then either (23) or (29) holds.

Suppose that (23) holds; this implies that (24) does not hold. Then let $\bar{x}_1$ and $\bar{x}_2$ be the vectors chosen respectively from the x_{1q} and the x_{2q} and such that

$$S_1(\bar{x}_1) \geqslant S_1(x_{1q}) \qquad \text{for} \quad q = t, ..., r \tag{30}$$
$$S_2(\bar{x}_2) \geqslant S_2(x_{2q}) \qquad \text{for} \quad q = 1, ..., r. \tag{31}$$

Consider the coalition C^2 formed of all the individuals except the type 1 individual (or one of the type 1 individuals) who receives $\bar{x}_1$ in E and the type 2 individual who receives $\bar{x}_2$. Equation (22) multiplied by $(r - 1)$ shows that this coalition can assign the following consumptions to its members:

$$k[(r - 1)x_1^1 + \bar{x}_1] \qquad \text{to the atom,}$$

$$\frac{1}{r}[(r - 1)x_{1q} + \bar{x}_1] \qquad \text{to the other type 1 individuals,}$$

$$\frac{1}{r}[(r - 1)x_{2q} + \bar{x}_2] \qquad \text{to the other type 2 individuals.}$$

Since (30) and (31) hold, but (24) does not, the strict quasi-concavity of S_1 and S_2 implies that C^2 blocks E except when all the x_{1q} and x_1^1 equal $\bar{x}_1$, and when all the x_{2q} equal $\bar{x}_2$, in which case (29) holds with an appropriate vector x_2^1. The reasoning makes use of the homothetic nature of the type 1 indifference curves since it assumes that $S_1(x_1^1) \leqslant S_1(\bar{x}_1)$ implies $S_1(krx_1^1) \leqslant S_1(kr\bar{x}_1)$.

Therefore (29) certainly holds, which is our required result.

6. Return to the theories of monopoly and duopoly

We have just investigated two market situations which are very similar to those previously discussed for monopoly in Chapter 3 and for duopoly in Chapter 6. How do our results relate to the results of these previous more classical theories? We shall see that the essential difference stems from the assumption adopted earlier, that all exchanges took place at the same prices.

Consider first the case of a single type 1 agent ($k = 1$), that is, in our illustrative case, a single supplier of the good 2. We can validly speak of monopoly here. Using the construction in Chapter 5, we can draw on the Edgeworth diagram the curve D_2 representing the consumptions demanded by the type 2 agents when exchanges take place at given prices (see Figure 6). At each point N on D_2 the budget line PN is tangential to the indifference curve $\mathscr{S}_2$ containing N.

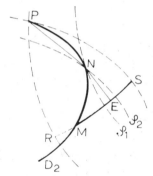

Fig. 6

If the monopolist must accept that all units are exchanged at the same price, the curve D_2 represents the locus of the points which he can realise, his consumption then being r times that defined by these points. Under these conditions, the monopolist chooses on D_2 the point N that is highest according to his system of preferences.

This point is analogous to the monopoly equilibrium investigated in Chapter 3. It does not belong to the core defined by the curvilinear segment MS. Relative to the locus of Pareto optima, it involves smaller-scale exchanges, which confirms the result of Chapter 3.

Obviously, the agents could agree to substitute for N a state E that is more favourable to all, a state chosen, for example, so that NE is tangential to the curve $\mathscr{S}_2$ passing through E. But this state cannot be realised if the agreement must consist in the choice of a price-vector applicable to all exchanges, a price vector that is to be adopted without obligation as to the quantities exchanged by the agents. On the budget line *PE*, the type 2 individuals would in fact choose a point other than *E* and less favourable than *N* to the monopolist.

Some other institutional arrangement is necessary for the state *E* to be realised. For example, the monopolist might conceivably fix the following tariff: for each buyer, the price of the good 2 relative to the good 1 is $\hat{p}_2$ for a quantity less than or equal to $\hat{e}_2$ and p_2^* for every unit bought in excess of $\hat{e}_2$. If $\hat{p}_2$ is defined by the normal to *PN*, p_2^* by the normal to *NE* and $\hat{e}_2$ by the projection of *NP* on the vertical axis, then the type 2 individuals will in fact choose *E*.

It is not surprising to find that the monopolist benefits from the right to introduce a tariff varying with the quantity exchanged. In fact, the monopolist with freedom to fix his tariff at will could regulate it by the indifference curve $\mathscr{S}_2^0$ passing through *P* and thus realise the state *S* (or at least, a state very near *S*). Need we add that, by too obviously exploiting the situation, he risks the formation of a buyers' syndicate and of finally having to accept a less favourable state than *E*? Once more we see the difficulty in defining an equilibrium in certain situations of imperfect competition.

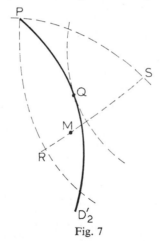

Fig. 7

Further considerations arise in the case of 'duopoly' where there are two type 1 atoms supplying good 2 and faced with a large number of buyers of good 1. To fix ideas, we can assume that the two atoms are of the same size ($k = 1/2$).

Let us look in particular at the Cournot equilibrium. In order to represent it by a point *Q* on the Edgeworth diagram, we have to draw the demand curve D_2' considered by one duopolist when he takes the other's supply as given and in conformity with Q (see Figure 7). The highest point on this curve according to the indifference curves $\mathscr{S}_1$ is the point Q. (The construction of D_2' from D_2 can be done iteratively and is not described here.) The point Q involves exchanges on a scale larger than the monopoly equilibrium point N but smaller than the competitive equilibrium point M.

We must take care not to confuse the core M obtained here with that discussed for duopoly in the previous chapter. We assumed then that all units were to be sold at the same price and that buyers took no part in forming any coalition. The core then referred to the 'game' between the two duopolists alone. On the other hand, our present core involves all the agents.

In particular, we can define the coalition that, according to the theory in Section 5, blocks the Cournot equilibrium. It consists of one of the duopolists, the first for example, and of more than half the type 2 agents. These agents agree to carry out their exchanges with the first duopolist, who therefore finds himself realising a point beyond Q to the right of PQ, and preferable to Q. To regain his 'share of the market', the second duopolist can only propose more favourable terms to the type 2 agents, terms with which the first duopolist must come into line. Competitive equilibrium alone then appears as stable.

Although it concerns an exchange economy and not the case of two producers supplying the same market, the above discussion reveals an aspect of things which we ignored in Chapter 6.

8

Determination of an optimum

1. The problem

The theory of the optimum is concerned with the definition and properties of certain states which are of particular interest from the point of view of the production and distribution of goods. Its results suggest certain advantages of market economies, but do not constitute an exhaustive investigation of the organisation of production and exchange. In fact they do not show how the optimum chosen by the community can in fact be established.

Of course, there is a possible formal solution to the problem. In Chapter 6 we established various systems of equations to be satisfied by states of maximum welfare. Conversely, the solutions of these systems all defined such states under conditions that did not generally appear very restrictive. For example, given a social utility function, and if the convexity assumptions are satisfied, the optimum can in principle be found by solving the system constituted by (22), (23), (26) and (35) in Chapter 6. But such a method cannot be used directly in a real situation. The central planning bureau responsible for applying it would have to know, apart from the social utility function U and primary resources ω_h, all the production functions f_j and all the utility functions S_i. The definition of each of these functions is liable to be complex, and there are very many of them; the central bureau would need an inconceivable mass of information and would be faced with impossible calculations. It is therefore necessary to consider less direct ways of determining the optimum.

Another conceivable solution is to institute a system of perfect competition† since, under the conditions discussed earlier, such a system leads to the

---

† It goes without saying that no actual social organisation can exactly realise perfect competition, which assumes the existence of a very large number of very well organised markets. It is therefore a question of judgment rather than of theory whether some particular set of institutions approximates sufficiently to perfect competition to have comparable efficiency.

establishment of an equilibrium which also maximises social welfare. This is in fact the aim of some reformers. But others think that the necessarily concomitant liberalism will be incapable of eliminating monopolies and other forms of imperfect competition. Still others consider that perfect competition results in an unacceptable distribution of wealth among consumers.

Most socialists have therefore proposed a more or less high degree of planning of production. Since they were faced with the impossibility of direct solution of the general equilibrium equations, the question arose of how the actual planning should be carried out. This is the object of 'the economic theory of socialism',† which has been investigated by some writers since the beginning of the century but has not yet produced very complete results. Its most important sections relate to the characterisation of the optimum, that is, to the properties discussed in Chapter 6. But some writers have also been concerned with the means by which an optimum can be determined and established.

The theory is much less fully worked out on this point than on the questions considered in previous chapters. Here we shall only state the problem and show various suggestions for solving it. We shall not attempt a deep investigation since we could not in any case put forward any very conclusive general results.

Yet the question is of obvious interest. It is basic to the understanding of the problems raised by the allocation of resources in societies subject to authoritarian planning. It is of interest to those who wish to make a full comparison of the performances of the competitive system and other systems of organisation. It necessarily arises in the institution of a mixed régime combining the price system with a certain degree of public intervention or with a guiding plan, which aims to provide all agents with a consistent and precise view of future economic development.

2. General principles‡

To the model used so far we must add a central agent, which we shall call the *planning bureau*, or simply the bureau. We must also define the information available to each agent *a priori*.

---

† This expression should not be taken as covering the economic analyses of socialist thinkers who were almost exclusively concerned with the capitalist society which they wished to reform or destroy. By far the best reference for our context in recent Russian literature is Kantorovich, *The Best Use of Economic Resources, 1959*, English Harvard University Press, 1965.

‡ This chapter is based fairly directly on Malinvaud, 'Decentralised Procedures for Planning', in Malinvaud and Bacharach eds., *Activity Analysis in the Theory of Growth and Planning*, MacMillan, 1967, in which detailed references to other original contributions to this subject can be found.

It is natural to suppose that each firm and each consumer knows his own particular constraints. The firm j knows its own production function f_j or its set Y_j. The consumer i knows to which set X_i his consumption vector must belong, and is perfectly aware of his preferences, that is, he knows his utility function S_i. In a private ownership economy, the ith individual also knows what resources ω_{ih} of the good h he owns.

A priori, the planning bureau knows little—the quantities ω_h of primary resources, if they are collectively owned. But it knows that feasibility demands equality of global supply and global demand for each good. Moreover, it has a criterion by which it can settle the problems raised by the distribution of incomes among consumers.

The bureau's task is to fix or to predict 'the plan', that is, the state to be achieved by the community: the consumption vectors x_i and production vectors y_j for each agent. In order to do so, it initiates a procedure that allows it to gather the necessary information.

In order to define and examine different procedures, we shall assume that the bureau transmits to the agents certain information about the plan that it is preparing, and we shall call this information *prospective indices*. On the basis of these indices, each agent sends a reply, called a *proposition*, to the bureau, this reply being determined by the application of certain *rules* fixed by the bureau. After several exchanges of this kind, the central bureau chooses the plan.†

If we let an index s denote the different stages of the procedure, letting A^s denote the agents' propositions, B^s the indices transmitted by the bureau at stage s and P^S the plan, we can represent a procedure as follows:

$$B^1 \to A^1 \to \dots B^s \to A^s \to B^{s+1} \to \dots B^{S-1} \to A^{S-1} \to P^S.$$

To define each procedure of this kind, we must say how the prospective indices, the propositions and the plan are determined. More precisely, in each case we must answer the following questions:

(i) To which quantities do the prospective indices relate? To which quantities do the agents' propositions relate? How does the procedure start?

(ii) What rules determine the agents' propositions at stage s?

(iii) How does the bureau calculate the prospective indices transmitted at stage s?

(iv) How does the bureau determine the plan P^S?

---

† Note that this formulation assumes the direct exchange of information between bureau and agents. Contrary to what generally happens in practice, the agents are not combined in representative groups. Similarly, the various procedures considered in existing theories assume that the bureau works on an unaggregated list of products and services. These obviously very severe simplifications affect the relevance of the results, but in a way that cannot for the moment be specified.

When a procedure has been defined in this way, when we are sure that the agents and the bureau can at each stage apply unambiguously the rules fixed for them, we can study the properties of the procedure, that is, the properties of the plan to which it leads. In particular, we ask if the plan P^S is near an optimum. An indication will be given in this direction if it is established that the plan P^S tends to an optimum in the obviously hypothetical case where the number S of exchanges of information tends to infinity.†

Up until recently those interested in the problem of determination of an optimum have suggested procedures based on the tâtonnement process that describes the adjustments to equilibrium in market economies (see Chapter 5, Section 5). The recent development of mathematical programming, and in particular of decomposition algorithms of solution, have led to other methods being suggested.

To illustrate the present state of knowledge, we shall go on to discuss three procedures, the first two in the context of the distribution economy (see Chapter 5, Section 2) and the third in relation only to the determination of a production programme. These three examples do not exhaust the extent of present knowledge, but are certainly adequate for the purposes of these lectures.

3. Tâtonnement procedure

The economists who first suggested procedures for determination of optimal plans in socialist economies started from the following idea. There is nothing to prevent the planning organism from simulating the operations that are held to take place in perfect markets. It may be guided directly by the models constructed for the theoretical description of competitive equilibrium and of the process by which it is realised. In order to determine an equilibrium corresponding to a satisfactory distribution of incomes, it need only obtain from the agents the information that they would spontaneously provide in the markets, and carry out the calculations describing the functioning of these markets.

To consider this solution to our problem in detail, we shall examine a distribution economy with m consumers among whom given quantities ω_h of the l commodities, quantities known to the central agency, are to be distributed. Let us assume that the planning bureau has instructions *to realise a given distribution of incomes* or, in other words, that the incomes R_i of the different consumers ($i = 1, 2, ..., m$) are fixed. We shall subsequently assume also that the R_i are known initially by the consumers.

---

† It is well known that science has often made effective use of the method consisting of the investigation of asymptotic properties when it is impossible to establish general results from finite formulations that are more representative of the real situation.

We can imagine the following way of simulating the tâtonnement process:

(i) The 'prospective indices' are prices and the individual consumers' 'propositions' are consumpton programmes. At stage s the bureau communicates a vector p^s of the prices of the different commodities. The consumer i replies with a vector x_i^s whose components x_{ih}^s represent his individual demands for the various goods. The first price vector p^1 can be chosen arbitrarily; common sense suggests, however, starting with a vector that gives a value for the available resources which is exactly equal to the sum of incomes:

$$p^1 \omega = \sum_{i=1}^{m} R_i = R. \tag{1}$$

For example, p^1 may conceivably be based on past prices or on observed prices in other communities. (Equality between $p^s \omega$ and R will not be rigorously maintained throughout the procedure, but achieved again in the limit.)

(ii) The ith consumer determines his proposition x_i^s as if the vector p^s were to be realised in markets where the individual consumers could acquire the different commodities. In other words, he must indicate which is his preferred vector x_i^s among all those vectors obeying the budget constraint

$$p^s x_i \leqslant R_i. \tag{2}$$

(As usual, we can also say that x_i^s maximises $S_i(x_i)$ subject to the constraint (2).)

(iii) At stage s, the bureau revises the price vector p^{s-1} so as to increase the prices of commodities that are too much in demand and to decrease the prices of commodities that appear to be over-supplied. This is in fact what happens in tâtonnement, which we formulated as a process continuous over time. We wrote

$$\frac{dp_h}{dt} = a_h \left[\sum_{i=1}^{m} x_{ih} - \omega_h \right] \qquad h = 1, 2, ..., , \tag{3}$$

with t denoting time during the adjustment process and a_h a positive constant. By analogy, we can set the following rule for the bureau's price revisions:

$$p_h^s - p_h^{s-1} = a_h \left[\sum_{i=1}^{m} x_{ih}^{s-1} - \omega_h \right] \qquad h = 1, 2, ..., l. \tag{4}$$

Obviously this rule must no longer be applied if it leads to a negative value for p_h^s, when a zero price is chosen.†

(iv) The supporters of this procedure have never indicated clearly how the plan is determined at the final stage S of the iterations. They seem to have

---

† If we wish to maintain the equality $p\omega = R$ throughout the procedure, it must not be based on (3), but on a very similar process

$$\frac{1}{p_h} \cdot \frac{dp_h}{dt} = \frac{1}{\omega_h} \sum_{i=1}^{m} x_{ih} - 1.$$

assumed that the last demands x_{ih}^{S-1} to be notified will define it satisfactorily. Of course, it will only then be by chance that global demands equal supplies ω_h. But a certain degree of inconsistency in the plan is allowable, either because existing stocks make supply relatively flexible, or because the many random factors involved in the future make perfect consistency to some degree illusory.

What are the possible properties of such a procedure?

Formula (4) shows that if at any stage the demands proposed by the consumers correspond exactly to the supplies then the procedure is halted. The plan achieved is in fact the required optimum since, as a market equilibrium, it defines a Pareto optimum and satisfies the income-distribution that was laid down *a priori*.

The discussion in Chapter 5 of the stability of the continuous process defined by (3) suggests that the iterative procedure resulting from (4) converges. In fact a property of this kind has been proved under certain conditions. However, it establishes only approximate convergence, which can be expressed more or less as follows:

Given any arbitrarily small positive ε, there exist numbers a_h (for $h = 1$, 2, ..., l) and S^0 such that the distance between the terminal price-vector p^{S-1} and the price-vector associated with the required optimum is less than ε when the number S of iterations exceeds S^0. As ε decreases, the a_h must decrease and S_0 must increase.

This property reveals a difficulty, which has also appeared in various experimental attempts to simulate the tâtonnement procedure. The desire for fairly rapid convergence favours the choice of values of the a_h that imply appreciable price revisions at each stage. But on the other hand, the need for precise convergence requires small values of these coefficients of adjustment.

The whole extent of the difficulty appears when we consider that the planning bureau does not have the available information to allow it to make a balanced assessment *a priori* of these two conflicting claims and to choose satisfactory values for the a_h. If the procedure is actually to be applied, then of course values of the a_h are chosen which decrease from one stage to the next. But this does not make the choice of these values any easier. Only experience can lead to good judgment.,

We note also that this inherent difficulty in the iterative tâtonnement process may affect not only the planning procedures based on it but also the advantages attributed to the spontaneous mechanism of competitive markets.† When they are faced with essentially new situations, are not these markets liable either to over-adjust, or to adjust too slowly?

---

† Some economists also question the ability of the tâtonnement process to describe correctly the adjustments that take place in existing markets. They hold that other processes such as those we are about to discuss are capable of describing the functioning of markets as well as planning procedures.

4. A procedure with quantitative objectives

According to the method described above, the bureau indicates prices to the agents and receives back propositions in terms of demands (or supplies) expressed in quantities. An alternative method has been suggested where the bureau indicates to each agent a quantitative programme concerning him.

He must then declare which marginal rates of substitution between the different goods the proposed programme implies for him. If the marginal rate for r with respect to q is higher for agent i than for agent α, this shows that it is advantageous to give i a little more of r and a little less of q, the inverse change being made in α's programme. Thus the bureau knows in which directions it has to modify the programmes of the different agents.

Let us consider this procedure in detail for the distribution economy, again assuming that income coefficient R_i for consumers are given *a priori*. It is convenient to assume that R_i represents not the ith consumer's income, but his share of the global income of the community, so that

$$\sum_{i=1}^{m} R_i = 1. \tag{5}$$

(i) The 'prospective indices' are consumption vectors; the individuals' 'propositions' are vectors of relative prices. At stage s the bureau informs i of the vector x_i^s which it proposes for him. The consumer i responds with a vector π_i^s whose component π_{ih}^s represents his marginal rate of substitution between commodity h and commodity l chosen as numéraire. The first vectors x_i^1 can be chosen arbitrarily subject only to the condition that they define a feasible plan:

$$\sum_{i=1}^{m} x_{ih}^1 = \omega_h \qquad \text{for} \qquad h = 1, 2, ..., l. \tag{6}$$

For example, the x_i^1 may assume a proportional distribution of available resources among the different individuals ($x_{ih}^1 = R_i \omega_h$).

(ii) The consumer i determines his proposition π_i^s as if he received the vector x_i^s and were free to state the terms on which he would be willing to exchange quantities of the different goods. He must therefore state his marginal rates of substitution between the different goods when he has x_i^s, namely:

$$\pi_{ih}^s = \frac{S_{ih}'(x_i^s)}{S_{il}'(x_i^s)} \qquad \text{for} \qquad h = 1, 2, ..., l - 1. \tag{7}$$

(Here we assume that the numéraire has been chosen so that its marginal utility S_{il}' is always positive for all agents.)

(iii) At stage s, the bureau revises the indices x_i^{s-1} on the basis of the propositions π_i^{s-1} of the different consumers. It first calculates the weighted mean of the marginal rates of substitution between any commodity h and the numéraire:

$$\pi_{.h}^{s-1} = \sum_{i=1}^{m} R_i \pi_{ih}^{s-1} \qquad \text{for} \qquad h = 1, 2, ..., l - 1. \tag{8}$$

For each consumer and each commodity it then defines

$$\phi_{ih}^{s-1} = R_i(\pi_{ih}^{s-1} - \pi_{.h}^{s-1}), \tag{9}$$

which is positive or negative according as the ith consumer attributes to the commodity h a higher or lower marginal utility than all the other consumers do on average. It follows from the definition of the $\pi_{.h}^{s-1}$ that

$$\sum_{i=1}^{m} \phi_{ih}^{s-1} = 0. \tag{10}$$

The bureau then calculates for each consumer a new vector x_i^s whose first $l - 1$ components are defined by

$$x_{ih}^s - x_{ih}^{s-1} = b_h \phi_{ih}^{s-1} \qquad h = 1, 2, ..., l - 1, \tag{11}$$

the b_h being fixed positive coefficients.

Thus the allocation of h to the ith consumer is increased or reduced according as his marginal rate of substitution for h is higher or lower than the average rate of the other consumers. (Here we ignore the fact that, in some cases, (11) may lead to a negative x_{ih}^s, which is clearly inadmissible. The procedure for finding the ϕ_{ih}^{s-1} would then need to be changed.)

It is clear that the x_{ih}^s as thus defined constitute a feasible programme for the distribution of the goods among the agents. For, (11), (10) and (6) imply that, for every commodity h other than l,

$$\sum_{i=1}^{m} x_{ih}^s = \sum_{i=1}^{m} x_{ih}^{s-1} = ... = \sum_{i=1}^{m} x_{ih}^1 = \omega_h.$$

It remains to allocate the numéraire for the complete definition of the new vector x_i^s. Consider

$$w^s = \sum_{i=1}^{m} \sum_{h=1}^{l-1} \pi_{ih}^{s-1}(x_{ih}^s - x_{ih}^{s-1}). \tag{12}$$

We shall see later that this quantity can be interpreted as a 'social surplus' emerging from the revision of the programme. We then set

$$x_{il}^s - x_{il}^{s-1} = R_i w^s - \sum_{h=1}^{l-1} \pi_{ih}^{s-1}(x_{ih}^s - x_{ih}^{s-1}). \tag{13}$$

It follows from (5) and the definition of w that the sum of the x_{il} is invariant and always equals ω_l, as is required.

(iv) Since the x_i^s define a feasible programme, the plan will naturally be determined at the last stage S of the iteration as the set of m vectors x_i^S defined as above on the basis of the x_i^{S-1} and the π_i^{S-1}.

Obviously if it happens in the course of this procedure that all the ϕ_{ih}^s are zero at a certain stage, then no change is made in the x_i^s, which then define an optimum since the marginal rates of substitution between the different goods are the same for all consumers. (Here we assume that the utility functions are quasi-concave.) The common value p_h of the π_{ih} then defines the price of h.

To this iterative procedure we can find a corresponding continuous process in which the x_{ih}^s are revised continuously according to the rules transposing (11) and (13). It is then easy to prove that this process converges, and does so in an interesting way. Let us see why.

Let $\dot{x}_{ih}$ and $\dot{S}_i$ denote the rates at which x_{ih} and S_i vary as a function of s, which is now considered to range from zero to infinity. We can write (12) and (13) as

$$w = \sum_{i=1}^{m} \sum_{h=1}^{l-1} \pi_{ih} \dot{x}_{ih}, \tag{12'}$$

$$\dot{x}_{il} = R_i w - \sum_{h=1}^{l-1} \pi_{ih} \dot{x}_{ih}. \tag{13'}$$

(We no longer state that the π_{ih} and w depend on s). We can find directly

$$\frac{\dot{S}_i}{S_{il}'} = \sum_{h=1}^{l-1} \frac{S_{ih}'}{S_{il}'} \dot{x}_{ih} + \dot{x}_{il} = \sum_{h=1}^{l-1} \pi_{ih} \dot{x}_{ih} + \dot{x}_{il} = R_i w.$$

Therefore the utilities of all the individuals vary in the same direction; the revisions treat the different consumers equitably. Moreover, taking account of (9) and (11), we can write

$$\dot{x}_{ih} = b_h R_i (\pi_{ih} - \pi_{.h})$$

and

$$\sum_{i=1}^{m} \pi_{ih} \dot{x}_{ih} = b_h \sum_{i=1}^{m} R_i (\pi_{ih} - \pi_{.h}) \pi_{ih} = b_h \sum_{i=1}^{m} R_i (\pi_{ih} - \pi_{.h})^2,$$

the last equality following from (8). Referring to the definition (12') of w, we see that w cannot be negative and is positive as long as the ϕ_{ih} are not simultaneously zero.

In short, the effect of the revisions is that the consumers' utility levels are all increasing so long as an optimum has not been attained. There is therefore no difficulty in principle in proving that the procedure converges. This property of the continuous process does not apply just as it is to the suggested iterative procedure. Remarks similar to those made on 'tâtonnement' could be made here, but repetition would be tedious.

On the other hand, we must certainly pause to compare the two procedures which we suggested for the distribution economy and can be generalised to less particular models.

Some authors try to contrast them as formulations of two different types of economic organisation. The tâtonnement procedure is taken as an idealisation of market functioning, where the central control needs only to know net demands and supplies and acts blindly to revise prices as a function of these global observations only. The second procedure is taken to represent the organisation of authoritarian economies where the planning bureau issues orders to the different agents and imposes precise programmes on them.

This is certainly an exaggerated contrast. At least in the present state of knowledge, there is no question of taking sides in the debate between the market system and planning on the basis of a comparison between the two types of suggested procedures. In principle, both can be applied for the preparation of a plan, which may in either case be imposed by authority or regarded as making public a collection of information that agents are left free to use as they wish together with the indications given by the market. The two procedures assume a certain degree of decentralisation in the preparation of the plan and a systematic exchange of information between agents and central authority. For the moment, their respective advantages should be investigated in the neutral and relatively technical context adopted for this chapter.

Since no other conclusions are possible, we shall only point out here that the second procedure involves a much greater burden of computation for the planning bureau since the prospective indices must be personalised. At each stage, the bureau must calculate the ml quantities x_{ih}^s while the l prices p_h^s are sufficient for tâtonnement. This difference is obviously particularly outstanding in the distribution economy since the number of consumers in it is generally high. It would be a less significant drawback in planning for the sphere of production, using a similar procedure, where the number of branches or the number of large firms is much smaller.†

5. A procedure involving the use of a model by the planning board

The two cases so far discussed have the common characteristic that they imply fairly direct calculations by the central board unaccompanied by any

---

† Note that the bureau's calculations may be somewhat decentralised. The determination of global demands in the first procedure, and of average rates of substitution $\pi_{.h}^s$ in the second, may be carried out in stages by intermediate bodies responsible for certain subgroups of agents.

attempt to represent the conditions in which each agent acts. In countries where there is some planning of production, the central agency usually works on a direct representation of the technology used by firms. It uses a model that is a simplified schema of both the equilibrium constraints on supply and demand and the technical constraints proper to each industry. The object of exchanging information with the agents is the progressive improvement of the central model and the plan that results from it.

If we think of the detailed organisation of national production in terms of a vast mathematical programme, we can say that this programme is 'decomposed' into as many partial programmes as there are producers, the whole being coordinated by a relatively simple central programme. Each partial programme takes as data elements determined by solution of the central programme. On its part, the central programme is continually revised as a function of the answers provided by the partial programmes. In the literature on mathematical programming, such methods for finding the solution come under the heading of 'decomposition methods'.

Here we shall confine ourselves to a simple example for which a quick and efficient procedure can be defined. This example is fairly typical of the more complex situations arising in the organisation of production.

We return to the model introduced in Section 5 of Chapter 5 for the discussion of the labour theory of value and we give it a slightly stricter specification. Each firm specialises in the production of a single commodity, under constant returns to scale. The last commodity is assume to be a primary factor (labour), which is non-consumable and available in a fixed quantity ω_l. We suppose further that each of the other commodities h is produced by a single firm and that $\omega_h = 0$. Finally, we assume the existence of a utility function $S(x_1, x_2, ..., x_{l-1})$ relating directly to the global consumptions x_h, which is equivalent to assuming that the central board knows the collective demand functions and represents them by a utility function (see the remarks on revealed preferences at the end of Chapter 2).

Such a model is obviously a schematic representation of production, where each 'firm' corresponds to a branch of production and the distribution of global consumptions among individuals is not taken into account.

It is convenient to number the firms ($j = 1, 2, ..., l-1$) so that the hth firm produces commodity h. Then y_{jj} is the output of the jth firm while $-y_{jh}$ is its input of h for all $h \neq j$. Returning to the notation of Chapter 5, Section 5, we let q_j denote the output y_{jj} of the good j and let a_{hj} be the *technical coefficient* of the input h in the production of j:

$$a_{hj} = \frac{-y_{jh}}{y_{jj}} \qquad h \neq j. \tag{15}$$

By convention, a_{jj} is zero. Let a_j be the l-vector corresponding to the jth firm's technical coefficients; let A be the square matrix of order $l-1$ consisting of the a_{hj} relating to the goods produced ($h, j = 1, 2, ..., l-1$); finally, let f be the ($l-1$)-vector consisting of the technical coefficients relating to the primary factor ($f_j = a_{lj}$).

With this notation, the equality conditions for supply and demand become

$$x_h + \sum_{j=1}^{l-1} a_{hj}q_j = q_h \qquad h = 1, 2, ..., l-1 \tag{16}$$

$$\sum_{j=1}^{l-1} f_j q_j = \omega_l, \tag{17}$$

or, using more compact matrix expressions,

$$x + Aq = q \quad \text{or} \quad x = (I - A)q \tag{16'}$$

$$f'q = \omega_l. \tag{17'}$$

(The vectors are considered as column matrices, f' denotes the transpose row matrix of f, and I denotes the unit matrix of order $l-1$.) System (16') is called the 'Leontief model', the matrix A being known as the 'Leontief matrix'.†

Since production is carried on under constant returns to scale in the jth firm, the technical constraints can be expressed directly in the vector a_j of its technical coefficients. We write them in the form

$$a_j \in A_j \qquad j = 1, 2, ..., l-1, \tag{18}$$

where A_j is a set of l-dimensional space. These constraints must obviously be obeyed by the pair composed of the matrix A and the vector f.

A fairly natural planning procedure for such an economy is that where, at stage s, each firm informs the central bureau of a vector a_j^s of technical coefficients. From these vectors the bureau first constructs a matrix A^s and a vector f^s, then reasons on the basis of the corresponding Leontief model as if A^s and f^s were completely fixed by technical exigences. Before defining this procedure in more detail, let us see how the bureau uses the Leontief model in question.

$S(x)$ is to be maximised subject to the constraints

$$x = (I - A^s)q \tag{19}$$

$$[f^s]'q = \omega_l. \tag{20}$$

We assume that the Lagrange multiplier relating to (20) is not zero in the optimum, which can be proved if, for example, all the f_j^s are positive. The first-order conditions then require the existence of a number λ and an

---

† Leontief models are currently used in theoretical and applied macroeconomics. See, for example, H. Chenery and P. Clark, *Interindustry Economics*, New York, 1959.

($l - 1$)-vector p such that the first derivatives with respect to the x_h and the q_j of

$$\lambda S(x) - p'[x - (I - A^s)q] - [f^s]'q + \omega_l$$

are zero. These conditions are respectively

$$\lambda S_h' = p_h \qquad (h = 1, 2, ..., l - 1) \tag{21}$$

$$p'(I - A^s) = [f^s]'. \tag{22}$$

Conditions (21) are exactly the same as the conditions for maximisation of $S(x)$ subject to the constraint that $p'x$ has a suitable value given in advance. Also (19), (20) and (22) show that $p'x$ must equal ω_l. It is therefore fairly obvious that the bureau must

(a) solve (22) to find the vector p,

(b) determine x so as to maximise $S(x)$ subject to the constraint $p'x = \omega_l$,

(c) find the corresponding vector q by solving (19).

Note that the p_h can be interpreted as the prices that the goods h must have when the primary factor is taken as numéraire. System (22) can be written:

$$p_j = \sum_{l=1}^{h-1} p_h a_{hj}^s + f_j^s.$$

It expresses the fact that the price of j must be equal to its unit cost of production when the technique represented by the vector a_j^* is chosen by the jth firm (cf. system (26) of Chapter 5).

Prices p_h are therefore adapted to the Leontief model constructed from the a_j^s. Are they also appropriate to the true technical constraints expressed by (18)? The simplest way to check up on this is to ask each firm j which is its most economic vector a_j of technical coefficients for the prices p_h. The closer these vectors stated by the firms approximate to the a_j^s, the greater the likelihood that the solution obtained by the central agency is satisfactory.

We are now in a position to define the procedure in detail:

(i) The 'prospective indices' are prices and the firms' 'propositions' are production techniques. At stage s, the bureau states a vector p^s of the prices of the different products, the primary factor being taken as numéraire. The jth firm replies with a vector a_j^s.

(ii) At stage s, the jth firm determines a_j^s so as to minimise its unit cost of production calculated at the prices p_h^s, that is, a_j^s minimises

$$\sum_{h=1}^{l-1} p_h^s a_{hj} + f_j \tag{23}$$

in A_j.

(iii) The bureau determines the vector p^{s+1} by solving the linear system (22).

(iv) Finally the bureau determines the plan (x^S, q^S) at stage S by calculating first of all the vector p^S as above from A^{S-1} and f^{S-1}, then by calculating x^S

so as to maximise $S(x)$ subject to the constraint $p^S x = \omega_l$ and last of all by finding q^S as the solution of the system

$$x^S = (I - A^{S-1})q.$$

We shall not linger over the properties of this procedure. It can be established that x^S converges to the optimal consumption vector. It can also be shown that, if the plan x^S is not yet optimal, the addition of a new stage necessarily leads to a plan x^{S+1} which is preferable to x^S provided that $S(x)$ is a strictly increasing function.†

Note that this procedure involves a "decomposition" of the total problem of maximisation of $S(x)$ subject to the constraints expressed by (16), (17) and (18). At stage s the 'partial programme' relating to the jth firm consists of minimising the linear form (23) in the set A_j. The central agency's problem consists of maximising $S(x)$ subject to the constraints (19) and (20). The data for each partial programme are the results of the immediately preceding central programme, just as the central programme uses the a_j^s resulting from the preceding partial programmes.

6. Correct revelation of preferences

Until now we have assumed that the agents, consumers or producers, who collaborate in the preparation of the plan, scrupulously follow the rules of the chosen procedure. Since the plan involves them directly, there is a risk that they may cheat so as to influence it in their favour. There is therefore an obvious advantage in procedures which are obeyed spontaneously by the agents even in the absence of control or of a social morality.

The aim of every procedure is to gather information about the preferences or the constraints that govern the activity of consumers and producers. Will they not try deliberately to give biased answers?

The question is all the more important since it has been claimed that the *market system ensures economically and correctly the collection of those bits of information which are the most relevant*. When he presents his demands and supplies at the prices that tend to be realised, when he revises them as prices vary, each agent spontaneously reveals the comparative utilities of the different goods for him in the neighbourhood of the equilibrium which is in process of being established. Now, this is just the information that a planner needs to organise the production and distribution of goods.

In fact the market system has this advantage only in perfect competition. As we have seen, a monopolist's supply takes account of the characteristics of the demand with which he is faced; it therefore does not reveal correctly, or at least not directly, the cost conditions governing production. But in

---

† See Part IV of the author's article 'Decentralized Procedures for Planning', op. cit.

atomless economies, the market system tends to the spontaneous realisation of competitive equilibrium.

Will the agents find it to their interest to reveal their preferences and costs correctly in the procedures we have discussed?

We note first that the adopted rules are not of a kind to encourage obvious fraud. If he considers each stage separately, without examining its repercussions on the outcome of the procedure, the consumer disposing of income R_i and confronted with prices p_h has every reason to state the same demand as in perfect competition. Similarly the producer, knowing prices p_h^s, finds it to his interest to choose the technique whose cost is least at these prices. Again, the consumer to whom a complex x_i^s is assigned will gain from marginal exchanges whose terms are favourable relative to his true rates of substitution. So in the second procedure, there is no obvious reason for the agent i to distort his answers π_{ih}^s. The three planning methods discussed in this chapter are not basically unrealistic.

However, if they consider the procedure as a whole, consumers and producers may find it to their advantage to distort their answers at stage s so as to obtain at stage $s + 1$ prices p_h^{s+1} or programmes x_i^{s+1} which are particularly favourable to them. This possibility does not exist in an atomless economy where each individual answer has only negligible effect on prices or on average substitution rates. But clearly it may arise in economies where competition is naturally imperfect.

Consider, for example, the first procedure in the particular case of two goods and two consumers, and where the procedure is so devised as to ensure always that $p\omega = R$. We can follow the successive stages on an Edgeworth diagram (cf. Chapter 4, Section 3 and Chapter 5, Section 2). The fact that incomes R_1 and R_2 are exogenous implies that the budget line passes through the point I on the diagonal OO' such that

$$\frac{OI}{IO'} = \frac{R_1}{R_2}.$$

The optimum is represented by the point M^0 such that the line IM^0 is tangential at M^0 to the two indifference curves passing through this point. Suppose now that the first consumer knows the preferences of the second consumer, and also knows that the latter obeys the procedural rules. The first consumer can then construct the second's demand curve IJ, which is defined by the condition that at each point M the line IM is tangential to the indifference curve $\mathscr{S}^2$ containing M. A particular point M^1 on this demand curve is preferred by the first consumer, this being the point that the second would choose if the budget line were IM^1.

If he considers each stage as being not the last one but rather a phase in the total procedure, it is to the first consumer's advantage to reply giving the

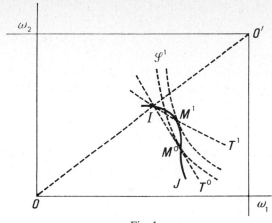

Fig. 1

impression that his preferences imply at M^1 an indifference curve tangential to IM^1. This allows him to obtain a plan near M^1 rather than near M^0.

This example shows that the suggested procedure does not eliminate all possibility of fraud. It also shows, let us note in passing, that the fact that incomes are given exogenously does not necessarily define unambiguously the distribution of welfare among the consumers.

9

External economies, public goods, fixed costs

1. General remarks

The model of production and consumption on which our discussion has so far been based has an important characteristic to which we must now turn our attention; it allows the strict minimum of interdependences among agents.

Consider the physical constraints. Those which are particular to one agent, the ith consumer's set X_i or the jth producer's set Y_j, do not depend on the other agents' activities. The only common constraints result from the necessary equality of global supply and global demand for each good. Similarly each consumer's system of preferences is unaffected by other consumers' or producers' decisions.

There are situations to which this model is inappropriate, situations where the physical constraints restricting the consumer α's vector x_α or the firm β's vector y_β obviously depend on the other agents' vectors x_i and y_j, situations where the consumer α's utility function S_α varies considerably with the values chosen for the x_i and y_j by other agents. The general terms 'external economies', 'external diseconomies' or simply 'external effects' are now used to characterise such situations. We shall see immediately how these terms arose.

The expression 'external economy' applies to the case where the production realised by one firm reduces costs for other firms. For example, a farmer's orchard increases his bee-keeping neighbour's output of honey. The installation or enlargement of an engineering factory in a town brings about the introduction of a female labour force (the workers' wives) which benefits a dress-manufacturer in the town. The professional training given to its employees by a very large firm often benefits other firms in the region when these employees leave the large firm.

Note also that these examples reveal a certain market imperfection: at no cost to himself, the beekeeper receives a service from his neighbour which improves his output; the dress-manufacturer, or the other firms in the region, can employ a more carefully selected or a better trained labour force at the same wages as before.

In these cases of external economy, the firm whose activity benefits others has no way of *excluding* them from this benefit. It cannot sell the service, which appears as a by-product of its own production. So to identify this service as a new good would not allow us to revert to our previous general model. Note also that it is the imperfections in market organisation which oblige us to take explicit account of external effects.

We can easily think of situations where there are 'external diseconomies', when one firm's activity damages the activity of others or the wellbeing of consumers. Air-pollution and water-pollution are frequent examples. In most cases, those who suffer from such diseconomies have no way of making the responsible firm or firms bear the cost of them.

The existence of collective services creates another type of interdependence among agents. Our previous general model assumes that goods are used strictly in private, that is, that the use of a given quantity of a good by one agent implies its destruction, so that this quantity is no longer available for other agents. Such an assumption is inappropriate to certain collective services from which all the individual consumers benefit without making private use of them; defence, fine arts, justice, sanitation, television, etc.

Microeconomic models have been augmented by the introduction of 'public goods', which have the property that they are used simultaneously by all consumers without individual exclusion, in order to take account of such services (they might more properly be called 'collective goods', but the other term is too well established). In certain cases, each individual might consume the total supply of the service in question. In other cases, he may either consume or abstain at will without causing the slightest change in the other resources available to the different consumers, and, in particular, to himself.

The case of external effects proper, like that of public goods defined above, corresponds to extreme situations. In real life, intermediate situations are often encountered. For example, the quality of a service rendered to consumers for their private use may depend on the extent of the demand to be satisfied: speedy, comfortable transport, the quality of water supplies in large urban areas, etc. Similarly, the fact that some productive activity is carried out under increasing returns to scale creates a kind of interdependence among consumers, since it is to the benefit of each that the others' demand is particularly high; an increase in global demand induces a decrease in average cost and therefore probably also in price or taxation.

The effect of urbanisation and progress in such areas as telecommunication is to cause more and more complex interdependences among agents in modern societies. So we must try to discover the necessary amendments to the general results of microeconomic theory when the model on which they have been based becomes insufficient.

The question arises for optimum as well as for equilibrium theory; but it is more serious in the latter case. The notion of Pareto optimum remains unchanged however complex the constraints or the definition of individual preferences. On the other hand, the very idea of equilibrium has to be re-formulated in certain cases.

The main formulations of equilibrium involve direct confrontation of producers and consumers without the intervention of any control to ensure that their actions are consistent. In these models, competition eliminates the need for any concerted organisation of production and distribution. But how can they be made to cover public goods which, by their very nature, involve all the individuals collectively? The market seems inadequate both for determining the production programme of such goods and for financing its execution. A new decision process becomes necessary. The definition of equilibrium is obviously affected by this.

The consideration of public goods and, as we shall see, of external effects, requires the formal representation of decisions that are taken collectively rather than individually. When faced with these questions, the economist must willy-nilly take account of the political organisation in whose context these decisions are taken. But he can certainly do so at a level of generality that avoids the need to construct a whole political theory.

One initial rule seems necessary: collective decisions are taken by the agents constituting the economy under investigation. Of course, it would be convenient to suppose that an omniscient State with sovereign powers determines all choices beyond the level of the individual. But this would be quite artificial, at least for the study of equilibrium. The aim of the theory must be to explain, at least partially and in general terms, how producers and consumers reach mutual agreement on the economic state to be realised.

A second rule has been adopted by the investigators of these problems. Just as a state of the economy is assessed in optimum theory on the basis of what it gives the individual consumers, so it is assumed that only these same individuals take part in collective decision-making. The citizen-consumer expresses his choices both on the market and through political representations which decide collective consumption and taxation, whose role we shall shortly investigate. The producer or the firm then appears to have a less important function, only to organise certain productive operations so as to ensure maximum profitability.

Economic science has not yet integrated into its general analytical framework the various complications just mentioned, although their nature is being better and better understood. So we shall confine ourselves to some simple examples and show some of the problems which they involve. In doing this, we shall touch on questions relating to *the economic theory of public finance*, but obviously shall not attempt to discuss the whole of this theory, even in summary.

In this chapter we shall be particularly concerned with the fairly detailed discussion of external effects occurring in production on the one hand, and on the other hand, with the case of completely public goods that are used by all the consumers collectively without affecting production. We shall make only brief mention of external effects in consumption, public goods used by producers and the case where the private consumption of certain goods directly concerns all the other individuals (services subject to congestion). We shall end the chapter with the discussion of the problems raised by the presence of fixed costs, which in some sense represent collective costs. The presence of fixed costs is the cause of the greatest deviations from convexity and requires that decisions are taken by procedures that are fairly comparable to those which occur in the treatment of public goods. This explains their place in this chapter.

2. External effects

Let us see how optimum and equilibrium theories must be modified when one firm's activity has an external effect on the conditions of production for other firms. It seems possible to lay bare the essentials of the problem by considering a very simple model with only two firms ($j = 1, 2$) and one consumer. Let us assume that there are three commodities, the first two being produced by each firm respectively, while the third one is the only input for both firms. This commodity therefore occurs in production as 'labour', but it can also be consumed by the individual consumer in the form of 'leisure'. We suppose finally that there is no primary resource other than the maximum quantity ω_3 of labour that the consumer can provide.

Let x_1 and x_2 be the outputs of the first two commodities and x_3 the quantity consumed of the third by the individual consumer. His system of preferences is represented by a utility function $S(x_1, x_2, x_3)$.

The external effects arising from a firm's activity depend in reality on a set of factors. But they tend to increase with the activity of the firm. So we can assume in our simple model that they are a function only of the volume of production. So the effect of the first firm's activity on the second firm depends on x_1, and the second firm's effect on the first depends on x_2.

The first firm produces x_1 from a labour-input a_{13}. The technical conditions are represented by a production function involving x_2:

$$x_1 = g_1(a_{13}; x_2). \tag{1}$$

Similarly the second firm produces x_2 from the input a_{23} and is subject to the production function

$$x_2 = g_2(a_{23}; x_1). \tag{2}$$

Let g'_{13} and g'_{23} denote the derivatives of g_1 and g_2 with respect to the respective labour-inputs. We also let g'_{12} denote the derivative of g_1 with respect to x_2 and g'_{21} the derivative of g_2 with respect to x_1. The derivative g'_{12} is positive (or negative) according as firm 1 benefits from external economies (or suffers from external diseconomies) resulting from the activity of firm 2.

We must add to (1) and (2) the equilibrium condition of supply and demand for the third commodity:

$$a_{13} + a_{23} + x_3 = \omega_3. \tag{3}$$

In this very simple economy a programme, or state, is defined by five numbers, the values of x_1, x_2, x_3, a_{13} and a_{23}. A programme is feasible if it satisfies (1), (2) and (3). In short, everything depends on the allocation of labour among its three uses, input for firm 1, input for firm 2 and leisure.

(i) *Optimum*

Let us first find the conditions under which a programme E^0 is an optimum. It must consist of five numbers which maximise S subject to the constraints (1), (2) and (3). So we can write the Lagrangian expression

$$S(x_1, x_2, x_3) + \lambda_1[x_1 - g_1(a_{13}, x_2)] + \lambda_2[x_2 - g_2(a_{23}, x_1)] +$$
$$\lambda_3[a_{13} + a_{23} + x_3 - \omega_3].$$

Equating the five first derivatives to zero, we have

$$\begin{cases} S'_1 + \lambda_1 - \lambda_2 g'_{21} = 0 \\ S'_2 + \lambda_2 - \lambda_1 g'_{12} = 0 \\ \quad S'_3 + \lambda_3 = 0 \\ -\lambda_1 g'_{13} + \lambda_3 = 0 \\ -\lambda_2 g'_{23} + \lambda_3 = 0. \end{cases}$$

After elimination of the Lagrange multipliers, these first-order conditions reduce to

$$\frac{S'_1}{S'_3} = \frac{1}{g'_{13}} - \frac{g'_{21}}{g'_{23}} \qquad \frac{S'_2}{S'_3} = \frac{1}{g'_{23}} - \frac{g'_{12}}{g'_{13}}. \tag{4}$$

Taking the third commodity as numéraire, we let p_1 denote the value for E^0 of the marginal rate of substitution S'_1/S'_3 between the first and third commodities. Similarly let p_2 denote the value of S'_2/S'_3. If the sufficient assumptions specified in Chapter 4 on optimum theory are satisfied,† then E^0 is an equilibrium for the consumer who is confronted with prices $(p_1, p_2, 1)$ and has

---

† This clause will not be repeated subsequently.

for his consumption of goods 1 and 2 an income from labour of $\omega_3 - x_3$ and an additional income of $p_1 x^0 + p_2 x^0 + x_3^0 - \omega_3$. But, for firms affected by external effects, the marginal conditions

$$p_1 g'_{13} = 1 - g'_{21}\frac{g'_{13}}{g'_{23}}, \tag{5}$$

$$p_2 g'_{23} = 1 - g'_{12}\frac{g'_{23}}{g'_{13}} \tag{6}$$

do not correspond to those for competitive equilibrium where firm 1 maximises its profit $p_1 x_1 - a_{13}$ and firm 2 maximises its profit $p_2 x_2 - a_{23}$:

$$p_1 g'_{13} = 1 \quad \text{and} \quad p_2 g'_{23} = 1. \tag{7}$$

The optimum no longer appears as a market equilibrium.

We must therefore find out in the first place how the equilibrium is likely to differ from the optimum, and in the second place, how institutions other than those of the market economy could bring about a good allocation of labour among its three uses. We shall make a preliminary examination of the additional terms in (5) and (6) with respect to (7). Let us, for example, fix attention on firm 1 and formula (5).

We note first that the new term $g'_{21}g'_{13}/g'_{23}$ is zero if g'_{21} is zero, that is, if the extent of the first firm's activity does not affect production conditions for the other firm. This term is therefore explained by the external effects caused by the first firm and not by external effects from which it suffers or benefits. More precisely, $g'_{21}g'_{13}$ measures the increase in production of good 2 caused by external effects for a unit of additional labour employed in firm 1. If production of good 2 is held at its previous level, the quantity of labour employed by firm 2 is reduced by $g'_{21}g'_{13}/g'_{23}$. In short, the additional term in (5) measures the quantity of labour which firm 2 can save without reducing output when an additional unit of labour is employed in firm 1.

Since g'_{13}, g'_{23}, S'_1, S'_2 and S'_3 can be considered positive, realisation of the optimum requires that $g'_{21}g'_{13}/g'_{23} < 1$ (see equation (5) above). The above interpretation suggests that this condition must be satisfied.

(ii) *Relations between equilibrium and optimum*

Before discussing in detail how the equilibrium allocation differs from an optimal allocation, let us consider the formulation of equilibrium. We assumed above for equations (7) that each firm maximises its profit, taking prices and *the other firm's activity* as given. We therefore adopted an assumption of behaviour comparable to that adopted in the theory of games for the definition of 'non-cooperative equilibria'. Is such behaviour plausible? Perhaps not in the context of our model, where there are only two firms. We shall therefore go on to consider alternatives. On the other hand, this assumption seems useful when the external effects are diffuse, that is, when they benefit or hinder a large number of agents who do not make up a coalition.

Suppose then for the moment that a competitive equilibrium E^1 is realised; equations (1), (2) and (3) are satisfied; prices p_1, p_2 and 1 exist; at these prices each firm maximises its profit, knowing and taking as given the effect on its own technical possibilities of other firms' decisions; (7) is therefore satisfied. How might the allocation realised by E^1 be improved?

The answer obviously depends on the specifications of the different functions. We shall consider two typical cases, the first where only firm 1 causes external effects ($g'_{12} = 0$), the second where the external effects caused by the two firms are 'symmetric'.

(a) Suppose first therefore that $g'_{12} = 0$. Obviously *if there are external economies* (or external diseconomies) *production and consumption in the equilibrium E^1 of the good whose manufacture gives rise to the external effect are too small* (or too high). Let us make the following small modifications to E^1: let a_{13} vary by du and a_{23} by $- du$, let x_1 vary by $g'_{13} du$ and x_2 by $- g'_{23} du + g'_{21} g'_{13} du$. Then the utility function S varies by

$$[S'_1 g'_{13} + S'_2 (g'_{21} g'_{13} - g'_{23})] du.$$

Now, in competitive equilibrium, $S'_1 g'_{13} = S'_3 p_1 g'_{13} = S'_3$ and $S'_2 g'_{23} = S'_3$. The variation in S is therefore

$$S'_3 g'_{13} p_2 \cdot g'_{21} du.$$

The first three terms in the product are positive. If g'_{21} is positive, that is, if there is external economy, the utility function increases following a reallocation of labour in favour of the first firm and against the second.†

(b) If the two firms both give rise to external economies of comparable importance, the allocation of labour brought about by competitive equilibrium is not necessarily bad. This case has a certain practical significance.

Thus, it has been pointed out that economies of scale related to the existence of vast markets are often external to each firm taken in isolation. Specialisation of labour, diffusion of technical information, the presence of diversified distribution circuits, etc., become increasingly effective with the increasing volume of the market. Thus, the higher the level of production in an economy, the more favourable the context to the firms' productivity. Each firm benefits from external economies because of the activity of all the others. Conversely, certain of the nuisances and costs of overcrowding due to mass production may constitute external diseconomies which affect the firms symmetrically.

---

† This is purely local reasoning, and does not allow a true comparison of the equilibrium and the optimum. But it is sufficient to show where the economic losses lie in the equilibrium.

In order to introduce this aspect of reality to the model, we shall assume that the last terms of (5) and (6) are equal:

$$g'_{21}\frac{g'_{13}}{g'_{23}} = g'_{12}\frac{g'_{23}}{g'_{13}} = e. \tag{8}$$

(This is so in particular if the two firms are identical.) The equality is apparently not sufficient to ensure that the equilibrium equations and the optimality conditions are identical. However, let us consider a case where the equilibrium and the optimum coincide.

If x_3 does not come into the utility function, that is, if all the available labour is allocated to production, then the optimality conditions are no longer (4), but

$$\frac{S'_1}{S'_2} = \frac{g'_{23} - g'_{21}g'_{13}}{g'_{13} - g'_{12}g'_{23}}. \tag{9}$$

The equilibrium equations are (7) and

$$\frac{S'_1}{S'_2} = \frac{p_1}{p_2}. \tag{10}$$

When (8) is realised,

$$g'_{23} - g'_{21}g'_{13} = (1 - e)g'_{23},$$

so that (9) reduces to

$$\frac{S'_1}{S'_2} = \frac{g'_{23}}{g'_{13}} \tag{11}$$

which is in fact realised in the equilibrium since it follows from (7) and (10).

But when the allocation must also specify the amount of leisure x_3 and when there are symmetric external economies, the equilibrium E^1 contains too large a quantity of leisure. To see this, we make the following small modifications in E^1: let x_3 vary by du and a_{13} by $- du$; let x_1 and x_2 vary correspondingly by $dx_1 = - \sigma g'_{13} du$ and $dx_2 = - \sigma g'_{13}g'_{21} du$ respectively, where σ is the inverse of $1 - g'_{12}g'_{21}$, which also equals $1 - e^2$. (It can be verified that these modifications are compatible with (1) and (2), which express the technical constraints.) Now $g'_{21}g'_{13} = eg'_{23}$, so that $dx_2 = - \sigma e g'_{23} du$. The utility function therefore varies by

$$[S'_3 - \sigma(S'_1 g'_{13} + eS'_2 g'_{23})] du.$$

In competitive equilibrium, $S'_1 g'_{13} = S'_3$ and $S'_2 g'_{23} = S'_3$. The variation in S is therefore

$$[1 - \sigma(1 + e)]S'_3 du = \frac{- e}{1 - e}S'_3 du,$$

the equality resulting from the fact that σ is the inverse of $1 - e^2$. We saw that e must be considered as less than 1 but positive in the case of external economy. The utility function will therefore increase if du is negative, that is, if the importance of leisure is reduced. The converse obviously is true in the case of external diseconomy.

(iii) *Payment for service or agreement*

There are various possible ways of improving the allocation of resources relative to competitive equilibrium. As we shall see, most of them appear particularly difficult to realise when it is a case of external diseconomies. So we shall first adopt the situation of external economies, which allows us a clearer understanding of the nature of the proposed solutions. We shall assume that only the first firm gives rise to external effects, since this is sufficient for the clear statement of the problems that now concern us.

The ideal solution would obviously be to identify an exact payment for the service that the first firm provides for the other. We should then have a new commodity, with index 4, whose output, completely absorbed as input a_{24} in the second firm, is equal to output x_1 of commodity 1. In the now amended competitive equilibrium, commodity 4 has a price p_4.

The first firm's profit is then $(p_1 + p_4)x_1 - a_{13}$, which gives the marginal equality

$$(p_1 + p_4)g'_{13} = 1. \tag{12}$$

The production function for firm 2 is $x_2 = g_2(a_{23}, a_{24})$ and its profit $p_2 x_2 - a_{23} - p_4 a_{24}$; hence the marginal conditions

$$p_2 g'_{23} = 1 \qquad p_2 g'_{24} = p_2 g'_{21} = p_4. \tag{13}$$

If we take account of this value of p_4 in (12), we find

$$p_1 g'_{13} = 1 - g'_{21}\frac{g'_{13}}{g'_{23}}.$$

This is just the optimality condition (5).

But this market equilibrium has no practical meaning, otherwise we should not talk of external effects. For one reason or another, the first firm cannot exclude the second from the service that it provides for it, and therefore cannot sell this service to it. In the case of diseconomies, the market does not allow compensation for the firm that suffers from external effects.

To resolve the difficulty, we might also think of a possible agreement between the firms. They then take a combined decision with a view to maximisation of the sum of their profits. If they operate in this way they will jointly determine the values a_{13} and a_{23} that maximise $p_1 x_1 + p_2 x_2 - a_{13} - a_{23}$, that is:

$$p_1 g_1(a_{13}) + p_2 g_2[a_{23}, g_1(a_{13})] - a_{13} - a_{23}.$$

These values will satisfy the equalities

$$\begin{cases} p_1 g'_{13} + p_2 g'_{21} g'_{13} - 1 = 0 \\ \qquad\qquad p_2 g'_{23} - 1 = 0 \end{cases}$$

which imply conditions (5) and (6).

This result is not surprising. The presence of external effects in production is not an obstacle to the definition of prices which correctly evaluate marginal rates of substitution for the community; but it is an obstacle to the decentralisation of production decisions.

In the case of external economies, the conclusions of agreements like that just discussed may also take place without having to be imposed on the firms. If, for example, g'_{23} is positive, as we assume here, it is to the advantage of the second firm to propose a change in the competitive equilibrium to the first firm, since an increase in x_1 benefits the former more than it costs the latter. Suppose for instance that there is a small positive change du in x_1 and the corresponding change du/g'_{13} in a_{13}. Since $p_1 g'_{13} = 1$ in competitive equilibrium, the decrease in the first firm's profit will be of second order with respect to du. On the other hand, the increase in the second firm's profit, $p_2 g'_{21} du$, is of first order. There is therefore a possible refund by the second firm to the first which makes the increase in x_1 advantageous to both firms.

In practice, the conclusion of such agreements is certainly a frequent corrective to highly localised external economies. However, many external economies are so diffuse in character that the beneficiaries cannot easily be identified. Moreover, when the activity of one agent results in damage to another, as happens in the case of external diseconomy, public opinion disapproves of the latter giving the former a reward for cutting down his activity.

These particular difficulties with regard to external diseconomies certainly explain why law and jurisprudence long ago introduced either restrictions on the exercise of property rights, or indemnities designed to correct those unfavourable external effects which can easily be localised.

(iv) *Taxes and subsidies*

An alternative solution lies in the institution of public aid for activities leading to external economies and taxation of activities responsible for external diseconomies. These subsidies or taxes could be so devised as to correct the reasons why competitive equilibrium does not bring about a good allocation of resources.

In the context of our model, and keeping to the situation where the second firm does not give rise to external effects ($g'_{12} = 0$), suppose that the first receives a subsidy, or pays a tax, proportional to its output. Let τ be the rate of subsidy ($\tau > 0$) or $-\tau$ the rate of tax ($\tau < 0$). Profit $(p_1 + \tau)x_1 - a_{13}$ is maximised when

$$p_1 g'_{13} = 1 - \tau g'_{13}.$$

This equation coincides exactly with the optimality condition (5) if τ is chosen correctly, that is, if

$$\tau = \frac{g'_{21}}{g'_{23}}, \tag{14}$$

which is positive in the case of external economies. If (14) is realised, the equilibrium achieves a good allocation of resources.

More generally, the optimality conditions can in principle be realised by the introduction of subsidies or taxes that are correctly calculated and sufficiently diversified to expand activities generating external economies and reduce activities responsible for external diseconomies.

Note, however, that two questions arise. In the first place, how can the public authority determine the appropriate rate τ of subsidy or tax? It must have some idea of the importance of external economies or diseconomies. The fact that they are diffuse greatly complicates the problem of determining the optimum and the corresponding rate τ.

In the second place, how will the subsidy be financed, or who will receive the yield from taxation? In our small model the only possible reply is that the corresponding sum must be substracted from or added to the consumer's income. This could be done by a levy or a transfer involving the consumer. But it is important that this should be devised in such a way that the presence of either does not result in marginal rates of substitution S'_1/S'_3 and S'_2/S'_3 differing from the prices p_1 and p_2. It is therefore necessary that the tax-regulations should make its amount independent of consumer decisions. Here again, the solution by subsidy or taxation is not easy.

(v) *External effects in consumption*

We have just made a fairly thorough investigation of a small model illustrating the problems raised by the presence of external effects in production. We can easily see that similar problems may appear if the needs or tastes of consumers are affected by the behaviour of other consumers. This is so when either altruism or the wish to emulate or impress their fellows causes some individuals to have preferences which no longer relate to the vector of their own consumption alone but to a vector involving also other individuals' consumption.

Without trying to go too deeply into this, we shall consider a very simple case of two consumers and two goods, where a state of the economy is represented by four numbers x_{11}, x_{12}, x_{21} and x_{22}. We assume that the physical possibilities require that these numbers satisfy

$$x_{11} + x_{12} + x_{21} + x_{22} = \omega,$$

where ω is a given number: from the point of view of production, the marginal rate of substitution between the two goods is 1.

If $h = 1$ corresponds to a staple good and $h = 2$ to a luxury good and if each of the two individuals is egoistic but aware of others, we can assume that the first consumer's preferences are represented by a function $S_1(x_{11}, x_{12}; x_{22})$ decreasing in x_{22} and the second consumer's preferences by a function $S_2(x_{21}, x_{22}; x_{12})$ decreasing in x_{12}. Let S'_{ih} be the derivative of S_i with respect to x_{ih}. Let Q'_1 and Q'_2 be the negatives of the derivatives respectively of S_1 and S_2 with respect to x_{22} and x_{12} (where $Q'_1 > 0$, $Q'_2 > 0$).

Clearly a Pareto optimum state satisfies the following marginal equations:

$$\frac{S'_{12}}{S'_{11}} = 1 + \frac{Q'_2}{S'_{21}} \qquad \frac{S'_{22}}{S'_{21}} = 1 + \frac{Q'_1}{S'_{11}}.$$

On the other hand, if an equilibrium is established in which the prices of the two goods are equal, because of production, and each individual takes as given the other's consumption, then the following equalities hold:

$$\frac{S'_{12}}{S'_{11}} = 1 \qquad \frac{S'_{22}}{S'_{21}} = 1.$$

Obviously consumption of the luxury good is too high in such an equilibrium; the utility levels of individuals could be improved by the simultaneous reduction, in some suitable way, of their consumption of 2 in favour of their consumption of 1.

Arguments similar to those dealing with external effects in production show that a Pareto optimum can be found by adequate taxation of the luxury good or by agreement between the two consumers to reduce their consumption of it.

3. Collective consumption

We now go on to discuss an example of a public good involving all consumers collectively. Suppose that there are three goods of which the first is 'public' and that a single firm produces this good from the other two according to a production function $y_1 = g(y_2, y_3)$. The ith consumer's utility function is then $S_i(x_1, x_{i2}, x_{i3})$ where x_1 represents the total available quantity of the public good.

(i) *Optimum*

Let us first find necessary conditions for a state E^0 to be an optimum, by considering the maximisation of S_1 subject to the following constraints:

$$
\begin{cases}
S_i(x_1, x_{i2}, x_{i3}) = S_i^0 & i = 2, 3, ..., m, \\
y_1 = g(y_2, y_3) \\
x_1 = y_1 + \omega_1 \\
\sum_{i=1}^{m} x_{ih} = y_h + \omega_h & h = 2, 3.
\end{cases}
\tag{15}
$$

After elimination of the Lagrange multipliers, the first-order conditions reduce to

$$
\sum_{i=1}^{m} \frac{S_{i1}'}{S_{i2}'} = -\frac{1}{g_2'}
\tag{16}
$$

$$
\frac{S_{i2}'}{S_{i3}'} = \frac{g_2'}{g_3'} \qquad \text{for} \qquad i = 1, 2, ..., m.
\tag{17}
$$

We are familiar with condition (17). It requires that the marginal rate of substitution between goods 2 and 3 is the same for all agents. But condition (16), which involves the public good, has a new form; it expresses the fact that the *sum of the marginal rates of substitution of the public good* 1 *with respect to the private good* 2 *must equal the marginal rate of substitution between these goods in production.*

(ii) *Market pseudo-equilibrium*

Can the optimum E^0 be realised as a market equilibrium? Let us try to find a price-system compatible with the establishment of E^0. We can think of it as follows.

Ordinary prices p_2 and p_3 exist for the private goods 2 and 3, and these prices apply for all agents. On the other hand, there are as many prices for the public good as there are agents; p_1 for the producing firm, p_{1i} for the ith consumer. So each unit of output of 1 brings p_1 to the firm while it costs the ith consumer p_{1i}. Under these conditions, p_1 must naturally be the sum of p_{1i}:

$$
p_1 = \sum_{i=1}^{m} p_{1i},
\tag{18}
$$

that is, the organisation that manages the public good receives contributions from the consumers, pays the price of the good to the firm and has a balanced budget.

If in E^0 the firm maximises its profit subject to the constraint of its production function, then the following equalities are satisfied:

$$
\frac{p_1}{p_2} = \frac{-1}{g_2'}, \qquad \frac{p_2}{p_3} = \frac{g_2'}{g_3'}.
\tag{19}
$$

If in E^0 the ith consumer maximises his utility function subject to the budget constraint

$$p_{1i}x_1 + p_2x_{2i} + p_3x_{3i} \leqslant p_{1i}x_1^0 + p_2x_{2i}^0 + p_3x_{3i}^0,$$

then the following equalities are satisfied:

$$\frac{p_{1i}}{p_2} = \frac{S'_{i1}}{S'_{i2}}, \quad \frac{p_2}{p_3} = \frac{S'_{i2}}{S'_{i3}}. \tag{20}$$

Thus in the optimum E^0, where (16) and (17) hold, appropriate prices exist and obey (18), (19) and (20). Conversely, in every feasible state E^0 where the firm maximises its profit and the consumers their respective utility functions, (19) and (20) are satisfied. By eliminating prices between (18), (19) and (20), we revert to (16) and (17).

It seems therefore that we can find a market equilibrium corresponding to the optimum E^0 by introducing individual prices p_{1i} for the public good and that conversely such a market equilibrium constitutes an optimum.

However a little reflection shows that the expression 'market equilibrium' is misused here. It is at most a 'market pseudo-equilibrium' in Samuelson's phrase. We assumed above that the consumer fixes his demand for the public good 1 exactly as he would for a private good with price p_{1i}. But, since he knows that 1 is a public good, *it is not in the consumer's interest to reveal his demand*, since if he does not claim it openly he can still benefit from it without having to bear its cost. So the quantity $p_{1i}x_1$ which represents the ith consumer's financial contribution to the production of x_1 will not be paid spontaneously. It can certainly take the form of a tax, but we are then no longer concerned with a pure market equilibrium and must find out how the amount of the tax can be decided.

(iii) *Equilibrium with subscription*

Before tackling this question, we shall try to find out which equilibrium is likely to be established in the absence of government authority or deliberate agreement among the agents. The only system that respects the complete autonomy of agents is of course the system whereby the public good is financed by *subscription*, with each consumer making a contribution to increase the production of the public good. However, when fixing the amount of his contribution, each individual is concerned only with the advantage that he personally will gain from the additional production, irrespective of the gain to others. It is therefore to be expected that he will fix his contribution at too low a level.

To see this in detail without too many complications, we shall simplify the model slightly. Let there be a single private good ($h = 2$) and let the production function of the public good be as follows:

$$y_1 = -ky_2,$$

where k is a constant. Also let $\omega_1 = 0$, and therefore $x_1 = y_1$.

Let s_i denote the ith consumer's subscription and let this subscription be made in terms of the good 2 (this does not restrict the generality of the analysis). The production of the public good is then

$$x_1 = k \sum_{i=1}^{m} s_i. \tag{21}$$

In addition, the ith consumer's consumption of the second good is

$$x_{i2} = \omega_{i2} - s_i, \tag{22}$$

where ω_{i2} denotes his initial resources of the good 2.

If he considers the contributions s_α of the other agents α as given, the ith consumer tries to fix x_i so as to maximise $S_i(x_1, x_{i2})$; in view of (21) and (22), this requires that

$$\frac{S'_{i1}}{S'_{i2}} = \frac{1}{k}. \tag{23}$$

Now, with the above simplifications to the model, the optimality conditions (16) and (17) reduce to

$$\sum_{i=1}^{m} \frac{S'_{i1}}{S'_{i2}} = \frac{1}{k}. \tag{24}$$

Comparison of (23) and (24) shows that, *in an economy where the public good is financed by subscription, the output of this good, as it results from the decisions of the individual consumers, is too small*; each fixes his contribution so that the marginal rate of substitution of the public good for him is $1/k$. The sum of the individual rates is then m times greater than the marginal rate of substitution of the first good with respect to the second in production.†

Clearly the equilibrium with subscription is properly speaking a non-cooperative equilibrium for the game corresponding to the economy under discussion, where each consumer has the 'pay-off function' S_i and chooses the 'action' s_i.

Now, it is often to the mutual advantage of the players in a game to discard a non-cooperative equilibrium in favour of a state that is attainable only by concerted agreement. This is the case here, contrary to the situation where there are neither external effects nor public goods.

---

† It is a useful exercise to verify that, if $\omega_{i2} = \omega_2/m$ and $S_i = \gamma \log x_1 + \log x_{i2}$, then the equilibrium with subscription E^1 is defined by

$$x_1^1 = \frac{k\gamma\omega_2}{m+\gamma}; \qquad x_{i2}^1 = \frac{\omega_2}{m+\gamma}; \qquad s_i^1 = \frac{\gamma\omega_2}{m(m+\gamma)}.$$

In addition, the market pseudo-equilibrium defined previously is

$$x_1^0 = \frac{k\gamma\omega_2}{1+\gamma}; \qquad x_{i2}^0 = \frac{\omega_2}{m(1+\gamma)}; \qquad \frac{p_1}{p_2} = \frac{1}{k}; \qquad p_{1i} = \frac{p_1}{m}.$$

This latter state is an optimum. It involves a higher consumption of the first good than in E^1.

(iv) *Politico-economic equilibrium*†

Suppose that a collective decision procedure is set up to determine collective consumption x_1 of the public good together with the contribution t_i of each individual. A public decision is now the choice of a 'budget' consisting of $m + 1$ quantities $(x_1; t_1, t_2, ..., t_m)$. Note that this decision, although motivated by the existence of the public good, may also aim at modifying the distribution of income or wealth by means of taxes t_i. What will the equilibrium be for a community like this where the individual consumers have set up a public authority to supervise and finance their collective needs?

To answer this, we return to the model used in our discussion of the optimum and of market pseudo-equilibrium. Private individual decisions determine consumptions x_{i2} and x_{i3}; the private decision of the firm determines (y_1, y_2, y_3). Public decision determines the budget

$(x_1; t_1, t_2, ..., t_m)$.

Let us assume that the markets for the three goods are competitive and that prices p_1, p_2, p_3 are established in them. This may seem a strong assumption for the market for the public good; we could make it more plausible by supposing that several firms, rather than only one firm, produce this good, but this further complication adds nothing in clarity to our analysis. At all events, we assume that the firm maximises its profit, taking prices as given.

Obviously the ith consumer makes his decision with the aim of maximising S_i; it is subject to the budget constraint

$$p_2 x_{i2} + p_3 x_{i3} = R_i - t_i, \tag{25}$$

where R_i is the ith consumer's disposable income before he makes his contribution t_i (if the initial resources are privately owned, R_i is the value $p\omega_i$ of the vector ω_i of i's resources). The firm makes its decision with the aim of maximising its profit; it must obey the production function. What of the public decision?

For a complete theory of equilibrium, we ought to represent in detail the process of collective decision-making. The attempt to do this is liable to distract us too far into the field of political science, since we should have to establish distinctions between different institutional systems. So, as we did previously in the discussion of the optimum, we shall be content with a partial theory, and make an assumption about the way in which the decision process works. This assumption will not be sufficient to characterise it, but will allow us a better grasp of our present problem.

---

† This section is based on Foley, *Resource Allocation and the Public Sector*, Yale Economic Essays, 7, Spring 1967.

Since the public decision results from organised consultation among the representatives of the individual consumers, it is natural to assume that the chosen budget will have the following property: *there is no further possible change in the budget that will improve the situation of one individual without causing a deterioration in the situation of any other individual*. In fact, it would be to no one's interest to reject an improvement of this kind, so that it would necessarily be adopted in every decision-making process where each individual is represented. In other words, the budget must not be rejected unanimously by the citizens.

A *politico-economic equilibrium* is therefore a feasible state with accompanying price-system and tax-system, where resources are compatible with uses for each good, the firm maximises its profit subject to the constraint of its production function, consumers maximise their utility functions subject to their budget constraints (25) and the public budget satisfies the above condition.

The assumption on the public budget is clearly analogous to the assumption that the outcome of a game necessarily belongs to its 'core'. In the language of games theory, we could say that the chosen budget must not be blocked by the coalition consisting of all the individuals. Now, as we saw previously in Chapter 5, information and communication costs, or a refusal to participate on the part of agents seeking special advantages, may prevent the assumption from being realised. It is therefore more restrictive than it appears at first sight. However, we shall show that, when it is satisfied, *every equilibrium is necessarily an optimum*.

Given our definition of optimality, this would obviously be a trivial result if the collective decision related directly to the state of the economy. It is interesting because this decision relates only to the budget and takes the prices of the different goods as given. Thus the economy preserves some degree of decentralisation with the consumers, the firm and the 'public authority' acting in a relatively autonomous way.

Let us examine more closely the conditions to be satisfied by the chosen budget. This budget is obviously balanced, which requires

$$p_1 x_1 = \sum_{i=1}^m t_i. \tag{26}$$

Our assumption also requires that x_1 and the t_i are chosen so as to maximise S_1 subject to the constraint that the values of $S_2, S_3, ..., S_m$ are fixed. This condition assumes implicitly that the private consumptions x_{i2} and x_{i3} of the ith individual are settled permanently so that S_i is maximised subject to the budget constraint expressed by (25).

In other words, the joint effect of the consumers' behaviour and the public authority's decision-making process is to determine x_{i2}'s and x_{i3}'s, x_1 and the t_i's which, for given values of p_1, p_2, p_3 and the R_i, maximise $S_1(x_1, x_{12}, x_{13})$ subject to the constraints

$$
\begin{cases}
S_i(x_1, x_{i2}, x_{i3}) = S_i^0 & i = 2, 3, ..., m \\
p_2 x_{i2} + p_3 x_{i3} = R_i - t_i & i = 1, 2, ..., m \\
p_1 x_1 = \sum_{i=1}^{m} t_i.
\end{cases}
\tag{27}
$$

After elimination of the Lagrange multipliers, the first-order conditions reduce to

$$
\sum_{i=1}^{m} \frac{S_{i1}'}{S_{i2}'} = \frac{p_1}{p_2}, \qquad \frac{S_{i2}'}{S_{i3}'} = \frac{p_2}{p_3}.
\tag{28}
$$

Suppose now that an equilibrium has been established. The decisions of the consumers and the public authority ensure that (28) holds, while the decision of the firm ensures that (19) holds. This equilibrium appears as a 'market pseudo-equilibrium' in which price p_{1i} equals $p_2 S_{i1}'/S_{i2}'$. The equalities (18), (19) and (20) are then satisfied. As we have seen, this state is Pareto optimal.

The proof suggests that the result does not depend on the form in which the individuals' contributions are expressed. Their basis and their method of calculation are irrelevant to optimality, since x_1, the t_i, the x_{i2} and the x_{i3} are decided simultaneously by the parallel behaviour of consumers and public authority. Of course, the fiscal system may be more or less favourable to such and such an individual; but, to the extent that our assumption is satisfied, the system finally adopted necessarily ensures that a Pareto optimum is established.

Conversely, suppose we have an optimum E^0; it satisfies (16) and (17). Let prices, taxes and incomes be defined so that (18), (26) and (25) are satisfied successively, as is always possible. This gives us a politico-economic equilibrium, which ensures that the optimum is maintained, provided that any change in the budget requires unanimous agreement among the individuals, and that the functions g and S_i satisfy the usual convexity assumptions. Equations (19) are then sufficient for maximisation of the firm's profit, and (27) and (28) are sufficient for a joint equilibrium of the consumers and the public decision.

The statement that every optimum corresponds to a politico-economic equilibrium can easily be misinterpreted. The only restriction on the public budget appearing in this equilibrium is that it should not be rejected unanimously by the citizens. Now, is it possible, by appropriate political organisation, to realise *any* budget that is not rejected unanimously? In fact, the adoption of some budgets among those of this kind may well require that certain individuals are given a dictatorial influence in the decision-making process.

To return to our particular example, we note also that the public good affects only the consumers and not production conditions for firms. This fact was used in the proof that every politico-economic equilibrium is an optimum. So what we said does not apply to the case where public goods affect firms.

Of course we could consider this case and see how taxes and subsidies, or participation by firms in collective decision-making processes allow the realisation of a Pareto optimum. But we should learn little new from this.

In real life there are many situations where external effects and collective consumptions are combined in varying ways. The formal analysis of such situations obviously becomes complex, but the principles established above remain valid.

4. Public service subject to congestion

We shall briefly discuss the example of a public service involving a good that can be used privately but whose quality depends on the global demand to be satisfied, which is typical of situations of congestion such as arise more and more frequently in urbanised communities.

Suppose then that there are only two goods and that the ith consumer's utility function is $S_i(x_{i1}, x_{i2}, x_2)$ where x_2 is total consumption of the second good. Suppose also that there is only one firm (the public service) producing the good 2 from the good 1 according to the production function $f(y_1, y_2) = 0$.

This case is intermediary to the two examples of pure external effect and pure public good discussed in Sections 2 and 3. As in Section 2, where an external effect appeared in the area of production, so here an external effect appears in the area of consumption, since i's preferences depend through x_2 on the other individuals' consumptions $x_{\alpha 2}$. Also, the good 2 can be considered in two ways: first as a private good, since it is privately used, and then as a public good since each particular individual is affected by its total production.†
In the case of congestion, the total consumption of x_2 in fact has disutility for the individuals, that is, the derivative of S_i with respect to x_2 is negative; for simplicity, we shall denote this derivative by S'_{i3}.

Let us first examine the conditions for an optimum. The following constraints are involved for maximisation of S_1:

$$\begin{cases} S_i(x_{i1}, x_{i2}, x_2) = S_i^0 & i = 2, 3, \ldots, m \\ f(y_1, y_2) = 0 \\ \sum_{i=1}^{m} x_{i1} = y_1 + \omega_1 \\ x_2 = \sum_{i=1}^{m} x_{i2} = y_2 + \omega_2. \end{cases} \qquad (29)$$

---

† Kolm proposes that the good 2 be said to cause 'collective concern'. See Kolm, 'Concernements et decisions collectifs; contribution a l'analyse de quelques phénomènes fondamentaux de l'organisation des sociétés'. *Analyse et Prévision*, July-August 1967.

After elimination of the Lagrange multipliers, the first-order conditions reduce to

$$\frac{f_2'}{f_1'} = \frac{S_{i2}'}{S_{i1}'} + \sum_{\alpha=1}^{m} \frac{S_{\alpha 3}'}{S_{\alpha 1}'} \qquad i = 1, 2, ..., m. \tag{30}$$

If the common value in an optimum E^0 of the ratios S_{i2}'/S_{i1}' is taken as defining relative price p_2/p_1, the pair (x_{i1}^0, x_{i2}^0) is an equilibrium for the ith consumer.

In order that the pair (y_1^0, y_2^0) should be an equilibrium for the firm, its relative price must be, not p_2/p_1, but

$$\frac{p_2}{p_1}(1 - \tau),$$

where, by definition, τ is the number:

$$\tau = -\frac{p_1}{p_2} \sum_{\alpha=1}^{m} \frac{S_{\alpha 3}'}{S_{\alpha 1}'}. \tag{31}$$

Since the derivative S_{i3} is negative, τ is generally positive. The public service must decide on its output taking account of the fact that the social value of an additional unit is not equal to the price p_2 paid by consumers but to a lower price $p_2(1 - \tau)$. It must fix output at the level where $p_2(1 - \tau)$ equals marginal cost. Conversely, we can say that the price p_2 paid by the consumer has two constituents: $p_2(1 - \tau)$, the marginal cost of production, and τp_2, the marginal social cost due to congestion. The absence of such a difference between marginal cost of production and price would lead the individuals to consume beyond the social optimum.

Here as before, the essential difficulty lies in the measurement of external effects, that is, in the determination of the marginal rates of substitution $S_{\alpha 3}'/S_{\alpha 1}'$ involved in the calculation of τ. The market tells us nothing about them. This gap could conceivably be filled by a suitable system of inquiries, or a collective decision-making process. To the extent that the same tax τp_2 must be paid by all the consumers, the difficulties relating to the revelation of preferences are less serious than in the case of pure public goods.

5. Public service with fixed cost

As we saw in Chapter 4, the existence of activities carried on under increasing returns to scale complicates the questions relating to the optimal organisation of production and distribution. We are now in a position to return to this problem and to see its nature more clearly.

We shall consider a simple model where a public service produces a private good but is subject to a high fixed cost and therefore to decreasing average costs. For reasons that will appear later, it often happens that activities carried on under increasing returns to scale are publicly managed, although this is not absolutely necessary. (We saw that a private monopoly may also find itself in equilibrium in spite of the presence of increasing returns.)

We note in passing that this model and the model discussed in Section 3 show that the distinctions of public and private goods on the one hand, and public and private firms on the other, must not be confused. A public good may be produced by private enterprise; a private good may be produced by public enterprise.

(i) *Optimum*

Suppose then we have an economy with m consumers, 2 firms and 3 goods. Suppose that there are no initial resources of the first two goods, which are consumable ($\omega_1 = \omega_2 = 0$), and positive initial resources ω_3 of the third good, which occurs only as input in the production of the first two goods. Let a_{13} and a_{23} be the inputs in question. The ith consumer's utility function is the quasi-concave function $S_i(x_{i1}, x_{i2})$. Production of the first good is governed by the production function $x_1 = g_1(a_{13})$, which obeys the usual assumptions and therefore involves non-increasing marginal returns. Production of the second good is governed by

$$a_{23} = \begin{cases} \beta + \gamma x_2 & \text{if} \quad x_2 > 0, \\ 0 & \text{if} \quad x_2 = 0; \end{cases} \tag{32}$$

where β and γ are two positive numbers representing a fixed cost, involved whenever production is non-zero, and a proportional cost respectively. This is obviously a particular form for increasing returns to scale. However, it has some relevance since it is based on the indivisibility of a fixed cost and indivisibilities are the real cause of increasing returns.

In the space (x_1, x_2) of total consumptions the set of attainable vectors is represented partly by the points within or on the curve BC defined by eliminating a_{13} and a_{23} in

$$\begin{cases} x_1 = g_1(a_{13}) \\ a_{23} = \beta + \gamma x_2 \\ a_{13} + a_{23} = \omega_3, \end{cases} \tag{33}$$

and partly by the points on the segment AB, where A has coordinates $(g_1(\omega_3), 0)$. The curve BC is concave downwards, since marginal returns for g_1 are non-increasing.

A priori, the optimal states can be represented in this space by the point A if there is zero production of the second good (cf. Figure 2, for the case of a single consumer), or by the points other than B on BC if there is positive production of the second good (cf. Figure 1).

An optimum represented by A is obviously a market equilibrium provided that the second good does not exist in the market. So we shall concentrate initially on an optimum represented by a point lying above the x_1-axis (the point M in Figure 1).

In such an optimal state E^0, $S_1(x_{11}, x_{12})$ is maximised subject to the constraints:

$$
\begin{cases}
S_i(x_{i1}, x_{i2}) = S_i^0 & i = 2, 3, ..., m \\
x_1 = g_1(a_{13}) \\
a_{23} = \beta + \gamma x_2 \\
x_1 = \sum_{i=1}^{m} x_{i1} \\
x_2 = \sum_{i=1}^{m} x_{i2} \\
\omega_3 = a_{13} + a_{23}.
\end{cases}
\tag{34}
$$

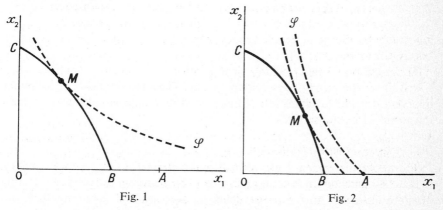

Fig. 1   Fig. 2

Let p_1, p_2, p_3 denote the Lagrange multipliers relating to the last three constraints. After elimination of the multipliers relating to the other constraints, the necessary first-order conditions for an optimum are:

$$
\frac{S_{i2}'}{S_{i1}'} = \frac{p_2}{p_1} \qquad i = 1, 2, ..., m;
\tag{35}
$$

$$
g_1' = \frac{p_3}{p_1};
\tag{36}
$$

$$
p_2 = \gamma p_3.
\tag{37}
$$

If p_1, p_2 and p_3 are interpreted as the prices of the three goods, we revert to the more general results of Chapter 4. The complex (x_{i1}^0, x_{i2}^0) appears as an equilibrium for the ith consumer and the complex (x_1^0, a_{13}^0) as an equilibrium for the first firm. Moreover, the price of the second good must equal its marginal cost γp_3. But (x_2^0, a_{23}^0) is not an equilibrium for the second firm since the corresponding profit $p_2 x_2^0 - \beta p_3 - \gamma x_2^0 p_3 = - \beta p_3$ is less than the zero profit from zero production.

If the optimum in question is to be realised in a market economy, the second firm must be required to produce the good 2 and to sell it at marginal cost. But it then incurs a deficit, which must be covered.

The covering of the deficit will naturally be ensured by taxes t_i imposed on the individuals and such that

$$\sum_{i=1}^{m} t_i = \beta p_3. \tag{38}$$

The definition of such taxes raises no particular difficulty since household incomes R_i can always be chosen so that

$$R_i = p_1 x_{i1}^0 + p_2 x_{i2}^0 + t_i. \tag{39}$$

Note however that t_i must be fixed independently of the consumption complex (x_{i1}, x_{i2}) chosen by the ith consumer, since it might otherwise be to his advantage to choose a complex other than (x_{i1}^0, x_{i2}^0) with a view to reducing his contribution t_i.

The conditions under which firm 2 must be managed therefore differ widely from the purely competitive system. They assume fairly strict public intervention. This explains why firms placed in similar situations often have the status of public services.

(ii) *Politico-economic equilibrium*

The above discussion deals with the characterisation of an optimum as a judiciously amended market equilibrium. The converse property is certainly of more interest: how can we define a decentralised economy that will achieve an optimum? At our present stage, the answer is fairly immediate.

We assume that the markets for the goods are competitive, and that firm 2 is required to sell its product at marginal cost in spite of its resulting deficit. A collective decision-making process is established which decides whether or not the good 2 is to be produced and in the former case, how the coverage of the deficit βp_3 is to be shared among the individuals.

We shall see that, if this process satisfies the assumption of section 3(iv), then an equilibrium is also an optimum.

Consider, for example, an equilibrium E^0 involving positive output of the good 2. In particular, let $(x_{i1}^0, x_{i2}^0, t_i^0)$ be the characteristics of the equilibrium for the ith consumer. We assume that, contrary to our required result, there exists a state E^1 that is preferable to E^0 for all the consumers. The case where E^1 involves positive output of the second good is eliminated by the theory in Chapter 4 (cf. proposition 6), since, *assuming that the fixed cost of* production of the second good *is covered*, the politico-economic equilibrium E^0 is a market equilibrium in the sense of Chapter 4; in particular, if no account is taken of the fixed cost, firm 2 maximises its profit. The state E^1 is therefore such that

$$S_i(x_{i1}^1, 0) \geqslant S_i(x_{i1}^0, x_{i2}^0) \qquad \text{for} \qquad i = 1, 2, ..., m \qquad (40)$$

where the inequality holds strictly at least once. Moreover, $x_1^1 = g_1(\omega_3)$, since we can always assume that resources are totally employed in the state E^1.

The concavity of g_1 implies

$$x_1^1 = g_1(\omega_3) \leqslant g_1(a_{13}^0) + g_1'(a_{13}^0) \cdot a_{23}^0 \qquad (41)$$

since $a_{13}^0 + a_{23}^0 = \omega_3$ (cf. theorem 1 of the appendix). In view of (33) and (36), which are satisfied in E^0, (41) becomes

$$x_1^1 \leqslant x_1^0 + \frac{p_3^0}{p_1^0}(\beta + \gamma x_2^0)$$

or, in view of (37),

$$p_1^0 x_1^1 \leqslant p_1^0 x_1^0 + p_2^0 x_2^0 + p_3^0 \beta. \qquad (42)$$

We set

$$t_i^* = p_1^0 x_{i1}^0 + p_2^0 x_{i2}^0 + t_i^0 - p_1^0 x_{i1}^1 = R_i - p_1^0 x_{i1}^1, \qquad (43)$$

where R_i is the income associated with E^0.

The relation (38) satisfied in E^0 and (42) then imply

$$\sum_{i=1}^{m} t_i^* \geqslant 0. \qquad (44)$$

A fortiori, there exist taxes t_i^1 at most equal to the t_i^* and whose sum is zero. The initial budget is therefore rejected unanimously in favour of the budget involving taxes t_i^1 and zero production of the good 2. The inequality $t_i^1 \leqslant R_i - p_1^0 x_{i1}^1$ shows that this new budget allows each consumer to obtain $(x_{i1}^1, 0)$, which by hypothesis is preferred to the best complex (x_{i1}^0, x_{i2}^0) compatible with the budget contained in E^0.

The existence of E^1 therefore contradicts the fact that E^0 is an equilibrium, which is what we had to prove. Completely similar reasoning applies to the case where E^0 involves zero production of the good 2.

Thus every politico-economic equilibrium is a Pareto optimum. This is not a surprising result by analogy with the result in Chapter 4 stating that every market equilibrium is an optimum. However, it is significant in so far as a politico-economic equilibrium involving positive production of the good 2 may exist even though there is no market equilibrium that has this characteristic.

However, we have not completely solved the problem raised by the decentralisation of decisions in our model, and *a fortiori* in more general economies where some firms operate under conditions of increasing returns to scale. For we have not really shown that every optimum can be realised as a politico-economic equilibrium, even with our very unrestrictive definition of the latter.

Consider what we did. We associated with the optimum a system of taxes t_i ensuring coverage of the deficit incurred by the public service. But we did not show that, if prices p_1, p_2, p_3 are taken as given, the budget defined by the production decision for the good 2 and by taxes t_i will in no circumstances be rejected unanimously. This can only be proved if g_1 is linear, when relative prices p_1/p_3 and p_2/p_3 are independent of the chosen state. If this particular condition is not satisfied, we can conceive of an optimum incompatible with the restricted decentralisation involved in our politico-economic equilibria.

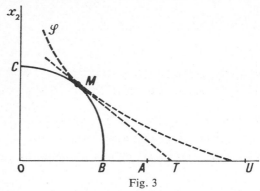

Fig. 3

Consider the situation illustrated by Figure 3, where there is a single consumer while the optimum is a point M involving positive consumption of the good 2. The prices p_1, p_2, p_3 corresponding to this optimum are well defined, up to a multiplicative constant, by (36) and (37). Also the tax t equals βp_3.

When he examines the budget on the basis of the prices p_1, p_2, p_3 and the tax t, the consumer thinks that by not paying the tax he could achieve a point U involving zero consumption of the good 2 and consumption x^U of the good 1 defined by

$$p_1 x^U = p_1 x_1^0 + p_2 x_2^0 + t. \tag{45}$$

The consumer therefore rejects the budget if the point U lies to the right of the indifference curve $\mathscr{S}$ passing through M. Now, U is always on the right of A when the first good is produced under decreasing marginal returns (g_1 is strictly concave) so that U may well be on the right of $\mathscr{S}$ even though by hypothesis A is on the left. The optimum cannot then be realised as a politico-economic equilibrium.

Let us verify that U is on the right of A when g_1 is concave. Let T be the point where the tangent at M to BC meets the horizontal axis. We can write (45) in the form:

$$x^U = x^T + \beta \frac{p_3}{p_1}, \tag{46}$$

or

$$x^U = x^T + \beta g_1'(a_{13}^0). \tag{47}$$

Also,

$$x^A = x^B + g_1(\omega_3) - g_1(\omega_3 - \beta). \tag{48}$$

Now, since g_1 is strictly increasing and concave,

$$x^B < x^T$$

and

$$g_1(\omega_3) - g_1(\omega_3 - \beta) < \beta g_1'(\omega_3 - \beta) < \beta g_1'(a_{13}^0).$$

These two inequalities imply that $x^A < x^U$.[†]

(iii) *An economic calculus*

The difficulty which has just been raised stems from the fact that the prices corresponding to the optimum M evaluate the marginal equivalences correctly only in the neighbourhood of M. To get round this difficulty, a rule of economic calculus has been suggested which takes account of the fact that prices must be revised progressively as we move along the boundary of the domain of attainable states. Let us examine this rule in the context of our model.[‡]

It is now convenient to choose the good 3 as numéraire and to let r_1 and r_2 denote the supposed prices of the first two goods, these prices being functions of the characteristics of the state to which they refer. More precisely, given a programme for the public service (a value of x_2), these prices must correspond to the marginal rates of substitution and transformation in the remaining sectors of the economy, these sectors being assumed to be optimally run. In other words, r_1 and r_2 permanently satisfy

$$r_1 = \frac{1}{g_1'(a_{13})}, \tag{49}$$

$$\frac{r_2}{r_1} = \frac{S_{i2}'}{S_{i1}'}. \tag{50}$$

[†] This proof also establishes that $x^A = x^U$ when g_1 is linear, in which case the optimum can always be realised as an equilibrium, as was stated earlier.

[‡] A general theory of this economic calculus is given by Lesourne, in 'A la recherche d'un critère de rentabilité pour les investissements importants,' *Cahiers du Séminaire d'Econométrie*, No. 5, 1959.

Suppose we have a situation where the production of the second good is zero, where the resource ω_3 is completely used in the production of the first good and where the output of this good is distributed among the consumers in a certain way. We now assume that production of the good 2 is increased progressively from zero and that each individual's utility remains constant at its level when production was zero; for the moment we are not concerned whether this transformation is technically feasible. The vatriaions in output of goods 1 and 2 must be distributed among the consumers so that

$$dx_{i1} = \frac{-S'_{i2}}{S'_{i1}} dx_{i2} = -\frac{r_2}{r_1} dx_{i2}; \tag{51}$$

it follows that, for total outputs x_1 and x_2,

$$dx_1 = -\frac{r_2}{r_1} dx_2. \tag{52}$$

Let us now examine the implications for inputs of the variations dx_1 and dx_2; but we still ignore the fixed cost, which must be incurred when we go from zero production to positive production of the second good. The negative variation dx_1 liberates a certain quantity $- da_{13}$ of good 3 while the positive variation dx_2 absorbs a quantity da_{23}. The net available surplus will be

$$- da_{13} - da_{23} = \frac{1}{g'_1} dx_1 - \gamma \, dx_2,$$

or, in view of (49) and (52),

$$(r_2 - \gamma) \, dx_2.$$

Clearly there is never any advantage in increasing x_2 beyond the quantity x_2^*, for which $r_2 = \gamma$, that is, for which (37) holds, since, with the usual convexity assumptions, r_2 decreases as x_2 increases (the marginal rate of substitution S'_{i2}/S'_{i1} decreases and g'_1 increases, therefore r_2/r_1 and r_1 both decrease). Beyond x_2^* a change keeping utilities constant no longer makes more of the good 3 available, but on the contrary absorbs a positive increasing quantity of it, because of variable costs; such a change is therefore disadvantageous.

But is it advantageous to go from $x_2 = 0$ to $x_2 = x_2^*$? It will be, if this releases a greater quantity of good 3 than that required to cover the fixed cost β.

To calculate the quantity of good 3 that is released, we need only consider the expression σ, called the 'surplus'† and defined by:

$$\sigma = \int_0^{x_2^*} (r_2 - \gamma) \, dx_2, \tag{53}$$

† There are many variants of the notion of surplus throughout economic theory. The reader must always check rigorously which particular version is used if he wishes to ensure that an argument is valid. In fact it is only rarely that the introduction of a 'surplus' helps toward the solution of the stated problem.

where the integral is taken for r_2 varying with x_2 along the transformations described above.

If $\sigma > \beta$, it will be possible to cover both the fixed cost and the variable cost of production of x_2^*, to maintain each consumer's utility at its level when x_2 is zero and to release an additional quantity of good 3, which can be used to produce either good 1 or good 2 and thus increase the utility of one or more consumers. Conversely, if $\sigma < \beta$, it is not possible to produce the second good and at the same time maintain the utility of all the consumers; consequently the optimum implies $x_2 = 0$.

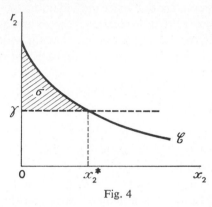

Fig. 4

This rule can be illustrated by a diagram with x_2 as abscissa, and, as ordinate, the value of r_2 corresponding to the marginal rate of substitution between goods 2 and 3 in the rest of the economy when it is optimally managed and the individuals' utilities remain constant. The surplus is equal to the area between the curve $\mathscr{C}$ representing r_2 and the horizontal with ordinate γ. It is advantageous to produce x_2^* if this area exceeds β.

Has this rule any practical relevance? Is it possible for the managers of the public service producing the good 2, or the citizens required to make a decision about it, to construct $\mathscr{C}$? It seems difficult to give a positive answer *a priori*. The variations in r_2 depend as a rule on all the elements of our model, namely the functions S_i, the function g_1, the initial state on which our reasoning is based. It seems as easy to determine the optimum directly as to construct the curve; in fact, both demand very full information. In short, the rule we have just established does not seem to allow real decentralisation of decisions.

Its supporters hold that a first approximation to the curve $\mathscr{C}$ can often be determined from very partial information and that such an approximation is sufficient. This is a question of fact which the reader can try to decide for himself.

The particular case where g_1 is linear has been given special consideration.

It is not surprising that it is favourable, since, as we have seen, it lends itself better to decentralisation than the general case. Let us consider it again.

Equation (49) shows that the price r_1 of the first good is then constant. Let us call it p_1 to remind us of this property. Price r_2 now depends only on individual utility functions since (50) becomes

$$r_2 = p_1 \frac{S'_{i2}}{S'_{i1}}. \tag{54}$$

Under these conditions, we can imagine a process for constructing a curve near $\mathscr{C}$. Let us fix the income of each individual at the value $R_i = p_1 x_{i1}^1$ of the quantity of the good 1 that he receives if the second good is not produced. We state successively decreasing prices r_2, starting with a value sufficiently high to correspond to zero demand for x_2. At each stated price r_2 we observe the demands x_{i2} of the different individuals and the corresponding sum x_2. Since 2 is a private good, we can assume that individual preferences will be revealed correctly and that individual demands will continually satisfy (54). The total demand x_2 will then define the abscissa of the point on a curve $\mathscr{C}'$ corresponding to the stated price. We can conceive that in practice determination of the demands at each price will be carried out by survey of a representative sample of individuals.

The difference between $\mathscr{C}$ and $\mathscr{C}'$ stems from the fact that the former is defined with reference to the indifference curves passing through the initial complexes x_i^1, while for the second incomes were fixed. The criterion discussed above for deciding whether to produce x_2 does not apply to the 'surplus' defined on $\mathscr{C}'$. But this surplus can be considered as an approximation to that defined on $\mathscr{C}$.

There is a tariff principle connected with this rule, as opposed to the sale at marginal cost justified in Chapter 4 and discussed above in Sections (i) and (ii). Let us discuss this briefly.†

Instead of assuming that all units of the second good are sold at the same price, let us assume that the public service sells each additional quantity at its marginal value to the individual buyer,‡ that is, at the value $p_1 S'_{i2} \, dx_{i2}/S'_{i1}$ of the quantity $dx_{i1} = S'_{i2} \, dx_{i2}/S'_{i1}$ that is equivalent to dx_{i2}. The abscissa of the point on $\mathscr{C}'$ with ordinate r_2 then represents the total number of units that will be sold at a price greater than or equal to r_2. If total output x_2^* is determined so that the last unit just covers the variable cost, the public service's

---

† This principle is due in particular to Dupuit and Colson. See the 'théorie du péage, in Colson, *Textes choisis*, edited by G.-H. Bousquet, Dalloz, Paris 1960, pp. 152-178.

‡ We could then speak of an 'ad valorem' tariff provided that we interpret this as a charge assessed in accordance with the value of the service rendered. But the expression is in fact used in a different sense to define transport tariffs that are proportional to the value of the freight.

net profit $\sigma - \beta$ will be positive or zero exactly when the optimum involves production of the good 2. The tariff principle in question is therefore advocated together with the rule that the public service must not suffer a loss.

Of course in practice it is impossible to apply a tariff schedule modelled exactly on demand. But the above principle may justify some discrimination among the units sold. The aim of such discrimination may be to balance the budget of the public service; the amount that each consumer pays in excess of the variable cost of the quantity he demands is then his contribution t_i towards the fixed cost β. According to some writers, this 'user-finance' often conforms to social justice.

The theory obviously gives us no cause to reject such a tariff principle, so long as an optimal quantity x_2^* is produced, that is, so long as each consumer's demand is the same as if he could acquire an additional unit at marginal cost γ. However, this last condition cannot easily be satisfied by a discriminatory tariff. In practice it assumes that individual demands are completely inelastic, and that the ith consumer does not reduce his demand when the price of the service to him is increased from γ to $\gamma + t_i$.

This concludes our discussion of some examples showing the directions in which economic science has sought the solution to the new problems arising from the complex interdependences among agents. As was pointed out at the beginning of the chapter, we have not given a full treatment of the questions raised. However, the reader can assess their importance and diversity.

10

Intertemporal economies

In principle, the theories examined up till now apply to models involving a time scale as well as to those which do not. However the problems raised by the choice between present and future consumption, or by capital accumulation, are sufficiently important in themselves to be considered explicitly, even if this only brings us back to the analyses already discussed. Also, interest and the discounting of values have a fairly subtle role. Their implications are important for the distribution of incomes, and we must therefore consider them in particular even if we have only to establish some direct consequences of what we already know about the general characteristics of the price system.

In addition, the development through time of production and consumption suggests the need to investigate new properties which have not been touched on up till now since they are meaningless in a static context. So this chapter will contain essentially new analyses in addition to the application of theories with which we are already familiar.

The questions now to be tackled have been discussed in the past under various headings without their essential unity being always understood: *the theory of interest, the theory of capital, the theory of growth* are so many extensions of optimum and equilibrium theories, which must obviously first be firmly established before the former can be developed.

Here we shall not attempt the complete treatment of interest, capital and growth, since too many difficult problems are involved. We shall introduce only those questions that follow most directly from our previous analyses. Thus we shall hope to make clear the common logic in microeconomic theories and lay the proper groundwork for further study.

In particular, we shall ignore that body of research concerned with the characterisation of possible growth paths in a competitive economy, or of interesting growth programmes resulting from planning.† In the author's

---

† See, in particular, Koopmans, 'Economic growth at a maximal rate', *The Quarterly Journal of Economics*, August 1964.

opinion, the results obtained thus far in the context of microeconomic formulations are too specialised for inclusion here.

(A) A DATE FOR EACH COMMODITY

As we saw initially, the theories discussed up till now apply to a time economy provided that two quantities available at two different dates are always considered to relate to different commodities even if their physical nature is the same.

There are some consequences of this remark which, although fairly straightforward, have not always been clearly understood. This first part of the chapter will be devoted to them, but will end with the discussion of a new concept, namely optimality in M. Allais' sense. In the second part we shall introduce a more specific formulation, which will be particularly useful for the investigation of stationary states and proportional growth programmes.

Suppose then that *commodities* are distinguished both by nature ($q = 1, 2, ..., Q$) and by date ($t = 1, 2, ..., T$). The former index h for a commodity is now replaced by the double index (q, t). To avoid confusion, we shall now use the term *good* for commodities of the same nature q considered at different dates ($t = 1, 2, ..., T$). The index q will then refer to goods.

We shall be concerned with the organisation of production, distribution and consumption over all dates. We wish to study individual or collective decisions in the period from $t = 1$ to $t = T$. We therefore place ourselves at the moment when these decisions are made, that is, *at the beginning of the period*. The date $t = 1$ can be considered as 'today', $t = 2, ..., T$ being future dates, which we assume to be ordered in time at regular intervals.

A complete specification of the activity of the various agents at the various dates constitutes a 'programme', which seems a preferable term here to the term 'state' used up till now. We are concerned with a programme adopted for the immediate and more distant future.

1. Market prices and interest rates

First of all we shall discuss the price system resulting from the theory developed particularly in Chapters 4 and 5. For the moment we do not have to state explicitly whether this system is introduced in order to allow the decentralised realisation of an optimum or if it arises from the existence of competitive markets for the different commodities.

In the first chapter, prices p_{qt} of the various commodities were defined in such a way that the ratio $p_{qt}/p_{r\tau}$ measures the quantity of the commodity (r, τ) that must be given in exchange for one unit of the commodity (q, t), that is, the quantity of the good r that, at date 1, must be guaranteed for delivery at date τ in return for the promised delivery at date t of one unit of the good q. Thus, by applying our general principles, the price-system defined by the p_{qt} is found applicable to forward contracts, the case of a spot contract corresponding to the particular situation where the two commodities exchanged are both available at the initial date ($t = \tau = 1$). These forward contracts are lending or borrowing operations when they involve the same good at two distinct dates.

Let us assume that the commodity (Q, 1) is the numéraire, that is, that p_{qt} is the quantity of Q which must be given at date 1 to buy the right to one unit of the good q deliverable at date t. This is said to be the 'discounted price' of the commodity (q, t). The origin of this expression will very shortly become clear.

We can define *'own interest rates' for a good* on the basis of prices p_{qt} relating to it when it is available at different dates. To do this, we call the ratio

$$\beta_{qt} = \frac{p_{qt}}{p_{q1}} \tag{1}$$

the 'own discount factor' β_{qt}. It is therefore the quantity of q which must be given today to obtain the promised delivery of one unit of the same good at date t (this discount factor is defined only if $p_{q1} \neq 0$). The own interest rate for period t, going from date t to date $t + 1$, is the number ρ_{qt} such that

$$\beta_{q,t+1} = \frac{1}{1 + \rho_{qt}}\beta_{qt} \tag{2}$$

(ρ_{qt} is defined only if $\beta_{q,t+1}$ is defined and differs from zero, that is, if $p_{q,t+1}$ and p_{q1} both differ from zero).

With this definition of the own interest rate, we can immediately verify, taking account of (1), that

$$p_{q,t+1} = \frac{1}{1 + \rho_{qt}}p_{qt}. \tag{3}$$

This equality shows that a loan contract involving the provision of one unit of q at date t and the return of $1 + \rho_{qt}$ units of the same good at date $t + 1$ conforms to the price-system, since the two values p_{qt} and $p_{q,t+1}(1 + \rho_{qt})$ exchanged are equal. We can also say that ρ_{qt} is the interest rate appropriate to a contract that stipulates the loan of one unit of the good q between the dates t and $t + 1$.

It may happen that the ρ_{qt} take values ρ_q that are independent of t. Then repeated application of (2) gives

$$\beta_{q,t+1} = (1 + \rho_q)^{-t}$$

(formula (1) shows that $\beta_{q1} = 1$). It then follows that

$$p_{qt} = (1 + \rho_q)^{-t+1}p_{q1}.$$

These two formulae, similar to those used in actuarial calculations, justify the terms 'discount factor' and 'discounted price' used for β_{qt} and p_{qt} respectively.

In general, own interest rates relating to different goods and the same period do not coincide. In order that they should, discounted prices must be such that the ratios $p_{q,t+1}/p_{q,t}$ have the same value for all goods. But *a priori*, there is no reason for this to happen (however, see Section B.2 below).

When we talk of *the* discount factor or of *the* rate of interest without specifying the good to which it refers, this good is understood to be that occurring in the definition of the numéraire; here it is identified by the index Q. In what follows, we shall use the term numéraire to denote the good Q, without the risk of confusion. We shall simply write β_t and ρ_t instead of β_{Qt} and ρ_{Qt}.

To say that prices are non-negative is equivalent to saying that discount factors are non-negative and that all the defined interest rates are greater than or equal to -1. However, we note that some interest rates may very well be negative.

Although the whole theory can be presented directly in terms of discounted prices, it is sometimes convenient also to define *undiscounted prices*, which are proportional, for a given date, to discounted prices but are such that the price of the particular good serving as numéraire is 1 on all dates. Undiscounted prices are determined uniquely from discounted prices, given the numéraire. Suppose again that the latter is the last good. The undiscounted prices $\bar{p}_{1t}, \dots, \bar{p}_{qt}, \dots, \bar{p}_{Qt}$ at date t must be proportional to the corresponding discounted prices $p_{1t}, \dots, p_{qt}, \dots, p_{Qt}$ and, in addition, $\bar{p}_{Qt}$ must equal 1. It is therefore necessary that

$$\bar{p}_{qt} = \frac{\bar{p}_{qt}}{\bar{p}_{Qt}} = \frac{p_{qt}}{p_{Qt}} \tag{4}$$

or,

$$\bar{p}_{qt} = \frac{1}{\beta_t} p_{qt}, \tag{5}$$

since $p_{Q1} = 1$ implies that, for the good Q, (1) can be written in the form

$$\beta_t = p_{Qt}. \tag{6}$$

Consider a complex of commodities defined by the quantities $z_{q\theta}$ of the different goods available at the dates $\theta = t, t + 1, \dots, t^*$. Let z_θ, p_θ and $\bar{p}_\theta$ denote the vectors with the Q components $z_{q\theta}, p_{q\theta}$ and $\bar{p}_{q\theta}$ respectively. For this complex, the *discounted value at date t*, or *the present value* at date t, is, by definition,

$$\frac{1}{\beta_t} \sum_{\theta=t}^{t^*} p_\theta z_\theta, \quad \text{which equals} \quad \sum_{\theta=t}^{t^*} \frac{\beta_\theta}{\beta_t} \bar{p}_\theta z_\theta.$$

In order to calculate the discounted value from the undiscounted prices $\bar{p}_{q\theta}$ and the coefficients β_θ, we can first determine the $\bar{p}_\theta z_\theta$, the undiscounted values of the bundles of goods available at the different dates, then associate with each of these terms the 'discount factor' β_θ/β_t, which discounts at date t the values concerning the later date θ. If the interest rate is the same for all periods ($\rho_\theta = \rho$), this discount factor is

$$\frac{1}{(1 + \rho)^{\theta - t}}.$$

It is less than 1 when the interest rate is positive.

For the same complex, we can also define the *capitalised value at date t^** as the quantity

$$\frac{1}{\beta_{t^*}} \sum_{\theta=t}^{t^*} p_\theta z_\theta, \qquad \text{which equals} \qquad \sum_{\theta=t}^{t^*} \frac{\beta_\theta}{\beta_{t^*}} \bar{p}_\theta z_\theta.$$

To find this value, we can start with the $\bar{p}_\theta z_\theta$ and multiply them respectively by the 'capitalisation factors' β_θ/β_{t^*}, which capitalise to date t^* the values concerning the previous dates θ. If the interest rate is constant, the factor β_θ/β_{t^*} equals $(1 + \rho)^{t^* - \theta}$; it is greater than 1 whenever ρ is positive.

2. The consumer

For the discussion of the consumer we can omit the index i. The consumption vector then has QT components, x_{qt} representing the quantity of the good q used by the consumer at date t; x is therefore in fact the 'consumption plan' covering the T dates from $t = 1$ to $t = T$.

No particular problem arises in the definition of the set X in R^{QT} which contains all physically possible consumption plans. So we turn to the utility function $S(x)$ representing the consumer's preferences among these different plans.

The marginal rate of substitution of the good q at date t with respect to the same good at date 1 can be considered as an own 'subjective discount factor' for this good; it is, in fact, the quantity by which consumption of q at date 1 must be increased to compensate for a decrease of one unit in consumption of q at date t:

$$- \frac{dx_{q1}}{dx_{qt}} = \frac{S'_{qt}(x)}{S'_{q1}(x)}. \tag{7}$$

In particular, if $q = Q$ is the numéraire, we can talk of the subjective discount factor without specifying the good Q to which it relates. *Subjective interest rates* defined by formulae similar to (2) correspond to the subjective discount factors. The values of the discount factors and the subjective interest rates clearly depend on the consumption plan x with respect to which they are defined.

Consider in particular the case of a single good and two dates. The consumer's indifference curves can be represented on a graph with x_{11} as abscissa and x_{12} as ordinate. With respect to a particular vector x, the subjective discount factor β (for the second period) is determined by the tangent to the indifference curve passing through x, as shown in Figure 1. It follows from (7) that it is in fact the gradient of the normal to this tangent. The definition of the subjective interest rate implies that the vector $(1 + \rho, 1)$ is collinear with the vector $(1, \beta)$ and is therefore parallel to the normal at x.

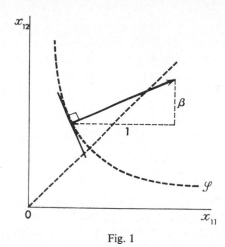

Fig. 1

It is usually assumed in actual observed situations that the subjective discount factors are in most cases less than 1 and that most subjective interest rates are positive. In the present example with only one good, this may result from the joint realisation of two assumptions and one particular circumstance.

According to the first assumption, individuals show a systematic psychological preference for the present over the future; this can be called 'impatience'. By this we mean that, if the consumption plan involves the same quantities at all dates for each good, then the increase in x_{qt} to compensate for a decrease of one unit in x_{q1} must be greater than 1. On Figure 1, at any point on the line $x_{11} = x_{12}$, the tangent to the indifference curve would have a gradient whose absolute value is greater than 1.

The second assumption is that the utility functions are quasi-concave (assumption 4 of Chapter 3). The effect of this on our graph would be to make the indifference curves concave upwards.

Finally, the consumption plans usually considered involve greater future than present consumption. In the particular case of Figure 1, x would lie above the line $x_{11} = x_{12}$. The gradient of the tangent to $\mathscr{S}$ at x would then be greater than the gradient of the tangent at the point of intersection with the bisector. The subjective interest rate would be higher at x than at this point of intersection, and therefore *a fortiori* would be greater than 1.

In order to make clear how the theory discussed in Chapter 2 for consumer equilibrium generalises to a situation involving time, we now examine the budget constraint

$$\sum_{t=1}^{T} \sum_{q=1}^{Q} p_{qt} x_{qt} = \sum_{t=1}^{T} \beta_t \sum_{q=1}^{Q} \bar{p}_{qt} x_{qt} \leqslant R. \tag{8}$$

The discounted value of the consumption plan must not exceed the value R of the resources that are available to the consumer *a priori*. In the static theory we have previously let R denote alternatively income or wealth. Only wealth is appropriate here since R relates to a budget covering not one particular date but the set of T dates under consideration.

The theory of consumer behaviour, as so far examined, assumes that the consumer considers discounted prices as given and chooses his whole consumption plan for the dates from $t = 1$ to $t = T$ so as to maximise his utility function subject to his budget constraint.

As thus interpreted therefore, the theory assumes that the consumer:

(i) has knowledge of all discounted prices (for all dates and all goods) as well as knowledge of all his future needs;

(ii) has the possibility of making forward contracts, that is, of buying or selling forward, for any date, quantities of products or services which he may wish to acquire or dispose of.

It is not indispensable that all forward contracts be concluded. It is sufficient that future prices are known and that the consumer may lend or borrow any quantity of numéraire at the interest rates ρ_t subject only to the constraint that he must balance his operations over all the T dates.

R can be considered as the consumer's initial wealth and $-\sum_q \bar{p}_{qt} x_{qt}$ as his 'savings' at date t. If e_t denotes this saving and A_t his net assets after taking account of e_t, then $A_1 = R + e_1$ and $A_t = (1 + \rho_{t-1})A_{t-1} + e_t$. We can easily verify that (8) is equivalent to $A_T \geqslant 0$ (we need only note that $\beta_t e_t = \beta_t A_t - \beta_{t-1} A_{t-1}$). The consumer must only end up with non-negative net assets at the terminal date T.

This theory therefore ignores uncertainty on future needs and prices, as well as possible stricter limitations on individuals' borrowing facilities than is required by their solvency over all the T periods considered (on the latter point, see the previous remarks in Chapter 2, Section 5).

3. The firm

Similarly, if we apply the general theory of Chapter 3 to an intertemporal economy, each firm must maximise its total profit, which can be written here:

$$\sum_{t=1}^{T} \sum_{q=1}^{Q} p_{qt} y_{qt} = \sum_{t=1}^{T} \beta_t \sum_{q=1}^{Q} \bar{p}_{qt} y_{qt}. \tag{9}$$

This is the discounted value of the net outputs of all periods. Like the consumer, the firm must know all discounted prices and have the possibility of concluding forward contracts for all goods, or at least of lending and borrowing amounts of numéraire which it either needs or has to dispose of.

The vector y of the QT net productions y_{qt} must be technically feasible. We have represented this constraint in two ways, either

$$y \in Y \tag{10}$$

where Y is a set of QT-dimensional space, or

$$f(y_{11}, ..., y_{qt}, ..., y_{QT}) \leqslant 0, \tag{11}$$

where f denotes a real function defined on this space and assumed to be differentiable.

In neither of these two representations are operations internal to the firm described; all that matters is what the technical constraints imply for the set of inputs acquired by the firm and for the outputs that it produces for disposal to others. There is nothing new in this: we noted it when defining production functions. Here it implies in particular that there is no call for detailed representation of the use of capital installations. Acquisitions of such equipment are dealt with in the same way as any other input; they are deducted as a whole in the calculation of the y_{qt} corresponding to the date of acquisition.

However, in this respect the initial and terminal dates are particular cases. The physical capital existing in the economy at date 1 is often treated as a primary resource available at that date. The part of this capital that is used by the jth firm must therefore appear among its inputs at date 1. Conversely, the capital equipment of the jth firm at the terminal date T is often considered as output at this date.

It may also happen that the initial capital of the firm does not appear explicitly in the model but is taken account of in the definition of the production set Y or the production function f. A vector y then belongs to Y if it represents the net productions of a programme that is technically feasible for the firm on the basis of its available capital.

A priori, (10) can accommodate itself to very diverse formulations of the technical constraints. So the following remark concerning the production function (11) does not apply to the general results established directly on the basis of (10). We have had occasion to point out that most of the properties discussed previously were generalised on the basis of models involving production sets Y instead of production functions f. So the following remark should not be taken as critical of the theories discussed here, but rather of the presentation we are giving of them in these lectures.

The existence of a differentiable production function of the type (11) implies that, without changing any other net productions, the firm can substitute an infinitely small quantity dy_{qt} of the net production of good q at date t for another quantity $dy_{r\theta}$ of the net production of any good r at any date θ, subject only to the condition that

$$-\frac{dy_{qt}}{dy_{r\theta}} = \frac{f'_{r\theta}(y)}{f'_{qt}(y)}. \tag{12}$$

The marginal rates of substitution of type (12) are supposed to be defined for all pairs with double indices $(qt, r\theta)$ and with respect to all the vectors y satisfying $f(y) = 0$ (except obviously in the cases where $f'_{qt}(y) = 0$). A priori, it may seem highly unlikely that such vast possibilities of substitution should exist. However, let us accept this assumption for the moment. We shall return to it at the start of part B.

Just as we can define 'subjective interest rates' from the consumer's marginal rates of substitution, so we can define *technical interest rates* from the producer's marginal rates of substitution defined by (12). The own technical discount factor of good r for date θ is the value of (12) when $q = r$ and $t = 1$. Technical interest rates can be deduced from technical discount factors by formulae similar to (2). Own technical interest rates can, *a priori*, be either positive or negative, as we shall see if we consider a simple particular case.

Suppose that there are two periods and a single good of which the firm possesses a certain quantity A a priori. At the first date, the firm may release of this good a quantity y_{11} that is subject only to the restriction that it must not be greater than A. At the second date it will possess and make available the quantity

$$y_{12} = (A - y_{11})(1 + \alpha),$$

where α is a fixed number. This representation is appropriate, for instance, if the firm stocks good 1, but the latter suffers some deterioration between dates 1 and 2, in which case α is negative and equal, apart from sign, to the proportion of deteriorated units. It is also appropriate if the firm is working a forest, when α is positive and equals the rate of growth of the standing timber (good 1) between the two dates.

In such a case, where the quantity A is not introduced explicitly in net productions, the function f is

$$f(y_{11}, y_{12}) = y_{12} - (1 + \alpha)(A - y_{11}):$$

consequently,

$$f'_{11} = 1 + \alpha, \qquad f'_{12} = 1,$$

these derivatives being well-defined to the extent that y_{11} and y_{12} are both positive.

The technical discount factor for good 1 is therefore

$$\frac{f'_{12}}{f'_{11}} = \frac{1}{1 + \alpha}.$$

The technical interest rate, α, is negative in the first case where the firm stocks good 1, and positive in the second example of forestry.

4. A positive theory of interest

Economic science must investigate how the interest rates that actually apply in borrowing and lending operations between agents are determined and how the rates of return in productive operations that employ capital are established. The theory of general equilibrium in perfect competition provides an answer to these questions, an answer that may be deceptive because of its lack of realism, but that must be thoroughly understood before its relevance can be discussed.

According to the generalisation with which we are now concerned, a competitive economy functions through markets which exist for all pairs (q, t). Thus for each good there are as many forward markets as there are dates. On the (q, t) market are confronted all the supplies and demands implied for good q and date t by the present plans of the agents. This confrontation leads to the determination of a discounted price p_{qt} which, together with the other discounted prices determined simultaneously on the other markets, ensures the equality of total supply and total demand. In addition, it is assumed that, in such an institutional context, agents fix their plans taking discounted prices as given, that is, that they behave as briefly described in the two previous sections.

We can state directly a certain number of results applying to such an economy and following from the theory in Chapters 2, 3 and 5. We shall do so without on each occasion stating the conditions required for the validity of each property. This would be tedious, and reference can easily be made back to previous chapters for the relevant material.

(i) The *consumer's equilibrium*, that is, the consumption plan maximising his utility subject only to his budget constraint, is such that the marginal rates of substitution are equal to the ratios of the corresponding discounted prices. In particular, *the subjective interest rates are equal to the corresponding market interest rates*, which are defined on the basis of discounted prices, as we saw earlier (Section 1). It is to the consumer's advantage to contract debts or make loans in such a way that this equality finally holds.

(ii) The *equilibrium for the firm*, that is, the net production plan maximising its total discounted profit (9) subject to its technical constraint, is such that the marginal rates of substitution (12) are equal respectively to the ratios of discounted prices $p_{qt}/p_{r\theta}$. In particular, *the technical interest rates are equal to market interest rates*.

It follows that the *'marginal rate of profit' for the firm between dates t and t + 1 is equal to the market rate* ρ_t. To define this 'rate of profit', let us consider a marginal investment implying inputs ∂a_{qt} at date t and giving outputs $\partial b_{q,t+1}$, which are all available at date $t + 1$. Introducing the Q-vectors $\bar{p}_t$, $\bar{p}_{t+1}$, δa_t and δb_{t+1}, we can define the marginal rate of profit as the net undiscounted revenue to the investment divided by the cost involved, namely

$$r_t = \frac{\bar{p}_{t+1}\delta b_{t+1} - \bar{p}_t\delta a_t}{\bar{p}_t\delta a_t}. \tag{13}$$

(We shall see later that such a definition may be open to criticism.) Given that we are concerned with an investment appearing as marginal *vis-à-vis* a criterion represented by discounted profit (9), we can write

$$- \beta_t\bar{p}_t\partial a_t + \beta_{t+1}\bar{p}_{t+1}\partial b_{t+1} = 0 \tag{14}$$

It then follows from (13), (14) and (2) that

$$r_t = \rho_t. \tag{15}$$

This expresses the fact that the firm will carry out a productive operation involving only the dates t and $t + 1$ precisely if the rate of profit from it is at least equal to ρ_t, otherwise it gains by lending the sum $\bar{p}_t\partial a_t$ that it is considering tying up in the investment.

(iii) *A competitive equilibrium* is defined by a set of discounted prices for all goods and all dates, by consumption plans and production plans that are equilibria for consumers and firms respectively and are also compatible with the equality of total demand and total supply for each good and each date. In a competitive equilibrium, the ratios between discounted prices are equal to the corresponding marginal rates of substitution both for each consumer and for each firm. In particular, for each good and each period, the own market interest rate is equal to the own subjective interest rate of all consumers and the own technical interest rate of all firms.

Let us examine briefly how a theory of interest can be derived from what has just been said. Even for an elementary period lasting between two successive instants t and $t + 1$, there are generally multiple interest rates ρ_{qt}. We must therefore state the choice of numéraire and assume Q to be determined so that the rates ρ_t can be considered truly representative of interest rates: ρ_t must have a central position in the set of ρ_{qt} relating to the same date. It is equivalent to say that the evolutions of the undiscounted prices $\bar{p}_{qt}$ of goods other than Q do not show a systematic trend, which would reveal the particular nature of Q. In fact, (5), (2) and (3) imply

$$\frac{\bar{p}_{q,t+1} - \bar{p}_{qt}}{\bar{p}_{qt}} = \frac{\rho_t - \rho_{qt}}{1 + \rho_{qt}}. \tag{16}$$

If ρ_{qt} is greater than ρ_t, this is because the undiscounted price of q decreases between t and $t + 1$. The choice of the numeraire would be inappropriate for ρ_t to define the *real* interest rate if either most $\bar{p}_{qt}$ would be decreasing or most $\bar{p}_{qt}$ increasing.

What factors account for the more or less high levels of market interest rates? How does it come about that these rates are positive? Since interest rates are elements of a complete price-system, since the theory presently under discussion follows from a generalisation of the theory of value examined in Chapter 5, we know that the explanation lies in various factors simultaneously: consumers' needs and preferences, the composition of the vectors of primary resources (and therefore also the way in which each ω_{qt} develops), the characteristics of production techniques. In Section 2 we saw why an assumption of 'impatience' is often adopted for individual preferences, which implies positive interest rates. We saw that the nature of certain technical processes such as in the forestry example of Section 3, has the same effect. But, at our present level of generality it is difficult to go further than this. We shall return to the question in the second part of this chapter, when we shall find that it is very complex.

For the moment we shall note only that stockpiling of a seasonal perishable foodstuff is covered by the model (the example of Section 3 with $\alpha < 0$). The own interest rate for the corresponding good q is negative during every period $(t, t + 1)$ in which it is stocked, because of the nature of the technical process. If the interest rate ρ_t is positive, as is usually the case, the undiscounted price of the foodstuff q increases between t and $t + 1$, in view of (16). However an equilibrium is realised when the good q fulfils needs existing at the date $t + 1$ since, apart from stocks, the available quantities are assumed to decrease between t and $t + 1$.

Can this theory, whose main elements have just been stated, help us to understand certain aspects of reality? Before answering this question, we must admit the very abstract character of the central part of the analytic apparatus: in no actual economy do there exist institutions which can be considered as making up a complete system of forward markets for all goods and all future dates, nor *a fortiori* for the relatively long periods involved in the installation and use of equipment.

To investigate the relevance of the theory, we must inquire into the actual role of prices and interest rates in economic decisions. The explicit or implicit calculations by which the various agents reach their decisions do in fact involve prices and interest rates. Present prices, of date $t = 1$, can be observed more or less precisely; similarly, there exist interest rates relating to the borrowing and lending of money for varying periods. But future undiscounted prices must be predicted by each individual. In fact consumers and producers have available information other than that assumed by the theory; they have less direct information on prices, but on the other hand, they often have some knowledge of the conditions of later economic development, which allows them to assess the advisability and profitability of the operations on which they are engaged. Of course, the consistency of individual plans is not completely assured since there is no systematic confrontation of the demands and supplies which result, for the different goods and the various future dates, from decisions taken today. Nevertheless the system of present prices and interest rates contributes to the partial consistency realised by existing institutions.

In the author's opinion, the positive theory discussed in this chapter must be considered to be aimed at the analysis of one aspect of reality, namely that concerning the intervention of prices and interest rates. For this analysis, it does not seem basically inadequate. In addition, we shall now see that the conceptual framework on which it is based is much better adapted to the examination of the normative problems raised by the organisation of economic activity over time.

5. Optimum programmes and the discounting of values

For the choice of public investments it has been suggested that the economist's aim should be to determine the discounted net value returned by each project and each of its variants (or, the 'discounted net revenue'). Such a rule receives some justification from optimum theory applied to an intertemporal economy.

As we saw earlier, a programme is a set of consumption plans and production plans, one for each agent. A programme is 'feasible' if each agent's plan is physically possible for him and if, in addition, for each good and each date, global supply is equal to global demand.

A programme is called a 'production optimum' if it is feasible and if there exists no other feasible programme giving at least as large a global net production $\sum_j y_{jqt}$ for all the pairs (q, t) and larger for at least one of them. Similarly, a programme is a 'Pareto optimum' if it is feasible, and if there exists no feasible programme which is considered at least equivalent by all consumers and preferable by one.

We saw in Chapter 4 that, with respect to an optimal programme, the marginal rate of substitution between two commodities (q, t) and (r, τ) is the same for all interested agents: all producers in the case of a production optimum, all producers and all consumers in the case of a Pareto optimum. It follows that, for a given good and period, the producers all have the same technical interest rate ρ_{qt} and, where a Pareto optimum is concerned, ρ_{qt} is also the subjective interest rate for all consumers.

Under the usual convexity assumptions, we can associate with an optimal programme a price-system with precisely the characteristics discussed in Section 1 of this chapter. If a numéraire is chosen, this system can be expressed by undiscounted prices $\bar{p}_{qt}$ for each good and each date, together with interest rates ρ_t. The latter are often rather called 'discount rates' in the present context, so as not to prejudice the possible equality of the numbers ρ_t thus defined with the interest rates actually applying in borrowing and lending operations.

An optimal programme is 'sustained' by the corresponding price-system when the agents involved use this system and make their economic calculations according to the rules discussed in Sections 2 and 3. In particular, each producer j must maximise the discounted value of his net productions, which can be calculated according to formula (9), namely

$$\sum_{t=1}^{T} \beta_t \sum_{q=1}^{Q} \bar{p}_{qt} y_{jqt} \tag{17}$$

where the β_t are 'discount factors'.

Suppose then that, relative to a programme P^0 containing for him the net productions y_{jqt}^0, the public producer j is considering an investment project which is not included in P^0, or a variant of an included project. Let ∂y_{jqt} be the net productions attributable to the project, or the changes in net productions if the variant is adopted instead of the project occurring in P^0. (We recall that the acquisition of capital equipment is accounted for among inputs and therefore appears as negative net production.) The producer j must verify that he has no grounds for carrying out the project in the first case, or for choosing the variant in the second. Maximisation of (17) implies the inequality

$$\sum_{t=1}^{T} \beta_t \sum_{q=1}^{Q} \bar{p}_{qt} \partial y_{jqt} \leqslant 0 \tag{18}$$

This is the discounted return from the project, or the difference between the discounted returns from the two variants, which must provide the criterion of choice.

Without going into more detail, we can also think of public decisions as resulting from a planning procedure similar to those discussed in Chapter 8. The prospective indices are undiscounted prices and discount rates; at each stage, the public firms fix their plans, choosing a set of projects that maximises the present value (17) calculated on the basis of previously announced discount rates. This ideal context in fact offers some justification for the rule usually put forward.

However, we must add two remarks here to those that are generally provoked in another way by the theories of Chapters 4 and 8. In the first place, this justification is valid only if *all* producers, private as well as public, reach their decisions after similar calculations and on the basis of the same prices and discount rates. It no longer applies rigorously if, for example, the private sector of the economy adopts different rules of choice. (Also, it is very difficult to determine exactly the best rules to be adopted then in the public sector for decentralised economic decisions.)

In the second place, knowledge of undiscounted prices $\bar{p}_{qt}$ for future dates is as important *a priori* as knowledge of discount rates. However the situation could conceivably arise where future prices $\bar{p}_{qt}$ are, for most goods q, equal to the corresponding present prices $\bar{p}_{q1}$. Given present prices and discount rates, fairly little additional information would then need to be obtained.

6. Optimality in Allais' sense†

In actual societies it seems to be common that social choices deviate from consumer preferences in the assessment of the relative importance of future needs with respect to present needs. It is frequently held that individual choices contain too marked a preference for present consumption, and that it is necessary to bring about a larger volume of savings than appears spontaneously. Public saving and legal arrangements such as compulsory pension schemes allow this objective to be realised.

The situation is represented in Figure 2, which applies to the case of only one good, two periods, one consumer and one firm. (The construction is similar to that in Figure 9 of Chapter 9). While production possibilities are not systematically more favourable for the first period than for the second, the consumer, who, by hypothesis, has a strong preference for the present, chooses a plan M that sacrifices his future consumption. If this is the situation, then it is often held that, in the choice between the present and the future, the consumer must have imposed on him a plan other than that which he chooses spontaneously.

It was in order to generalise optimum theory to such a collective attitude that M. Allais put forward the concept of 'rendement social généralisé'. His idea is to define and investigate a notion of optimum in which individual preferences are retained for the choice between consumptions relating to the same date, but not necessarily between those relating to different dates. For

---

† See Allais, *Economie et Intérêt*, Paris, Imprimerie Nationale, 1947, particularly Chapter VI and Appendix III.

simplicity, the theory will be given here for only two dates $(T = 2)$; it can easily be generalised to any number of dates.

Let x_{iqt} be the consumption of the good q by the consumer i at date t (where $t = 1, 2$). Let x_{i1} and x_{i2} be the vectors with Q components representing the consumptions of the different goods by the consumer i at dates 1 and 2 respectively. At date 1, his utility function S_i depends on the values of the two vectors x_{i1} and x_{i2} (this function represents a preorder on complete consumption plans); we can write it $S_i(x_{i1}; x_{i2})$.

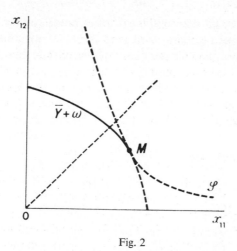

Fig. 2

Now we must also introduce a utility function at date 2, that is, a function $S_{i2}(x_{i2})$ representing the ith consumer's preferences at date 2 between the different vectors x_{i2}. Obviously this function is not independent of S_i; if it were, there would be little reason to refer to individual preferences for choices internal to future periods. Moreover, for Allais' theory, the definition of S_{i2} must be independent of the vector x_{i1}. We therefore adopt the following assumption†:

ASSUMPTION 1. There exists a function S_{i2} of the vector x_{i2} such that the function S_i can be written in the form $S_i^*(x_{i1}; S_{i2})$, where S_i^* increases with S_{i2}. The function $S_{i2}(x_{i2})$ represents the ith consumer's choices at date 2.

On reflection, we see that this assumption implies a certain independence of choices at different dates. If a change in prices at date 1 brings about a change in x_{i1}, this should not change i's preferences among the different vectors x_{i2}.

---

† Instead of expressing the assumption directly in terms of the functions S_i and S_{i2}, we could formulate it in terms of the preferences expressed by these functions. However, this seems an unnecessary refinement.

We can now define optimal programmes in Allais' sense. To do this, we must refer to a partial preordering of programmes, a preordering that respects individual preferences at each of the two dates, but is not necessarily conclusive for choices between these dates. Hence the following definition:

DEFINITION 1. A programme P^0 is said to be an 'Allais optimum' if it is feasible and if there exists no feasible programme P such that

$$S_i(x_{i1}; x_{i2}) \geqslant S_i(x_{i1}^0; x_{i2}^0) \quad \text{for} \quad i = 1, 2, ..., m \tag{19}$$

$$S_{i2}(x_{i2}) \geqslant S_{i2}(x_{i2}^0) \quad \text{for} \quad i = 1, 2, ..., m, \tag{20}$$

where at least one of all these $2m$ inequalities holds strictly.

In short, P^0 cannot be changed so as to increase one consumer's utility at date 1 without decreasing another consumer's utility at date 1 or at date 2, or the first consumer's utility at date 2.

Consider a programme P which is optimal in the Pareto sense. There exists no feasible programme P satisfying (19) and consequently no such programme satisfying both (20) and (19). A Pareto optimum is therefore an Allais optimum. But clearly, the converse is not true. Thus, in the example of Figure 2, M is the only point representing a Pareto optimum while all the programmes on the boundary $\bar{Y} + \omega$ to the left of M are also Allais optima since movement along the boundary from the vertical axis up to M implies an increase in $S(x_{11}; x_{12})$ but a decrease in $S_2(x_{12})$.

What are the properties of an Allais optimum?

To answer this question, we can use the constrained maximisation techniques widely used in Chapter 4. But we can also adopt direct reasoning.

Let $S_{i2}(x_{i2}^0) = S_{i2}^0$. If P^0 is an Allais optimum, then there exists no feasible programme P such that

$$S_i^*(x_{i1}; S_{i2}^0) \geqslant S_i^*(x_{i1}^0; S_{i2}^0) \quad \text{for} \quad i = 1, 2, ..., m \tag{21}$$

$$S_{i2}(x_{i2}) \geqslant S_{i2}(x_{i2}^0) \quad \text{for} \quad i = 1, 2, ..., m \tag{22}$$

where at least one inequality holds strictly. For, if such a programme exists, we can write, in view of (21) and the fact that S_i^* increases with S_{i2}:

$$S_i(x_{i1}, x_{i2}) = S_i^*(x_{i1}; S_{i2}) \geqslant S_i^*(x_{i1}; S_{i2}^0) \geqslant S_i^*(x_{i1}^0; S_{i2}^0) = S_i(x_{i1}^0; x_{i2}^0). \tag{23}$$

Since (23) and (22) are identical to (19) and (20), the existence of a feasible programme satisfying (22) and (21) contradicts the assumption that P^0 is an Allais optimum.

We see now that P^0 can be formally considered as a Pareto optimum in the following fictitious economy: it is identical to the economy under consideration in respect of firms and primary resources, but contains $2m$ consumers; the first m consumers have consumption vectors x_{i1} and utility functions $S_i^*(x_{i1}; S_{i2}^0)$ considered as functions only of the vector x_{i1}; the last m consumers have consumption vectors x_{i2} and utility functions $S_{i2}(x_{i2})$. Therefore each consumer of this imaginary economy lives in one and only one period. The fact that no feasible programme P satisfies (22) and (21) shows that P^0 is a Pareto optimum for the fictitious economy.

We can therefore apply the usual optimum theory and state the marginal equalities to be satisfied.† Thus we have directly, both for time $t = 1$, where S'_{iq1} is equal to $\partial S^*_i / \partial x_{iq1}$, and for time $t = 2$,

$$\frac{S'_{iqt}}{S'_{irt}} = \frac{S'_{\alpha qt}}{S'_{\alpha rt}} = \frac{f'_{jqt}}{f'_{jrt}}, \tag{24}$$

for all $i, \alpha = 1, 2, ..., m; j = 1, 2, ..., n; q, r = 1, 2, ..., Q$.

We can also write

$$\frac{f'_{jq2}}{f'_{jq1}} = \frac{f'_{\beta q2}}{f'_{\beta q1}} \tag{25}$$

for all $j, \beta = 1, 2, ..., n; q = 1, 2, ..., Q$; technical interest rates must be the same for all firms.

On the other hand, *for the real economy we can no longer equate subjective and technical interest rates, nor can we equate the subjective interest rates of the different consumers.* For, in the above fictitious economy, each consumer acts in one period only; his marginal rates of substitution are defined only for pairs of commodities relating to a single period.

Under the usual convexity assumptions, every Allais optimum appears as a market equilibrium for this fictitious economy. With respect to the initial economy, this state is also a market equilibrium for firms since all the necessary marginal equalities are satisfied. In this equilibrium, firms are in particular assumed free to conclude forward contracts at fixed interest rates. Each consumer can freely acquire his consumptions at market prices, but his net expenditures in each period are not necessarily equal to what he would choose if free to borrow and lend as he pleases on the markets.

To establish this, we need only apply proposition 5 of Chapter 4 to the fictitious economy. Associated with P^0, there exist discounted prices p_{qt} (for all goods and both dates) and incomes $R_{it} = \sum_q p_{qt} x^0_{iqt}$ such that, in particular,‡

---

† The part played by assumption 1 becomes clear here. If it is not satisfied, the consumer's choices at time 1 depend not only on the level of utility at time 2 but also on the chosen vector x_{i2}. In the fictitious economy, an 'external effect' then appears between the two imaginary consumers corresponding to i.

‡ (i) can be interpreted in two ways. On the one hand we can assume that, given prices p_{q2} and his income R_{i2} at date 2, the ith consumer chooses first x^0_{i2} then the complex x^0_{i1} that is best for him at date 1. On the other hand, we can consider that, at date 1, the consumer does not know income R_{i2} and prices p_{q2}, but that his choices at date 1 are not affected by S^0_{i2}. This second interpretation therefore assumes that assumption 1 is strengthened.

9

(i) the vector x_{i1}^0 maximises $S_i^*(x_{i1}; S_{i2}^0)$, and therefore also $S_i(x_{i1}; x_{i2}^0)$ subject to the constraint $\sum_q p_{q1} x_{iq1} \leqslant R_{i1}$, for $i = 1, 2, ..., m$;

(i') the vector x_{i2}^0 maximises $S_{i2}(x_{i2})$ subject to the constraint

$$\sum_q p_{q2} x_{iq2} \leqslant R_{i2} \qquad \text{for} \qquad i = 1, 2, ..., m.$$

This theory can clearly be generalised to any number T of dates. A slightly more complex assumption than assumption 1 must imply some independence of the preference systems relating to each period. A fictitious economy can be defined where i is split up into T distinct consumers. With an Allais optimum we can associate a system of discounted prices and a market equilibrium whose only special feature is that consumers have given 'incomes' for each period and can neither lend nor borrow.

The fact that they disregard the possibility of consumer saving makes the new equilibria introduced by M. Allais' theory appear somewhat unrealistic. However, their discussion can usefully round off the knowledge acquired from the study of classical market equilibria.

(B) PRODUCTION SPECIFIC TO EACH PERIOD

Until relatively recently, the theory of capital and interest has been based on the study of stationary régimes in which each period repeats the previous one. Still today, the real nature of some problems can be more easily understood if they are examined in a stationary context.

To investigate such régimes, we must introduce a new representation of technical constraints, which will also be useful for less simple models of development and which does not contradict the representation used so far. Its particular feature is that it applies directly to the production operations relating to an elementary period and is thus more analytic than the production function (11).

The questions to be tackled in this second part of the chapter are almost uniquely concerned with the organisation of production in its relationships with prices, interest rates and incomes. Consumers will only occasionally be considered explicitly.

1. The analysis of production by periods

Let us consider one particular firm, omitting the index j for the moment. Up till now, we have discussed its operations over all T dates $t = 1, 2, ..., T$, using only the net productions y_{qt} made available for use by other agents. Let us now try to represent its operations between two successive dates t and $t + 1$, this time-interval being called the 'period t'.

At date t, the firm puts into operation inputs a_{qt} of the various products or services; as a result of its activity, it obtains outputs $b_{q,t+1}$, which are available at date $t + 1$. Since as economists we need not know the mechanism by which inputs are transformed into outputs, we can describe production during period t by the pair of vectors $(a_t; b_{t+1})$.

For this representation to be meaningful, the a_{qt} must describe all the inputs including inputs of new and old capital equipment available to the firm in period t and possibly also including articles in course of manufacture at date t. Of course, a new piece of equipment and an existing piece of the same kind must be considered as two different goods; the same is true of an article in course of manufacture and the corresponding finished article. This is not a very serious constraint, since there is no restriction on the number Q of goods. However, for equilibrium it implies that there are well-defined prices for existing equipment and for products in course of manufacture.

In short, the vector a_t represents the set of products and services immobilised for production in period t. We shall call it the firm's *capital* at date t, without disguising the fact that such a definition, like that used in the nineteenth century, in particular by Karl Marx, is wider than that commonly accepted. As thus conceived, capital is a stock of goods. Its value, which will be discussed in Section 3, is also called 'capital'. The particular interpretation will be clear from the context. Capital thus includes quantities of labour, (Marx's 'variable capital'), current inputs of raw materials, power, etc. as well as durable equipment. It is therefore both 'circulating capital' and 'fixed capital'.

The vector b_{t+1} likewise represents not only the firm's outputs properly so called, but also all its equipment in whatever state it may be at the end of period t, and also articles in course of manufacture at date $t + 1$.

How does this new representation of the firm's operations relate to that given in part A of this chapter? This can be simply illustrated (see Figure 3).

Net production y_{qt} of good q at date t is obviously the quantity of q made available by the firm, that is, the excess of output in period $t - 1$ over input in period t:

$$y_{qt} = b_{qt} - a_{qt}. \tag{26}$$

We again let y_t denote the vector of the y_{qt} at date t.

The equipment remaining in use in the firm during periods $t - 1$ and t appears both in b_{qt} and a_{qt}; therefore it is not included in y_{qt}. However, for (26) to apply to the initial and terminal dates, we set

$$b_{q1} = 0; \qquad a_{qT} = 0. \tag{27}$$

This convention also agrees with our discussion at the beginning of this chapter since equipment existing at date 1 is in most cases counted negatively

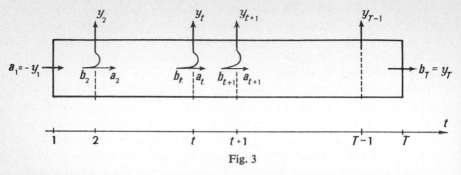

Fig. 3

in the y_{q1} and equipment surviving at date T is counted positively in the y_{qT}.

With this new formulation, it is natural to represent the technical constraints which limit production during period t by

$$g_t(a_t; b_{t+1}) \leqslant 0, \tag{28}$$

where g_t is a real-valued function with $2Q$ arguments, called the 'production function for period t'.

At the beginning of Chapter 3 we made a careful examination of the meaning of production functions and the exact bearing of assumptions made about them. What was said then applies rigidly to the g_t, and there is no point in repeati ng that discussion.

2. Intertemporal efficiency

From the production functions (28) relating to each of the $T - 1$ elementary periods we can obviously deduce a production function of the type (11) referring directly to the y_{qt} and relating to all $T - 1$ periods. We need only take account of the fact that the firm will naturally choose for each period input and output combinations in such a way that they lead to 'technically efficient' net productions in the sense of Chapter 3. Without reference to the price-system or to the market structure, the firm must already impose certain conditions of *intertemporal efficiency* on the sequence of pairs $(a_t; b_{t+1})$.

To make these conditions clear in general, we can assume that all the y_{qt} except one are given, say y_{QT} is not given, and assume that production in the period from 1 to T is organised so that y_{QT} is maximised. The constraints are then equations (26), (27) and (28) written for all suitable periods and dates. The maximisation conditions express the requirements of intertemporal efficiency. Moreover, the problem as thus stated has generally a solution, which varies with the y_{qt} that are assumed as given. The equation $f(y) = 0$, satisfied by the vector of the y_{qt} when y_{QT} is determined in this way, is, by definition, the production function for the whole period from 1 to T.

It will certainly be instructive to examine this question in detail in a simple case. Consider the case where $Q = 2$ and $T = 3$. Let quantities of each of the two goods be represented on a Cartesian graph. Let a point A_1 represent a vector a_1^0 of inputs at date 1, these inputs being considered as fixed. Then let Γ_2 be the locus of the extremities of the vectors a_2 that are feasible on the basis of a_1^0 when net production at date 2 is restricted to a fixed vector y_2^0. The vectors a_2 of Γ_2 are restricted to satisfy

$$g_1(a_1^0; y_2^0 + a_2) = 0. \tag{29}$$

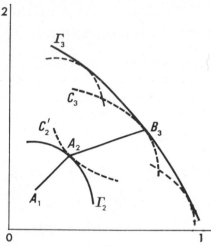

Fig. 4

Similarly, from a point A_2 on Γ_2 we can draw the curve C_3 of the extremities of the vectors b_3 which can be established from a_2, that is, which satisfy

$$g_2(a_2; b_3) = 0.$$

When A_2 moves along Γ_2, the curve C_3 is also displaced. Let Γ_3 be the envelope of C_3 in this displacement. Starting from $a_1^0 = -y_1^0$ and having to provide y_2^0, the firm may realise any vector $y_3 = b_3$ whose extremity belongs to Γ_3, but no vector whose extremity lies beyond it. Therefore Γ_3 is the locus of the y_3 of the technically efficient vectors. Its equation can be written in the form:

$$f(y_{11}^0, y_{12}^0, y_{21}^0, y_{22}^0, y_{31}, y_{32}) = 0, \tag{30}$$

in which there appear explicitly the quantities $y_{11}^0, y_{12}^0, y_{21}^0, y_{22}^0$ on which the position of Γ_3 depends. Considered as a function of its six arguments, f is therefore the production function for the whole period from 1 to 3.

From a point B_3 on Γ_3 corresponding to a vector b_3^0 satisfying (30), we can also construct the curve C_2', the locus of the extremities of the vectors a_2 which allow B_3 to be achieved, that is, of the vectors a_2 such that

$$g_2(a_2; b_3^0) = 0. \tag{31}$$

Clearly C_2' and Γ_2, which both contain a_2^0, are tangents, otherwise B_3 could be reached from a point on the left of Γ_2, and could be exceeded from a properly chosen point on Γ_2, at least if g_2 is increasing in b_3 and decreasing in a_2, a property that can be assumed.

It is convenient to introduce the following notation for the partial derivatives of g_t, which is assumed differentiable:

$$g'_{qt} = \frac{\partial g_t}{\partial a_{qt}}, \qquad \gamma'_{q,t+1} = \frac{\partial g_t}{\partial b_{q,t+1}}. \tag{32}$$

The fact that C_2' and Γ_2 are tangents can then be expressed as:

$$\frac{g'_{12}}{g'_{22}} = \frac{\gamma'_{12}}{\gamma'_{22}}, \tag{33}$$

the derivatives being evaluated for the values a_1^0, b_2^0, a_2^0 and b_3 of the vectors that are their arguments. Thus, *the marginal rate of substitution between the two goods at date 2 is the same whether it is calculated from the production function relating to period 1, the goods appearing as outputs, or from the production function relating to period 2, the goods appearing as inputs.*

This last result characterises an organisation of production that is efficient relative to the whole period from 1 to 3. It can obviously be generalised to any number of periods and products.

In fact, the conditions of intertemporal efficiency are

$$\frac{g'_{qt}}{g'_{rt}} = \frac{\gamma'_{qt}}{\gamma'_{rt}} \qquad q, r = 1, 2, ..., Q \tag{34}$$

as can be seen from the general solution to the maximisation problem defined at the start of this section.

It is obviously not necessary to assume the existence of differentiable functions g_t in order to establish a correspondence between the technical constraints expressed for the pairs $(a_t; b_{t+1})$ and a similar constraint expressed for the vector y with the QT components y_{qt}. For, let P_t be in $2Q$-dimensional space the set containing the pairs $(a_t; b_{t+1})$ that are technically feasible during period t. The vector y is technically feasible if and only if there exist $T - 1$ vectors a_t (for $t = 1, 2, ..., T - 1$) and $T - 1$ vectors b_t (for $t = 2, 3, ..., T$) such that:

$$\begin{cases} (a_t; b_{t+1}) \in P_t & t = 1, 2, ..., T - 1; \\ \left. \begin{array}{r} - a_{q1} = y_{q1} \\ b_{qT} = y_{qT} \end{array} \right\} q = 1, 2, ..., Q; \\ b_{qt} - a_{qt} = y_{qt} \begin{cases} q = 1, 2, ..., Q, \\ t = 2, 3, ..., T - 1. \end{cases} \end{cases}$$

This condition then defines the set Y of feasible vectors y. It is easily verified that, in particular, the convexity of Y follows from the convexity of the P_t.

Using the general properties of maximisation, for example the Kuhn-Tucker theorem, we can establish the conditions of intertemporal efficiency by demanding that the sequence of the $(a_t; b_{t+1})$ leads to a technically efficient vector y. This generalises relations (34).

3. Interest and profit

We now return to the price-system, with which the first section of this chapter was concerned, and examine its implications for the operations in one period in more detail. This leads us to the investigation of the distribution of the incomes created in each period.

Incomes originate in production, and we must therefore first consider how the calculation of values is affected when productive operations are analysed for a single period. Only thereafter can we establish consistent definitions for the different types of income.

In Section A.3, equilibrium for the firm was described as resulting from the maximisation of discounted total profit (9). The expression for the latter is now:

$$\sum_{t=1}^{T} p_t y_t = \sum_{t=1}^{T} (p_t b_t - p_t a_t).$$

In view of (27), it can also be written:

$$\sum_{t=1}^{T-1} (p_{t+1} b_{t+1} - p_t a_t) = \sum_{t=1}^{T-1} \pi_t \tag{35}$$

with, by definition,

$$\pi_t = p_{t+1} b_{t+1} - p_t a_t. \tag{36}$$

The quantity π_t is basically the profit, discounted at date 1, from the production realised during period t. We can also define the undiscounted profit available at the end of the period, that is, at date $t + 1$:

$$\bar{\pi}_t = \frac{\pi_t}{\beta_{t+1}} = \bar{p}_{t+1} b_{t+1} - (1 + \rho_t) \bar{p}_t a_t, \tag{37}$$

the last equality following from (5) and the definition of the interest rate ρ_t.

Thus we see that, by applying the general rules for finding discounted values, the profit $\bar{\pi}_t$ resulting from production during period t must be computed as the difference between the undiscounted value of outputs and a cost comprising both the value of inputs and an interest charge applied to all inputs. This definition applies at the level of the firm in isolation as well as at the level of the whole community.

If we wish to define a 'value added' equal to the sum of incomes created by production, we must distinguish two categories of inputs: inputs of labour and 'material inputs'. The vector a_t is then written as the sum of two vectors, l_t which has zero components for all goods other than the various services provided by labour, and m_t which on the other hand has zero components for these services. The value R_t added by production in period t is defined as the difference between the value $\bar{p}_{t+1}b_{t+1}$ of outputs and the values $\bar{p}_t m_t$ of 'material inputs';

$$R_t = \bar{p}_{t+1}b_{t+1} - \bar{p}_t m_t. \tag{38}$$

In view of (37), and since $a_t = l_t + m_t$, we can also write

$$R_t = \bar{p}_t l_t + \rho_t \bar{p}_t a_t + \pi_t. \tag{39}$$

According to (39), the 'value added' or 'global income' is equal to the sum of three terms:

—the return to labour $\bar{p}_t l_t$,
—interest on capital $\rho_t \bar{p}_t a_t$,
—profits $\bar{\pi}_t$.

There are certain remarks to be made about this decomposition of global income.†

In the first place, it applies not only to the economic calculus concerning the programmes of a society where markets for future commodities exist but obviously also to operations taking place currently. It does not assume a competitive system underlying the determination of prices and interest. It allows in fact a particular *theory of distribution* to be derived from each price theory.

In the second place, the term 'profit' is the source of some ambiguity in economic literature as in everyday language. Here we obtained the definition of profit $\bar{\pi}_t$ for period t by the natural generalisation of a concept first defined for an economy that did not explicitly involve time. It is therefore 'pure profit', which appears as residual when the whole interest charge on the capital engaged has been deducted. The term 'profits' is often given to all incomes other than incomes from labour, or 'unearned incomes' as they are sometimes called, that is, the sum $\rho_t \bar{p}_t a_t + \bar{\pi}_t$. It is therefore necessary to check the definition used by the author of any theoretical or applied work using the term profit.

---

† We must also note that, for a given programme and a given system of discounted prices, the definition of value added varies with the choice of numéraire for each date. If $\bar{p}_t$ remains fixed, and $\bar{p}_{t+1}$ is multiplied by a number ϕ, the 'income' R_t increases by $(\phi - 1)\bar{p}_{t+1}b_{t+1}$, profit $\bar{\pi}_t$ is multiplied by ϕ and interest increases by $(\phi - 1)(1 + \rho_t)\bar{p}_t a_t$, the rate of interest varying by $(\phi - 1)(1 + \rho_t)$. The numéraire should therefore be chosen so that the income has satisfactory practical significance.

In scientific literature the most common reference is to pure profit $\bar{\pi}_t$; but a *rate of profit* is sometimes also discussed, this being defined as the ratio between the sum of unearned incomes and the value of the capital employed, i.e. in the present case:

$$\frac{\rho_t \bar{p}_t a_t + \bar{\pi}_t}{\bar{p}_t a_t}. \tag{40}$$

We shall not attempt to avoid this ambiguity and shall occasionally talk of (40) as the average rate of profit and call

$$r_t = \frac{\rho_t \bar{p}_t \, \mathrm{d}a_t + \mathrm{d}\bar{\pi}_t}{\bar{p}_t \, \mathrm{d}a_t} \tag{41}$$

the *marginal rate of profit*, where $\mathrm{d}a_t$ is a small variation in the input vector and $\mathrm{d}\bar{\pi}_t$ the resulting variation in pure profit. This expression has already been used in Section A.4 in the discussion of competitive equilibrium when we stated that the marginal rate of profit was equal to the rate of interest (see (13) and (15)). In the following section we shall see that, in competitive equilibrium, the pure profit $\bar{\pi}_t$ for each period is maximised, so that $\mathrm{d}\bar{\pi}_t = 0$ and we again have $r_t = \rho_t$.

In the third place, the decomposition of R_t according to (39) corresponds to an analysis of the source of incomes; it does not generally correspond to the distribution of income among different agents or *a fortiori* among different social categories. Not only does it ignore all transfers, particularly those due to the fiscal system, which is quite natural since collective services are not taken into account here, but it can be accommodated to very varied distribution systems according to the assumptions made about property rights and the conventions governing payments.

For their distribution theories the major economists often started from different assumptions about the social structure. Thus, at the beginning of the nineteenth century,[†] Ricardo distinguishes three classes: workers, who sell their labour, landlords who rent their land, and finally farmers and capitalist entrepreneurs who organise production and put up capital other than land. So to proceed from (39) to the distribution of income, the input vector a_t must be split into two: a vector f_t corresponding to land and a vector g_t corresponding to other inputs. The return to labour, assumed to be received at date t, is then $\bar{p}_t l_t$, the return to landlords, received at $t + 1$ and called 'rent', is $\rho_t \bar{p}_t f_t$ and the return to capitalists is $\rho_t \bar{p}_t g_t + \bar{\pi}_t$. Marx[‡] distinguishes only two classes: workers, who receive $\bar{p}_t l_t$ and capitalists, who organise production and put up the total capital required, and receive

---

[†] Ricardo, *On the Principles of Political Economy and Taxation*, reprinted at C.U.P., 1953.

[‡] Marx, *Capital*, English transl., George Allen and Unwin, Ltd., London 1946.

$\rho_t \bar{p}_t a_t + \bar{\pi}_t$. The classical writers at the beginning of the century† follow (39) more strictly by identifying not only workers and capitalists, who lend capital, but also 'entrepreneurs' whose only function is to organise production without contributing either labour or capital. These three categories then receive the incomes $\bar{p}_t l_t$, $\rho_t \bar{p}_t a_t$ and $\bar{\pi}_t$ respectively.

We should also pay attention to dates. For example, in the last case it is assumed that, at date t, capitalists make the value of inputs $\bar{p}_t a_t$ available to entrepreneurs. The latter immediately acquire and pay for these inputs, in particular for inputs of labour l_t. At date $t + 1$, entrepreneurs sell all their outputs $\bar{p}_{t+1} b_{t+1}$ and repay capital $\bar{p}_t a_t$ and interest $\rho_t \bar{p}_t a_t$ to capitalists; so they have left a profit $\bar{\pi}_t$. (This description assumes that operations in period t are considered independently of those in other periods, a point which will not be emphasised here since we return to it in the next section.) But other assumptions can be made as to dates. For example, if the elementary period is considered to be of short duration, we can assume that the workers receive only at date $t + 1$ the return for their efforts during period t. Then the entrepreneur borrows no more than $\bar{p}_t m_t$, the capitalists' income becomes $\rho_t \bar{p}_t m_t$ and the workers' income $(1 + \rho_t) \bar{p}_t l_t$.

In the next section we shall see that, if the production function for period t has constant returns to scale, pure profit $\bar{\pi}_t$ is zero in competitive equilibrium. Decreasing returns to scale leads to a positive profit $\bar{\pi}_t$; but it could only be due to the existence of scarce resources available in limited quantities in the productive sphere and not taken explicitly into account in the definition of inputs (site, particular skills of the managing director, etc.). The return $\bar{\pi}_t$ is then in reality the result not of an organising activity but of the employment of the resources in question.

In such cases, the classical writers of the beginning of the century held rightly that clarity was gained by treating this revenue as due to the owners of resources rather than to 'entrepreneurs'. It was not really a case of profit, but of 'rent', comparable to that which Ricardo identified as due to landlords. In competitive equilibrium, every scarce resource of this type must have a value, which conforms to the rent that it brings in. If v_t is its value at date t, then to let it must bring in a return $\rho_t v_t$, which must be equal to the rent. The latter can therefore be considered as interest.‡

Therefore if all scarce resources are clearly identified among inputs, interest includes all rent, returns to scale are constant and pure profit becomes zero in competitive equilibrium.

---

† See, for example, Knight, *Risk, Uncertainty and Profit*, Boston 1921.

‡ Failure to account for such scarce resources brings in a bias in the evaluation of global income whenever their value varies with time. The increase (or decrease) $v_{t+1} - v_t$ in the value of a resource should in principle be accounted for in the value added $\bar{p}_{t+1} b_{t+1} - \bar{p}_t a_t$.

Is this not paradoxical? Why should an entrepreneur bother organising production if his income must be zero? This question obviously preoccupied economic theorists. Schumpeter gave a persuasive answer.[†] If the entrepreneur obtains a profit, this is because the economy is never perfectly competitive nor in perfect equilibrium.[‡] Positive pure profit exists either because of monopoly positions, or of temporary deviations of actual prices from equilibrium prices. More precisely, the entrepreneur keeps looking for 'innovations', that is, for profit possibilities not yet exploited. By discovering such possibilities and putting them into operation, he makes a temporary monopoly for himself and realises a disequilibrium profit (an 'extra surplus-value' according to Marx) so long as competition from other entrepreneurs does not appear; the size and duration of these profits varies according to the difficulty of the productive and commercial processes which the innovation involves and according to the degree of rigidity in the economy's institutional structure.

Competitive equilibrium analysis is therefore inadequate to explain the importance of pure profit. On the other hand, it should be informative about the factors that may take part in the division of value between return to labour and interest on capital. We shall discuss this question in Section B.8.

4. Short-sighted decisions and transferability of capital

Let us now return to the decisions of firms in a competitive market. The firm tries to maximise its discounted total profit subject to the technical constraints which govern it. For the representation of production in periods, the constraints are expressed by the sequence of production functions g_t, that is, the inequalities (28). Each pair of vectors $(a_t; b_{t+1})$ appears as argument in only one of these inequalities, that for period t. Now, (35) shows that the discounted total profit $\Sigma_{p_t y_t}$ can be expressed as a sum of discounted profits π_t relating to the different periods and that the choice of the pair $(a_t; b_{t+1})$ affects only one of these profits. Consequently, to maximise $\Sigma_{p_t y_t}$ subject to the set of inequalities (28) written for $t = 1, 2, ..., T - 1$, *it is sufficient for the firm to maximise the profits π_t successively and independently*, taking account in each period only of the production constraint relating to it.

We shall presently see why this apparently rather surprising result follows from the model under consideration. For the moment, let us look at its consequences.

Maximisation of

$$\pi_t = p_{t+1}b_{t+1} - p_t a_t$$

---

† Schumpeter, *The Theory of Economic Development*, Cambridge 1934, Chapter IV.
‡ We must also mention the presence of uncertainty, to be discussed in the next chapter.

subject to the constraint

$$g_t(a_t; b_{t+1}) = 0$$

imposes the following first-order conditions:

$$\begin{cases} p_{qt} = -\lambda_t g'_{qt} & q = 1, 2, ..., Q \\ p_{q,t+1} = \lambda_t \gamma'_{q,t+1} \end{cases} \tag{42}$$

where λ_t is a Lagrange multiplier and the notation (32) is used for the partial derivatives.

From these equations, and taking account of formula (8) defining ρ_{qt}, we obtain directly

$$\rho_{qt} = \frac{p_{qt} - p_{q,t+1}}{p_{q,t+1}} = -\frac{g'_{qt}}{\gamma'_{q,t+1}} - 1 \tag{43}$$

showing that the *own rate of interest of good q during period t is equal to the ratio between the net increase in supply of this good,*

$$d(b_{q,t+1} - a_{qt}),$$

and the increase in the input of the same good, da_{qt}, when only a_{qt} and $b_{q,t+1}$ vary from the equilibrium state for the firm. (Indeed, the equality $g'_{qt} da_{qt} + \gamma'_{q,t+1} db_{q,t+1} = 0$ implies that the ratio in (43) equals the ratio of $d(b_{q,t+1} - a_{qt})$ to da_{qt}).

We note also that conditions (42) imply conditions (34), which we obtained when investigating intertemporal efficiency. This result is not surprising, since a Pareto optimum is obviously 'intertemporally efficient'. Now, in Chapter 4 we discussed a property that applies perfectly in a time context and states that every competitive equilibrium is a Pareto optimum.

The necessary first-order conditions for maximisation of π_t subject to the constraint $g_t = 0$ are also sufficient when a suitable convexity assumption is satisfied. More precisely, let P_t be the set of $2Q$-dimensional space which contains the pairs $(a_t; b_{t+1})$ satisfying the technical constraints

$$g_t(a_t; b_{t+1}) \leqslant 0.$$

We shall then state the following assumption:

ASSUMPTION 2. The sets P_t are convex; the functions g_t are differentiable, non-decreasing with respect to the $b_{q,t+1}$, and non-increasing with respect to the a_{qt}.

Discussion of the validity conditions for this assumption takes us straight back to the remarks in Chapter 3. In particular, the assumptions about the direction of increase of g_t express the fact that a technically feasible pair cannot be reached from an unfeasible pair simply by reducing inputs or increasing outputs.

We saw in Chapter 3 that the convexity property found practical justification in two other properties, which can often be considered to be approximately satisfied, namely additivity and divisibility. But we saw also that then production must be carried out under constant returns to scale; if the pair $(a_t; b_{t+1})$ is technically feasible, then so also is the pair $(\mu a_t; \mu b_{t+1})$, for any positive number μ. Now, if the first pair returns a profit π_t, the second returns the profit $\mu\pi_t$. The maximum value of π_t is therefore necessarily zero, and the consequences of this property have been discussed in the previous section.

Let us now examine the origin of the property established at the beginning of this section; for a firm in a 'competitive market', the optimal policy is separate maximisation of the profits relating to each period.

This property assumes the existence of perfect markets for all commodities including equipment in use and products in course of manufacture. In particular, it implies that no transaction cost hinders the sale or purchase of second-hand material.

Without this assumption, the choice of the optimal policy must involve simultaneously the operations over all periods.

To see this clearly, we shall consider a very simple example, of a machine that can be used in the two successive periods 1 and 2. Let p_1 be its price new at date 1 and p_2 its discounted second-hand purchase price at date 2. The firm can also resell the machine at date 2 after having used it during period 1, but at a discounted price p_2^v which is less than p_2. The discounted gross receipts for the firm are u_1^0 and u_2^0 in the two periods when the machine is not used, u_1^1 and u_2^1 when it is.

The firm must make a decision for each period: to use (1) or not to use (0) the machine. There are therefore four 'programmes' leading to the following discounted total profit:

$$\pi(0, 0) = u_1^0 + u_2^0$$
$$\pi(0, 1) = u_1^0 + u_2^1 - p_2$$
$$\pi(1, 0) = u_1^1 + u_2^0 - p_1 + p_2^v$$
$$\pi(1, 1) = u_1^1 + u_2^1 - p_1.$$

This total profit cannot be expressed as the sum of a first term depending on the decision taken for period 1 and of a second term depending on the decision taken for period 2. For then we should have

$$\pi(1, 1) - \pi(0, 1) = \pi(1, 0) - \pi(0, 0),$$

that is, $p_2 = p_2^v$. In such an example we can no longer define the profit relating to each period as a function only of the decisions involving this period.

In short, the property under consideration assumes that capital is freely transferable at each date, at well-defined prices. In the real situation, a large part of capital is 'fixed'. The cost of transferring it from one use to another is often prohibitive. Thus the general theory with which this chapter is concerned ignores one aspect of reality which is important in certain cases.

Unfortunately it seems impossible to achieve general theoretical results when we consider the practical irreversibility of investment operations, i.e. when it is no longer feasible for existing installations to change their use. So in what follows, we shall ignore the possible effects of non-transferability. This will not be a serious drawback since we shall mainly be discussing stationary programmes or proportional growth programmes where no transfer of existing equipment is required.

5. Efficient stationary states and proportional growth programmes

A stationary regime or state is a programme in which the quantities representing the activity of the different agents have the same values in all periods so that production and consumption in one period are the same as in the previous period.

Stationary states are unlikely to be realised if the conditions governing the activity of consumers and producers vary over time, and in these circumstances there is nothing special to be gained from their investigation. For this reason *the theory of stationary states assumes the environment invariant over time.*

Confining ourselves for the time being to production operations, we can define precisely what is meant by a stationary environment. In each firm j, the production functions $g_{jt}(a_{jt}; b_{j,t+1})$ are the same for all periods, which excludes all technical progress. Moreover, in a stationary state inputs a_{jqt} and outputs b_{jqt} are also the same in all periods. So we shall use simply g_j to denote the production function, a_j for the input vector and b_j for the output vector. We shall let $y_j = b_j - a_j$ be the vector of the net productions available at all intermediary dates, where obviously $y_{j1} = - a_j$ at the initial date and $y_{jT} = b_j$ at the terminal date.

A production programme is in general a set of vectors a_{jt}, b_{jt} for all firms and all dates. Such a programme is feasible if it obeys the inequalities

$$g_j(a_{jt}; b_{j,t+1}) \leqslant 0 \tag{44}$$

for all j and all t, as well as the conditions at the extreme dates. It is a production optimum if it is feasible and if there is no other feasible programme giving a higher level for at least one global net production:

$$y_{qt} = \sum_{j=1}^{n} (b_{jqt} - a_{jqt}) \qquad \begin{cases} q = 1, 2, ..., Q \\ t = 1, 2, ..., T, \end{cases}$$

and giving a lower level for none.

More precisely, the stationary programme E^0 is a production optimum if it is feasible and if there exists no feasible programme E such that, for all q,

$$- \sum_{j=1}^{n} a_{jq1} \geqslant - \sum_{j=1}^{n} a_{jq}^0$$

$$\sum_{j=1}^{n} (b_{jqt} - a_{jqt}) \geqslant \sum_{j=1}^{n} (b_{jq}^0 - a_{jq}^0) \qquad t = 2, ..., T - 1$$

$$\sum_{j=1}^{n} b_{jqT} \geqslant \sum_{j=1}^{n} b_{jq}^0$$

where at least one inequality holds strictly.

We are now in a position to establish the following result.

PROPOSITION 1. Let E^0 be a stationary state which is a production optimum. If the functions g_j satisfy assumption 2, then there exists a non-zero vector p with Q components and a number ρ (where $p_q \geqslant 0$ and $\rho > - 1$) such that $(a_j^0; b_j^0)$ maximises $pb_j - (1 + \rho)pa_j$ over the set of pairs of vectors $(a_j; b_j)$ satisfying $g_j(a_j; b_j) \leqslant 0$.

For, consider the vectors y_j whose components are the QT numbers y_{jqt}; consider also the inequalities $f_j(y_j) \leqslant 0$ representing the technical constraints on the y_j which can be deduced from (44). It is easy to verify that assumption 2 on the g_j implies that the sets Y_j are convex and the functions f are differentiable and non-decreasing with respect to each of the y_{jqt}.

Since, by hypothesis, E^0 is a production optimum, proposition 3 of Chapter 4 implies that there exist QT numbers p_{qt}, not all zero, such that y_j^0 maximises py_j over the set of y_j satisfying $f_j(y_j) \leqslant 0$. As we saw earlier in Section B.4, this implies that for each t from 1 to $T - 1$, $(a_j^0; b_j^0)$ maximises $p_{t+1}b_{j,t+1} - p_t a_{jt}$ over the set of $(a_{jt}; b_{j,t+1})$ satisfying (44).

Let us consider the marginal equalities resulting from this last property. They are expressed by:

$$\begin{cases} p_{qt} = - \lambda_{jt} g'_{jq} & q = 1, 2, ..., Q \\ p_{q,t+1} = \lambda_{jt} \gamma'_{jq} & t = 1, 2, ..., T - 1, \end{cases} \qquad (45)$$

where g'_{jq} and γ'_{jq} denote the values of the derivatives of type (32) for the pair of vectors $(a_j^0; b_j^0)$. (The stationarity of E^0 means that these derivatives do not depend on t.) System (45) implies conditions on the g'_{jq} and γ'_{jq}. We shall not emphasise them here, since they have already been discussed on other occasions in similar contexts. But this system also implies conditions on the p_{qt}. In fact, the ratio p_{qt}/p_{rt} must equal g'_{jq}/g'_{jr}; it is independent of t, which means that the vectors p_t relating to different dates differ by at most a multiplicative constant. So we shall write

$$p_t = \beta_t p, \qquad (46)$$

where p denotes a suitable vector with Q components.

System (45) also implies that the ratio $p_{q,t+1}/p_{qt}$, which equals β_{t+1}/β_t, has the value $-\gamma'_{jq}/g'_{jq}$, which is independent of t and can be denoted by β. Adopting the convention $\beta_1 = 1$, which is always possible, we can deduce $\beta_t = \beta^{t-1}$ and

$$p_t = \beta^{t-1}p. \tag{47}$$

The form at which we have just arrived shows that discounted prices p_{qt} are such that *the interest rates relating to the different goods are all equal and the interest rates relating to the different periods are also equal.* We can therefore let ρ denote this common rate for all goods and all periods. The maximised expression $p_{t+1} b_{j,t+1} - p_t a_{jt}$ is then proportional to $pb_{j,t+1} - pa_{jt}/\beta = pb_{j,t+1} - (1 + \rho)pa_{jt}$. This completes the proof of proposition 1.

This proposition shows the sense in which relative prices p_q and the interest rate ρ are defined uniquely with respect to every programme corresponding to a stationary regime which is a production optimum. It can easily be generalised to the case of proportional growth.

A state of *proportional growth* is a programme in which the quantities representing the activity of the different agents all increase at the same rate $\alpha - 1$ from period to period. If the a_{jq} represent inputs at date 1, then

$$a_{jqt} = \alpha^{t-1}a_{jq} \qquad t = 1, 2, ..., T - 1$$

Similarly, if the b_{jq} represent outputs at date 2, then

$$b_{jqt} = \alpha^{t-2}b_{jq} \qquad t = 2, 3, ..., T.$$

States of proportional growth are almost as special cases as stationary regimes (the case $\alpha = 1$). In fact, they assume that *the environment is stationary and that production is carried on under constant returns to scale.* So that the condition that the growth is technically feasible can be expressed simply as

$$g_j(a_j; b_j) \leqslant 0.$$

In order to substain a state of proportional growth which is a production optimum, the price system must also satisfy (45). It must therefore have the form (47).

6. Capitalistic optimum

In the previous section we applied optimum theory purely and simply, and confined ourselves to production. In particular, in order to establish a programme of proportional growth as an optimum, we compared it with all other feasible programmes, whether or not they were of proportional growth.

We might also think of comparing proportional growth programmes with each other directly, concentrating on the net productions which they yield. For this, we consider the following definition.

DEFINITION 2. A proportional growth programme E^0 is said to be a 'capitalistic optimum' if it satisfies the technical constraints

$$g_j(a_j; b_j) \leqslant 0 \qquad j = 1, 2, ..., n \tag{48}$$

and if there is no other programme E of proportional growth which satisfies the same constraints, grows at the same rate α^0, gives a higher net production of at least one good and does not give a lower net production of any other:

$$\sum_{j=1}^{n} (b_{jq} - \alpha^0 a_{jq}) \geqslant \sum_{j=1}^{n} (b_{jq}^0 - \alpha^0 a_{jq}^0) \qquad q = 1, 2, ..., Q \tag{49}$$

where the inequality holds strictly at least once.

This definition reveals a certain relationship between production optimum and capitalistic optimum. However, there is a fairly clear-cut difference between the two notions. For the second, no explicit account is taken of the initial and terminal situations of the programme, which on the other hand are involved in the production optimum. In the comparisons to which the latter concept gives rise, the inequalities (49) must be supplemented by the following, which result directly from the constraints relating to the initial and terminal dates respectively:

$$-\sum_{j=1}^{n} a_{jq} \geqslant -\sum_{j=1}^{n} a_{jq}^0,$$
$$\sum_{j=1}^{n} b_{jq} \geqslant \sum_{j=1}^{n} b_{jq}^0. \tag{50}$$

In other words, we can say that, when determining a capitalistic optimum, we can leave the a_{jq}, the quantities relating to capital, completely unrestricted since, in comparisons between programmes of proportional growth, we do not consider the a_{jq} directly, but only the $b_{jq} - \alpha^0 a_{jq}$. In a *capitalistic optimum, the equipment, stocks and current inputs represented by the a_{jq} are, in a certain sense, optimal from the standpoint of the net productions which they yield under proportional growth. But, in the initial concrete situation in an economy, there is no reason a priori for existing equipment and stocks to be extensive enough to allow the immediate realisation of such an optimum.* This is the reason why capitalistic optima are also often called in the literature 'golden age' programmes.

We can now establish

PROPOSITION 2. Let E^0 be a proportional growth programme, which is a capitalistic optimum. If the functions g_j satisfy assumption 2 and, when $\alpha^0 \neq 1$, have constant returns to scale, there exists a non-zero vector p such that $(a_j^0; b_j^0)$ maximises $pb_j - \alpha^0 pa_j$ over the set of pairs of vectors $(a_j; b_j)$ satisfying the technical constraints (48).

The proof is similar to the proof of proposition 3 in Chapter 4, so only the main elements will be given here.

If E^0 is a capitalistic optimum, it maximises

$$\sum_j (b_{j1} - \alpha^0 a_{j1}) \tag{51}$$

subject to the constraints

$$\begin{cases} \sum_j (b_{jq} - \alpha^0 a_{jq}) = \sum_j (b_{jq}^0 - \alpha^0 a_{jq}^0) & q = 2, 3, ..., Q; \\ g_j(a_j; b_j) = 0 & j = 1, 2, ..., n. \end{cases} \tag{52}$$

Therefore there exist Lagrange multipliers $\sigma_1 = 1$, σ_q and μ_j ($q = 2, 3, ...,$ Q; $j = 1, 2, ..., n$) such that E^0 equates to zero the derivatives with respect to the a_{jq} and b_{jq} of the function that consists of (51) added to the constraints (52), each multiplied by its Lagrange multiplier. Equation to zero of the derivatives in question is expressed by

$$\begin{cases} \sigma_q + \mu_j \gamma'_{jq} = 0, \\ -\alpha^0 \sigma_q + \mu_j g'_{jq} = 0. \end{cases} \tag{53}$$

On the other hand, the first-order conditions for maximisation of $pb_j - \alpha^0 pa_j$, subject to the constraint (48), are

$$\begin{cases} p_q = \lambda_j \gamma'_{jq} \\ \alpha^0 p_q = -\lambda_j g'_{jq}. \end{cases} \tag{54}$$

These conditions are satisfied by E^0 if $p_q = \sigma_q$ and $\lambda_j = -\mu_j$. Finally, they are sufficient for maximisation of $pb_j - \alpha^0 pa_j$ when the function g_j obeys assumption 2. This completes the proof of proposition 2.

The price-system introduced by proposition 3 has the special feature that it involves an interest rate equal to the growth rate $\alpha^0 - 1$, and, in particular, a zero interest rate in the case of a stationary regime. In fact, the value of inputs is accounted for in the profit $pb_j - \alpha^0 pa_j$ with the addition of an interest charge equal to $(\alpha^0 - 1)pa_j$.

This result may seem more natural, and the relation between production optimum and capitalistic optimum may become clearer if we consider the simple case of stationary programmes in an economy with a single good and a single firm.

The curve in Figure 5 represents the variations in $b - a$ as a function of a when $g(a; b) = 0$. Any point M^1 situated on the increasing part of this curve defines a stationary state E^1, which immediately appears as a production optimum. (To increase $b - a$ beyond $b^1 - a^1$ implies an increase of capital beyond a^1, that is, a decrease in 'initial net production' $y_1 = -a$). The gradient of the tangent to the curve at M^1 defines the interest rate ρ corresponding to E^1, since M^1 must maximise profit, which here becomes $(b - a) - \rho a$ when the good serves as numéraire. The point M^0, the maximum of the curve, defines a stationary state E^0, which is obviously a capitalistic optimum. The tangent at M^0 is horizontal, consequently the rate of interest is zero.

Thus, in a stationary economy the return to capital disappears if capital is sufficiently plentiful, if production is organised efficiently, and if the price-system correctly reflects marginal equivalences. It is remarkable that this statement is no longer exact for a programme of proportional growth corresponding to true expansion ($\alpha^0 > 1$). If capital is optimal in such a state of growth, then the rate of interest remains positive. This must be so *a fortiori* if capital is too scarce to allow immediate realisation of a capitalistic optimum.

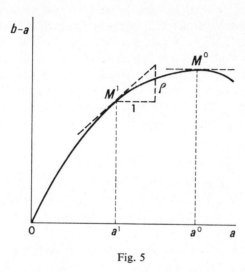

Fig. 5

7. The theory of interest once again

This naturally leads us to conceive of a relation between the rate of interest and the 'scarcity' of capital, or between interest and 'capital-intensity'. In a given state of technique, that is, for given production functions or sets, the price-system varies *a priori* as a function of (i) the resources available to the economy, (ii) consumer preferences and (iii) the distribution of property rights. The description of such variations may be very complex. However, are they not compatible with the existence of a simple relation between the rate of interest and certain physical characteristics of the programmes under consideration?

Most economists who have approached this question have believed it possible to give a positive answer, at least so long as the investigation is confined only to stationary regimes. However, we must now recognise that there is no simple universal relation between the rate of interest and capital intensity. Certainly a tendency exists, but it is often contradicted by examples which are not particularly abnormal.

For a clear grasp of the subject we shall first establish an inequality resulting from profit maximisation. This inequality leads to clear-cut conclusions for the most aggregative model; but it has no simple implication when even a small number of goods is being considered. We shall then discuss a small example that should help to reveal where the difficulties lie. We shall conclude the chapter with another example that gives rise to reflection on the special features of 'stationary equilibria'.

Let us try to apply the idea that the study of production conditions alone allows us to establish a relation between the rate of interest and capital intensity.

Let us assume that there are two categories of goods: primary resources, which can neither be produced nor consumed, and products. Let z denote the input vector of primary resources and w their price vector. We let a, b, y and p denote the vectors relating to the products. With this new notation, the profit $\bar{\pi}$ realised in an elementary period is

$$\bar{\pi} = py - \rho pa - w'z \tag{55}$$

where, by convention, w' denotes $(1 + \rho)w$.

We now refer to two stationary equilibria: E^0 (with quantities defined by y^0, a^0, z^0 and prices by p^0, w^0, ρ^0) and E^1 (with similarly y^1, ..., p^1). We set, for example

$$\Delta y = y^1 - y^0.$$

Maximisation of profit with respect to the price-system of E^0 implies

$$p^0\Delta y - \rho^0 p^0 \Delta a - w^{0\prime}\Delta z \leqslant 0. \tag{56}$$

Similarly, profit maximisation with respect to the price-system of E^1 implies

$$p^1\Delta y - \rho^1 p^1 \Delta a - w^{1\prime}\Delta z \geqslant 0. \tag{57}$$

It follows from the last two inequalities that

$$\Delta p \Delta y - \Delta(\rho p)\Delta a - \Delta w' \Delta z \geqslant 0. \tag{58}$$

Inequality (58), which can be called the 'relation of comparative dynamics', sets a condition on the variations which, affecting quantities (Δy, Δa, Δz) and prices (Δp, $\Delta(\rho p)$, $\Delta w'$) simultaneously, are compatible with the given production possibilities. To make use of this inequality, we assume further that E^0 and E^1 use the same primary inputs $\Delta z = 0$. We then say that the capital-intensity of E^1 is greater than that of E^0 if all the components of Δa are positive; using the same inputs of labour, E^1 uses more products—equipment, power, raw materials, etc. When $\Delta z = 0$, inequality (58) becomes

$$\Delta p \,.\, \Delta y - \Delta(\rho p) \,.\, \Delta a \geqslant 0. \tag{59}$$

It has a simple implication in an aggregate model where y, a and p have each a single component: the same product represents both 'production goods' and 'consumption goods'. This product can be taken as numéraire so that $\Delta p = 0$ and $\Delta(\rho p) = \Delta\rho$. It then follows from (59) that

$$\Delta\rho \cdot \Delta a \leqslant 0. \tag{60}$$

The greatest capital-intensity corresponds to the lowest interest rate.

But, apart from this model to which economists have tended to attribute too much general significance, (59) does not necessarily lead to such a clear-cut result. As we shall see, we can construct examples in which a family of stationary equilibria is not ranked in inverse order according as capital intensity or the rate of interest is being used as the ranking criterion.

Suppose then that there is a single primary resource (z and w are scalars), a 'subsistence good' taken as numéraire and not used as input, and finally a 'durable good' with price p. The input of the latter is denoted by a, its net production by y_2, and that of the subsistence good by y_1. The technical constraints are represented by the production function

$$y_1^\beta + y_2^\beta = A^\beta a^\alpha z^{\beta-\alpha} \tag{61}$$

where α and β are two parameters.† Assumption 2 is satisfied when $\beta \geqslant 1$ and $0 < \alpha < \beta$.

We shall assume that $z = 1$, so that a will be taken as a measure of capital intensity. A stationary equilibrium then depends on two numbers, a and, for example

$$s = \frac{y_2}{y_1},$$

the third number being determined by (61). The number s increases as consumption is directed more to the durable good, to the detriment of the subsistence good (y_1 and y_2 are naturally used for consumption).

Profit is

$$\bar{\pi} = y_1 + py_2 - \rho pa - w'z; \tag{62}$$

its maximisation subject to (61) implies

$$\begin{cases} \beta y_1^{\beta-1} = \lambda \\ \beta y_2^{\beta-1} = \lambda p \qquad \alpha\dfrac{u}{a} = \lambda\rho p \\ \qquad\qquad (\beta - \alpha)\dfrac{u}{z} = \lambda w' \end{cases} \tag{63}$$

where λ is a Lagrange multiplier and u is the expression $A^\beta a^\alpha z^{\beta-\alpha}$.

---

† The reader can verify that we revert to this function with $\alpha = 1$ and $z = 1$ if we consider an economy with two primary resources, one of which can only be used for product 1 and the other for product 2, and in which the net outputs of the two products are $y_1 = Aa_1^{1/\beta}$ and $y_2 = Aa_2^{1/\beta}$ when the primary resources are all used, the numbers a_1 and a_2 denoting capital inputs of the 'durable good' in each production.

From this system we can deduce directly

$$\frac{w'}{\rho p} = \left(\frac{\beta}{\alpha} - 1\right)a \tag{64}$$

when $z = 1$. *Capital intensity is related directly to the ratio between the current cost of labour (w') and the current cost of capital (ρp)*. But w' and p depend on the characteristics of equilibrium so that the relation between a and ρ is not simple.

We can also deduce from (63):

$$p = s^{\beta-1} \tag{65}$$

which, combined with (64), gives

$$\frac{w'}{\rho} = \left(\frac{\beta}{\alpha} - 1\right)a \cdot s^{\beta-1}. \tag{66}$$

The ratio between the 'rate of wages' and the 'rate of profit' increases as capital-intensity increases and as consumption tends to be more directed towards the durable good.

But the expression for w' as a function of a and s is complex. We can deduce from (63):

$$w' = \left(1 - \frac{\alpha}{\beta}\right)uy_1^{1-\beta}. \tag{67}$$

Now,

$$u = y_1^{\beta} + y_2^{\beta} = A^{\beta}a^{\alpha},$$

and so

$$uy_1^{-\beta} = 1 + s^{\beta}$$
$$y_1^{\beta}(1 + s^{\beta}) = A^{\beta}a^{\alpha}$$
$$y_1 = Aa^{\alpha/\beta}(1 + s^{\beta})^{-1/\beta}. \tag{68}$$

Finally,

$$w' = A\left(1 - \frac{\alpha}{\beta}\right)a^{\alpha/\beta}(1 + s^{\beta})^{1-1/\beta} \tag{69}$$

which, combined with (66), gives

$$\rho = \frac{\alpha A}{\beta}a^{\alpha/\beta-1}(1 + s^{-\beta})^{1-1/\beta}. \tag{70}$$

The rate of interest certainly decreases as a increases, since $\alpha < \beta$; but it also depends on s. Two stationary equilibria E^0 and E^1 can be such that $\rho^1 > \rho^0$ and $a^1 > a^0$ on condition that $s^1 - s^0$ is negative and large enough in absolute value.

To make things more precise, we can imagine that, for each level a of capital intensity, there exists a single combination (y_1, y_2) of net outputs, that is, a single value of s compatible with the consumers' preferences between the 'subsistence good' and the 'durable good'. Figure 6 illustrates such a situation for the case of a single consumer. In the plane (y_1, y_2), the curve UV represents the set of combinations that are feasible in a stationary equilibrium for a given level of a, and the curve $U'V'$ corresponds to a higher value of a. Indifference curves are drawn in dotted lines. To each level of a there corresponds an equilibrium represented by the point on the curve of production possibilities which is highest in the consumer's preferences: P on UV, or P' on $U'V'$.

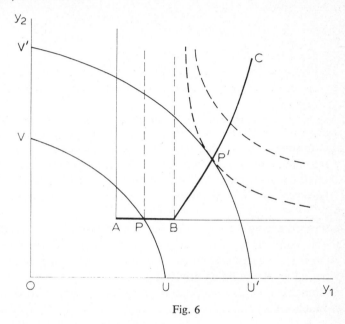

Fig. 6

The indifference curves have been drawn so that, for increasing levels of a, the equilibrium point moves first along the horizontal segment AB and then on an increasing curve BC. We can verify that, if $\alpha > 1$, the rate of interest *increases* along AB while capital intensity also increases.

In fact, (68) implies

$$y_2 = sy_1 = Aa^{\alpha/\beta}(1 + s^{-\beta})^{-1/\beta}.$$

When y_2 remains constant, $(1 + s^{-\beta})$ varies proportionally with a^α. In view of (70), the rate ρ varies proportionally with

$$a^{\alpha/\beta - 1} \cdot a^{\alpha(1 - 1/\beta)} = a^{\alpha - 1}.$$

Figure 7 illustrates how ρ then varies with the increase in capital intensity: the rate of interest increases initially and only decreases after y_2 increases.

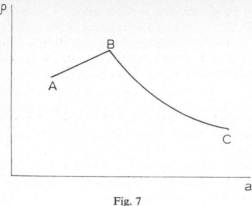

Fig. 7

8. Stationary equilibria

Apart from a reference to consumer preferences in the last example, we have so far considered only production. A stationary equilibrium can be completely formulated in different ways. In order not to lengthen this chapter unduly, we shall consider only a very simple case, which yet reveals certain particular features of the definition of equilibrium in intertemporal economies.†

Suppose there is a single good (close scrutiny shows that the model also applies if it also contains labour, considered as a primary resource available in a fixed quantity). We can set the undiscounted price of this product as 1, that is, we can adopt the good as numéraire.

Let us assume that there is a single firm whose technology is invariant over time. Its production function is

$$g(a; b) = 0$$

and its capitalised profit at the end of the period:

$$\bar{\pi} = b - (1 + \rho)a. \tag{71}$$

We also assume that each consumer lives during exactly two periods, that his consumption of the product is x_1 and x_2 in the first and the second half of his existence respectively, that his discounted income at the beginning of

---

† This case is borrowed from Samuelson, 'An Exact Consumption-Loan Model of Interest with or without the Social Contrivance of Money', *The Journal of Political Economy*, December 1958.

his life is R and his utility function is $S(x_1, x_2)$. If he is free to borrow and lend, his budget constraint is

$$R = x_1 + \frac{x_2}{1 + \rho}. \tag{72}$$

Let us assume that exactly one consumer is born at each date, that is, that two consumers exist in each period, one young and one old. At each date, the equilibrium condition in the market for the good is

$$x_1 + x_2 = b - a. \tag{73}$$

What shall we say is a stationary competitive equilibrium in such an economy? Obviously, values of the different variables $(a, b, x_1, x_2, \rho, \bar{\pi}, R)$ which are such that:

(i) The firm maximises $\bar{\pi}$ subject to the constraint of its production function (that is, it determines $\bar{\pi}$, a and b as a function of ρ, which is considered as given for the firm: hence three equations);

(ii) Each consumer maximises S subject to the constraint of his budget equation (72) (that is, he determines x_1 and x_2 as a function of R and ρ: hence two equations):

(iii) Equilibrium is realised in the market for the good (equation (73)).

These three conditions imply 6 equations among the seven variables. If there are no other conditions for equilibrium, then it has one degree of freedom *a priori*.

Looking at the situation more closely, it seems that equilibrium can be meaningful in such a model only if we define how profit is distributed to the consumers and if they have no other source of income. Let us assume that a fraction α of profit is distributed at the end of the period to the consumer who has just been born, and a fraction $1 - \alpha$ to the consumer starting the second half of his life. In these conditions, the discounted income of a consumer at the beginning of his life is

$$R = \bar{\pi}\left(\alpha + \frac{1 - \alpha}{1 + \rho}\right), \tag{74}$$

which completes the six previous equations for the determination of equilibrium. This equilibrium will then be a function of α.

Let us discuss in particular the cases $\alpha = 0$ and $\alpha = 1$. If $\alpha = 0$, equations (74), (71) and (72) imply

$$x_1 + \frac{x_2}{1 + \rho} = \frac{b}{1 + \rho} - a$$

or

$$x_1 + a = \frac{b - x_2}{1 + \rho}.$$

But this is compatible with the market equilibrium condition (73) only if $\rho = 0$. A stationary equilibrium is possible only with a zero rate of interest, and this is so for any functions S and g. We can easily think of examples where no stationary equilibrium exists. We need only choose for g a function such that $b - a$ tends to infinity with a.

If $\alpha = 1$, this situation disappears. Equations (74), (71) and (72) imply

$$x_1 + \frac{x_2}{1 + \rho} = b - (1 + \rho)a$$

or

$$b - x_1 = \frac{x_2}{1 + \rho} + (1 + \rho)a$$

but the equilibrium condition (73) implies $b - x_1 = x_2 + a$.

Therefore

$$(x_2 + a)(1 + \rho) = x_2 + (1 + \rho)^2 a,$$

that is,

$$x_2 = (1 + \rho)a$$

which, taken in isolation, imposes no particular value for the rate of interest.

This example confirms the conclusion of the previous section; the interest rate does not depend only on the technical conditions of production. It shows also that the *existence* of stationary equilibria has aspects not previously encountered with the static model and that the particular way in which income is distributed may play an important part, according to circumstances. However, we shall leave the question of existence at this point, since no general results for it are available.

Uncertainty

In the models discussed so far, we have assumed that agents have perfect knowledge of the consequences of their decisions and that these decisions determine the equilibrium completely, provided that they are mutually consistent. There was no element of risk or uncertainty in the situation.

Around 1950, equilibrium and optimum theories could be accused of thus neglecting a basic aspect of the real world. It was difficult at that time to decide how far the simplifying assumption of the absence of uncertainty affected the relevance of the results. Thanks to recent progress in the theory of decision-making under uncertainty, this very considerable gap has largely been filled in. Generalisation of the abstract properties discussed up till now may still appear insufficient for the theoretical description of the real situation, which can be very complex. But the logical extension of microeconomic theories to situations involving uncertainty has been well elucidated. We must devote some time to it.

1. States and events

How does uncertainty affect our general formulation? Here are some examples: such and such agricultural production may be feasible on the basis of such and such inputs only if the composition of the soil has some particular characteristic and if weather conditions are favourable; a consumer may tomorrow prefer one entertainment to another according as his mood will be happy or sad; some proposed factory will be profitable only if a newly discovered geological deposit has sufficient reserves beyond those already known. Thus, the sets of feasible activities (X_i and Y_j), the preferences (S_i) and the resources (ω_h) in the economy may depend on elements as yet unknown.

To represent this situation, we must identify all the elements affecting the equilibrium or optimum: soil composition, weather conditions, the consumer's future mood, the extent of undiscovered reserves, etc. *A priori*, each element can have two or more values. Uncertainty disappears if we know the value of each of them.

So the following theoretical formulation is required: let *e* be a particular set of values given to each of the uncertain elements in the situation under consideration and let Ω be the set of *e*'s that are possible *a priori*. Uncertainty is represented by Ω; it disappears if we know which *e* of Ω is realised. It is customary nowadays to call *e* the '*state of nature*', or more simply, the *state*.† In short, the agents of the economy must make their decisions in the knowledge of the set Ω of possible states, but not knowing which of the *e*'s is 'true'.

An uncertain *event* is then a subset *H* of Ω; for example, the fact that the consumer will be happy tomorrow is the event defined by the set of all states for which this takes place. In most cases, the consequences of a particular decision depend on events comprising a certain number of states. But we shall scarcely be concerned with this in what follows.

At this point there are three remarks which must be made about this formulation:

(i) *Uncertainty and time.* Uncertainty is mostly concerned with the future. But this is not always so; for example, the extent of geological deposits is as much a characteristic of the present as of the future. The theories which we shall be discussing assume nothing about the temporal nature of the set of states. So there is no point in going into more detail here.

However, when the model involves uncertainty and time simultaneously, we must remember that a 'state' specifies all uncertain elements which may be important, that is, the whole 'story of nature', whether it involves unknown past, present or future facts.

(ii) *Uncertainty and probability.* When we say that the state *e* belongs to Ω, is this sufficient to represent the available information completely? Certainly not, since some states of Ω may be more probable than others.

Clearly there is nothing to prevent us from assuming a distribution on Ω defining the probabilities that the agents attribute to the different states and the different events.‡ We shall do so in Sections 5 and 6 below. But the most direct generalisation of microeconomic theories need not concern itself in principle with such a distribution, even when it exists. So we can ignore it at least for the next two sections.

Thus, our theory will cover the case where different agents have different

† Of course, this notion of state must not be confused with the notion of 'state of the economy' used previously. To avoid confusion, the latter expression will not be used in this chapter.

‡ If Ω is not a finite set, the definition of the distribution assumes previous definition of probabilisable events. There is no point in dwelling on this here.

distributions on Ω. Each of these individual distributions can properly be called 'subjective' since it depends on the subject to which it applies. The fact that different agents attribute different probabilities to the same state is no more inconvenient for our theory than the fact that different consumers have different tastes.

(iii) *Uncertainty and information.* To define Ω is to define the information common to *all* agents in the community; all know that the true state belongs to Ω. However, we have just seen that they do not necessarily agree on the probabilities to be attributed to the different states, which we can now interpret to mean that they have differing information.

We can go even further. Some consumer or some producer may know that some event H^1, more restricted than Ω, is true; so he knows that the true state belongs to the subset H^1 of Ω. Some other agent may know that this same state belongs to another subset H^2.

We shall pay no particular attention to this. It considerably complicates the proof of the existence of an equilibrium.† But especially, it explains the appearance of a new type of activity: before making their decisions on consumption or production, individuals or firms may find it useful to exchange or seek out information. We shall go no further into this question, for which the most useful results are certainly still to be established.

2. Contingent commodities and plans

We shall adopt a similar approach to that used in the treatment of inter-temporal economies, and first try to apply to an uncertain economy the concepts and theories examined in earlier lectures. This will be an aid to clearer discussion of the general problems raised by the organisation of economic activities affected by random influences. It must therefore provide a basis for the more specific studies which may be required because of the presence of uncertainty.

How does the elementary concept of a commodity apply to an economy whose state of nature is uncertain? Two equal quantities of the same good are not equivalent if they must be available for different sets of states, the first when the true state belongs to the event H^1, and the second when it belongs to H^2 (where $H^1 \neq H^2$). *So the complete characterisation of a commodity must specify the states in which it is available.* In other words, the commodities which we shall now be discussing must be 'contingent', that is, their existence must be related to the realisation of certain events.

Consider also a contract stipulating that a certain quantity of a good must be delivered if a particular event H comprising three states e^1, e^2 and e^3

---

† See Radner, 'Competitive Equilibrium under Uncertainty', *Econometrica*, vol. 35, No. 3, 1967.

is realised. It will be convenient subsequently to say that this contract implies a complex of three elementary commodities, the first being the good in question subject to the condition that e^1 is realised, the second the good if e^2 is realised, and the third the good if e^3 is realised. This procedure allows us to describe any contract stipulating conditional delivery; we need only introduce a complex of elementary commodities, each consisting of a specified good which is due if and only if a particular state is realised. This concept of elementary commodity is sufficient for theoretical purposes.

In short, a commodity is now defined not only by its physical characteristics, its location, the date at which it is available, but also by a particular state of nature, that which must be realised in order that a stipulated delivery of this commodity should take effect.

We have no reason here to take location or date in isolation. So we shall say that such and such a 'commodity' consists of such and such a 'good' available if such and such a 'state' is realised. We shall talk of 'commodities' without mentioning each time that we are concerned with elementary contingent commodities. The index h previously used to characterise commodities will now correspond to the pair (q, e) where q refers to the good and e to the state.

In our theoretical investigation we assumed that the number of commodities was finite. So for the moment we shall assume that the number N of states is finite: $e = 1, 2, ..., N$. If there are Q goods, then there exist $l = NQ$ commodities.

The activity vectors of the agents, x_i for the ith consumer, y_j for the jth firm, then define quantities for each good and each state. These vectors represent 'uncertain prospects', 'plans of action', or what are sometimes called 'strategies'. To choose the vector x is to choose to consume $x_{11}, x_{21}, ..., x_{Q1}$ if the first state is realised, $x_{12}, x_{22}, ..., x_{Q2}$ if the second is realised, etc. In fact, a consumption strategy is chosen. In the generalisation of equilibrium and optimum theories, each agent no longer has to fix his activity, but rather to decide on his strategy.

This change of outlook does not basically affect the definition of sets of feasible vectors, X_i for the ith consumer, Y_j for the jth firm. It remains true to say that certain plans of action are physically or technically possible for the individual while others are not. The general assumptions introduced for the X_i and Y_j seem to raise no particular difficulty in the actual context.

Similarly, the ith consumer's choices here must relate to plans of action rather than to activity vectors. This fact does not seem likely to affect either the general assumptions on individual preferences nor the definition of utility functions. We shall have occasion to look at this more closely very shortly. We must first consider the prices of contingent commodities and the nature of the markets for such commodities.

3. The system of contingent prices

The generalisation of the basic concepts being now clear, we can examine, in the context of an uncertain economy, the nature of the price-system and the market equilibria with which our theories have dealt so far. We shall then consider the possible role of such prices or equilibria in positive and normative theories.

The price p_{qe} of the commodity (q, e) is the price to the purchaser in a contract stipulating that a unit quantity of the good q must be delivered if the state e is realised, but that otherwise, nothing is due from the seller. Note that the price p_{qe} applies firmly to the contract; it represents the value of the contract involving conditional delivery, and does so independently of the realisation of the event. In other words, the price p_{qe} must be firmly tendered by a purchaser wishing to obtain the promise of a conditional delivery.

Of course, it is also possible to define the price of a 'conditional contract' which will come into force, both as regards payment by the purchaser and delivery by the seller, only if the state e is realised.

Let us now express prices as quantities of the good Q. We shall call this good the 'numéraire', although this is an abuse of language relative to our general concepts, where the numéraire is a particular commodity.

The price $\hat{p}_{qe}$ in the conditional contract proposed above is

$$\hat{p}_{qe} = \frac{p_{qe}}{p_{Qe}}. \tag{1}$$

In fact, this contract is equivalent to the simultaneous conclusion of two firm contracts between the agents A and B. According to the first contract, A is bound to pay the price p_{qe} while B must deliver one unit of q if e is realised. According to the second, B must pay the price p_{qe} while A is bound to deliver $\hat{p}_{qe}$ units of Q if e is realised. The conditional price $\hat{p}_{qe}$ must be such that the second contract is fair relative to the price-system which has been introduced, that is, that the firm value $p_{Qe}\hat{p}_{qe}$ of the conditional delivery given by A is equal to the firm value p_{qe} given by B. This justifies formula (1).

It is also possible to define firm prices for conditional deliveries depending on the realisation of events H compatible with several states. Thus, the delivery of one unit of good q subject to the condition that H is realised, consists of the delivery of a 'complex' of elementary commodities: one unit of each of the commodities (q, e) for which e belongs to H. The price of this delivery is

$$p_{qH} = \sum_{e \in H} p_{qe}. \tag{2}$$

In particular, we can let $\bar{p}_q$ denote the price of a firm delivery of one unit of q. Formula (2) applies here with $H = \Omega$, that is:

$$\bar{p}_q = \sum_{e=1}^{N} p_{qe}. \tag{3}$$

Since we are considering the good Q as numéraire, we shall normalise prices so that $\bar{p}_Q = 1$. (Note that then p_{Qe} is generally less than 1, and so $p_{qe} < \hat{p}_{qe}$, as is required.)

This price system defines a value for each consumption plan or production plan. For example,

$$px = \sum_{q=1}^{Q} \sum_{e=1}^{N} p_{qe} x_{qe} \tag{4}$$

is the value of the consumption plan x. Here we are concerned with a firm value determined before the true state of nature is known. We can also write

$$px = \sum_{e=1}^{N} p_{Qe} \cdot \hat{p}_e x_e \tag{5}$$

where $\hat{p}_e$ and x_e denote the vectors with the Q components $\hat{p}_{qe}$ and x_{qe} respectively. The scalar product $\hat{p}_e x_e$ is the 'conditional value' of the plan x if the state e is realised. The firm value px is then the average of the conditional values weighted by the p_{Qe}, whose sum is equal to 1.

In a 'market equilibrium' defined as in Chapter 4, each consumer i chooses that plan which he prefers among all plans belonging to X_i and whose value does not exceed a numerical income R_i. Each firm j chooses a plan whose value is maximum among all plans belonging to Y_j. Moreover, the usual conditions of equality of global demand and global supply are satisfied for each commodity, that is, for each good and each state.

How relevant is this concept of equilibrium to the description of actual economies in so far as they are affected by the presence of uncertainty?

The critical assumption lies in the existence of prices for all pairs (q, e), prices known to all agents and at which any contracts containing conditional clauses can be concluded, prices ensuring equilibrium in the markets for all goods and doing so in each conceivable state of nature. Because of the existence of markets for contingent goods, each consumer i can choose any consumption strategy x_i subject only to the constraints that the value of x_i does not exceed income R_i and that x_i belongs to X_i.

There is another noteworthy consequence of this assumption: the firm's decisions entail no risk as to the profit to be realised, since the firm can conclude contracts thanks to which it can immediately realise the sure and firm value of its production plan. Consequently it is not concerned with risk;

it need only compare its returns from certain different strategies whose physical consequences are partly uncertain but whose values are determined here and now by the market.

Note that the consumer has to consider risk. He certainly has sure knowledge of the cost of each consumption plan; but he must choose from among more or less uncertain plans. His attitude towards risk is reflected in the fact that his chosen plan contains consumptions which vary to a more or less marked degree with the states of nature. We shall return to this point later.

In a market equilibrium as thus conceived, the structure of contingent prices expresses the joint result of consumer preferences and of the influence that the state of nature has both on the conditions of production and on the availability of primary resources.

In practice, contracts involving contingent commodities are relatively rare. *A fortiori*, there are few 'markets' involving such commodities, that is, few institutional systems determining the prices to apply in such contracts through the confrontation of supply and demand. The best three examples are in insurance, lottery tickets and the Stock Exchange.

The buyer of an insurance policy agrees to pay the firm value of the benefit that will be due to him from the insurer if a particular event occurs. The buyer of a lottery ticket is in a similar position. The buyer of a share in an industrial company pays the discounted firm value of future profits which will depend on events involving the particular company.

An insurance market can validly be held to exist. Stock Exchanges are often put forward as prototypes of well-organised markets. So some actual prices are very similar to our theoretical contingent prices. But they are obviously too few to define the multitude of p_{qe}'s relating to a fairly complete sample of goods and states of nature. Thus the market equilibrium discussed above is a quite abstract idealisation of the way in which real markets function.

As in certain other of its aspects, microeconomic theory may be of more normative than descriptive interest. The theory of the optimum, applied here, states that, subject to conditions which we shall not restate, there exist contingent prices corresponding to every optimal programme, and that with these prices, the programme appears as a 'market equilibrium'. Determination of these prices may improve the conditions in which decentralised economic decisions are taken, and thus ensure that risk is more adequately taken into account.

Finally, the theory offers a precise conceptual framework, which is both rigorous and has wide generality. So it is very likely to prove fruitful in the investigation of more specific questions involving the influence of uncertainty on the conditions of economic management.

10

4. Individual behaviour in the face of uncertainty

We shall now look more closely at the behaviour of the individual consumer confronted with risk; there are some useful results bearing on this subject. Let us fix attention on the simple case of a single good and two states ($Q = 1$; $N = 2$) and, for simplicity, omit the index q relating to goods.

Figure 1 represents an indifference curve in the plane whose coordinates are the consumptions obtained if the first state is realised (abscissa) and if the second state is realised (ordinate). To fix ideas, we shall assume that the first state is 'it will rain tomorrow', and the second 'it will be sunny tomorrow'. To choose a vector x is to fix the consumptions that will take place in each of these eventualities.

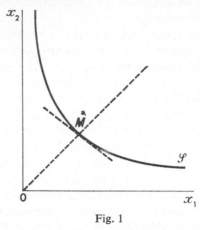

Fig. 1

For the indifference curve to be meaningful, it is obviously necessary that *a priori*, the individual should be able to consider any complex on this curve, that is, that he can acquire a title giving him the right to receive x_1 if it rains and x_2 if it is sunny. Suppose that this condition is satisfied, as is required by the general formulation given in the previous sections. Two distinct points on the same indifference curve represent two titles ('plans of action' or 'uncertain prospects') considered as equally advantageous by the individual.

The points lying on the first bisector are of particular interest since they correspond to sure consumptions, that is, to complexes ensuring the same consumption in both states. What is the significance of the marginal rate of substitution defined by the tangent to the indifference curve at the point M where it cuts the bisector? This rate, $- \mathrm{d}x_2/\mathrm{d}x_1$, indicates the amount by which the individual agrees to diminish his consumption in sunny weather in order to obtain the guarantee that he will increase his consumption by one unit in rainy weather. Why is it not necessarily 1?

There may be two reasons for this. In the first place, the individual may have differing needs in the two states. He may think it necessary to increase his consumption in rainy weather over his consumption in sunny weather, for example by buying an umbrella. In order to increase his consumption by one unit in rainy weather, he is willing to make a bigger reduction in his consumption in sunny weather. In the second place, he may think that it is more likely to rain than to be sunny. If his needs are the same in both states, it is to his advantage to obtain an additional unit of consumption in the more probable state if to do so, he need only agree to a unit decrease in consumption in the less probable state.

Thus the fact that marginal rates of substitution differ from 1 in the neighbourhood of certainty is explained both by changes in needs and tastes as a function of states of nature and by differences in the likelihood attributed by the individual to the different states.

If it can be assumed that needs and tastes do not depend on the state, then the marginal rates in question reveal the likelihood or the '*subjective probability*' of each of the different states for the individual. In the particular example, if we know that $- \, dx_2/dx_1 = 2$ in the neighbourhood of certainty and that needs are unchanged whether it is rainy or sunny, then it seems in fact that the individual thinks there are 2 chances out of 3 that it will rain.

Subject to certain axioms about choices between uncertain prospects, it has in fact been shown that the individual behaves as if he had constructed a (subjective) distribution on the set Ω of states of nature. This theory will be mentioned again in more detail at the end of Section 6.

Let us assume that, for one reason or another, the marginal rate in the neighbourhood of certainty is 2. Suppose that there exist markets for contingent commodities and that prices are such that p_1/p_2 also equals 2. (So now to obtain an additional unit of consumption in rainy weather, the assurance of 2 units in sunny weather must be given up.) Will the individual then decide on a certain consumption plan? Not necessarily; everything depends on his 'attitude to risk'. He will certainly be indifferent to any *infinitely small* displacement in the neighbourhood of certainty along his budget line. But a finite displacement may seem advantageous to him.

Figures 2 and 3 illustrate two different types of behaviour. The budget line *PR* is the same in each case. It is tangential to an indifference curve at the point *M* where it intersects the bisector. In Figure 2, where the indifference curve is concave upwards, the individual chooses *M*, that is, certainty. In Figure 3 he chooses another point *N* which lies on a higher indifference curve. It is very natural to say that Figure 2 shows an individual with an aversion to risk, while Figure 3 shows an individual who enjoys risk.

More generally, we can say that, in the application of our model to situations involving uncertainty, quasi-concavity of the utility function $S(x)$ implies *aversion to risk* in the sense that certainty appears optimal whenever contingent prices correspond to the marginal rates of substitution calculated in this state of certainty.† We have had sufficient discussion of the role of quasi-concavity of S to understand directly which properties depend on this aversion to risk.

5. Linear utility for the choice between random prospects

What we have just said is sufficient for generalisation of microeconomic theory to the case of uncertainty. However, individual preferences have often been given a more restrictive form, which allows more specific results to be proved.

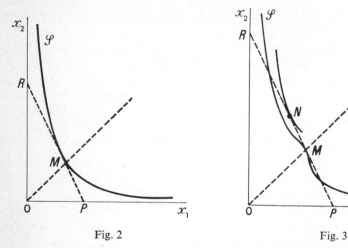

Fig. 2   Fig. 3

In the situation most frequently considered, there exists, given *a priori*, a distribution on Ω. In other words, with each state e there is associated a known, well-defined probability π_e. We also talk of *objective probabilities*, meaning by that the given π_e. The economist F. Knight introduced the distinction between *risk* and *uncertainty*, suggesting that the former word be kept for situations in which objective probabilities exist. So we shall now deal with risk.

In such a situation, the utility function is often given the particular form

$$S(x) = \sum_{e=1}^{N} \pi_e u(x_e), \tag{6}$$

where x_e denotes the vector with the Q components x_{qe} ($q = 1, 2, ..., Q$) and u denotes a function, which we shall call the elementary utility function.

---

† Note that, with this definition, aversion to risk has a fairly wide meaning since it covers the case where the individual considers the certain prospect as equivalent but not preferable to uncertain prospects.

Thus, the global utility function S, with NQ arguments, is written as the expected value of the elementary utility function. The global utility function is therefore *linear with respect to the probabilities*.

Such a form was first postulated directly as a good representation of behaviour in the face of risk. Nowadays its existence is established from a system of axioms on individual preferences, a system to be discussed in Section 6.

Note that expression (6) is still very general. If the function u is suitably chosen, we can represent, at least approximately, very varied systems of preferences. To see this, we shall consider the particular case of a single good ($Q = 1$).

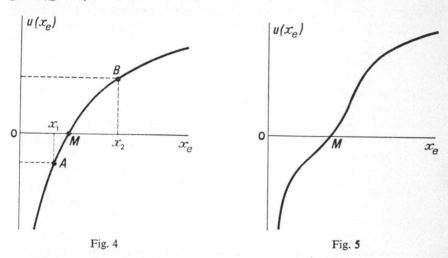

Fig. 4   Fig. 5

Figure 4 represents the variations of $u(x_e)$ as a function of x_e.

It allows us to construct point by point an indifference curve similar to that in Figure 1. Consider, for example, the curve corresponding to $S(x_1, x_2) = 0$, a value which has no particular virtue since the addition of the same constant to $S(x)$ and to $u(x_e)$ affects neither equation (6) nor the system of preferences. Let us also assume that the two states have the respective probabilities $\pi_1 = 2/3$ and $\pi_2 = 1/3$.

The abscissa of the point M where the curve in Figure 4 cuts the x-axis corresponds to the abscissa of the point where the indifference curve cuts the bisector in Figure 1 (certain prospect corresponding to $S(x) = 0$). To construct another point on the indifference curve, consider some abscissa x_1 and the point A with coordinates x_1 and $u(x_1)$ on Figure 4. The abscissa of the point B with ordinate $- 2u(x_1)$ defines the quantity x_2 such that the point (x_1, x_2) lies on the indifference curve in question in Figure 1. (For, $u(x_2) = - 2u(x_1)$, and so $\pi_1 u(x_1) + \pi_2 u(x_2) = 0$.)

By applying this construction it can be verified that the functions $u(x_e)$ represented in Figures 4 and 5 lead to indifference curves of the same appearance as those drawn in Figures 2 and 3 respectively.

The global utility function is partly arbitrary since an increasing transformation applied to S does not change the system of preferences. Clearly nothing is changed in this general property, which still holds. But all the equivalent functions S cannot simultaneously have the form (6). If we wish to keep this form, we must allow only increasing linear transformations on S (or equivalently on u).

A priori, the elementary utility function u has no other significance than to serve, through (6), in the representation of the system of preferences. It has sometimes been interpreted as an 'absolute utility function' between certain prospects, that is, as allowing comparisons between differences in utility (cf. Chapter 2, Section 10). Because he has absolute utility u, so the argument goes, the individual tries to maximise the expected value of u. For example, when he compares the certain prospect containing x_0 and an uncertain prospect containing x_1 with probability 2/3 and x_2 with probability 1/3, the individual tries to find out if the gain in utility when x_2 is substituted for x_0 is twice as great as the loss in utility when x_1 is substituted for x_0. Conversely, observation of choices among uncertain prospects would reveal the underlying absolute utility function, which can thus be estimated indirectly. Obviously there is no need to take sides on this question. Elementary utility u and absolute utility between certain prospects (function $\bar{S}$ in Chapter 2), can very well be considered as essentially different, even when both are considered to exist.

We can immediately verify that the quasi-concavity of $S(x)$ implies that $u(x_e)$ is also quasi-concave. For, let ξ^1 and ξ^2 be two vectors with Q components such that

$$u(\xi^1) = u(\xi^2).$$

Consider two uncertain prospects x^1 and x^2, which are identical except for a state e with non-zero probability, for example, the state $e = 1$, and such that $x_1^1 = \xi^1$ and $x_1^2 = \xi^2$. Then $S(x^1) = S(x^2)$ and the quasi-concavity of $S(x)$ implies $S[\alpha x^1 + (1 - \alpha)x^2] \geqslant S(x^1)$ for any number α such that $0 < \alpha < 1$. Given the form (6) for S and the definitions of x^1 and x^2, the inequality in question can also be written

$$\pi_1 u[\alpha \xi^1 + (1 - \alpha)\xi^2] \geqslant \pi_1 u(\xi^1),$$

which proves that $u(x_e)$ is quasi-concave.

Conversely, the *concavity* of $u(x_e)$ implies the concavity of $S(x)$ as defined by (6), and consequently also the quasi-concavity of any other function representing the same system of preferences. (Note here that the quasi-concavity of $u(x_e)$ is not sufficient.) For, let x^1 and x^2 be any two vectors with NQ components:

$$u[\alpha x_e^1 + (1 - \alpha)x_e^2] \geqslant \alpha u(x_e^1) + (1 - \alpha)u(x_e^2)$$

for all e and for any number α such that $0 < \alpha < 1$; consequently

$$S[\alpha x^1 + (1 - \alpha)x^2] \geqslant \alpha S(x^1) + (1 - \alpha)S(x^2).$$

Thus a concave elementary utility function represents the choices of an individual with an aversion to risk.

In fact, *when choices are represented by a linear utility function, concavity of* $u(x_e)$ *can be taken directly as defining aversion to risk.* Given some prospect x^0, we associate with it the sure prospect $\bar{x}$ defined by

$$\bar{x}_{qe} = \sum_{e=1}^{N} \pi_e x_{qe}^0 \qquad \text{for all } q \text{ and all } e.$$

($\bar{x}_{qe}$ is therefore independent of e; it is the expected value of x_{qe}^0). Aversion to risk can be defined naturally as the property that the individual always finds the sure prospect $\bar{x}$ at least equivalent to the corresponding uncertain prospect x^0.† This is expressed by:

$$u\left[\sum_{e=1}^{N} \pi_e x_e^0\right] \geqslant \sum_{e=1}^{N} \pi_e u(x_e^0), \tag{10}$$

an inequality that must be satisfied for every set of non-negative numbers π_e whose sum is 1. This inequality then defines precisely the concavity of u.

6. The existence of a linear utility function

We must now show that the existence of a utility function of the form (6) can be deduced from some axioms relating to individual behaviour in the face of risk. To deduce this, we must modify the model so far used, since the property to be proved does not apply without additional restriction when states of nature are only finite in number.‡ However, the first axiom will allow us to define a relatively simple formulation.

AXIOM 1. Preferences do not involve the states of nature, in the sense that they concern only the probability distribution of the vector x_e.

In other words, *to classify a prospect x in the scale of preferences, we need only give the values of the vectors x_e and the probability with which each value is realised;* there is no point in identifying the states for which the values in question appear. If there are only two states with the same probability

---

† As before, aversion to risk then covers the case of indifference between x^0 and its expected value $\bar{x}$.

‡ See Maitra, *Sur la théorie de la decision dans le cas d'un nombre fini d'états*, Cahier No. 9, Série recherche du Bureau Universitaire de Recherche Opérationelle, Paris, 1966.

(rainy and sunny weather, for example, or heads and tails in the toss of a coin), the uncertain outlook defined by $x_1 = \xi_1$ and $x_2 = \xi_2$ should, according to axiom 1, be equivalent to that defined by $x_1 = \xi_2$ and $x_2 = \xi_1$, this being true for any ξ_1 and ξ_2.

This axiom may obviously appear debatable in certain concrete situations. It seems particularly valid in lotteries and games of chance since the preferences of the individual player do not depend on the random events determining that some particular ticket, number or card will be drawn. On the other hand, in the example discussed at the beginning of this section, we assumed that needs might differ in the case of rain or of sunshine.

In fact, the axiom assumes that three concepts have been carefully distinguished: states, actions and consequences, all of which are precisely defined in decision theory. *Individual choices relate solely to consequences*, which are functions of states and actions. But the list of consequences must be complete. For example, if the individual has chosen (action) a complex of contingent commodities containing no umbrella in the case of rain, then the consequence in the case of rain (state) must specify that the individual will be wet. His preferences therefore relate to consequences whose description is supposed to be sufficiently precise to ensure that the states causing them do not directly affect choice. Thus, in principle there always exists a formulation of the problem which makes the axiom valid; but this formulation is sometimes too complex to be useful.

Be that as it may, axiom 1 allows a new representation of uncertain prospects. In fact, a prospect can be characterised sufficiently well by finding the probabilities with which there appear in it the different values ξ which the vector x_h can take *a priori*. For example, if x_e must belong to a subset X of R^Q, a prospect defines a distribution on X; two prospects defining the same distribution are equivalent (axiom 1) and will therefore be taken as identical in what follows.

We shall now assume that x_e can take only a finite number of values $\xi_1, \xi_2, ..., \xi_R$. This will greatly facilitate our following discussion, and is justified by the needs of exposition, while it does not play an essential part in the theory. There is no reason why we should not think of R as very large. We shall subsequently call the ξ_r 'sure prospects'.

To find a prospect (uncertain or sure) is to find the R probabilities μ_r relating to each of the values ξ_r (for $r = 1, 2, ..., R$), given that

$$\mu_r \geqslant 0 \qquad \text{for } r = 1, 2, ..., R \tag{11}$$

$$\sum_{r=1}^{R} \mu_r = 1. \tag{12}$$

By definition, μ_r equals the sum of the probabilities π_e of all the states e for which the vector x_e equals ξ_r in the prospect under consideration. We shall also let μ denote the vector of the R numbers μ_r and talk of 'the prospect μ' instead of the prospect x. Similarly, the consumer's choices may be defined by a function $S^*(\mu)$ as well as by a function $S(x)$ satisfying axiom 1. Thus, to prove the existence of a utility function of the form (6), we must find R numbers u_r and establish that

$$S^*(\mu) = \sum_{r=1}^{R} \mu_r u_r \tag{13}$$

provides an indicator of the individual's system of preferences among the different possible prospects μ.

We shall do this, assuming that the vector μ can be chosen arbitrarily provided that it satisfies conditions (11) and (12). The individual can obtain the prospect defined by any μ if he wishes to and has sufficient resources to cover its value. It is here that we assume the existence of an infinite number of states, since, if there is a finite number of states with specified probabilities π_e, each component μ_r of μ must be either zero or equal to one of the π_e's, or to the sum of several π_e's (those of the states in which the vector resulting from the prospect coincides with ξ_r).

Given any two particular prospects, μ^1 and μ^2, the vector $\mu = \alpha\mu^1 + (1 - \alpha)\mu^2$, where $0 < \alpha < 1$, defines a precise prospect which attributes the probability $\alpha\mu_r^1 + (1 - \alpha)\mu_r^2$ to ξ_r. In fact, this vector satisfies conditions (11) and (12). The prospect μ thus defined constitutes a sort of 'lottery ticket', which gives the prospect μ^1 with probability α and the prospect μ^2 with probability $1 - \alpha$. The prospects μ^1 and μ^2 can themselves be lottery tickets, in which case μ corresponds to a lottery whose lots are the tickets for other lotteries.

Consider now the individual's system of preferences. It implies a pre-ordering on the vectors μ, that is, a relation which is complete, transitive and reflexive. Let $\mu^1 \succsim \mu^2$ indicate that the prospect μ^1 is judged preferable or equivalent to the prospect μ^2. Similarly, let $\mu^1 \sim \mu^2$ indicate that μ^1 and μ^2 are considered equivalent ($\mu^1 \succsim \mu^2$ and $\mu^2 \succsim \mu^1$), and finally let $\mu^1 \succ \mu^2$ mean that μ^1 is preferred to μ^2 ($\mu^1 \succsim \mu^2$ but not $\mu^2 \succsim \mu^1$). We need the second axiom:

AXIOM 2. If $\mu^1 \succ \mu^2$, if μ is some prospect and if $0 < \alpha < 1$, then

$$\alpha\mu^1 + (1 - \alpha)\mu \succ \alpha\mu^2 + (1 - \alpha)\mu.$$

Similarly, if $\mu^1 \sim \mu^2$, then

$$\alpha\mu^1 + (1 - \alpha)\mu \sim \alpha\mu^2 + (1 - \alpha)\mu.$$

This axiom appears fairly natural if we consider the choice between two lottery tickets both giving μ with probability $1 - \alpha$, the first also giving μ^1 with probability α and the second μ^2 with probability α. If μ^1 is preferred to

11

μ^2, it seems that the first lottery ticket should be preferred to the second. If μ^1 is equivalent to μ^2, it seems that the two tickets must also be equivalent.

However, this axiom has been criticised by those who do not admit certain of its implications.† Suppose, for example, that there is a single good, money, and three sure prospects ξ_1 giving the right to 10,000 francs, ξ_2 giving the right to 1,000 francs, and ξ_3 the right to 0 francs. Consider the three prospects:

$$\mu^1 = [0.10 \quad 0.90 \quad 0]$$
$$\mu^2 = [0.20 \quad 0.60 \quad 0.20]$$
$$\mu = [0 \qquad 0 \qquad 1],$$

and $\alpha = 0.1$. Then

$$\mu^3 = \alpha\mu^1 + (1 - \alpha)\mu = [0.01 \quad 0.09 \quad 0.90]$$
$$\mu^4 = \alpha\mu^2 + (1 - \alpha)\mu = [0.02 \quad 0.06 \quad 0.92]$$

Suppose that some prudent individual prefers μ^1 to μ^2 because μ^1 gives him at least 1,000 francs, which is quite a valuable sum of money, and because the risk of getting nothing with μ^2 (1 in 5) is not compensated for him by the increased probability of winning 10,000 francs (this probability increases from 1/10 to 2/10). If he obeys axiom 2, he must also prefer μ^3 to μ^4. Some economists have disputed that the second choice follows from the first. They say that the individual in question may quite logically prefer μ^4 to μ^3 since the two prospects have similar probabilities of gaining nothing while μ^4 gives a probability of gaining 10,000 which is twice that in μ^3.

The reader must judge for himself whether axiom 2 is compatible with real behaviour, as a first approximation, and whether it constitutes a norm that he would think reasonable to impose on his own choices, or on collective choices for which he might be responsible.

We still need an axiom of continuity for the system of preferences:

AXIOM 3. Given any three prospects μ^1, μ^2 and μ^3, if $\mu^1 \succsim \mu^2 \succsim \mu^3$, then there exists a number α, where $0 < \alpha < 1$, such that

$$\alpha\mu^1 + (1 - \alpha)\mu^3 \sim \mu^2.$$

In other words, there exists a lottery ticket that combines the two extreme prospects with appropriate probabilities and is equivalent to the intermediary prospect.

To construct a preference indicator of the form (13), let us first consider the sure prospects ξ_r. Since their number is finite, there exists one to which no other is preferred and one that is not preferable to any other. We can assume without loss of generality that the former is ξ_1 and the latter ξ_R.

---

† See the discussions at the colloquium organised by the C.N.R.S., the reports of which are published in the volume *Econométrie*, Paris, C.N.R.S., 1953.

We can also assume that $\xi_1 \succ \xi_R$, without which all prospects are equivalent, We then set

$$u_1 = 1, \qquad u_R = 0. \tag{14}$$

Let us apply axiom 3 to the sure prospects ξ_1, ξ_r, and ξ_R, where $1 < r < R$. There exists a number α such that $\alpha\xi_1 + (1 - \alpha)\xi_R$ is equivalent to ξ_r; let this number equal u_r. The utilities u_r of the sure prospects are then fixed. We must show that the function $S^*(\mu)$ defined by (13) is an indicator of the individual's preferences. We shall do this for the case where $R = 3$, generalisation to any value of R raising no difficulty of principle.†

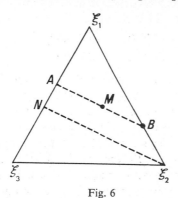

Fig. 6

The vectors μ restricted by (11) and (12) are easily represented on a classical triangular diagram in which μ_1, μ_2 and μ_3 measure distances to the three sides (cf. Figure 6). At each vertex of the triangle we represent the corresponding sure prospect ξ_1, ξ_2 or ξ_3. The first ξ_1 is, for example, the vector $(1, 0, 0)$. In this triangle, the prospect $\mu = \alpha\mu^1 + (1 - \alpha)\mu^2$ is represented by the centre of gravity M of the points M_1 and M_2 representing μ^1 and μ^2 with which the masses α and $1 - \alpha$ are associated respectively. On the side $\xi_1\xi_3$ we can let N denote the prospect $\mu^N = (u_2, 0, 1 - u_2)$ which is equivalent to ξ_2. In order to prove that

$$S^*(\mu) = \mu_1 + \mu_2 u_2 \tag{15}$$

is an indicator of individual preferences, it is necessary and sufficient to establish that the indifference curves are straight segments parallel to $\xi_2 N$. It is necessary because (15) implies this property of indifference curves. It is also sufficient since the contours of the function (15) coincide with the indifference lines and are classed in the same order.

Let M be a point in the triangle corresponding to some prospect μ. To fix ideas, let us assume that M lies on the same side as ξ_1 of the line $\xi_2 N$. Draw

---

† See Marschak 'Rational Behaviour, Uncertain Prospects and Measurable Utility', *Econometrica*, April 1950.

the parallel through M to $\xi_2 N$; it cuts $\xi_1\xi_3$ and $\xi_1\xi_2$ at A and B respectively. Moreover,

$$\frac{A\xi_1}{N\xi_1} = \frac{B\xi_1}{\xi_2\xi_1}. \tag{16}$$

The prospects μ^A and μ^B represented by A and B are equivalent. Indeed let λ denote the common value of the ratios (16). We can write

$$\mu^A = \lambda\mu^N + (1 - \lambda)\xi_1 \qquad \text{and} \qquad \mu^B = \lambda\xi_2 + (1 - \lambda)\xi_1.$$

But μ^N and ξ_2 are equivalent; axiom 2 then implies that μ^A and μ^B are also equivalent. The same axiom implies that any prospect represented by a point on AB is also equivalent to μ^A or μ^B (in the statement of the axiom, take $\mu^1 = \mu^A$, $\mu^2 = \mu = \mu^B$, with α denoting the probability of μ^A in the intermediate prospect under consideration).

To establish the required result completely, we need only show that the indifference class contains no points other than those on AB. If it contains another such point, then we can show by the above reasoning that it contains the whole segment parallel to AB and passing through this point. It therefore contains a point A' of $\xi_1\xi_3$, distinct from A. But it is impossible for two distinct points of this segment to be mutually equivalent. To show this, we shall assume, for example, that A' lies between A and ξ_1. In view of axiom 2, the relation $\xi_1 \succ \mu^A$ implies $\mu^{A'} \succ \mu^A$, which contradicts the equivalence of A' and A. But, if A, A' and ξ_1 are all equivalent, then $\mu^{A'} \succ \xi_3$ and axiom 2 implies $\mu^{A'} \succ \mu^A$, which is also a contradiction. This completes our proof.

The theory whose main argument has just been given was introduced first in 1944 by von Neumann and Morgenstern as one of the foundations of their theory of games. It can usefully be generalised to the case where the probability of events is not given *a priori*. Subject to a certain number of axioms on individual behaviour in the choice among uncertain prospects, we can prove the existence of an elementary utility function and a (subjective) probability on the space of states, this function and this probability being representative of individual choices in the sense that, when calculated with the probabilities in question, the expected value of the elementary utility function is an indicator of preferences.† We have tried to show in Section 4 how an agent's choices reveal the probabilities that he attributes to the different states. The property just stated makes use of this.

7. Risk premiums and the degree of aversion to risk

The economic literature dealing with situations involving uncertainty attributes an important role to 'risk premiums'. We must see how they can be defined within our formulation.

---

† See Savage, *The Foundations of Statistics*, John Wiley, New York, 1954.

Let x be a consumption prospect containing elements of risk in the sense that the vectors x_e corresponding to the different states are not all equal in this prospect. The sure prospect $\bar{x}$, the expected value of x, is defined by

$$\bar{x}_q = \bar{x}_{qe} = \sum_{e=1}^{N} \pi_e x_{qe} \qquad \text{for all } q \text{ and all } e, \tag{17}$$

this formula having already been given at the end of Section 5. The concept of risk premium is related to the fact that $\bar{x}$ is usually preferred to x so that we can deduce from $\bar{x}$ a 'premium' for obtaining another sure prospect that is equivalent to x. More precisely, let ρ be the number such that

$$u[(1 - \rho)\bar{x}] = \sum_{e=1}^{N} \pi_e u(x_e), \tag{18}$$

where $\bar{x}$ is considered as a vector with Q components. The sure prospect $(1 - \rho)\bar{x}$ is equivalent to the risky prospect x. The number ρ can be called the 'risk premium rate'.† With the definitions given at the end of Section 5, this premium is positive if the individual has a genuine aversion to risk, and zero if he is indifferent to risk.

A parallel is often drawn between the risk premium and the subjective rate of interest defined in Chapter 10. The former results from a systematic preference for certainty and the latter from a systematic preference for the present. We saw that the rate of interest may be positive for reasons other than 'impatience'. But there is a more important reason why this parallel is dangerous.

We saw that, for optimal organisation of production and distribution or for competitive equilibrium, subjective interest rates must be the same for all individuals and must equal technical interest rates. These rates are a characteristic of the price system. Nothing similar exists for risk premiums; they cannot play a role similar to that of interest rates in economic calculus. Only the system of contingent prices has solid justification here.

However, consideration of risk premiums leads naturally to a measure of the degree of aversion to risk. Let x be a prospect which is fairly near certainty:

$$x_e = \bar{x} + \xi_e \tag{19}$$

where ξ_e is a vector with Q components considered as small, and zero expectation:

$$\sum_e \pi_e \xi_e = 0 \tag{20}$$

---

† It might be thought preferable to establish a marginal definition of risk premium by comparing the risky prospect x with infinitely close prospects with diminishing risk. But such a marginal definition does not seem to lead to any significant new result.

We can approach $u(x_e)$ by a limited expansion:

$$u(x_e) \sim u(\bar{x}) + \xi'_e \operatorname{grad} u + \tfrac{1}{2}\xi'_e U \xi_e$$

where ξ'_e denotes the transpose of ξ_e, $\operatorname{grad} u$ is the vector of the derivatives of $u(\bar{x})$ with respect to its Q arguments $\bar{x}_q$ and U is the matrix of the second derivatives of the same function. It follows from (20) that

$$\sum_e \pi_e u(x_e) \sim u(\bar{x}) + \tfrac{1}{2} \sum_e \pi_e \xi'_e U \xi_e. \tag{21}$$

Let V be the covariance matrix of x_e:

$$V = \sum_e \pi_e \xi_e \xi'_e \tag{22}$$

(this is a square matrix of order Q). We can write:

$$\sum_e \pi_e \xi'_e U \xi_e = \operatorname{tr} UV$$

(if A is a square matrix, $\operatorname{tr} A$ denotes the sum of its diagonal elements). Formula (21) can then be written:

$$\sum_e \pi_e u(x_e) \sim u(\bar{x}) + \tfrac{1}{2} \operatorname{tr} UV \tag{24}$$

Since the risk premium rate ρ is necessarily small whenever the ξ_e are small, we can similarly approach $u[(1 - \rho)\bar{x}]$ by

$$u[(1 - \rho)\bar{x}] \sim u(\bar{x}) - \rho \bar{x}' \operatorname{grad} u. \tag{25}$$

In view of (18), comparison of (24) and (25) implies

$$\rho \sim \frac{\operatorname{tr} UV}{2\bar{x}' \operatorname{grad} u}. \tag{26}$$

Therefore the risk premium rate ρ depends on the covariance matrix of x_e and on the matrix $- U/\bar{x}' \operatorname{grad} u$. The latter can be taken as a measure of the aversion to risk.

In the particular case where there is a single good ($Q = 1$), the matrix V reduces to σ^2, the variance of x_e, and (26) becomes

$$\rho \sim - \frac{u''\bar{x}}{2u'} \cdot \frac{\sigma^2}{\bar{x}^2}. \tag{27}$$

This is why $- \bar{x}u''/u'$ is called the 'relative degree of risk aversion' while $- u''/u'$ is called the 'absolute degree of risk aversion'. If the function $u(x_e)$ is concave, this degree is positive and increases with the curvature of the graph of u.

8. The exchange of risks

We can see intuitively that, in an exchange economy, individuals with the least aversion to risk accept the most uncertain prospects and so in a sense act as insurers for the other individuals. We can illustrate this graphically for the simple case of a single good, two equally probable states, and two exchanging agents.

In an Edgeworth diagram, let P be the point representing initial resources, which we assume to be equally distributed between the two parties to exchange; resources are much greater in state 1 than in state 2. If we adopt assumption 1 and recall that $\pi_1 = \pi_2$, we know that the first consumer's indifference curves have a slope of 45° where they cut the bisector of the angle O, and so also have the second consumer's indifference curves where they cut the bisector of the angle O'. If the first consumer has a greater aversion to risk than the second, the concavity of his indifference curves is more marked. The

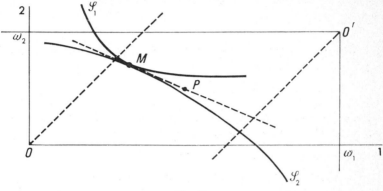

Fig. 7

equilibrium point is therefore to the left of P. It obviously involves a higher contingent price for state 2 than for state 1. At these prices, the first exchanger ensures for himself a consumption that does not greatly depend on the state of nature; the second exchanger is willing to give up part of his resources if state 2 is realised, in exchange for a larger quantity that he will receive if state 1 is realised.†

Let us look at this question in more general terms.

Suppose that, in a competitive equilibrium where markets exist for contingent commodities, the risky prospect x has been chosen by a consumer who has an aversion to risk. Then the sure prospect $\bar{x}$, the expected value of x, must be greater than x in value, otherwise it would have been chosen in preference to x. Consequently

$$\bar{p}\bar{x} > \sum_{e=1}^{N} p_e x_e \qquad (28)$$

---

† If there are no objective probabilities for the states, the exchange can be explained both by differences in needs or attitudes to risk and by differences in the subjective probabilities that the exchangers attribute to the states.

where $\bar{p}$ is the vector with Q components defined by

$$\bar{p}_q = \sum_{e=1}^{N} p_{qe} \qquad q = 1, 2, ..., Q. \tag{29}$$

This is the price vector for unconditional delivery already discussed in Section 3.

With the definition of $\bar{x}$ given by (17), the inequality (28) can be written:

$$\sum_{e=1}^{N} (\pi_e \bar{p} - p_e) x_e > 0. \tag{30}$$

But (29) and the fact that the sum of the π_e is 1 imply

$$\sum_{e=1}^{N} (\pi_e \bar{p} - p_e) = 0. \tag{31}$$

Comparison of (30) and (31) shows that, for a given good, x_{qe} must in most cases be large when $p_{qe} < \pi_e \bar{p}_q$.

Inequality (30) applies to a specified consumer. If all consumers have an aversion to risk, the corresponding inequalities can be summed so that (30) applies to the aggregate consumption prospect. In particular, in an exchange economy the latter must equal the prospect ω of initial resources, and therefore

$$\sum_{e=1}^{N} (\pi_e \bar{p} - p_e) \omega_e > 0.$$

If there are two states and if ω_{qe} varies from one state to the other only for a single good $q = g$, then in view of (31) the inequality becomes

$$(\pi_1 \bar{p}_g - p_{g1})(\omega_{g1} - \omega_{g2}) > 0.$$

If, for example, $\omega_{g1} > \omega_{g2}$, then contingent prices must be such that

$$\frac{p_{g1}}{\pi_1} < \bar{p}_g < \frac{p_{g2}}{\pi_2}. \tag{33}$$

The ratio between the contingent price and the probability of the corresponding state is smaller for the state in which the resource is less scarce.

9. Individual risks and large numbers of agents

Up till now we have assumed that uncertain events involve all agents directly. There are some events of this type, but many risks are in fact very localised; the risks against which one insures in most cases concern a single person or a small number of persons. Similarly, the physical or technical risks affecting many productive activities are fairly largely independent of each other.

We can easily imagine that the social consequences of individual risks are quite different from those of collective risks affecting all agents or a large proportion of them. In particular, it seems that, for efficient allocation of individual risks, the price of an insurance contract should be equal to the value of the risk covered multiplied by its probability. More precisely, if there is a large number of agents and if only individual risks exist, conditional prices should be independent of the states to which they refer, and contingent prices should be proportional to probabilities. We shall see this illustrated by a simple case, without trying to give a rigorous proof.†

Let us consider an exchange economy for which the vector ω of resources is sure. Let us assume that the risks affect only the needs of individual 1, to whom assumption 1 does not therefore apply. The utility function of the other consumers is

$$\sum_e \pi_e u_i(x_{ie}), \qquad i = 2, 3, ..., m \tag{34}$$

With an optimum we can associate a system of contingent prices p_{qe} such that each consumer maximises his utility function (34) subject to a budget constraint

$$\sum_e \sum_q p_{qe} x_{iqe} \leqslant R_i. \tag{35}$$

The equality between marginal rates of substitution and price-ratios implies here, for a given good q and two distinct states e and ε:

$$\frac{u'_{iq}(x_{ie})}{u'_{iq}(x_{i\varepsilon})} = \frac{p_{qe}}{p_{q\varepsilon}} \cdot \frac{\pi_\varepsilon}{\pi_e}. \tag{36}$$

If there is a large number of individuals, then in all circumstances the first consumer takes up only a small part of the resources. The quantities $\omega_q - x_{1qe}$ distributed among the others do not depend to any great extent on the state e. We can therefore assume that the allocation received by a consumer $i \neq 1$ does not depend much on e. The ratio on the left of (36) is therefore near 1 and the p_{qe} are nearly proportional to the π_e.

In short, we can write

$$p_{qe} \sim \pi_e \bar{p}_q. \tag{37}$$

In view of (1) and since $\bar{p}_Q = 1$, it follows that

$$\hat{p}_{qe} \sim \bar{p}_q. \tag{38}$$

This conclusion is unrelated to the fact that a single individual is affected by uncertainty. If all were subject to distinct personal risks, a 'state of nature' e

---

† The property is stated in the context of production problems by Arrow, *Essays in the Theory of Risk-bearing*, Chapter 11, North-Holland Publ. Co., 1970. See also Malinvaud, 'Equilibrium in Large Markets and the Allocation of Individual Risks', *Journal of Economic Theory*, 1972.

would be a complete specification of the situations of the different individuals. By comparison with a given state e, there would exist states ε which differ from e only in the situation of one single individual. Equation (36), written for such pairs of states e and ε then implies that p_{qe}/π_e approximately equals $p_{q\varepsilon}/\pi_\varepsilon$, which can be generalised to all states step by step.

The approximate formulae (37) and (38) lead us back to a remark at the end of Section 3. We then saw that there were too few existing markets to determine the very numerous p_{qe} relating to a fairly exhaustive sample of goods and states. But if we know that p_{qe} is equal to $\pi_e \bar{p}_q$, then we need only know the $\bar{p}_q$ applying to sure deliveries. The markets necessary for the formation of an appropriate price system are therefore much less numerous than it appeared at first sight. Those relating to contingent commodities are required only to the extent that collective risks are involved.

10. Profit and allocation of risks

In Section 3 we saw that, in a market equilibrium generalising those investigated in Chapters 4 and 5, producers were not subject to any risk; they could immediately realise the sure value of their chosen production plans. In other words, they would insure against the risk of loss.

When (37) applies, the value of a production plan y_j of the jth producer is

$$P_j = \sum_e \pi_e \bar{p} y_{je} \tag{39}$$

where y_{je} is the vector with the Q components y_{jqe}. Now, $\bar{p} y_{je}$ is the profit P_{je} realised by j in the eventuality e. The value P_j of the production plan is therefore the *expected value of the profit*. The reason why the producer can restrict his attention to this expected value P_j is that he is able to contract by giving up the difference $P_{je} - P_j$ when it is positive but covering himself against it when it is negative.

Such contracts are extremely rare in reality. It is nevertheless true that, for an efficient allocation of resources, producers ought to maximise the expected value of their profits, at least to the extent that they are subject only to individual risks.

It is often assumed that, in real life, firms behave in the face of risk as consumers do. Unable to insure, they give greater weight to losses than to gains of equal probability. Instead of maximising P_j, the expectation of the P_{je}, the jth producer maximises

$$\sum_e \pi_e u_j(P_{je}) \tag{40}$$

where the function u_j represents the 'utility' attributed to the profit P_{je} and is strictly concave because of aversion to risk. Such an attitude would give rise to some inefficiency in the organisation of production.

It would also have repercussions on the distribution of income. If competition is free, if in fact firms maximise their expected profit, pure profit, excluding rent and interest on capital, is on average zero in the equilibrium. Indeed we know that constant returns to scale imply that the equilibrium values of the P_j are zero; therefore on average, the P_{je} are zero. (We shall not repeat the reasons justifying constant returns to scale.)

But, if firms maximise a function such as (40) and if the u_j are strictly concave, profits are positive on average. Indeed, consider small variations $dP_{je} = P_{je}\, d\lambda$ relative to equilibrium profits P_{je}; such variations are possible since there are constant returns to scale. The variation in (40) must be zero $(d\lambda \gtrless 0)$:

$$\sum_e \pi_e P_{je} u'_j(P_{je}) = 0. \tag{41}$$

Also, the strict concavity of u_j implies

$$(P_{je} - P_j)[u'_j(P_{je}) - u'_j(P_j)] \leqslant 0$$

where the inequality holds strictly if $P_{je} \neq P_j$ (see theorem 1 of the Appendix). Consequently

$$\sum_e \pi_e(P_{je} - P_j)[u'_j(P_{je}) - u'_j(P_j)] < 0 \tag{42}$$

except in the trivial case where all the P_{je} are equal. Since P_j is the expectation of the P_{je}, we can write

$$\sum_e \pi_e(P_{je} - P_j)u'_j(P_j) = 0. \tag{43}$$

Now, (41), (42) and (43) imply directly

$$- P_j \sum_e \pi_e u'_j(P_{je}) < 0$$

and, since the multiplier of $- P_j$ is obviously positive,

$$P_j > 0. \tag{44}$$

Aversion to risk, which, according to prevailing opinion characterises the behaviour of firms, is thus a new cause for the existence of positive profits. Apart from competitive imperfections, apart from disequilibria related to innovations, the caution of firms in the face of the risk of loss explains why pure profits are on average positive.

Conclusion

The theories which we have investigated are built round a central model whose exact significance we have attempted to make quite clear. The student may go on to round off his knowledge of each of the questions discussed either by referring to deeper and more general proofs of the essential properties or by extending the analysis to situations so far unconsidered.

He may also think of the most serious limitations of microeconomic theory as a model for private or collective decisions relating to the organisation of production and exchange. In particular, it will be remembered that on several occasions we had to ignore transaction costs and information costs. These have been discussed by various authors in particular contexts. But they have not been incorporated in general economic theory because they complicate matters considerably.

In particular, this explains why we have not discussed monetary phenomena. The holding of money is due essentially to the transaction and information costs which agents must bear if they wish to dispense with cash. Monetary theory must therefore deal preponderantly with factors that do not figure largely in microeconomic theory. To go on now to monetary questions would divert us from the main line of development of these lectures. It seems preferable to end at the point we have now reached.

Appendix

The extrema of functions of several variables with or without constraint on the variables

by J.-C. MILLERON

The object of this appendix is to give succinct justification for a certain number of simple mathematical methods concerning maxima and minima of functions of several variables. In various chapters of this book we have to find the maximum of a function $f(x)$ of the variables $x_1, x_2, ..., x_n$ either when they can be chosen arbitrarily or when they are subject to constraints of the form $g_j(x) = 0$ or $g_j(x) \geqslant 0$, for $j = 1, 2, ..., m$. In classical mathematics text-books this problem generally is not considered with sufficient precision for our needs.

We shall see that the methods discussed here are not completely general, but a certain number of particularly interesting cases can be dealt with in full.†

1. Useful definitions

(a) *The notion of maximum*

Let $f(x)$ be a real function defined on R^n and X a set of R^n. In this appendix we shall use the expression 'maximum of $f(x)$' to designate not only the largest value taken by f but also any maximising vector $\hat{x}$ for which this value is achieved. More precisely:

(i) $\hat{x}$ is said to be *a maximum of* $f(x)$ *in* X, or $\hat{x}$ is said to be *a constrained maximum* of $f(x)$ subject to the condition that x belongs to X, if $\hat{x}$ is in X and $f(\hat{x}) \geqslant f(x)$ for all x of X.

This is said to be an *unconstrained maximum* if X is the whole space R^n.

(ii) $\hat{x}$ is said to be a *local maximum* of $f(x)$ if there exists a neighbourhood $U(\hat{x})$ of $\hat{x}$ in which $f(x)$ is never greater than $f(\hat{x})$.

---

† See also Frisch, *Maxima et Minima* (Dunod, Paris, 1960) who gives a very detailed introduction to the methods presented here.

This is said to be an *absolute maximum* if $\hat{x}$ maximises $f(x)$ in the whole set X, that is, if $\hat{x}$ is a local maximum for which the neighbourhood $U(\hat{x})$ can be identified with X.

The above concepts can easily be superimposed.

We then obtain the following definitions of a maximum.

	Unconstrained	Constrained
Local	There exists $U(\hat{x})$ such that $$f(\hat{x}) \geqslant f(x)$$ for all $x \in U(\hat{x})$	$\hat{x} \in X$ and there exists $U(\hat{x})$ such that $$f(\hat{x}) \geqslant f(x)$$ for all $x \, \varepsilon \, U(\hat{x}) \cap X$
Absolute	$$f(\hat{x}) \geqslant f(x)$$ for all x	$\hat{x} \, \varepsilon \, X$ and $f(\hat{x}) \geqslant f(x)$ for all $x \in X$

We sometimes introduce the concept of *strict maximum*, keeping the same definitions as in the above table, but replacing the sign $\geqslant$ by the sign $>$ (strict inequality) and requiring that $x \neq \hat{x}$. For example, $\hat{x}$ is, in the strict sense, a constrained absolute maximum of $f(x)$ in X if $\hat{x}$ belongs to X and if $f(\hat{x}) > f(x)$ for all $x \in X$ such that $x \neq \hat{x}$.

(b) *Concave functions*

A set X of R^n is said to be convex if the vector $x = \alpha x^1 + (1 - \alpha)x^2$ belongs to X whenever x^1 and x^2 belong to X and $0 < \alpha < 1$.

A function $f(x)$ defined on a convex set X of R^n is said to be *concave* if, for all x^1 and all x^2 of X and for every scalar α lying between 0 and 1, the following inequality holds:

$$\alpha f(x^1) + (1 - \alpha)f(x^2) \leqslant f[\alpha x^1 + (1 - \alpha)x^2].$$

When the inverse inequality is realised under the same conditions, the function f is said to be *convex*.

It is equivalent to say that, if $f(x)$ is concave, the set of vectors (x, y) of R^{n+1} such that $y \leqslant f(x)$ is convex and that, if $f(x)$ is convex, the set $\{(x, y) \in R^{n+1} | y \geqslant f(x)\}$ is convex.

Figures 1 and 2 illustrate these definitions for the case of a function $f(x)$ of a single variable.

We now prove the following important property:

THEOREM I. If $f(x)$ is differentiable and concave,† then

$$f(x) \leqslant f(x^0) + (x - x^0)' \operatorname{grad} f(x^0) \quad \text{for all } x \text{ and all } x^0 \text{ of } X.$$

---

† 'Prime' notation will be used for the transposes of vectors and matrices; $\operatorname{grad} f(x^0)$ represents the vector of the first derivatives of f at the point x^0.

Using the definition of concavity with $x^1 = x$, $x^2 = x^0$ and an infinitely small positive number α which we can denote by dt, we get:

$$dtf(x) + (1 - dt)f(x^0) \leqslant f[dtx + (1 - dt)x^0],$$

which can also be written,

$$dt[f(x) - f(x^0)] \leqslant f[x^0 + (x - x^0) dt] - f(x^0).$$

Since dt is positive, this inequality implies

$$f(x) \leqslant f(x^0) + \frac{f[x^0 + (x - x^0) dt] - f(x^0)}{dt},$$

which must hold for all dt and therefore also in the limit when dt tends to zero through positive values. The limiting inequality is precisely that stated in theorem 1, which is therefore proved.

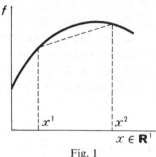

Fig. 1

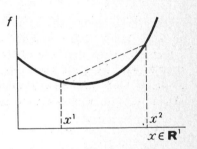

Fig. 2

(c) *Quadratic forms*

A quadratic form of the variables $x_1, ..., x_n$ is any homogeneous polynomial of second degree in $x_1, ..., x_n$;

$$Q = \sum_{i=1}^{n} \sum_{j=1}^{n} b_{ij}x_ix_j.$$

If x denotes the vector with components $x_1, ..., x_n$ and A the symmetric square matrix whose elements a_{ij} are defined by

$$a_{ii} = b_{ii}; \qquad a_{ij} = \frac{b_{ij} + b_{ji}}{2} \qquad \text{for} \qquad i \neq j,$$

then the quadratic form Q can also be written

$$Q = x'Ax.$$

Q is said to be

— positive definite   if $x'Ax > 0$ for all x other than the null-vector
— negative definite   if $x'Ax < 0$ for all x other than the null-vector
— positive semi-definite if $x'Ax \geqslant 0$ for all x
— negative semi-definite if $x'Ax \leqslant 0$ for all x.

2. Unconstrained maximum of a function of several variables

Confining our analysis to functions with continuous first and second derivatives, we shall try to characterise a local unconstrained maximum x^0 of the function $f(x)$ defined on R^n.

(a) *Necessary first-order conditions*

We shall prove the following property:

THEOREM II. In order that the differentiable function $f(x)$ should have a local unconstrained maximum at x^0, it is necessary that $\operatorname{grad} f(x^0) = 0$.

Since $f(x)$ is differentiable, we can write

$$f(x) = f(x^0) + \sum_{i=1}^{n} (x_i - x_i^0)[f_i'(x^0) + \varepsilon_i(x)], \tag{1}$$

where $f_i'(x^0)$ denotes the value at x^0 of the derivative of f with respect to x_i and $\varepsilon_i(x)$ tends to zero as x tends to x^0.

Let us assume that one of the derivatives $f_i'(x^0)$ is not zero, for example that $f_j'(x^0)$ is positive. Let us then choose the vector x so that all its components are equal to those of x^0 except for x_j, which we take as equal to $x_j^0 + a_j$, where a_j is positive (if $f_j'(x^0)$ is negative, we take a_j as negative). Equation (1) can then be written:

$$f(x) = f(x^0) + a_j[f_j'(x^0) + \varepsilon_j(x)]. \tag{2}$$

If now a_j tends to zero through positive values, then x tends to x^0 and $\varepsilon_j(x)$ to zero; therefore $f_j'(x^0) + \varepsilon_j(x)$ necessarily becomes positive for sufficiently small values of a_j. Equation (2) then shows that $f(x) > f(x^0)$. But, for sufficiently small values of a_j, x, which tends to x^0, belongs to the neighbourhood $U(x^0)$ within which, by hypothesis, x^0 maximises f. It is therefore a contradiction for $f(x)$ to exceed $f(x^0)$, and this proves the theorem.

This theorem provides a necessary condition for a maximum. The same condition applies for a local unconstrained minimum x^0 of $f(x)$ since this is a maximum of $-f(x)$ and since $\operatorname{grad}[-f(x^0)] = -\operatorname{grad} f(x^0)$ is zero when $\operatorname{grad} f(x^0)$ is zero.

(b) *A case where the first-order conditions are sufficient; f is concave.*

THEOREM III. A differentiable concave function has an unconstrained absolute maximum at $x = x^0$ if and only if $\operatorname{grad} f(x^0) = 0$.

Every absolute maximum is a local maximum. In view of theorem II, the condition that $\operatorname{grad} f(x^0) = 0$ is necessary. Conversely, if this condition is satisfied, it follows immediately from theorem I that we can write $f(x) \leqslant f(x^0)$ for all x, which proves that x^0 maximises $f(x)$.

(c) *Necessary second-order conditions*

Let us assume that x^0 is a local maximum of a twice differentiable function $f(x)$. In view of theorem II we can write

$$f(x) = f(x^0) + \tfrac{1}{2}(x - x^0)'\{[f''(x^0)] + [\varepsilon(x)]\}(x - x^0), \tag{3}$$

where $[f''(x^0)]$ is the matrix of the second derivatives of f for $x = x^0$ and $[\varepsilon(x)]$ is a square matrix of order n whose elements tend to zero as x tends to x^0.

We wish to establish

THEOREM IV. If x^0 is a local maximum of a twice differentiable function $f(x)$, then $[f''(x^0)]$ is negative semi-definite.

We must prove that, for all x,

$$(x - x^0)'[f''(x^0)](x - x^0) \leqslant 0.$$

Suppose that there exists x^* such that

$$(x^* - x^0)'[f''(x^0)](x^* - x^0) > 0. \tag{4}$$

We can then find a sufficiently small positive number λ so that simultaneously:

(a) $x^1 = x^0 + \lambda(x^* - x^0)$ belongs to the neighbourhood $U(x^0)$ in which x^0 maximises $f(x)$;

(b) $|(x^* - x^0)'[\varepsilon(x^1)](x^* - x^0)| < (x^* - x^0)'[f''(x^0)](x^* - x^0).$

But $x^1 - x^0 = \lambda(x^* - x^0)$ so that, since λ is positive, (4) and (b) imply

$$(x^1 - x^0)'\{[f''(x^0)] + [\varepsilon(x^1)]\}(x^1 - x^0) > 0.$$

It then follows from (3) that

$$f(x^1) > f(x^0) \qquad \text{where} \qquad x^1 \in U(x^0),$$

which contradicts the assumption that x^0 maximises $f(x)$ in $U(x^0)$. The theorem is therefore proved.

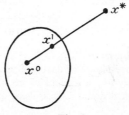

Fig. 3

(d) *A case where the second-order conditions are sufficient; the matrix of the second derivatives is negative definite.*

THEOREM V. Let $f(x)$ be a twice differentiable function. If grad $f(x^0) = 0$ and if $[f''(x^0)]$ is negative definite, then x^0 is a strict local maximum of $f(x)$.

We can define a neighbourhood $U(x^0)$ such that, for all x in $U(x^0)$ and not equal to x^0, we have

$$|(x - x^0)'[\varepsilon(x)](x - x^0)| < -(x - x^0)'[f''(x^0)](x - x^0).$$

In fact, the left hand side is bounded above by $\|x - x^0\|^2$ multiplied by the largest latent root $\bar{\mu}(x)$ of $[\varepsilon(x)]$ while the right hand side is bounded below by $\|x - x^0\|^2$ multiplied by the smallest latent root v of $[-f''(x^0)]$. The root v is positive and $\bar{\mu}(x)$ tends to zero† as x tends to x^0.

Equation (3) then implies:

$$f(x) < f(x^0) \text{ for all } x \text{ other than } x^0 \text{ and belonging to } U(x^0).$$

Note. The above theorems can be transposed immediately to the case of a minimum. In theorem III, $f(x)$ must be a convex function since $-f(x)$ must be concave. In theorems IV and V $[f''(x^0)]$ must be positive semi-definite and positive definite respectively.

3. Extremum subject to constraints of the form $g_j(x) = 0; j = 1, 2, ..., m$

From now on, we shall assume that not only f, but each of the functions g_j is twice differentiable.

(a) *Necessary first-order conditions; Lagrange multipliers.*

THEOREM VI. Let X be the set of x's satisfying the constraints $g_j(x) = 0$, for $j = 1, ..., m$. If x^0 is a local maximum of $f(x)$ in X and if the matrix $G^0 = [\partial g_j(x^0)/\partial x_i]$ has rank m, then there exists a vector λ^0 of R^m such that

$$\text{grad } f(x^0) + \sum_{j=1}^{m} \lambda_j^0 \text{ grad } g_j(x^0) = 0. \tag{5}$$

The numbers λ_j^0 are called 'Lagrange multipliers'.

Consider the system of m equations

$$g_j(x) = z_j \qquad j = 1, 2, ..., m \tag{6}$$

---

† In fact the latent roots of a matrix tend to zero as it tends to the zero matrix. Let λ be a root of A and let x be a corresponding latent vector: $Ax = \lambda x$. Let us define the norms $\|A\|$ and $\|x\|$ as equal respectively to the maxima of the absolute values of the elements of A and x. If n is the order of A and i, j the indices of its elements, we can establish directly:

$$|\lambda x_i| \leqslant \sum_{j=1}^{n} |a_{ij}| \cdot |x_j| \leqslant n\|A\| \cdot \|x\|$$

and therefore

$$|\lambda| \cdot \|x\| \leqslant n\|A\| \cdot \|x\| \qquad \text{and} \qquad |\lambda| \leqslant n\|A\|,$$

which implies the stated result.

in which the z_j are real variables. Since G^0 has rank m, we must have $n \geqslant m$. Moreover, the theorem of implicit functions† ensures that, in a neighbourhood of x^0, we can express m of the variables x_i as differentiable functions of the other $n-m$ variables and the z_j. Suppose, for example, that the first m variables x_i are expressed in this way:

$$x_k = \xi_k(z_1, z_2, ..., z_m; x_{m+1}, ..., x_n) \qquad k = 1, 2, ..., m.$$

Substituting these expressions in f, we define a new differentiable function:

$$f(x) = F(z_1, z_2, ..., z_m; x_{m+1}, ..., x_n).$$

To say that x^0 is a local maximum of $f(x)$ in X is to say that $x^0_{m+1}, ..., x^0_n$ locally maximise the function $F(0, 0, ..., 0; x_{m+1}, ..., x_n)$.

It follows from theorem II that the derivatives of F with respect to the $x_{m+1}, ..., x_n$ are zero. Thus, the differential of f, identically equal to the differential of F, can be written:

$$df = dF = \mu_1 \, dz_1 + ... + \mu_m \, dz_m$$

where the $\mu_1, \mu_2, ..., \mu_m$ are the partial derivatives of F with respect to $z_1, z_2, ..., z_m$. Setting $\lambda^0_j = -\mu_j$ and taking account of (6), we can transcribe the last equation as follows:

$$df + \sum_{j=1}^{m} \lambda^0_j \, dg_j = 0,$$

which expresses precisely the equality to be proved.

Remarks

(1) To determine the coordinates of the constrained maxima (or minima) x^0, of a function $f(x)$, we may write that the necessary conditions (5) are satisfied and that also

$$g_j(x^0) = 0 \qquad \text{for} \qquad j = 1, 2, ..., m. \tag{7}$$

Equations (5) and (7) are equal in number to the components of the vectors x^0 and λ^0. The solutions for x^0 and λ^0 of the system that they constitute include the maxima and minima of f, but possibly also certain other vectors (saddle-points of the function, etc.). Stronger conditions are necessary for the precise determination of maxima and minima.

(2) With each x^0 that satisfies (5) there is associated one or more λ^0, which we shall call vectors of the dual variables at x^0, in accordance with recent usage.

(3) The following two propositions are naturally equivalent:

---

† See, for example, Dieudonné, *Foundations of Modern Analysis*, Academic Press, New York, 1960.

(i) x^0 is a maximum of $f(x)$ in the set X defined by $g_j(x) = 0$ for $j = 1, ...,$ m.

(ii) x^0 is a maximum of $f(x) + \sum\limits_{j=1}^{m} \lambda_j^0 g_j(x)$ in the same set X.

For, for every x in X,

$$f(x) = f(x) + \sum_{j=1}^{m} \lambda_j^0 g_j(x).$$

(b) *Necessary second-order conditions for a local maximum of* $f(x)$

We saw that, if $\|\partial g_j(x_0)/\partial x_i\|$ has rank m, the existence of a local maximum of $f(x)$ in $X = \{x | g_j(x) = 0; j = 1, 2, ..., m\}$ is equivalent to the existence of an unconstrained local maximum of $F(0, ..., 0; x_{m+1}, ..., x_n)$. We could therefore proceed directly to find the matrix of the second derivatives of this function and to write that this matrix is negative semi-definite (theorem IV).

It is simpler to investigate the function

$$l(x) = f(x) + \sum_{j=1}^{m} \lambda_j^0 g_j(x),$$

also written for simplicity $f(x) + \lambda^0 g(x)$, which we shall call the 'Lagrangian', and take account of the fact that $l(x)$ has a maximum at x^0 in X (remark (3) above).

Considering $x_1, ..., x_m$ as implicit functions of $x_{m+1}, ..., x_n$, we can write, as on page 305:

$$L(x_{m+1}, ..., x_n) = l[\xi_1(x_{m+1}, ..., x_n), ..., \xi_m(x_{m+1}, ..., x_n), x_{m+1}, ..., x_n].$$

The arguments $z_j = 0$ of the ξ_j are omitted for simplicity. Our problem therefore reduces to finding the matrix of second derivatives of L.

Now, we have

$$d^2 L = dx' \left\| \frac{\partial^2 l}{\partial x_i \partial x_h} \right\| dx + \sum_{i=1}^{n} \frac{dl}{\partial x_i} d^2 x_i. \tag{8}$$

If no simplification were possible, we should have to eliminate the terms in dx_i and $d^2 x_i$ between (8) and the equations $dg_j = 0$, $d^2 g_j = 0$; we should then have to identify the coefficients of the terms in $dx_i\, dx_h$ ($i, h = m + 1,$ ..., n) as second derivatives of L.

It is possible to use more simple reasoning. We see that, in the expression for $d^2 L$, the terms in $d^2 x_i$, $i = 1, ..., m$ disappear, since the first-order conditions imply

$$\frac{\partial l(x^0)}{\partial x_i} = 0.$$

Therefore we need only require that the quadratic form

$$d^2L = dx' \left\| \frac{\partial^2 l}{\partial x_i dx_h} \right\| dx$$

is negative semi-definite in a subspace defined by the equations $dg_j = 0$ for $j = 1, ..., m$.

Hence the theorem:

THEOREM VII. Let X be the set of x's such that $g_j(x) = 0$, for $j = 1, ..., m$. Suppose that $f(x)$ and $g_j(x)$ are twice differentiable. If x^0 is a local maximum of $f(x)$ in X, and if λ^0 is a dual vector associated with x^0, the quadratic form

$$d^2L(x^0) = dx' \left\| \frac{\partial^2 f(x^0)}{\partial x_i \partial x_h} + \lambda^0 \frac{\partial^2 g(x^0)}{\partial x_i \partial x_h} \right\| dx$$

is negative semi-definite subject to the constraints

$$\sum_{i=1}^{n} \frac{\partial g_j(x^0)}{\partial x_i} dx_i = 0 \qquad j = 1, ..., m.$$

(c) A case where the second-order conditions are sufficient

We can also apply theorem V to the case of a constrained maximum:

THEOREM VIII. Let $f(x)$ and $g_j(x)$, $(j = 1, ..., m)$, be twice differentiable functions. If there exists a vector λ^0 of R^m such that

$$\text{grad } f(x^0) + \sum_{j=1}^{m} \lambda_j^0 \text{ grad } g_j(x^0) = 0$$

at a point x^0 such that $g_j(x^0) = 0$, for $j = 1, ..., m$, and if, in addition, the quadratic form

$$d^2L = dx' \left\| \frac{\partial^2 f(x^0)}{\partial x_i \partial x_h} + \lambda^0 \frac{\partial^2 g(x^0)}{\partial x_i \partial x_h} \right\| dx$$

is negative definite subject to the constraints

$$\sum_{i=1}^{n} \frac{\partial g_j(x^0)}{\partial x_i} dx_i = 0 \qquad j = 1, ..., m,$$

then x^0 is a local maximum of $f(x)$ in $X = \{x | g_j(x) = 0, j = 1, , m\}$.

Suppose that this is not the case. There exists a sequence x^s of vectors of X tending to x^0 and such that $f(x^s) \geqslant f(x^0)$. If η^s is the length of $x^s - x^0$, the vectors $u^s = (x^s - x^0)/\eta^s$ belong to the unit sphere, which is a compact set. We can therefore extract from the sequence of the u^s a sub-sequence tending to a vector u, which is obviously non-zero. Let us confine attention to this sub-sequence. In view of the fact that $g_j(x^0) = 0$ and grad $l(x^0) = 0$, we can write

$$0 = g_j(x^s) = \eta^s u^s [\text{grad } g_j(x^0) + \delta^s]$$

and

$$l(x^s) = l(x^0) + \tfrac{1}{2}(\eta^s)^2 u^{s'}\{[l''(x^0)] + \varepsilon^s\}u^s$$

where $[l''(x^0)]$ is the matrix that occurs in the expression for d^2L. Reasoning similar to that in the proof of theorem V shows that the vector δ^s and the matrix ε^s are negligible for sufficiently large s.

Thus, in the limit,

$$u \cdot \operatorname{grad} g_j(x^0) = 0$$

and therefore

$$u'[l''(x^0)]u < 0$$

and consequently also

$$u^{s'}[l''(x^0)]u^s < 0$$

for sufficiently large s. It then follows from the limited expansion of $l(x^s)$ that, for sufficiently large s,

$$f(x^s) = l(x^s) < l(x^0) = f(x^0).$$

This is the required contradiction, which establishes the theorem.

(d) *A case where the first-order conditions are sufficient*: the Lagrangian is a concave function

THEOREM IX. If $f(x)$ and $g_j(x)$ are differentiable and if there exists λ^0 of R^m such that, at a point x^0 of X,

$$\operatorname{grad} f(x^0) + \sum_{j=1}^{m} \lambda_j^0 \operatorname{grad} g_j(x^0) = 0$$

and such that the associated Lagrange function

$$l(x) = f(x) + \sum_{j=1}^{m} \lambda_j^0 g_j(x)$$

is concave, then x^0 is an *absolute* maximum of $f(x)$ in

$$X = \{x | g_j(x) = 0, \quad j = 1, 2, ..., m\}.$$

Since $l(x)$ is concave, theorem 1 implies

$$l(x) \leqslant l(x^0) + (x - x^0)' \operatorname{grad} l(x^0)$$

or

$$f(x) + \sum_{j=1}^{m} \lambda_j^0 g_j(x) \leqslant f(x^0) + \sum_{j=1}^{m} \lambda_j^0 g_j(x^0) + (x - x^0)' \operatorname{grad} l(x^0).$$

Since $\operatorname{grad} l(x^0) = 0$ and $g_j(x^0) = 0$,

$$f(x) \leqslant f(x^0)$$

for all x such that $g_j(x) = 0; j = 1, 2, ..., m$.

Particular case. If $f(x)$ is concave and if the $g_j(x)$ are linear, the Lagrangian is concave; the first-order conditions are sufficient to establish that x^0 is a maximum.

4. Extremum subject to constraints of the form $g_j(x) \geqslant 0, j = 1, ..., m$†

In what follows we shall have to use a theorem known as Farkas' theorem. Its proof is fairly laborious so we shall assume

THEOREM X. Given a matrix Q, a row vector r and a variable vector x, then in order that $Qx \geqslant 0$ should imply $rx \geqslant 0$ it is necessary and sufficient that there exist a row vector p with non-negative elements such that $r = pQ$.

From now on we shall let Y denote the set of x's such that

$$g_j(x) \geqslant 0, \qquad \text{for} \qquad j = 1, ..., m.$$

Let x^0 be a maximum of $f(x)$ in Y.

By convention, E is the set of indices j such that $g_j(x^0) = 0$ and $\bar{E}$ is the set of the other indices ($g_j(x^0) > 0$). Finally, K is the cone of the vectors x for which

$$(x - x^0)' \text{ grad } g_j(x^0) \geqslant 0, \qquad \text{for all } j \text{ in } E.$$

We make the following assumptions:

ASSUMPTION 1. $f(x)$ and the $g_j(x)$ have first derivatives.

ASSUMPTION 2. For every x of K, there exists in Y an arc which is a tangent at x^0 to the line $x - x^0$.

More precisely, given x in K, there exists a line segment with equation $\xi = e(\theta), 0 \leqslant \theta \leqslant 1$, such that

$$e(0) = x^0$$

$$\frac{de(0)}{d\theta} = \rho(x - x^0) \tag{9}$$

where ρ is a positive number.

Note that the condition is not generally satisfied if the matrix G^0 of theorem VI has rank smaller than m.‡

Figure 4 illustrates assumption 2 in the case of two variables and two constraints. The following constraints provide an example where the assumption is not satisfied:

$$\begin{cases} g_1(x) = -x_1^3 + x_2 \geqslant 0 \\ g_2(x) = x_1^4 - x_2 \geqslant 0 \end{cases}$$

---

† Here we follow the approach given in Huard, *Mathématiques des programmes économiques*, Dunod, 1965.

‡ Assumption 2 is often called the 'constraint qualification' as a reminder that the assumption relates to the set of functions defining the constraints and not to the function f to be maximised.

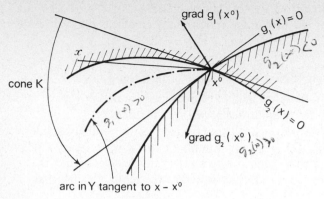

arc in Y tangent to x - x⁰

Fig. 4

If x^0 is the origin, the cone K is identified with the x_1-axis. The condition in the assumption is not satisfied for any x belonging to the positive part of this axis (cf. Figure 5).

We wish to establish the following theorem:

THEOREM XI (Kuhn-Tucker theorem). If x^0 is a maximum of $f(x)$ in Y and if assumptions 1 and 2 are satisfied, there exists a vector λ none of whose components is negative, and which is such that simultaneously

$$\operatorname{grad} f(x^0) + \sum_{j=1}^{m} \lambda_j \operatorname{grad} g_j(x^0) = 0$$

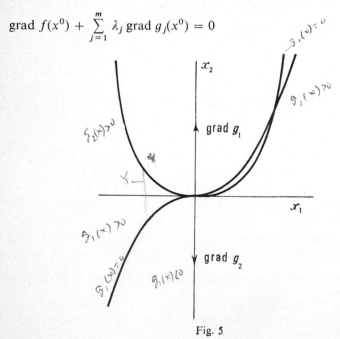

Fig. 5

and

$$\sum_{j=1}^{m} \lambda_j g_j(x^0) = 0.$$

For applying Farkas' theorem, we shall first prove that

$$\begin{cases} \text{if } (x - x^0)' \text{ grad } g_j(x^0) \geqslant 0 \text{ for all } j \text{ of } E \text{ (therefore if } x \in K), \\ \text{then } (x - x^0)' \text{ grad } f(x^0) \leqslant 0. \end{cases} \tag{10}$$

Let $\xi = e(\theta)$ be the arc whose existence is guaranteed by assumption 2. Consider the function $\Phi(\theta) = f[e(\theta)]$ for $0 \leqslant \theta \leqslant 1$. Since the points $e(\theta)$ are in Y, we have

$$\Phi(0) = f(x^0) \geqslant f(\xi) = \Phi(\theta);$$

hence,

$$\frac{d\Phi(0)}{d\theta} \leqslant 0$$

or

$$[\text{grad } f(x^0)]' \frac{de(0)}{d\theta} \leqslant 0.$$

In view of (9). the last inequality can be written:

$$[\text{grad } f(x^0)]' \rho(x - x^0) \leqslant 0$$

and, since ρ is positive,

$$(x - x^0)' \text{ grad } f(x^0) \leqslant 0.$$

Let us now apply Farkas' theorem to preposition (10). There exists a vector with components $\lambda_j \geqslant 0$, for all the j's of E, such that

$$- \text{ grad } f(x^0) = \sum_{j \in E} \lambda_j \text{ grad } g_j(x^0). \tag{11}$$

We also set $\lambda_j = 0$ for all the j's of $\bar{E}$. Then (11) becomes

$$\text{grad } f(x^0) + \sum_{j=1}^{m} \lambda_j \text{ grad } g_j(x^0) = 0. \tag{12}$$

But $g_j(x^0) > 0$ implies $\lambda_j = 0$, according to the definitions of the λ_j and of $\bar{E}$.

On the other hand, $\lambda_j > 0$ implies $g_j(x^0) = 0$, so that $\lambda_j g_j(x^0)$ is zero for all j and so

$$\sum_{j=1}^{m} \lambda_j g_j(x^0) = 0. \tag{13}$$

This proves the existence of the vector λ specified in theorem XI.

Particular case. The domain Y is frequently defined by conditions of the form

$$\begin{cases} g_j(x) \geqslant 0 & j = 1, ..., m. \\ x_i \geqslant 0 & i = 1, 2, ..., n. \end{cases}$$

When we apply theorem XI, we know that, if x^0 is a maximum, there exists in R^{m+n} a vector $\begin{bmatrix} \lambda \\ \mu \end{bmatrix}$ with no negative component and such that

$$\text{grad } f(x^0) + \sum_{j=1}^{m} \lambda_j \text{ grad } g_j(x^0) + \mu = 0, \tag{14}$$

where

$$\sum_{j=1}^{m} \lambda_j g_j(x^0) + \mu x^0 = 0. \tag{15}$$

μ is then the vector of the dual variables of the constraints $x_i \geqslant 0$.

Let us introduce the Lagrange function

$$l(x, \lambda) = f(x) + \sum_{j=1}^{m} \lambda_j g_j(x) \dagger$$

Remembering that μ has no negative component, we can write (14) and (15) in the form

(i) $x^0 \geqslant 0$; $\partial l(x^0, \lambda)/\partial x_i \leqslant 0$ for all $i = 1, ..., n$; in addition, if $\partial l/\partial x_i < 0$ for a particular index i, then $x_i^0 = 0$ for this index.

(ii) $\lambda \geqslant 0$; $\partial l(x^0, \lambda)/\partial \lambda_j = g_j(x^0) \geqslant 0$, for all $j = 1, ..., m$; in addition, if $\lambda_j > 0$ for a particular j, then $g_j(x^0) = 0$ for this j.

Taking the inverses, we note that the implications of (i) and (ii) are equivalent to

$$x_i^0 > 0 \Rightarrow \frac{\partial l}{\partial x_i} = 0 \quad \text{and} \quad g_j(x^0) > 0 \Rightarrow \lambda_j = 0.$$

A case where the Kuhn-Tucker conditions are sufficient

THEOREM XII. If $f(x)$ and the $g_j(x)$ are concave, then the Kuhn-Tucker conditions imply that x^0 is a maximum.

Suppose that x^0 satisfies the conditions

$$g_j(x^0) \geqslant 0 \quad j = 1, ..., m$$

and that there exist $\lambda_j \geqslant 0$ such that

$$\text{grad } f(x^0) + \sum_{j=1}^{m} \lambda_j \text{ grad } g_j(x^0) = 0,$$

---

† Note that here, as opposed to the case in Section 3, l is interpreted as a function of x and of λ.

with

$$\sum_{j=1}^{m} \lambda_j g_j(x^0) = 0.$$

Let us apply theorem 1 to the concave functions f and g_j:

$$f(x) - f(x^0) \leqslant (x - x^0)' \operatorname{grad} f(x^0),$$
$$g_j(x) - g_j(x^0) \leqslant (x - x^0)' \operatorname{grad} g_j(x^0).$$

For all x such that $g_j(x) \geqslant 0$, we can therefore establish directly the sequence of inequalities:

$$f(x) - f(x^0) \leqslant (x - x^0)' \left[-\sum_{j=1}^{m} \lambda_j \operatorname{grad} g_j(x^0) \right]$$

$$\leqslant \sum_{j=1}^{m} \lambda_j [g_j(x^0) - g_j(x)]$$

$$\leqslant -\sum_{j=1}^{m} \lambda_j g_j(x) \leqslant 0,$$

which completes the proof of theorem XII.

Index

Absolute satisfaction, 41
Accounting economy, 9
Activity analysis, 51
Additivity, 51
Agents, 3
Allais, V, 39, 55, 155, 164, 231, 244, 245, 246, 248
Arbitrage, 155
Arrow, 295
Atomistic economy, 163–164
Atomless economy, 163–164
Aversion to risk, 281, 282, 285, 290–292

Bacharach, 185
Berge, 131
Bertrand, 145
Bilateral monopoly, 147, 150
Blocking of an imputation, 154
Brouwer's theorem, 131
Budget, 215
Budget constraint, 23, 24, 29

Capital, 249
Capital intensity, 265
Capitalistic optimum, 262–265
Capitalized value, 234
Cardinal utility, 39
Cassel, 41
Champsaur, 174
Chenery, 195
Clark, 195
Coalition, 153
Collective concern, 218
Collective consumption, 211-219
Collective good, 201
Collusion, 175

Colson, 228
Commodity, 2, 231, 275
Comparative dynamics, 266
Comparative statics, 64
Compensated variation in income, 35
Competition (perfect), 56, 106
Competitive equilibrium, 106, 143
Complements, 38
Complex of goods, 3
Concave function, 300
Conditional price, 277
Congestion, 218
Constraint qualification, 309
Consumer, 4, 12–42
Consumer equilibrium, 13, 26–33
Consumption plan, 8
Consumption programme, 8
Contingent commodity, 275
Contingent price, 277
Convex function, 300
Convex hull . . ., 166
Convex set, 21
Convexity, 53, 165–168
Core, 149, 152, 154, 157–161
Cost function, 64–68
Cournot, 145, 150–151
Cournot equilibrium, 150–153, 182

Date, 7
Debreu, V, 6, 19, 101, 170
Decomposition methods, 194, 197
Demand function, 14, 34–39
Dieudonné, 27, 305
Differentiated sector, 55, 164
Discount factor, 233
Discounted price, 233

Discounted value, 233
Distribution economy, 106–109
Distribution optimum, 79–86
Distribution theory, 125–130, 253–257
Divisibility, 52
Domination, 174–181
Dorfman, 51, 118
Duopoly, 150–153, 182
Dupuit, 228

Economic theory of public finance, 203
Economic theory of socialism, 185
Economy, 5
Edgeworth, 16, 81, 112, 155, 157, 158, 160, 161, 172, 176, 181
Efficient, 87
Elementary utility function, 282
Entrepreneur, 256
Equilibrium, 5
Equilibrium for the firm, 55–59
Event, 274
Exchange economy, 109–113, 157–162
Exchange value, 14
Existence of equilibrium, 130–136
External economies, 200–211
External effects, 200–211

Farkas' theorem, 309
Feasible state, 77, 87
First-order conditions, 302, 304, 308
Fixed cost, 219–229
Fixed point, 131
Foley, 215
Free disposal, 23
Free entry, 174–181
Frisch, 299

Games, 144–147
General equilibrium, 5, 105
Golden age, 263
Good, 2, 231
Gross substitutability, 113

Hahn, 156
Hicks, 39
Houthakker, 41, 42
Huard, 309
Hyperplane, 101

Impatience, 235
Imperfect competition, 144–162

Imputation, 154
Income, 12, 23, 24
Income distribution, 125–130, 253–257
Income effect, 35, 36
Increasing returns, 92–93
Individual risks, 294–296
Inferior good, 38
Information, 154, 184–187, 275
Initial resources, 4
Input, 4
Intercomparison of utilities, 97
Interest, 231–234, 239–242, 253–257, 265–270
Intertemporal economies, 230–272
Intertemporal efficiency, 250–253
Isoquant, 46

Jevons, 14

Kahutani's theorem, 131
Kantorovich, 185
Karlin, 103
Knight, 256, 282
Kolm, 218
Koopmans, 100, 230
Kuhn, 310

Labour, 4, 5
Labour income, 254
Labour theory of value, 117
Lagrange multiplier, 304
Lagrangian, 306
Lange, 1
Laroque, 174
Leontief, 118, 195
Lesourne, 225
Lexicographic ordering, 19
Linear utility, 282–290
Location, 7
Long-run, 69

McKenzie, 115, 119
Maitra, 285
Malinvaud, 7, 185, 295
Marginal cost, 66
Marginal productivity, 47
Marginal rate of substitution, 15, 47
Marginal rate of transformation, 47
Marginal returns, 53, 54
Marginal utility, 14

Market equilibrium, 78
Marschak, 289
Marx, 44, 249, 255, 257
Material input, 254
Maximum, 299
Menger, 14
Merit wants, 77
Microeconomic theory, 2
Minkowsky, 103, 104
Money illusion, 34, 62, 108
Monopoly, 70–75
Monopsony, 71
Morgenstern, 290

Negative definite, 301
Negative semi-definite, 301
Negishi, 140, 143, 156, 161
Net production, 4
Non-cooperative equilibrium, 146, 205
Non-increasing marginal returns, 53, 54, 58
Numeraire, 4

Ophelimity, 16
Optimal state, 76–78
Optimum programme, 242–244
Optimum theory, 5, 76–104
Ordinal utility, 18
Output, 4
Own discount factor, 232
Own interest rate, 232

Pareto, 16, 44, 78
Pareto optimum, 78
Partial equilibrium, 5
Pay-off function, 145
Perfect competition, 56, 106, 170–174
Plan, 8, 276
Planning theory, 184–199
Politico-economic equilibrium, 216
Positive definite, 301
Positive semi-definite, 301
Preference relation, 16–20
Preordering, 19
Present value, 233
Price, 3, 4
Private ownership economy, 123–125
Producer, 4, 43–75
Production function, 45–51, 250
Production optimum, 86–92, 260–262

Production set, 45
Profit, 56, 253–257, 296–297
Programme, 8, 231
Proportional growth, 262
Proposition, 186
Prospect, 276
Prospective indices, 186
Pseudo-equilibrium, 212–213
Public good, 201, 211–219
Public service, 218–229

Quadratic form, 301
Quality, 6
Quasi-concave, 26

Radner, 275
Rate of profit, 240, 255
Recontracting, 160
Relative utility, 18
Rent, 124, 256
Resources, 4
Return to enterprise, 124
Return to labour, 254
Returns to scale, 52–53
Revealed preference, 40–42
Revelation of preferences, 197–199, 213
Ricardo, 14, 255
Risk, 282
Risk premium, 290–292
Robbins, 1

Samuelson, 40, 41, 42, 51, 118, 213, 270
Satisfaction, 13, 16
Savage, 290
Scarcity, 114
Scarf, 170
Schumpter, 14, 257
Shapley, 155, 161
Shubik, 155, 161
Second order conditions, 303, 306, 307
Separation theorem, 101, 103
Short run, 69
Short-sightness, 257–260
Slutsky coefficients, 37
Slutsky equation, 37
Social utility function, 97
Solow, 51, 118
Stability, 138–143
Stable allocation, 156
State, 5, 274

State of the economy, 5, 76
State of nature, 274
Stationary equilibrium, 265–272
Stationary state, 260
Strategy, 146, 276
Subjective discount factor, 234
Subjective interest rate, 234
Subjective probability, 275, 281, 290
Subscription, 213, 214
Subsidies, 209, 210
Substitute, 38
Substitution coefficient, 37
Substitution effect, 35
Substitution (marginal rate of), 15, 47
Supply, 61
Surplus, 226
Survival condition, 134
Sustain, 100

Tatonnement, 138, 187–189
Taxes, 209, 210, 215
Technical coefficient, 194
Technically efficient, 44
Technical interest rate, 238

Theory of capital, 230
Theory of distribution, 125–130, 253–257
Theory of games, 145
Theory of growth, 230
Theory of interest, 230, 239–242, 265–270
Theory of value, 105, 113–123
Time, 7
Transferability of capital, 257–260
Tucker, 310

Uncertainty, 273–298
Undifferentiated sector, 55
Uniqueness of equilibrium, 136–138
Use value, 14
Utility function, 14–20

Vajda, 145
Value, 3, 113–123, 161
Value added, 254
Von Neumann, 290

Walras, 14, 44, 138, 139, 161
Walras' law, 111, 125, 142
Welfare economics, 4